Because I Said So

Also edited by
Camille Peri and Kate Moses

Mothers Who Think:
Tales of Real-Life Parenthood

FROM THE EDITORS OF
MOTHERS WHO THINK

CAMILLE PERI
& KATE MOSES

Because I Said So

33 Mothers Write About Children, Sex, Men, Aging, Faith, Race, & Themselves

HarperCollins*Publishers*

HarperCollins books may be purchased for educational, business, or sales promotional use. For information, please write: Special Markets Department, HarperCollins Publishers Inc., 10 East 53rd Street, New York, NY 10022.

FIRST EDITION

Designed by Nancy B. Field

Printed on acid-free paper

Library of Congress Cataloging-in-Publication Data
Because I said so: 33 mothers write about children, sex, men, aging, faith, race, and themselves / edited by Kate Moses and Camille Peri.
    p. cm.
    ISBN 0-06-059878-6
    1. Motherhood. 2. Child rearing. 3. Family. 4. Mothers—Social conditions. I. Moses, Kate. II. Peri, Camille.

HQ759.B37 2005
306.874'3—dc22   2004062007

05 06 07 08 09 ❖/RRD 10 9 8 7 6 5 4 3 2 1

This book is dedicated to the children
who have lost parents to war or terrorism
since the turn of the new century,
and to the hope that their children
will be spared the same fate.

ACKNOWLEDGMENTS

This collection was a team effort from start to finish. We'd like to thank, first, Ellen Levine and Marjorie Braman for their enthusiasm, wisdom, good humor, and extended deadlines as this book evolved.

We owe a debt of enormous gratitude to our children and husbands—Joe and Nat and David Talbot; Zachary and Celeste and Gary Kamiya—for being gracious and patient as we ruined vacations, forgot groceries, left you in front of the TV for far too many hours, or feigned only the most superficial interest in your work during our single-minded sprint to the finish on this book. We especially want to thank Celeste, Zachary, Nat, and Joe for giving more to us as our children than we could ever hope to give you as parents. Much appreciation and love to Gary and David for keeping us fortified with unwavering dedication, unerring editorial insight, dry martinis, great home cooking, and boundless love.

Our thanks and apologies go out to our contributors' children for letting your mothers ignore you while they wrote about you for us. We'd also like to thank Ruth Henrich, Beth Kephart, Debra Ollivier, Susan Straight, and Joan Walsh for acting as our on-call team of farsighted, trenchant readers. And many thanks to "Dr. Ed" Mechem for his nonjudgmental technical expertise and good cheer.

Camille wishes to express her deepest gratitude to Dr. Hope Rugo and Dr. Laura Esserman, and a thumbs-up to Karen Bayuk for making sure she had a life to go back to. Heartfelt thanks also to Teri, Bob, Don, and Sue Peri, and to Louise Rubacky, Cheryl

Nardi, Margaret Weir, and Ruth Henrich for giving so much of themselves to help Camille get well.

Kate wishes to thank those friends, old and new, who so generously outfitted her for her quest to find Demos, supplying everything from encouragement and safe harbors to Pimm's cups and chocolate on pillows: Tracy Brain, Sohair Hosny, Joanna Lincoln, Ruth Lopez, Diane Middlebrook, Laila Moussa, Mrs. Abdul Razik Sabah, Ahdaf Soueif, Mrs. Zienab Tawfic, and especially Euphrosyne Doxiadis, for whom thanks will never be enough.

Together we'd like to thank the many embedded women on the mothering front who have shored us up over the months of this book's gestation, with child support, escapist fantasies, baked goods, babies to squeeze, coffee to go, and hilarious, heart-wrenching, and unforgettable stories and ideas about the ebb and flow of motherhood. You have been our backup and our backbone: Tammy Anderson, Za Berven, Marni Corbett, Jodi Douglass, Tacy Gaede, Charo Gonzalez, Season Jensen, Beth Kephart, Connie Matthiessen, Chris Myers, Rachida Orr, Sylvia Ortiz, Susan Straight, Fufkin Vollmayer, Ayelet Waldman, Joan Walsh, and Katherine Whitney.

Finally, we'd like to thank our contributors and all the mothers we've met on the journey from *Mothers Who Think* to *Because I Said So*, women who helped us know that whatever else we're doing wrong, we did this right.

CONTENTS

INTRODUCTION

Mothers Who Think, Again

It was, like young motherhood itself, naïve if not purely delusional: Two conversation-starved and over-caffeinated mothers on a zoo outing with their children started to talk about how underserved they felt by the standard motherhood books and magazines. They ranted about the treacly mom testimonials and recycled how-tos. They decided they would create an alternative—a website where mothers could read honest, unsentimental essays by women who were struggling with the same serious issues they were. They would do this working part time, so they wouldn't miss out on decorating tomato soup with Goldfish crackers or spray-painting Halloween costumes with their four children, two of whom were under three years old. They would call their creation Mothers Who Think, in homage to Jane Smiley's essay "Can Mothers Think?," which ponders the question of whether motherhood turns women's brains to mush.

They would, in short, create a Narnia for mothers, a place where mothers could disappear through their computer screens, day or night, always miraculously on time no matter how late they showed up, always welcome to join the ongoing conversation, free to revive or chat or let off steam, and to come back later after some small elf had, inevitably, demanded their attention.

In one sense, the mothers succeeded. Their website, part of the online magazine *Salon* (and hatched with *Salon* editor Joyce

Millman), became very popular, so popular that they decided to put together a book of essays, also called *Mothers Who Think*, which they would write and edit in addition to putting out the daily website while still working part time.

Boy, were they deluded. Their husbands, both professionally supportive if not totally clear on the concept of shared parenting, failed to come through on their ends of the expected childcare partnerships. The two mothers ended up working fifty-hour weeks at *Salon*. Their professional lives leaked like spilled juice into the cracks of their other, "real" mothering lives, leaving a sticky mess—the mothers could often be seen behind piles of papers in the bleachers at soccer practice, for example, or editing copy while waiting at the pharmacy for amoxicillin prescriptions. They resorted to holding their daily editorial meetings by phone late at night, after their children and husbands were fast asleep.

They found themselves in the awkward position of writing and editing a book about motherhood while they hardly ever saw their own children. When they did see their kids, it was often to shoo them away like pigeons so they would not leave little criss-cross tracks on their mothers' thoughts. Other times they tried to ignore their children altogether, a skill they found themselves bio-logically impaired to master. Their shrewd children, who had already taken to slipping nonsensical sentences into conversations with their fathers to see if their dads were actually listening, were not about to put up with such behavior from their mothers.

Still the mothers huffed and puffed, "We think we can! We think we can!" while their children memorized the phone number of the pizza delivery place. From their makeshift desks at home, closed off from whatever domestic goings-on they had no choice but to ignore to meet their deadlines, they heard their toddlers muttering to them-selves, "Mommy's behind the door again." When the mothers would finally go to bed, images of Lewis Hine waifs and smirking little boys lobbing hand grenades disturbed their sleep.

Spring came. Their book was published. Theoretically more rested, the two mothers got themselves together for a publicity tour. Never mind that they would be gone only half the time it took them to create their exit memos listing the helpers and scheduling that would keep their children's lives running smoothly in their absence. They were the Runaway Mommies who would see their children's faces in the floral arrangements in hotel lobbies, in cloud formations scudding between high-rises in distant cities. But they were headed, eagerly, for intelligent conversation, and they had it all under control. They were Thinking Mothers with a capital TM. They were, they thought, getting good at this.

In cities across the nation, they found the village of real mothers that they had known thus far only virtually—warm, sharp, lively women who were starved for a night out and for someone to read to them. Ironically, you could not hear yourself think at these readings: they were raucous events, a cross between a Baptist testimonial and open-mike night at a stand-up comedy club. For all these mothers, the kindling of real-time, face-to-face, uninterrupted conversation had been dry for a while; it didn't take long to set it ablaze.

Each day the two mothers headed out for TV and radio appearances from their tidy hotel rooms, confident that the toilet seats would remain dry and down in their absence and that there were no jam fingerprints on the backs of their white silk blouses. In Manhattan they sipped Cadillac-size martinis under Maxfield Parrish's mural of jolly King Cole, and revived their own old souls with seaweed facials and eyelids soothed by cucumber slices at a fancy day spa. One morning they opened the *New York Times* to see "A Night Out with . . . the Mothers Who Think." And the headline wasn't meant to be some kind of oxymoron, like "military intelligence." There they were with their contributors, in living color, talking about sex, good cheese, gun control, and "Bill Nye the Science Guy."

At last the mothers returned home, triumphant. Their husbands kissed them like Adrien Brody at the Oscars, and their children squealed with delight. But the next day, they assessed the damage. Healthy, perishable food they had stocked up on before they left was still in the refrigerator, seeping and glued to the shelves; the goldfish were dead. Their husbands had run out and bought the children new clothes in lieu of learning to use the washing machine. Piles of unsigned field trip slips, homework never turned in, bills for piano lessons and diaper services were shoved into random drawers. At pickup time, a preschool teacher said to one of the mothers, "I knew you were home because her hair was brushed." The mothers were stricken by the realization that they owed weeks of carpooling and sleepovers to other mothers as payback on the huge debt they had incurred for leaving home. Bags reappeared under their once coolly cucumbered eyes. They took to drinking martinis while watching—perhaps even because they were watching—*SpongeBob SquarePants*.

They were exhausted, and so were their children. The mothers decided that the daily website was too much, and they left their jobs for other pursuits: Kate to write a novel, Camille to care for an ailing mother; both to sprinkle Goldfish on tomato soup while their kids were still young enough to care. Without its birth parents to feed and sustain it, Mothers Who Think at *Salon* eventually went the way of a Grimm fairy tale orphan, wandering unwittingly too far into the wood, leaving a diminishing trail of crumbs that was hard to follow on the forest floor.

We too had wandered off, sort of. In the midst of where our lives had taken us, there were still a few fat crumbs of nostalgia for the camaraderie and stimulation of our website and book. Like the memory of childbirth, we knew the process had been painful, but the pain itself had disappeared, and all that was left was the heady relief of having gotten through it, and the lasting pleasure of the bundle of optimism we took home when we were done.

But it wasn't just nostalgia that made us long to return to the roots of Mothers Who Think; it was a sense of necessity. We discovered it was not true that the longer we did this, the better we were at it. We did not, actually, have motherhood all figured out. We often felt like the flailing mother in British novelist Helen Simpson's short story "Golden Apples," who flags down strangers on the street to help dislodge a bean that has found its way up her child's nose. We recalled the wise observation of a seasoned mother and contributor who said that after those early, intensive years of babyhood and toddlerhood, there was a moment of calm when her work as a mother seemed to lessen, and her children seemed so independent and grown up. Then adolescence struck, and she felt again like the mother of toddlers, who needed physical closeness, support, and guidance in a way she'd thought was past.

Motherhood and time had challenged our lives, and the lives of our friends and contributors, in ways enormous and even unimaginable. Our parenting experiences were colored by war, terrorism, and increasing environmental havoc. Amid the moments of personal glory and professional success we had all experienced, there were also cancer and divorce, and cancer and divorce narrowly averted. There were pregnancies lost, and families uprooted or scarred by violence or financial disaster; there were mothers who had left their children. There were mothers losing sleep over their decision to go back to work, and mothers losing sleep over their decision to stay home. There were antidepressants, against-better-judgment PTA presidencies, playground infatuations, and full-fledged affairs. There were mothers scorned by their once-adoring daughters, and sprouting chin hair along with their adolescent sons. As we tumbled over the Niagara of our lives, we wondered why no one who had survived the drop had sent back word about the perils that lay ahead of us.

The world had shifted drastically—for our children and for us—since our last book, published in the final months of the twentieth century. As one of our contributors discovered, those five years spawned an acronym for the growing phenomenon of childhood innocence lost: KGOY—kids growing older younger. Mouseketeer turned "virgin" sex tease Britney Spears—now married to a man who shortly before fathered a second child with another woman—has matured into the young woman we least want our daughters to become. Lindsey Lohan, the freckled star of the heartwarming Disney remakes of *The Parent Trap* and *Freaky Friday*, has had her coming-of-age party in the form of a lip-licking *Rolling Stone* cover that read, "Hot, Ready, and Legal!" Boys are finding it harder to be boys without also being labeled ADD or ADHD, or saddled with some other psychiatric diagnosis that requires that they be fed drugs daily by the school nurse. With little room to run—literally and figuratively—and with sports heroes and other role models tarnished by charges of rape and drug use, perhaps it was inevitable that boys would come to idolize rappers, with their defiant, open glorification of machismo and violence. Even preschool boys are sagging their pants, no easy feat when your jeans still have an elastic waistband, while little girls jiggle their skirts down to better show their underwear.

Every school day—as we have done since our kids started kindergarten—we trace each others' paths during commutes across town from our homes on opposite ends of our city, unsettled by a deepening sense of the world encroaching ominously on our children's lives even as we shepherd them safely to school. One of our teenage sons wants to listen to hip-hop in the morning to get psyched for his classes; the other begs his mother to turn off NPR because he "can't start his day" listening to the relentlessly bleak, bloody news. And who can blame him? Childhood asthma, obesity, diabetes, and autism are on the rise, a function of the deteriorating environment, corporate avarice, or both. In four years, the U.S. budget surplus of $230 billion became a stunning deficit of $422 billion, a debt that will be shouldered by our children and their children. As we write this, just after the 2004 presidential election, welfare programs, other federally funded assistance for families, and assault weapon bans have been all but scrapped; health care is a mess; American education is falling farther and farther behind. One public school teacher in our overeducated community asked each of the assembled parents on Back-to-School Night to donate the price of a chair so that all of their children could have a seat in history class.

In fact, all of us seem to be living in the shadow of something lost, an innocence shaped like two towers. In the introduction to our book *Mothers Who Think*, we pay tribute to the origins of Mother's Day, envisioned by Julia Ward Howe in the aftermath of the American Civil War as a day for mothers to unite for peace and strategize how to make the world a better place for all children. We could not have imagined then that the good will that would unite Americans with each other and with the world in the days after 9/11 would evaporate in four short years, leaving much of the world alienated from America and the nation torn apart from within.

As the recent election made clear, politically and socially America is a nation of deep divisions: urban versus rural, liberal versus conservative, single women versus married women, white versus black, women versus men, red states versus blue states. In the United States as we know it now, the one-size-fits-all how-tos still being recycled in the parenting literature are not only useless, they are laughable, even irresponsible, as the subjects of some of the stories in this book make clear. What's a black mother to do when people assume she's the hired nanny of her biracial child? What's a modern Muslim mother to do when her American mosque tries to banish her for having a child but no husband? What's a widow to do when her son asks why his father was killed by terrorists? What's a husband to do in the waiting room while his wife's eggs are being transferred to the uterus of the woman who may carry their child to term?

Certainly, the profound issues that affect our children are as important to fathers as they are to mothers. As journalists, our husbands have been fighting to keep an independent voice alive in the arena of American politics, something vital to them not just as citizens but as parents. Yet how mothers and fathers view political and social issues often differs. Discounting "security moms" as a new, influential voting bloc—they turned out to be staunch Bush supporters whose votes were never really in question— American women still vote more consistently than men against guns and war, and in favor of increased spending on education, childcare, and social services. Given the complex and jumbled-up nature of mothers' lives, it seems that the political continually spills over into the personal, and vice versa. You aren't likely to hear men at the playground discussing the evils of high-fructose corn syrup or how the broadcast of a political event conflicts with piano practice—but you'll likely hear this from mothers.

As many of these stories also reflect, even as profoundly important issues preoccupy our thoughts and change our lives, mothers are still by and large responsible for keeping the domestic trains running on time—in the words of one contributor, providing our children with hope, strength, and dinner. Under the headline "Things You Knew But Could Never Prove," the *New York Times* recently ran the results of a survey confirming that the average working mother still spends twice as much time on household chores and the care of children compared to the average working father. It seems fittingly ironic that this moment in time saw the ignoble downfall of domestic dictator Martha Stewart and her endlessly variable recipe for complicating our lives and making us feel inadequate, alongside the rise of clean-lined *Real Simple* magazine, whose promise that we can streamline our Martha-fied lives is so alluring it has managed to hoodwink some of us into taking on more tasks in order to simplify.

While childhood may have become more sexualized, parenthood hasn't. American magazines have been flooded in the last few years with articles about sexless marriages. Allison Pearson's novel *I Don't Know How She Does It* begins with working mother Kate Reddy up late "distressing" mince pies for the school Christmas party so she can avoid sex with her husband and therefore skip a morning shower, a ruse that might give her a chance to catch up on her e-mails. In a recent British survey, a majority of fathers said they did not wake up when their babies cried during the night, and more than half admitted to sleeping on, or pretending to, even after their wives got up to tend to the child. Not surprisingly, the majority of mothers who said they preferred sleep over sex—75 percent—was precisely the same as that of fathers who preferred sleep over tending to a bawling infant. (Any mother knows that once sex goes from being recreational to procreational, it's never the same, and sleep, as one of our contributors once quipped, is very sexy.) Our contributors' admissions about sex may come as a surprise to the curious man who opens this book. Mothers love sex as much as the next guy; it's just that our idea of what makes good foreplay has changed, and any man who wants to find the right key to that door would do well to read further.

What has continued to surprise and amaze *us* is our children, with their resilience, their compassion, and their optimism even as the world seems to be chipping away at the safety and innocence of their childhoods. Forced to be more attuned to the multimedia onslaught of politics, spin, cynicism, and extreme everything, our children critique the statements of politicians and toss their pennies to wish for peace. Growing up in more diverse communities and more knowledgeable of world culture and religion, they are accepting of—even blasé about, as one of our contributors found—the many different kinds of families they encounter, despite the heated public debate over gay marriage. "If I get gay-married, I'm going to marry Miranda," said Kate's third-grade daughter recently, "and if I get regular-married, I'll marry Vikram."

A sense of this resilience and tenderness—the best of our imperfect selves reflected back to us—came up again and again as we lived and wrote and read these stories. While Camille was recovering from chemotherapy, her two boys lined her bedroom with photographs of bald-headed Sinead O'Connor, Grace Jones, and Demi Moore, to provide her with solidarity, company, and strength. One of our contributors' teenage sons complimented her on the "buff" arms that she had developed cleaning and painting houses after losing her home, her business, and her self-esteem to the plummeting economy. Another contributor's grown daughter wrote to praise her mother for working, even when it meant having to juggle her children's needs against her own—an example that inspired her daughter's career.

We chose to title this book from a position of maternal strength. *Because I Said So*—the very words conjure images of fierce mothers in aprons, hands planted on their hips, imposing boundaries that will not be breached. And these four words also evoke the emphatic telling of mothers' truths, so deeply understood and felt that their explanations are self-evident.

The stories in *Because I Said So* reflect real motherhood just after the turn of a new century, as we find ourselves living, like Julia Ward Howe, in the shadow of many battles. A reminder that motherhood is a lifelong experience, the book welcomes back eight of the contributors to *Mothers Who Think*, and features twenty-five new contributors wrestling with the personal and the political, the minutiae that occupies their days and the larger concerns that keep them awake at night, and their sense of themselves as it evolves and deepens. Some of these mothers are well known for their fiction, poetry, and journalism; others are appearing in print for the first time. None of them fails to hold to the light the jewel-like, shifting facets of astonishment, bliss, humor, and ferocious love that having children has brought to their lives, or the darker shimmer of anxiety over the endlessly conflicting decisions they are forced to make as mothers. To put it another way, motherhood, as one of our contributors once observed, is like a *mille-feuille* pastry: countless flaky layers—both buttery and sweet, crunchy and delicious—and there, deep at the creamy center, is guilt. Yet as we brush the flaky remains from our laps, we are inspired and humbled by these stories' reminder that no role is more powerful in the shaping of the future than is motherhood. It is this profound, daily responsibility to the next generation—our future teachers and soldiers and artists and presidents—that keeps giving mothers more to think about, not less.

Are we doing this right yet? Or are we forever like the mother whose child has a bean up her nose? We don't know. We do know that the two mothers who blithely stumbled through the zoo seven years ago searching for nonfat lattes and sure that they could do this motherhood thing better could never have predicted the intensity and the range of stories that fill this book. Whether you read these essays while breastfeeding, sleepless during a teenager's late-night joyride in the family car, or waiting for a prune-skinned child to allow her removal from an ice-cold bathtub, we hope they will draft you instantly into a dream mother's group of warm, sharp, lively women whose shared and vastly different experiences unite us to one another, and to mothers through time. Quirky, tender, funny, and harrowing—filled with true shock and awe—these stories helped us reconnect to something vital that has not changed: our belief, as mothers, that it is essential to look squarely at the dark and the light. As different as our stories are as mothers, we believe that all of them are part of our own story. To paraphrase another smart contributor, to share them makes us all better.

Camille Peri and Kate Moses
San Francisco
November 2004

Because I Said So

The Scarlet Letter *Z*

Asra Q. Nomani

Ugly whispers about me began long before I found myself, in the summer of 2004, standing before a massive green door that led into the mosque in the town that I have known as my home since I was a girl of ten. The door stood in front of me like an entryway into my own personal hell.

My local community of Muslims—interconnected via the Internet with like-minded Muslims globally—had rebuked me for giving birth to a child out of wedlock and living without shame with this fact, then writing about it publicly to defend the rights of women who were quietly punished for similar cultural trespasses in the far corners of the world. From the pulpit of our mosque, a Ph.D. student called unchaste women "worthless." In the grocery store, an elder I had called "uncle" since my childhood days averted his eyes from mine when I passed him in the fruit section. A professor told his children to stay away from me. My family lost Muslim friendships of thirty years, relationships considered solid since we first made this town our home.

Criticism and condemnation seemed to come from everywhere: a Charleston, West Virginia, man wrote that I should stay in the shadows: "It would have been best if the facts of [your son's] birth had not been so callously flaunted. . . . Do you HAVE to rub it in?" When a Muslim immigrant said I was unfit to be a leader because of my unwed motherhood, an American convert responded, ". . . why not just make her wear a big red *Z* on all of her clothes, for *zina*, so everyone can steer clear and judge her for the rest of her life, like the adulteress in *The Scarlet Letter*?" Finally, the men at my mosque were putting me on trial, trying to banish me—a symbolic exile from our community.

It was my mother, Sajida, strong and supportive and curious, who first sought out Nathaniel Hawthorne's novel. "You are Hester Prynne," she told me when she closed the cover. I read it next, and she was right: the elders of our mosque were like the seventeenth-century Puritans in *The Scarlet Letter* who sentenced a single mother, Hester Prynne, to forever wear the letter *A* on her chest as punishment for the adultery in which she had conceived a child.

Three hundred years later, I was being subjected to the same experience of religious scrutiny, censure, and community rejection in a country that was founded on religious freedom. But could I garner anywhere near the strength of Hester's inner character in the inquisition that I faced? To walk into my house of worship was to invite the demons of hatred into my life. With a deep breath I opened the door, my son scampering inside ahead of me.

> *A throng of bearded men, in sad-colored garments and gray, steeple-crowned hats, intermixed with women, some wearing hoods, and others bareheaded, was assembled in front of a wooden edifice, the door of which was heavily timbered with oak, and studded with iron spikes.*

An assembly of my community sat, mostly men with beards, crocheted prayer caps, and dim-colored pants and T-shirts; others were clean-shaven, intermixed with women hooded with *hijab*, the head covering of Muslim women. I tucked my jet black hair into the hood of the oversize black, hooded jacket I had won in a beach volleyball tournament in my younger days. Like Hester most of her life, hiding her lush hair under a cap, I was making myself asexual in this world in which my sexuality had become the evidence of my criminality. But my jacket had the label "Six Pack," insider volleyball lingo for the power of a hard-driven spike hitting an opponent's face.

I took a seat at one end of the cafeteria-style tables arranged in a *U*. At the head of the table, a gray-haired, bearded, casually dressed elder, a university professor, got down to business. He pulled strips of paper with names typed on them out of a plastic Ziploc sandwich bag. He read the names on the slips of paper as if he were the master of ceremonies at a carnival drawing winners for raffle prizes. In fact, these were the names of those who would be the jury for the secret tribunal that the professor and the other leaders of the mosque had initiated against me. The judges at this "Ziploc justice" trial would be the five-member board of trustees that ran the mosque.

My crimes? In October 2003, I had walked through the front door of my mosque on the first night it opened, my infant son, Shibli, on my hip, instead of taking the rear entrance designated for women. I sat in the secluded women's balcony that night, but eleven days later, I walked through the front door and into the main hall, which is reserved for men. Then, when the mosque elders wouldn't meet with me, I wrote about the rights denied women in mosques such as mine, drawing attacks on my family and myself. But questioning the leadership and policies of the mosque wasn't enough to earn the full wrath of my community. My greatest offense was being an unwed mother.

> *She had wandered, without rule or guidance, in a moral wilderness; as vast, as intricate and shadowy, as the untamed forest, amid the gloom . . .*

From my first memories, my life has been defined by a search for community. I was born in India but came to America at the age of four to join my mother and father, arriving with my older brother, Mustafa. Our parents had settled in New Jersey so that my father, Zafar, could pursue his academic career. I loved the one-story red house that we called home. It was part of a colony of World War II barracks converted to student housing. Animals stared at me out of a dense jungle scene on my bedroom walls; above me, glow-in-the-dark stars twinkled, and the sweet scent of honeysuckle swept inside from beyond my bedroom window. Here I felt safe from the outside world, where I was always reminded that I had been transplanted.

I remember standing on the curb outside my elementary school one December day. Raised in traditional Muslim families in India, my parents knew nothing about Christmas gift exchanges in America, and bought me Barbie dolls to give to my schoolmates year after year. By the fifth grade, the girls in my class protested. On the day of the gift exchange, I placed a desperate call home from the school office. My father promptly rounded the corner in our Plymouth Valiant and dropped McDonald's gift certificates into my hand.

"Thank you." I sighed, clutching the gift certificates, and I leapt back to class to exonerate my reputation under the Christmas tree.

When I was ten, my family moved to Morgantown, West Virginia, a small community tucked into the hills of Appalachian coal country. My father taught at the university; I became a National Honor student and a Who's Who among American high school students. But I never felt as if I belonged.

Throughout my teens, I challenged my cultural ethos, with my protests often aimed at my father as the embodiment of the restrictions I felt. When I was nine years old, he laid down the law that I could no longer wear skirts because I was now too old to show my legs. Nevertheless, I whipped around the coliseum track in the 880-yard run and played on the high school volleyball team in shorts and a sleeveless shirt, my devout father still cheering me from the bleachers. As a good Muslim girl, I also wasn't allowed to date: I turned down our senior class president when he asked me to the prom, and another boy who asked me on a theater date. By the time I hit my sophomore year as a West Virginia University co-ed, though, I couldn't resist the natural temptations of life: at eighteen, I fell in love with my first boyfriend, a white, Catholic, Special Forces Reservist who tucked Skoal chewing tobacco into the back pocket of his Levi's.

Knowing that the enticements of the West lay before me, still my father drove me to New York City for a summer internship at *Harper's* magazine. Such independence was unorthodox in Muslim households, where the strictest families wouldn't allow a girl to travel without a chaperone, but my father believed I should pursue my dream to be a journalist. No dummy, though, he deposited me at a women-only boarding house in Manhattan.

I had started on the slippery slope to my own empowerment. In my junior year, I sat across from my father at a Chinese buffet restaurant and broke the news that he had hoped he would never hear: "Dad, I want to move out." A good Muslim girl left her father's house only for her husband's house, not for a bachelorette pad with Annette and Debbie, the sports editor and news editor, respectively, of the student *Daily Athenaeum*. My father struggled with my decision, but I finally received a letter with roses on the stationery.

"*Behti*," he wrote, using the Urdu word for "daughter," "I love you."

As a twenty-year-old, I swept through my college graduation ceremony with my shins visible under my gown, wearing a skirt for the first time as an adult. Despite the many times my father had shown pride in and acceptance of me throughout my life, I could sense his discomfort and disapproval, and I hated him for it. Seven years later, when my short-lived marriage to a Muslim man ended, I buried my face in a pillow in shame. My husband's father had complained that I hadn't cooked three meals a day at home. My father tried to assure me that I didn't have to blame myself. He didn't expect me to sacrifice my self-esteem for a bad marriage. "I don't care about the marriage. I care about you. I don't want to lose you," he said, trying to comfort me.

"Leave me alone!" I yelled. "I hate you."

He embraced me in the proper, Muslim fatherly way that ensured he didn't have too much frontal contact, and whispered, "I love you, *behti*," before quietly slipping out of the room. I felt worthless.

For years, I chafed under the harness that people of my religion—and so many other religions—had put upon women to control them. Unfairly, in my mind my father became the manifestation of centuries of male domination. I continued to fight the patriarchy in my career as a globetrotting journalist for the *Wall Street Journal,* and then as a book author.

After the terrorist attacks of September 11, 2001, I went to Pakistan on assignment as a journalist for the online magazine *Salon,* and fell in love with a man while wading in the warm waters of the Arabian Sea, off the shores of Karachi.

He was a friend of a family friend's friend's son—in my native land, that virtually made him family. He was a young and hip Muslim, part of the Karachi elite that spent weekends at a place called French Beach. We fell madly in love and consummated our devotion on the shore where we had first met, the stars twinkling above us, just as they had in my childhood bedroom. He told me he wanted to marry me. When I discovered I was pregnant, however, he changed his mind and scorned me.

I could barely tell my mother about my pregnancy. I didn't dare tell my father, but eventually she did. Later I learned that he wept, not from any shame he personally felt but because of the suffering he anticipated I would experience as an unwed Muslim mother.

She turned her eyes downward at the scarlet letter, and even touched it with her finger, to assure herself that the infant and the shame were real. Yes!—these were her realities,—all else had vanished!

The letter I would wear was Z, for *zina,* a crime considered one of the most serious in Islam: illegal sex—extramarital and premarital sex. In a Muslim state such as Pakistan, *zina* is a violation of *shari'a,* or Islamic law. While Hester Prynne's punishment was to stand on the pillory for three hours of public disgrace and to wear the letter A for the rest of her life, the *shari'a* sentence for adultery is stoning to death. The punishment for premarital sex in Pakistan is one hundred lashes and, often, exile. To appease

Muslim purists, some countries have been strengthening these laws and their enforcement. Increasingly, women charged with *zina* end up in jail, often with their babies. In 1980, few women were imprisoned in Pakistan. By 2002, most of the nearly 1,500 women in Pakistani jails were imprisoned for having crossed societal boundaries, much as Hester Prynne and I had done.

In 2002, a previously lenient Malaysian province passed a law making *zina* a criminal offense. An Iranian actress received a suspended sentence of seventy-four lashes in 2003 for kissing a male director on the cheek during an awards ceremony. He was a student of her late husband. Not surprisingly, the director wasn't prosecuted. It is women, rarely men, who become targets of these punitive sex laws.

In 2002, Islamic judges sentenced a Nigerian mother, Amina Lawal, to death for having had a baby while unmarried. Her sentence was to be buried to her shoulders and pelted with stones until she died. I was pregnant with my son at the time, and I followed Lawal's case closely, horrified. There was one common bit of evidence used to convict women like Amina Lawal: their babies. Every day untold numbers of Muslim women aborted their pregnancies, dumped their babies in rubbish piles, or secretly abandoned their children so they themselves wouldn't face the consequences of having had a child out of wedlock.

"I have thought of death," she said,—"have wished for it,— would even have prayed for it, were it fit that such as I should pray for any thing."

My despair was so deep during my pregnancy that I looked for ways to end my life. I scanned the Internet and searched words on Google: *poison* and *suicide*. I found a website that lists the pros and cons of various methods, and I studied the success rates, printing out the list and marking the best possibilities. My future seemed so bleak. I loved the father of my baby, but clearly he had abandoned me.

I left Pakistan for Morgantown, pregnant and angry. I

returned home to West Virginia and found my father redecorating a room for my baby and me, his fingernails coated with paint. I was not to be imprisoned or lashed. I had the support of loving parents and was shielded by progressive laws and societal notions that had largely decriminalized consensual adult sex in a country where religion and state are separated.

> *Man had marked this woman's sin by a scarlet letter, which had such potent and disastrous efficacy that no human sympathy could reach her, save it were sinful like herself. God, as a direct consequence of the sin which man thus punished, had given her a lovely child, whose place was on that same dishonored bosom, to connect her parent for ever with the race and descent of mortals, and to be finally a blessed soul in heaven!*

"He is beautiful," I whispered as I took my son into my arms for the first time in the protected space of my hometown hospital's maternity ward.

It was a death-defying delivery, as so many are, in which my baby's heartbeat slowed suddenly and dangerously, sending me into the operating room for a C-section. When I emerged from the slumber of my anesthesia, I felt as though my son had given me new life. He was *so* beautiful. None of the trauma of my pregnancy had soiled his perfection. He had lashes that flapped like butterfly wings, long and graceful. He breathed gently and softly. And, my father insisted, he had smiled when he emerged.

When my baby was born, it was my father who whispered the *azan*, or Muslim call to prayer, into his ear, a responsibility usually reserved for a baby's father. I named my son Shibli, meaning "my lion cub" in Arabic, evoking the most famous ancestor in my paternal lineage, a late-nineteenth-century Islamic reformer and scholar by the name of Shibli Nomani.

I had new life. I did not have to accept the dishonor that had marked my state of mind during my pregnancy. My body had shaken with so many tears during those months. No more, I told myself. With my son, I was reborn.

Alone in the world, cast off by it, and with this sole treasure to keep her heart alive, she felt that she possessed indefeasible rights against the world, and was ready to defend them to the death.

My father had helped to build the new mosque in Morgantown, and I was excited to join the local Muslim community. When Shibli was three months old, I had taken him with me, bouncing on my chest in his baby carrier, to Mecca for the holy pilgrimage of the *haj*; on his first birthday party, I initiated him into life as a Muslim with a ritual Muslim naming ceremony. But when I tried to enter the mosque with Shibli on its opening night, the president of the board stood at the door and barked at me to take the door reserved for women. "Sister, please, take the back entrance!"

The men at the mosque expected women to take the rear entrance to an isolated balcony, denying the rights Islam had granted women centuries ago, which allowed them to participate and pray in mosques without having to be hidden behind a partition. I walked through the front door despite the board president's protests.

Days later, I entered the main hall with Shibli in my arms. I had no intention of praying right next to the men, who were seated at the front of the cavernous hall. I just wanted a place in the main prayer space, not up in the balcony, where women who wanted to participate in the activities did so long distance, through notes sent down to the men. As my mother, my niece Safiyyah, and I sat twenty feet behind the men, a loud voice broke the quiet. "Sister, please! Please leave!" the mosque president yelled at me. "It is better for women upstairs."

"Thank you, brother," I said firmly. "I'm happy praying here."

The president went to the mosque's lower floor, where my father had taken Shibli so that my mother and I could pray. I couldn't make out all of their words, but I could hear my father's voice filter upstairs with proclamations such as "equal rights" and "justice."

The next day the men on the board met and passed a rule to make the front door and main hall solely for the use of men. In protest, my father choked on his tears as he appealed to them to open their doors—not shut them—to his daughter and other women who were trying to find their place in the mosque. "Please have mercy on me!" my father cried. They remained firm, and through the months that followed, my father, too, remained solid in his support for my position.

Another night, I sat respectfully behind the men for a weekly study session in the mosque. The men exploded with anger that I had dared join their class, usually attended only by men. A member of the congregation, one of my father's colleagues at the university, wildly gesticulated at my father and lashed out at him verbally. "You are an idiot!" he thrice exclaimed, making his point with this logic: "Look at the kind of daughter you raised!"

Shaken, I returned home, hurt and angry. My father stood by me. "They do not like losing their men's club," he said. "Do not let their words hurt you."

Paradoxically, I had also begun to feel free. I was ruffling feathers because I was not hiding the fact that I was an unwed mother. But this gave me the strength to overtly challenge the system: writing about it, refusing to be silenced, fighting for inclusiveness and tolerance. I wrote an essay for the *Washington Post* about reclaiming the rights Islam had granted to women in mosques in the seventh century. In it I mentioned that the kindness of many Muslims to my single motherhood had buoyed my hope in the Muslim community.

So I wasn't surprised when the matronly wife of one of the mosque elders, neighbors of my parents, called me shortly after I walked through the front door of the mosque. I had heard a rumor sweeping through the community: her husband was insisting on marrying a second wife in their native country, against her wishes. I was fighting for women like her, whose husbands filled the mosque with chauvinist chatter. At the mosque, her husband had won support for polygamy.

When I arrived at the woman's house, she opened the door with a smile. She invited me to tea and I settled into her oversize sofa, absorbed the Qur'anic verses framed and hanging from the walls, and readied for her secret expression of support. Instead, through smiles, she admonished me.

"You are young and pretty. The men, they are weak. They are selfish. Let them have their place," she argued.

I sat, dumbfounded. She took issue with my argument that unwed mothers shouldn't be stoned to death or lashed. "It is God's law," she said. "You should spend the rest of your life praying for repentance."

Not long after my neighbor's reproof, I gathered with our community for a holy feast marking the day that Abraham was prepared to slaughter his son Ishmael in response to God's call, an act meant to symbolize the challenge of every person to sacrifice that which gets in the way of their spiritual practice.

A clown entertained the children in a spacious restaurant. After the clown was finished, the women scampered off with their children to a cramped private room with a security guard posted out front to guard them from intruders. The men took over the main dining room and bounced from table to table in festive conversation.

Overheating with the pulse of so many women and children in our small space, I greeted a young woman ripe with new motherhood. Her newborn on her lap, she tore into me. "I don't agree with the way you are trying to bring about change. People are going to think you're crazy."

With my son ready to tumble a tray of basmati rice to the floor, she continued: "I'm not saying it, but others are going to say, 'Look, she's an unwed mother. She breaks rules.'"

By this point, Shibli had lost interest in the rice and turned to a tray of salad. "I am trying to make our communities welcome all women," I tried to explain.

The young woman was only interested in making her point. "I'm not saying it, but others are going to say, 'Look, she's an unwed mother' . . ."

I stopped listening to her chiding of me, only to hear her complain a moment later, "We have nothing to drink while the men have everything."

> *In all her intercourse with society, however, there was nothing that made her feel as if she belonged to it. Every gesture, every word, and even the silence of those with whom she came in contact, implied, and often expressed, that she was banished, and as much alone as if she inhabited another sphere . . .*

I continued to publish articles and opinion pieces about sexism and intolerance in the Muslim community, reporting on the appeal of Amina Lawal, the Nigerian mother who had escaped being stoned to death when her conviction was overturned. My public stance gave my detractors the opportunity to scrutinize and discredit everything about me. I was equated scornfully with novelist Salman Rushdie, who had gone into hiding after a *fatwa* that ruled he should be killed for his writings, which had been deemed blasphemous; and with Taslima Nasreen, who also had a *fatwa* on her head in her native Bangladesh for her writings challenging traditional Muslim society. Muslim readers complained via e-mail that I was trying to force "progressive" ways onto the traditions of Islam, that I didn't cover my head with a scarf, and that I had had a photo taken by a male photographer who wasn't my *mahram*—an adult male chaperone from my family. My maternal instincts were questioned for my not shielding my son from the shame of his birth, and it was predicted that he too would be ostracized. I was devastated when I read an e-mail from a Muslim man who insisted that I should give my son up for adoption. Not one of the people who denounced me raised the issue of my baby's father's responsibilities.

I received notice of my twenty-first-century inquisition via e-mail. The elder who was president of the mosque's management committee wrote that "about thirty-five" members of the mosque had signed a petition to revoke my membership and expel me from the mosque. It was alleged that I had engaged in actions and

practices that were "disruptive to prayer, worship and attendance" and "harmful to members of our community."

This elder, a university professor active in the Muslim
Students' Association, had earlier complained about "the sound
of Ms. Nomani writing notes and flipping pieces of paper" during
Friday sermons. In the spirit of Ziploc justice, he had led a
takeover of the mosque and gotten elected president in a rushed
election. Students who preached hatred became volunteer *imams*,
religious leaders who give sermons at the pulpit.

The professor gave me two days' notice before my trial would
begin.

. . . it may seem marvellous, that this woman should still call
that place her home, where, and where only, she must needs
be the type of shame. . . . Here, she said to herself, had been
the scene of her guilt, and here should be the scene of her
earthly punishment; . . . Hester Prynne, therefore, did not flee.

The night of the trial arrived. My stomach was in turmoil. A
terrible pain pierced my head in the minutes before the trial was
to begin. I wanted to flee.

My mobile phone rang. It was Amina Wadud, an African
American scholar of Islam. "They have no Islamic right to banish
you from the mosque," she told me firmly. "Stay strong."

I lay down at home, trying to draw whatever reserves I could
find. Instead, I found myself doubled over in suffering on my bed.
"They are trying to drive me from my home," I cried. "I feel so
alone." But I wasn't. As the moment arrived for me to leave, my
father embraced me and said, "You are not alone. We are here."

My mother, too, stood by me. "This does not upset me," she
said, looking me straight in the eye. "It should not upset you."
With that, she gave me the simple jumpstart kick only a mother
can give a child. I splashed cold water on my face and knew that I
would not run away.

• • •

While the world watched Saddam Hussein's courtroom defiance on TV, I wasn't even allowed to turn on my digital recorder in our mosque.

I asked for a copy of the complaint against me. Denied. I asked for the names of the complainants. Denied. I asked for a delay so I could find legal counsel. Denied. Muslim civil rights groups had demanded and won due process rights for Muslim prisoners-of-war in Guantánamo Bay, but here in my own country, I was being denied them.

My mosque leaders reduced me to lining up in front of me the slips of paper with the jurors' names, in an effort to cross-check them against the mosque's membership list. My mother alone was with me, because my father had been rushed to the hospital. The stress had weakened his health; he hadn't been able to catch his breath. As he rested with electrodes attached to his body, his brothers in the mosque put his daughter through the first steps of her trial.

An American convert, chairwoman of the committee to educate non-Muslims about Islam, tried to talk to me as I kept order of the papers. She used to be the mosque's bell ringer. After all my clamoring about equal rights, she had won a position at the table, but I had heard not a peep of support from her. Now she whispered, "Asra, I want you to know that a lot of people don't support this petition to ban you."

That could very well have been true; her name was not among those of the thirty-five members who had signed the petition. But that left about one hundred members who hadn't taken a stand. They were just another part of the silent, moderate majority who allow extremists to define Islam in the world.

". . . a father's kindness towards the poor, deserted babe."

"Mama! Dada! Mama! Dada! Mama! Dada!" my young son cooed every night, lulling himself to sleep by singing my name and the Urdu name he called my father.

Literally, *dada* means "paternal grandfather," and it was the word that Shibli had heard my brother's children call my seventy-two-year-old father. This gentle man has taken to calling himself a "soccer mom" in his retirement days, shuttling his grandchildren to the arts center and soccer field, changing diapers. Whenever I hear Shibli comfort himself with his names for my father and me, my heart swells.

For so many years I had held the forces of my culture's paternalism against my father—my loving, accepting father. But as religiously orthodox as he might have seemed to my rebellious younger self, he always tried to be open-minded and compassionate. His rejection of the social stigma of Shibli's conception had been a public manifestation of his unconditional love for me. And by showing me that unconditional love, he helped free me to be a mother who could show unconditional love to her son. Making peace with my father meant making peace with myself.

My son helped me realize that my father is an extraordinary man. He could have bowed to societal and extended family pressure to live a public lie about my child, but he urged me to be truthful. Through the circle of life, these two generations, boy and man, had encouraged me to be a strong, powerful woman.

In a gesture of our solidarity, before my trial my father and I had written an article on the battle at the mosque for the *Journal of Islamic Law and Culture.* We had traveled so far together, as father and daughter, to transcend our traditional boundaries. It was not a victory just for Islam, I told him when the article was published, but for us.

As my trial wore on, I sat through a night in my father's room at the hospital where Shibli had been born. Earlier that evening, my father had patiently hosted a visit from his busy, toddler grandson, who turned the sink faucet into a fountain, spraying the room. Now I watched my father sleep; the gentle sound of his breath filled the quiet room. The water dripped in the apparatus that sent him fresh oxygen. My father's body was feeling the burden of challenging the dark forces in this world with the only weapon he had: love.

Here, where vulnerability pierced ego, I was able to see my father with clarity. Earlier, he had wept in the emergency room for the way puritans, with their divisive ideology, had overtaken our local Muslim community. "I love everybody," he cried. When he awoke in the morning, it would be my turn to echo the words that had allowed me to rewrite Hester Prynne's legacy in the twenty-first century. "I love you," I would tell him.

There were two Latin words that separated my fate from the destinies of women such as Hester Prynne: *pro bono.* I knew it was time to hire a lawyer. Amina Lawal did not have one when an all-male jury of Muslim men sentenced her to death; but for her appeal, she had Nigerian attorney and human rights activist Ayesha Imam. Imam helped Lawal win her freedom.

I had a powerful legal team headed by an American Jewish lawyer and an Egyptian American Muslim attorney. Attorney David Remes supported my case as he concurrently represented Muslim prisoners in Guantánamo Bay. He identified my defense immediately in the mosque constitution: "Each member shall exercise tolerance and respect the right of other members and their opinions." Mr. Remes wanted to invoke Islamic justice, because he knew it should prevail when it came to truth-telling.

I was also blessed to have standing by me Khalid Abou El Fadl, one of the greatest scholars of Islamic law. Dr. Fadl said that Islamic jurisprudence did not allow political expediency to override a morally compelled duty such as speaking the truth. "The Prophet says a person who conspires is a silent devil," he told me. "No one has a right to put you on trial. This is nothing less than an inquisition."

As my trial continued, I took to heart acts of faith in which my twenty-one-month-old son revealed to me the divine providence of following my instincts as his mother and as a truth-teller. I knew that this effort to exile me, if successful, would be a de facto ban not only on my son but also on the future of truth-telling in the Muslim world. And I knew that truth and righteousness would prevail; my son told me so.

The Ziploc justice meeting broke up as the man who had

declared that I was worthless recited the *azan,* or call to prayer, which starts, "Allahu Akbar."

Listening to the call spill into the room, Shibli paused from his spinning around the room with his Foosball.

"Ababooboo," he said through a grin, imitating the sound of the *azan.*

As my mother and I gathered to leave, Shibli scampered upstairs into the main hall and stood in the sacred space where my mother and I had taken to sitting. He lay in full prostration in the darkness, just like a good Muslim man, then jumped up with a smile and caught my hand in his own.

"Hester," said he, "hast thou found peace?"

In the end, Hester Prynne becomes a heroine to her community and in American literature. She perseveres. Her daughter, Pearl, marries into a royal family and, though Hester leaves her cottage at the outskirts of the village for some years, she returns to give counsel to others who carry a psychic scarlet letter on their hearts.

As I write this, I remain under trial. Even if I am ultimately banished from my mosque, I consider the trial and the cultural examination it has opened a victory, for myself and for others. A gay man from the Arab world wrote to ask me how he could overcome the despair of being considered a criminal in his native land. A crowd of Muslims, young and old, male and female, mobbed me in support after I made a presentation at a large Islamic organization's convention about women's rights in Muslim communities. A young woman from Pakistan hugged me again and again in appreciation of my efforts to reclaim women's rights in Islam. A young woman from Boston thanked me for my work and said, "Give a kiss to Shibli from me."

I reject the letter Z that many in my community want to thrust upon me. The message I stand for, instead, is women's rights and truth. One night, in downtown Morgantown, holding Shibli's hand, I walked with a poster board I had created emblazoned with an "Islamic Bill of Rights for Women in Mosques." Standing in front of a notorious underage bar was one of my greatest detractors at the mosque, a Muslim man whose family operates the club; ironically, the bar is named Club Z. Surrounded by co-eds in micro-miniskirts, he avoided my eye. I stood strong and proud, firmly holding my son's hand and my poster. I knew the spirit of Hester Prynne walked with me.

> *Her sex, her youth, and the whole richness of her beauty, came back from what men call the irrevocable past, and clustered themselves, with her maiden hope, and a happiness before unknown, within the magic circle of this hour. . . . All at once, as was with a sudden smile of heaven, forth burst the sunshine, pouring a very flood into the obscure forest, gladdening each green leaf, transmuting the yellow fallen ones to gold, and gleaming adown the gray trunks of the solemn trees.*

Feeling triumphant about standing before my community, regardless of the final resolution of my trial, I took my mother and son to California for a few days' respite. My father was recuperating at home, trawling Internet message boards discussing my case. "Death to Asra," said one that called for me to be stoned to death. On the other side of the country, I took Shibli to the shore of the Pacific Ocean. The wind snapped his face into wide grins, the sun glittered off his untamed curls. My mother quietly smiled. I took to flight and flipped through the air in a cartwheel, free.

Two Heads Are Better Than Three

Mary Roach

In the early days of transplant science, a horribly enthusiastic surgeon named Vladimir Demikhov grafted the head of a puppy onto the neck of a full-grown dog—a dog that already had a head, thank you very much. In the files for my last book, I have a photograph of the aftermath of this ill-advised undertaking. The severed head is sewn into the front of the neck of the intact dog, nose up, so that the two canines are face-to-face, constantly reminded of each other's presence. You can almost see the Wellbutrin bottle in the background.

Bear with me, I'm working on a metaphor here.

Seven years ago, I met a man and fell in love. He had been married before and had two young daughters. Because I was in love, and because at that time his children lived with their mother in another state and our visits with them went well, I did not give the complexities of the situation all that much thought. I did not read even one of the dozen or so books out there about "blended families." (I love the term "blended." I love the ridiculous optimism of it. It suggests an outcome that is smooth and delightful and effortless to attain. "I'll be the mango!" *"I'll* be bananas!" "Dad, you push FRAPPE!")

After a couple years, the man's family moved back to our city.

Do you see what I wrote? "The man's family." They were his family, and I was his second wife. His parents are her kids' grandparents, which gives his ex-wife a permanent slot there between the generations on the family tree. I don't know if there's even a protocol for adding second wives to family trees. I'm imagining a faint dotted line of the sort used by mapmakers to delineate unpaved roads or proposed subway extensions that have been in the works since the Eisenhower administration. There is an inalterable solidity to the ties of matrilineage. These are people attached to one another by the uncorrodable bonds of blood and ancestry and family photo albums. A second wife is a flimsy, sewn-on thing.

This became clear to me shortly after their return. My husband's ex-wife gave me a present and a card that said, "Welcome to the family." This was an extraordinarily nice gesture, for she is an extraordinarily nice and generous person, but for some reason it did not sit right with me. When you first fall in love with someone, you have a sense of the two of you as a complete and perfect universe. Like any new couple, you want to feel like the core of a family unit. It was naïve and self-centered, but such is the nature of new love. Reading that card was my Demikhov moment. You are the stitched-on dog head, it might as well have said. No, I thought, *you* are. No, YOU are!

Then I forgot about it, because things were going well. My husband's kids liked me, and when the four of us were together, I permitted myself to think of us as a family. The transplant, it seemed, had taken. Of course, this probably made my husband's ex-wife—"my ex-wife," as I sometimes slip up and call her—feel like the unwanted dog head. (With stepfamilies, it seems, someone always has to be holding the "big fat loser alone at recess" card. I once saw a book entitled *How to Win as a Stepfamily*. I imagined opening it up and finding 213 blank pages with the last page saying, "Ha, ha, ha, ha, ha, ha YOU CAN'T!!!!")

As it turned out, the ex-wife did not have to feel this way for long. Soon it was my turn. Like transplanted appendages, stepparents are allowed to thrive and feel good for a short while before the rejection stage begins. Family counselors call this the "honeymoon period." Inevitably and all too soon, the honeymoon ends. Someone starts to have issues.

Often this coincides with someone hitting puberty. Up until puberty, you can pretty much get a kid to go along with anything. All kids have issues with a parent's remarriage, but the issues remain more or less subcutaneous until adolescence. As long as the equilibrium holds, stepparents—provided they are not abusive, overbearing boors—are treated like any other adult in the child's universe: one more person to play Chinese checkers or spring for lip gloss. Not the greatest thing in the world, but not the worst.

Then comes puberty. Now the issues demand to be heard. They unionize. They organize demonstrations and carry signs. This is a period when everything is annoying, and a stepmother, especially to a girl, can top the list. A stepmother is a random extraneous adult thrown into a girl's life, day in and day out, taking up her dad's time and attention, which she doesn't want anyway these days but she's going to resent its absence nonetheless. The child who just last year was walking hand-in-hand with you to the corner store is now refusing to laugh at your jokes or look you in the eye.

I was no longer me; I had become the things I represented: someone standing in the way of Mom and Dad's remarriage, someone who usurps dad's love. When I look at the situation from a stepchild's perspective, I can understand the resentment. Of course they have issues. I would too. That doesn't mean I enjoy it or handle it well. Issues breed issues. It is not easy to enjoy the company of someone who makes it clear, however subtly, that she wishes you'd go away. Not surprisingly, the odds are not in favor of the stepfamily living happily ever after. I read somewhere that 60 percent of marriages involving "blended" families end in divorce. Rocks in the Osterizer.

Part of the problem is this loaded and mostly outmoded word *stepparent*. It's a holdover from the days when divorce was uncommon and stepparents were mainly people married to widows and widowers. Unless an actual parent has died and the step-parent functions as an ersatz actual parent, the word just makes everyone uncomfortable. It sets up confusing expectations. (Under the heading "relationship" on my older stepdaughter's high school emergency contact form, it says, for me, "Dad's wife.") If people are referring to you as a stepparent, you imagine you will be occupying some sort of vaguely parent-like post, and that even if you don't behave like a parent and mete out discipline or pick them up at school, there will be some sort of familial bond. But why should there be? A child who has two loving parents does not need or want a third. Especially a bogus one who didn't give birth to you and who can't be relied on to send letters while you're at summer camp and who doesn't know the songs you all sang in the car together when you were growing up. Who is this woman? What is she doing at parents' night? How did she get into a book about mothers?

While I'm not wild about my status as stitched-on appendage, I view it as just. No one owes me otherwise. And there have been times—there *are* times—when I feel genuinely loved and appreciated by one or another of my stepkids. To feel the affection or love of someone who has cause and cultural rubber-stamp to resent you is a uniquely precious thing. Unlike the love between parent and child, this love you don't take for granted. It's an Indian summer kind of love—maybe it'll show up this week, maybe it won't. But when it does, it's a gift, and you run out and bask in it.

We're an odd, ungainly thing, this three-headed family of ours, but we seem to have adapted to our condition. All families have some sort of metaphorical deformity. There are ripped-out hearts and overactive spleens, forked tongues and wandering loins. Relatively speaking, we're as normal and healthy as the next dog.

Material Girls

Margaret Talbot

I don't have anything against dolls, but part of me has always found them a little creepy—their inert perfection, their blinky eyes, the way you find them in odd corners of the house, limbs akimbo, as if dropped from a great height. As a child, I had a Barbie with a frothy black cocktail dress and a Heidi doll I was fond of, though I could never get her hair rigged back up into those cinnamon buns on either side of her head after I'd unbraided it. I was impatient and a klutz, so buttons and bows, especially tiny ones, were a trial. In any case, I was more of a stuffed-animal girl myself, and my daughter, who is five, seems to be one too. She's had a few baby dolls, which she has graced with peculiar names—Ha-Ha, Pogick—but her interest in them, though warm, is intermittent. They spend most of their time upside down in the toy basket, missing crucial garments, which is why, I suppose, I don't care much for that genre of children's story in which toys come to life and bemoan their little masters' neglect of them.

So it was something of a surprise to me when, about a year ago, I developed a mild obsession with American Girl dolls. I read the catalogs; I read the books. I made a special trip to American Girl Place, the vast doll emporium in New York, where, without my children, I felt like a doll stalker or one of those self-styled hobbyists with a little too much time on her hands. (I kept thinking of a little amusement park we sometimes go to that has an ominous placard forbidding adults to enter unaccompanied by children.) I drifted by the clusters of mothers and grandmothers and little girls in satin-lined winter coats, their noses pressed against glass cases of doll accessories, their expressions sweetly avid. Sales people kept asking pointedly if they could help me.

Could they? I didn't know. The American Girl story fascinated me partly because of its sheer, almost shocking success. Mostly it fascinated me because of what it seemed to say about American girlhood. Parents I knew with girls on the brink of adolescence seemed anxious to prolong their daughters' childhoods, and some had specific advice on how to do so. Encourage an interest in horses—that was my sister's idea. She was certainly relieved that her thirteen-year-old spent most of her afternoons mucking out stables and soaring over jumps rather than, say, IMing trash talk to her friends. Sports, in general, other people recommended—unless they were the kinds of sports that led to extreme dieting. But for more and more families, it seemed, American Girl dolls were the chosen talisman against unwanted precocity.

How odd, when you think of it, that such an idea should exist. Who would have predicted that here in America, at the start of the twenty-first century, girls in high-necked Edwardian dresses, girls in bonnets, girls with labor-intensive *chores,* would seem so sturdy, competent, and admirable—so much like the girls we hoped our little girls would want to be? But there it is: perhaps the most popular strategy for protecting your young daughter from Britneyhood and Paris Hiltonville, for holding her from the brink of mall-haunting, 'ho'-dressing tweendom, is to get her interested in American Girl dolls. It is a strategy that involves buying something in order to try and be something: the mother of a girlish girl, an innocent girl, a girl who, at nine or ten, still likes playing with old-fashioned dolls. But then again, there aren't that many options for parents who don't wish to succumb to what the toy industry calls "age compression," or "kids getting older younger"—KGOY, for short. "The girls these days grow up so fast," a seven-year-old girl's grandmother explained to *Newsday* in 2003. The woman and her husband were waiting patiently in line at the opening of American Girl Place in Manhattan. They had already paid about four hundred dollars for Kaya, the Nez Perce American Girl doll and various accessories, but they did not regret it. "These toys," the woman said, "help them be girls for a little longer." These toys, she implied, were *needed*.

American Girl dolls are a very big deal, though if you have sons and no daughters, you may have to take my word for it. But this, in brief, is the story: In 1986, a forty-five-year-old woman with the fateful name Pleasant T. Rowland started a new career as a doll entrepreneur. Rowland had been an elementary school teacher, a TV news reporter, and a textbook author, but in 1984, when she accompanied her husband on a business trip to Colonial Williamsburg, she had something of an epiphany about what she wanted to do next. She loved the material culture of history, the stuff you could touch—the wood, the pewter, the parchment. Rowland wondered whether there was a new way to market this tangible history to children, and she was still wondering when she headed into a toy store that Christmas to buy dolls for her eight- and ten-year-old nieces. She didn't want Barbie and she wasn't crazy about the other choices either. "Here I was, in a generation of women at the forefront of redefining women's roles," she recalled years later, "and yet our daughters were playing with dolls that celebrated being a teen queen or a mommy."

Soon Rowland hit on the idea of combining her love of history with her drive to create an uplifting girl culture. She would accomplish her aim by marketing dolls that represented little girls from different periods in American history. Eventually there would be eight of them: Kaya, an "adventurous" Nez Perce girl; Felicity, a "spunky" colonial girl; Josefina, a "hopeful" girl living on a New Mexican rancho in 1824; Kirsten, "a pioneer girl of strength and spirit"; Addy, a "courageous" girl who escapes slavery; Samantha, "a bright, compassionate girl living with her wealthy grandmother

in 1904"; Nellie, who is Irish and also "practical and hardwork-
ing," which is just as well, since she was "hired to be a servant in the
house next door to Samantha"; Kit, a "clever resourceful girl growing up during America's Depression"; and Molly, "a lively, loveable
schemer and dreamer growing up in 1944." The dolls would be
exceptionally well made—Rowland went all the way to Germany
for doll eyes that met her exacting standards for realism—and outfitted in costumes that could pass some sort of muster for historical
accuracy without sacrificing any girl appeal. (Nellie, the servant girl,
for instance, would not be clad in anything too practical or gray, nor
would Addie, the slave, look too disheveled. Their boots, however,
would have a lot of buttons.)

Each girl had a book and eventually a series of books that
told her story, and each book was sprinkled with historical
details: steamboats, breadlines, Victory Gardens. In a sense, all
the girls are pretty much the same girl— the historical backdrops
change, but the same basic personality type cycles cheerfully
through all of them. All American Girls are "plucky," "spunky,"
and mildly adventurous but not overtly rebellious, and they are
never misfits. They often have a pesky boy in their lives: a brother
or neighbor who annoys them to no end. They are inclined to
help the less fortunate, useful to the household economy, talkative
without being mouthy, and bright without being egg-headed.
Because all the leading characters in the books have a second and
more compelling life as dolls (though pleasant enough, the books
are not great children's literature), they must be pretty. Some of
the most memorable children's book heroines are not pretty—
though it is understood that they may grow up to be handsome or
striking or even, to the discerning eye, beautiful—which is one
reason so many generations of awkward, intellectual girls have
loved them. Jo in *Little Women* is famously plain and tomboyish;
Meg in *A Wrinkle in Time* describes herself as "snaggle-
toothed," "myopic," and "clumsy," a bespectacled frump in the
shadow of her gorgeous mother; even dear Laura in the *Little
House* books compares herself unfavorably to her golden-haired,
lady-like sister Mary, who always remembers to save her com-

plexion by wearing her hat. In a freestanding book, a homely or an unkempt heroine is fine. In a book that supplies back story for a doll, it won't do.

The girls of color—Josefina, Addy, and Kaya—came later, but neither late arrival nor cultural distinctness did anything to alter their essential personality or, in some respects, their appearance. All American Girl dolls are plump-cheeked and sturdy-legged (the dolls look younger—and hence cuddlier—than the girls illustrated in the books), with round eyes and small smiles that reveal precisely two teeth. The catalogs often show girls matched to dolls by race: Addy is snuggled by an African American girl, Josefina by a Hispanic one. But in real life, girls quickly exhibited a happy disregard for such conventions. Kaya, the native American doll, for instance, has entranced girls of various ethnic backgrounds. (She is, after all, a nine-year-old with ready access to fast horses, beaded dresses, and the wide-open plains.)

The concept was, almost from the beginning, a remarkable success. Pleasant Company did not advertise and made its wares available by catalog only, but between September and December of its first year, 1986, it sold $1.7 million worth of products. By 2003 it had sold seven million dolls and eighty-two million books, still without advertising. In 1998 it opened its first store— American Girl Place—in Chicago, which became, in its first year, the top-selling store on Chicago's prime shopping street. In 2003 it opened a second American Girl Place, on Fifth Avenue in New York. "Place" was a significant word, for both the Chicago and New York stores were meant to be more than stores: they were destinations for families, safe harbors for innocent girlishness and mother-daughter bonding. Each store featured a doll hospital; a hair salon, where, for fifteen dollars, doll tresses could be styled by an adult; a theater with a live, Broadway-meets-Branson–style stage show, in which young actresses playing the American Girls belted out original tunes; and a classy black-and-white-and-fuchsia tearoom, where mothers could eat smoked salmon–and-cucumber sandwiches with orange fennel butter and daughters could eat grape jelly flag sandwiches, and dolls got "treat seats" of their own. In 1998, Rowland sold the brand that was essentially the anti-Barbie to Mattel, the Barbie maker, for $700 million. And since then, American Girl has done the amazing: it has nearly displaced the venerable, vacant Barbie as the best-selling doll in America.

Ours, it's clear, is a moment in consumer history when middle-class American parents will spend, pretty much happily, a great deal of money on what they perceive as quality goods for their children, particularly if those goods can be seen as in any way educational. A Samantha starter kit, which includes the doll, a slim paperback book, and a few teensy accessories, sells for $98. Samantha's cunning little wooden school desk, with its historically accurate wrought-iron legs, costs $68. Her trunk, with its oval mirror and three wee hangers, costs $175. Josefina's carved wooden chest, in tasteful Santa Fe style, goes for $155. And so on. For many American girls, these are, of course, unimaginable luxuries. At an economically and racially diverse private school where a friend's daughter goes, American Girl dolls are a dividing line—and an early introduction to class in America—for a group of third-graders. Two of the girls are from families who cannot afford the dolls, let alone the fripperies that go with them. And, lately, these two girls have been getting left out of play dates and playground games, which often center on American Girl fantasies. Ironic, in a way, since these particular girls are from newly arrived immigrant families of modest means, whose life stories are, therefore, classic American Girl. The "Barbie as Halle Berry in *Catwoman*" doll may come swathed in stereotypes, but at least it has the virtue of being available at your local Target for $14.99.

For middle-class and upper-class families, however, the American Girl brand seems to work in part *because* it is so expensive. "Few goods are purchased as flat-out status symbols; each one carries a subtle message about its owner and user," writes Michael Silverstein, the co-author of *Trading Up: The New American Luxury*, and a great fan of Pleasant Rowland's vision. "When a mother gives her child an American Girl doll, she is telling the child, 'I love you and care about your emotional and intellectual development.'" There are easier and less expensive ways, perhaps, to convey such things, but maybe we don't consider them as surefire, or as likely to please our little girls. Or maybe they require more time and resourcefulness than harried mothers feel they have to give.

But the other reason the American Girl brand succeeds is that it aims to please both mothers and daughters in equal measure. For years, moms with feminist leanings had been complaining about Barbie and her ilk. But previous attempts to sell edutaining alternatives to Barbie—dolls in lab coats, dolls with briefcases—had failed. Sometimes they failed because they were too transparent, too earnest—kids could see that adults were aiming straight for their self-esteem, as zealously as Mormon missionaries. Sometimes they failed because their trappings of empowerment seemed faintly absurd—okay, it's Barbie, and she still has those torpedo boobs and those pointy little feet that fit only into stilettos, but now she's a dentist! And the doll Emme, the plus-size model, which came out a few years ago—how literal-minded could you get? Since dolls are role models, the thinking went, a size-twelve doll will help big little girls accept themselves—as though any doll, let alone a doll of a model, could be entrusted with such a task. Even the GetRealGirl dolls, the well-meaning attempt to introduce more "athletic figures," fell short. "They're active girls," crowed a toy website, "who have all kinds of toys and they can kick Barbie's butt like you wouldn't believe." Well, all right! I guess. But the GetRealGirls were still babes—it's just that they were in the babe mode of today (tanned and toned surfers, snowboarders, and soccer players), not of the 1950s. And, anyway, wouldn't a girl who loved action sports prefer to be out doing them to playing with dolls?

American Girl dolls set out in a different direction, going backward in time and in age: the American Girls were nine-year-old girls, not happenin' teenagers or blowzy adults. Parents liked the idea that their girls might be learning history from them. (The company has a new line of contemporary dolls, American Girl Today, but the historical dolls are still the brand's most distinctive franchise.) And Rowland understood that, for kids, history is in part a fantasy realm, a distant land of eternal dress-up and inscrutable, vigorous chores, such as churning butter and pounding flax seed, a place sufficiently different that it might as well be Oz or Hogwarts. American Girl offered a festive view of history, one that was full of character-building hardship but also of really neat stuff—little lockets and fringed shawls, sun bonnets and bee veils, washstands and split-log school benches, jelly biscuits and rock candy.

Of course, there are sober-minded critics—mostly of the ideological left or right—who fault the dolls and their books for offering too anodyne a view of history. Peter Wood, writing in the conservative *National Review* a few years ago, chided American Girl for creating "cloying p.c. play worlds." He particularly loathed Kaya because, he contended, she is shown at "the apex of the Nez Perce culture" to which she belonged, while the other American Girls are shown living through periods of "ethnic oppression and social crisis." But then, American history pretty much consists of "periods of ethnic oppression and social crisis." And, besides, the American Revolution and World War II (the backgrounds for Felicity and Molly) are generally considered heroic moments in our history, social crises though they may also be. What did Wood expect—a Kaya doll who works the night shift in a reservation casino?

From the other end of the spectrum, Cynthia Peters, writing in the left-wing *Z Magazine*, complained that the Pleasant Company's multiculturalism didn't go nearly far enough. The Kirsten books ignored the "fact that the pioneer presence in the area, made possible by fraudulent U.S. treaties with the various Ojibwe bands, leads to the displacement of most of the Native people." Peters is disappointed that Kirsten's cousin Lisbeth says, the Indians might get angry, but "we need the land, too." Yet that seems more or less what a pioneer girl in 1854 might say—at least a pioneer girl willing to acknowledge the feelings of native Americans at all, which would already make her slightly ahead of her time. What did Peters expect? That little Lisbeth would run off and join a nineteenth-century version of AIM, shaking her blonde pigtails and denouncing fraudulent treaties all the way? The truth is there is history that evokes, that summons up a brightly colored though flickering and incomplete picture of the past, like a home movie or a dream. And there is history that analyzes and criticizes. History written for eight-year-old girls about their dolls is probably going to do the former. Eventually eight-year-old girls grow up and some of them, with appetites for history piqued by the kind of sunny, commercial culture that some purists disdain, go on to read the critical and analytical kind. When I was a kid in L.A. in the sixties, my family used to go to a restaurant called the Old North Woods. It was meant to be a log cabin, though it was surely made of fiber glass and Sheetrock, and I was utterly taken in by it. I still remember the hurricane lamps on the tables, the waitresses in calico, the peanut shells you were encouraged to throw on the floor—in keeping with some agreeably old-timey, and probably made-up, custom. It was my first intimation that the past could be simultaneously cozy and alien, recondite and inviting—and I loved it.

What the American Girls phenomenon best represents, though, is the fact that fathers and mothers, even if they do not consider themselves social conservatives, want help in keeping at bay certain aspects of the pop culture. And they want help they can buy.

"Mothers are tired of the sexualization of little girls," Pleasant Rowland said in an interview with *Fortune* magazine. Dolls based on girls of the past are appealing because girls of the past presumably weren't being pressured to give blow jobs or sending sexually explicit videos of themselves to the guys they liked. Girls of the past weren't hip-hop like the Flava dolls or diva-esque like the Bratz dolls. They were, or so we are content to imagine, "good girls." This was a supreme irony: that in an era when feminism had given American girls so many more opportunities to exercise ambition of all kinds, there was still a way in which a girl who was growing in the 1940s or the 1930s or even the 1700s and 1800s could seem less encumbered—freer, if that is the word—to work on the content of her character rather than on the condition of her skin.

In part, of course, this was a simplification, if not a whitewash. The notion that kids, and girls especially, "just grow up too fast today" is a cliché now, and it was probably a cliché in our parents' time, and in their parents'. It's too easy to embrace; it dovetails too neatly with the common feeling that each of us has about our own children— that childhood really is a fleeting thing, which is both just as it should be and deeply sad. And it is also a convenient shorthand for expressing a generalized nostalgia, a sense that the world is no longer as we knew it, to its great misfortune and ours. Moreover, to answer the question "Are children growing up faster today?" you first have to ask which children you're talking about. For child laborers in nineteenth-century mills and factories and, of course, for children born into plantation slavery, childish innocence could scarcely have been supplanted any more swiftly and cruelly.

And yet there is some truth tangled in the proverbial longing for a "simpler" time, when a girl, or at least a white, middle-class girl could be a girl, in the bosom of her family, as they say, for just a little longer. For all our precious gains, for all the opening-up of the wider world, for all the possibilities that I would never, ever want to foreclose for my daughter, there is a way in which girls enjoyed a sense of themselves as vitally needed and yet protected by their families that they do not quite have today. In a book called *The Essential Daughter: Changing Expectations for Girls at Home, 1797 to the Present,* historian Mary Collins argues that although the kind of work that daughters did to help their mothers throughout much of our history—sewing, canning, taking care of brothers and sisters—narrowed their horizons in ways we would never accept today, it also accomplished something good: it imparted competence. And there might be "something in that culture of usefulness," Collins argues, that is "worth salvaging." The hale, resourceful, family-minded American Girls are always pitching in—Kit sells eggs door-to-door to help her family make ends meet during the Depression; Kirsten milks cows and catches fish enough to feed "nine hungry people"—and though the emphasis on their can-do helpfulness might seem treacly at times, it's also a big part of what makes their characters appealing.

Life for American girls of the nineteenth and early twentieth centuries was not characterized by unrelenting oppression, as we used to think, in the early, sometimes smug, days of feminist history. In that sense, the high-spirited American Girls are not necessarily anachronistic. "Little girls lived as unfettered and vigorous an outdoor life as their brothers," writes Anne Scott McLeod in her essay "The Caddie Woodlawn Syndrome: American Girlhood in the Nineteenth Century." Indeed, mothers were advised to encourage open-air exercise for their daughters to counteract "artificial habits" and maladies that afflicted genteel girls. "Millions of us lived in small towns where we . . . had complete freedom of movement on foot, roller skates, and bicycles," recalled one woman about her early-twentieth-century girlhood. In surveys about toy use taken in the late nineteenth century—yes, apparently there were such things, even then—girls preferred jumping rope, playing tag or hide-and-seek, and bicycling to more sedate pastimes such as playing with dolls or doing embroidery, according to Miriam Formanek-Brunell, the author of *Made to Play House: Dolls and the Commercialization of American Girlhood, 1830–1930*. Girls "walked fences, flew kites, belly-bumpered down hills on [their] own sleds." And, though the American Girl characters aren't usually intellectual types, the truth is that in the late nineteenth century, middle-class urban girls, at least, did have opportunities to exercise their minds. Many of them attended intellectually rigorous boarding schools, wrote and read constantly, challenged themselves to improve their minds and characters, and led rich interior lives, illuminated by the poetry and novels they cherished. It isn't really such a stretch, in other words, to make role models out of Victorian girls.

For all that, though, the curatorial meticulousness of the American Girl world can seem a bit oppressive. Silverstein argues that the dolls appeal to middle-class buyers who want something with a pedigree—in this case, the elaborate back story that comes with each of them. But in a way, that's what is disappointing about this doll world. An American Girl doll comes with so *much* story, so much baggage, it's hard to know whether a girl could approach play with an untrammeled imagination—making of the doll whatever she wants. The catalog copy for Kaya's pretend food is a typical study in detail-oriented pedantry: "Help Kaya gather huckleberries and camas roots in her woven basket—cover it with huckleberry branches to keep all her food safe inside. Later, she can lay everything on a tule mat to dry: her berries, some salmon, and a bowl of mashed cama to make into finger cakes." (Or maybe you could just put some mud in a cup and call it soup.)

And it might be harder still when a girl's parents are deeply invested—both emotionally and financially—in a particular kind of child's play. "When you own dolls and accessories that cost thousands of dollars, you really like to keep it going," as one mother told a Massachusetts paper, explaining why she had enrolled her daughter in an American Girl doll club whose meetings they attended together. Sometimes, evidently, kids begin to feel a bit encumbered by the particular intensity of adult interest in their hobby. Ten-year-old Talia, writing in for advice from a teenage counselor on a PBS website, described this scenario: "A few years ago, I begged my mom to get me a doll that everyone had," writes Talia. "Now I never touch it, even though it was very expensive. My mom wants to take me to a place in New York that's all about the doll: American Girl Place. Since I never play with my doll, I don't want to waste $500 on a trip there. My mom is all excited about it. Should I go or not?" I don't blame Talia's mother—it's an entrancing world she wants to linger in with her daughter, an elegant and a safe one. And besides, the moment when a daughter relinquishes those dolls is poignant. A few years ago, when I was writing a magazine article about "mean girls," I sat in on several classes in which twelve- and thirteen-year-old girls were meant to apologize to one another. One girl said she was sorry for having spread it around that her friend still had an American Girl doll. It was apparent that this was somehow worse than saying you still had a Barbie. It was more like saying you cried for your mother every night at sleep-away camp. It was something that could make you hot-faced with embarrassment. It was saying that this was a girl in conspiracy with her mother—or at least her elders—to remain, for a little while longer, a little girl.

Sometimes at night I lie awake and think about how fast time goes with children. For years adults said this to you and you never knew what it meant. And then you had children and the baby time was molasses slow and then it seemed to go faster and faster, and you could imagine far too clearly all the things your children, who are so sweet and full of blooming affection now, wouldn't want to do in just a few years time—like hug you in public. I see the ridiculousness of brooding about the inevitable and desirable—we want our children to grow up, which means, in part, away from us—not to mention the not-even-here-quite-yet. But there it is. Talia's mother probably feels something like the same sentiment, and Talia probably senses it.

It's odd what will draw a child into history, and into history's particular way of vouchsafing a sense that our world is not the only world. And it's odd how we can't know or always plan for the edifying moments. Not long ago, on a trip to Boston, my husband and I and our two children wandered into a very old graveyard. It was a place I'd always liked when I'd lived near it in my early twenties—a quiet place on a hill, with a view of the Boston Harbor, gleaming like a nickel in the sun. We had planned to stop there for a few minutes on our way to get pizza. But our children loved it and wanted to linger. The seven-year-old lay on his stomach in front of a stone and read the inscriptions as though he were cracking a code, which in a way he was. His younger sister traced the words with a long stalk of grass and rubbed her fingers over the little death's heads with wings that you see in old New England graveyards—not quite angels, something harsher. They asked a lot of questions. What did the skeletons look like? Where were their souls? Where was their skin? Why were African Americans buried in a separate part of the cemetery? Why did people die so young then? What sort of a name was Hephzibah?

Children are like us, but they are not us. That's the thing we forget sometimes: that their world is in some sense ineffable for us, as passionately as we love them. And in that sense, imagining their inner lives—as immediate as a horse's in some ways and yet much more mystical than mine—is like imagining history. I can no more remember what it felt like to be four years old or seven, not really, than I can know what it felt like to be a person of the eighteenth or nineteenth century. I have little pictures, just as I do of history—magic lantern slides, backlit, endlessly fascinating, and somehow just beyond my grasp. We've all heard that "the past is a foreign country; they do things differently there." Well, childhood is too. American Girl dolls are one way to visit both those foreign countries, I suppose. But every day my children surprise me with where they want to go, and how they want to get there.

Prayin' Hard for Better Dayz

Camille Peri

I have to tell you: I hate rap. I hate the bitches and the asses and the 'ho's. I hate the in-yo'-faceness, the pumped-up testosterone, the butted-out chests, the finger-jabbing, the ice, the six-packs, the balloon pants, the rings like brass knuckles. The pervasive boxer shorts, the Jockey bands where belts used to be. In yo' face is not an attempt to connect. It means shut up, stay away. *Move bitch. Get out the way,* as the song says.

I know the socioeconomic justifications and the political roots. I like some of the bravado and the clever wordplay. There are songs that have opened my eyes and forced me to think. But most of it pretends that glamorizing guns and gangstas is keeping it real; it is misogyny decked out like a Courvoisier ad. *I'm into havin' sex, I ain't into makin' love,* 50 Cent sings. No intimacy or mystery or love, God forbid any allusion to or regard for what comes next. Just poses and postures selling a crude idea of what it means to be a man.

The hills are alive with the sound of rap—blasting in suburbs, in Paris clubs, out of the cars that cruise up our street from the projects down the hill. Ghetto is a state of mind. To kids of every color—black, Asian, Latin, or white, like my son Joe—it's an adjective, the coolest, the best. *Now dat's ghetto,* you say if you're ghetto. It came out of the ghetto, but now it's not anywhere, it's in kids' heads. You can live in the ghetto and not be ghetto. On the other hand, my son Joe doesn't live there, but he's ghetto.

For the past couple of years, since the summer Joe turned ghetto, I have felt like I live in a rap video—rappers crowding the camera frame above me, looking down like they just kicked my butt and are ready to do it again. As my husband, David, and I have watched Joe take on the gangsta swagger and pout, we have wandered around like the iguana in Eddie Murphy's *Dr. Dolittle,* muttering, "So young, so angry. Damn that rap music!" What did we do that our kid has embraced such a dark view of the world? Where did all we raised him with go? Where did who he was go? The star athlete, the student leader, the boy who wrote screenplays and directed the neighborhood kids in films, the kid who composed music on the piano so beautiful that other mothers cried . . . *He thuggin? Oh he a thug. On da real.*

Looking back, there was no way that summer could have been normal. It began not with a party at the beach or a banana split. It began with me taking off my wig.

The autumn before, I had been diagnosed with breast cancer. Two things stand out from the misty light that bleached most of those first few days from my memory. One is that I had not been given a death sentence; there was a lot I could do to fight it. The other is Joey on the soccer field the day after we told him about my diagnosis. He said he was going to make a goal for me, and he did. In the slow-motion replay in my head, I can see him right after, his summer blond hair gone brown, turning to find me in the stands, pointing to me from the field. *Just do it,* his burning eyes said. He was eleven years old.

I began chemotherapy after Thanksgiving and started brushing out handfuls of my shoulder-length hair just before Christmas. As part of the instructions on helping kids cope with that side effect of chemo, they suggest making it fun, having your kids draw funny faces on your bald head. Joey and his younger brother, Nat, wanted no part of that. The coping mechanism for them was not to see my smooth, bare head ever, if possible. I searched out a wig that approximated my tight, dark, Italian curls, but the standard dealers had only shiny flips and big loopy ringlets. Then I found a woman who specialized in wigs for women of color. Through her, I bought a hand-me-down from a wealthy black woman that was a near-perfect match for my hair.

It wasn't that the cancer was a secret. Everyone knew. But the boys could cope with my occasional nausea and fevers as long as we kept the rhythms of our routine—as long as I could pick them up at school and look normal. This worked pretty well until my eyelashes and eyebrows started thinning out too. Without those familiar signposts on my face, my hair seemed to get bigger. I looked like a country singer. So I switched sometimes to a cheap, short pageboy wig that I could wear with a baseball cap pulled down low. That had its problems too. Arriving at school in our family car with straight hair was one thing, but the day I told Nat I'd be coming with a friend in her car, it was too much. "You *will* have curly hair though, won't you?" he asked with a worried look.

By summer I had a feathery mantle of baby hair, just enough to let me abandon my wig. "It looks good, Mom," Joe said cheerfully. "You look like Cal Ripken." Actually, I wish I had looked as good as Cal Ripken. With a pale man-in-the-moon face still puffy from chemo, I scared even myself sometimes when I caught a glimpse of me in a mirror. Taking off my fake hair was supposed to be a relief. Instead, it seemed to lay open all our anxieties and fears that had somehow stayed tucked neatly away under my wig.

Through the long winter and spring, I had just wanted life to go back to normal. But there was no normal, or at least normal wasn't going to be what it used to be. We went through the usual motions of summer—the drive from swimming lessons to art camps to piano lessons to the grocery store—and sometimes we had an extra stop: radiation. I was required to go for fifteen minutes a day and therefore, some days, so were my sons. They would sit in the waiting room with women in hospital pajamas doting over them—two brave little men, their arms folded across their chests. Only God knows what they were thinking; I chose not to ask.

Sometimes we stopped at Mission Dolores on the way home. I was a long-lapsed Catholic; my religion by then was incense, candles, and the "Ave Maria" sung in Latin. David and I and the children had gone to church recreationally, mostly for the spectacle of the Christmas pageant, where children dressed as angels and shepherds tripped on their robes down the usually austere aisle—accompanied by live goats, donkeys, and bunnies—and everyone prayed that the Baby Jesus stand-in would make it to the altar without slipping from little Mary's arms. One Christmas, in a fabulous faux pas, a pregnant goat went into untimely labor in the vestibule, her screams punctuating the telling of the Christmas story, something that perhaps only a mother could appreciate: a truly wrenching evocation of birth in a manger.

But now I was back at church, slipping in after my treatments, guilty as only a Catholic can be, daring to ask for whatever mercy could be spared, trying this time to deal directly with God and ignore the angry voices of my childhood, which demanded, Why do you deserve this? What have you done for God lately? One day, as I lit a candle at a time when the thought of leaving my children was particularly tormenting, warmth spread through my fingertips to my toes, a sense of calm I had never felt, telling me that everything would be all right. On another visit, as I sat silent in the dark, cavernous church, alone except for a caretaker fussing with the kneelers, the sun suddenly broke through a stained-glass window, drenching only me in a circle of gold, green, and purple light. My mind rationalized that Catholic architects had designed the church for just that effect and that tomorrow it would happen again to whoever was sitting in my spot, but my heart hoped it was a sign from God.

I didn't talk to my sons about this. I just took them a few times to Mission Dolores to light a *veladora*, and I hoped that in the cool stone and serene faces of the saints, in the red light that is always lit to signify God's presence, they would breathe in some of the security that Catholicism gave me as a child. Nat, who was eight at the time, seems to have an innate feel for both the simplicity and profundity of things. (He keeps scented candles by his bed to smell at night and once took an empty M&M bag to preschool so the other kids could share its faint odor of chocolate, its nostalgic whiff of sweetness.) As I had expected, the mystery of the church did its magic on him: He told me that the wooden eyes of Saint Joseph had looked at him, and another time he saw the statue move.

As summer went on, the boys cut their hair short, shorter than mine. I checked mine daily to see if it had grown. We made jokes about the cancer, but mostly we were quieter that summer. Strangely, what carried us through, what helped us cope, was rap. It drifted into our lives through the car radio and became the background rhythm to the strange dance that we were stumbling through. That relentless beat had always seemed so annoying when it boomed from the open windows of cars. Suddenly, it was something reliable, dependable, comforting almost.

And so were the words. The struggle to survive, the defiance, the loss of friends and family, the anger at being dealt a crooked hand, even the fragility of here and now sealed us in a trance. This was not a Beach Boys summer. We weren't havin' fun all summer long. We were shell-shocked street soldiers, trying to get to the next stop. The "angel thug" Tupac Shakur—whose premonition of his own violent death six years before had infused his songs with a poignant intensity—spoke to us from the grave: *Baby, don't cry. You gotta keep your head up. Even when the road is hard, never give up.*

The rap poet Nas sang to his mother, who had died of breast cancer two years before:

> *They playing our song the lifebeat my hand on your waist*
> *I grab your other hand and try not to step on your toes*
> *Spin you around with my eyes closed*
> *Dreaming I could have*
> *One more dance with you mama*
> *. . . I'd give my life up ... to have*
> *One more dance with you mama*

We never changed the dial when that came on. We listened in silence. It spoke to us more than any cancer self-help manual could.

• • •

David and I are liberals in a cosmopolitan city that considers itself one of the outposts of progressivism. We were committed to putting our children in a diverse public elementary school and lucky enough to get them into one where the parents were very involved and the racial mix mirrored that of the nation. This is no easy feat in San Francisco because much of the black middle class has immigrated to Oakland, driven out largely by rising housing costs.

When Joe's adolescence came on with a bang during the fall when my treatments ended, we were blindsided: a basketball jersey, a headband, a pair of Air Force Ones, and before we could catch our breath, he was talking the gangsta talk. The first time I heard it, I thought it was some other kid outside our door. *I done got locked out,* an excessively manly voice said. Then I heard it again and again, and like a scary movie, the voice was inside the house. *De popo's comin. You mess wit dat breezy? Neva dat. She jockin me. I don chill wit dem.*

For a while, friends and family hung up the phone when they heard Joe's super-cool new voice and talk on our answering machine, thinking they had gotten the wrong number. When Joe did pick up the phone, they were bemused by the throaty voice that greeted them. "Yo' mama's on the phone," he said one day as he handed me the receiver. My mama? Wasn't she still *his* grandma? His man voice was moving him away from us and from his childhood.

We had always congratulated ourselves that Joe had built a rainbow coalition of friends at school. But overnight he stopped chillin' with his white buddies. His sudden need, and to a lesser extent Nat's, to be black (or more correctly, to be "ghetto," the popular teen definition of being "authentically" black) took us by surprise. Of course, Joe denied it and laughed at other white kids who tried to act "black."

"But you're trying to be black," I said one day in the car.

"I'm just trying to be a cool white guy."

Nat threw up his hands. "I admit it. I'm a *wigga.*"

It's true, Nat was a "wannabe *nigga.*" Although he still fell asleep clutching a furry little bunny, he had also taken to wearing a do-rag and oversize white T-shirt to bed, which made him look more like an angel than a thug. At his birthday party, he was the token white kid. Actually, Nat had been conferred the status of *nigga* by one of his friends, a term that still burned my ears though I knew it was considered a form of endearment among some African Americans. "And Natty," his friend had added, "I mean it in the nicest possible way."

Nat's foray into ghetto was mild and fanciful, but Joe's, like everything Joe, was with great heart and a vengeance. "Our school is so white," he complained one day. "There are only three black kids in my class." I started to count off all the African American and biracial kids, but it was all he could do to be patient with me. "Oh her—she's so white," he huffed. "Him—you call him black?" By his definition, there were really only three "authentic" blacks, and he was one of them.

To a city boy like Joe, urban street-corner society was simply more interesting. The sidewalks were livelier, the styles hipper, the banter wittier, the music better, and the extended families of cousins and aunties and siblings more fun. White kids at school snickered at his transformation. "Didn't that used to be Joey Talbot?" one mother giggled to a teacher. Although black kids are routinely expected to fit into white culture, the idea of a white kid becoming "black" seemed laughable to everyone but Joe's African American friends.

We knew Joe's need to define himself separately from us was a natural part of adolescence. "I'm trying to figure out who I am," he reflected one day. "I think this is who I am." But all attempts to convince him that he could not erase his white middle-class roots were to no avail.

When he was thirteen, we took him to see *The Godfather,* to expose him to an American classic and revive his interest in his Italian American roots—but that backfired. Soon after, describing how he averted fights between neighborhood kids, he explained to me, "I'm kind of like the Godfather. People come to me with their problems, and I help them work them out." I looked at him—the thin arms that were lifting weights to get buff, the ethnic nose he was trying to grow into—and I immediately regretted that choice of films.

I realized then, with some awe, that he was still young enough to believe he could reinvent himself as anyone he wanted to be. I knew that, someday soon, his ghetto persona would probably not be accepted by either blacks or whites. But I marveled that, for now, by his definition, skin color was superfluous.

Maybe, after all we had been through, Joe's need to reinvent himself as someone else was simply stronger than most adolescents'. Maybe he needed to go to a world where his parents and his old friends couldn't go. Maybe my cancer had accelerated his hardening himself to be a man. But it was something else too. Once, a writer told me that after her divorce her son dropped out of the school band to become a loner skateboarder. When she asked him why, he said, "Mom, kids whose parents are divorced don't play in the school band." I think that, for Joe, the world of shiny soccer trophies and smiling two-parent families busying themselves for school bake sales just didn't seem important anymore. Inside, he needed to connect with people whose lives seemed as hard and scary as his must have suddenly felt. And in his inner-city friends, he found that connection.

In bookstores, the titles on helping kids cope with cancer in the family are shelved with those on raising children who are biracial or disabled. But none of the books tells you what to do when your cancer crashes up against your son's becoming ghetto. I came out of a year of treatments with a childlike appreciation for life's humble things. The pale clouds of winter, a glittery spider web could bring tears to my eyes. But I had also lost my son's last year of boyhood, and I wasn't ready. I'd get hurt by his sulking street self. While his eyes darted around to make sure he was not being seen with us at movies and on other family outings, I still wanted every second of our time together to count. I had no right to ask that of him, I knew. *Give him time to find himself,* I thought. But I also wondered sometimes how much time I had to give.

David and I were concerned with Joe's transformation for other, more rational reasons. His lapses into bad grammar were to us like a jarring car alarm on a deserted street at night. All his interests—school, piano, film, soccer—seemed to shrivel against the pounding rhythms coming from behind his door. Sometimes I'd hear him working out a beautiful refrain on the keyboard, but then there would be the familiar grunts and shouts, and I knew it was just background for the main event: rap.

After all our family talks about the civil rights movement and African American history, we were actually appalled. Didn't Joe know that most people were trying to get out of the ghetto, not into it? Joe and his pals weren't thugs, but they all wanted to look like it. They studied the short lives and violent deaths of rap stars as if they were Martin Luther King, Jr. or Malcolm X. We worried about what serious risks could lay ahead if Joe pursued the gangsta persona into the more dangerous years of high school.

But Joe's new identity challenged our own assumptions and awareness as well. With Joe's new friends in the picture, neighborhoods that we usually drove through only on our way somewhere else now became our destinations. I remember walking through double-locked gates into a labyrinth of concrete halls to drop off one of Joe's friends at a unit that had only a TV and a PlayStation—no chairs, no kitchen table, no beds. Dropping off another child meant driving through acres of public housing staggering down to the shipyards in San Francisco's Hunter's Point. Years ago I often went into these projects when I worked with teenagers in juvenile court, and later wrote about kids who were struggling to get out of them. But when had they built so many more of them? Why didn't I know how the projects had multiplied? They might have been communities of Amish or Hasidic Jews for all my life intersected with them now.

The insidious face of inner-city poverty seemed to raise the stakes on everything—even the simplest get-together. Should we let Joe sleep overnight at the home of his new best friend, who lived in public housing? Would Joe be a target in a tough inner-city neighborhood, or just an unlucky victim of a stray bullet? Should I be honest about my fears with his friends' mothers or make excuses? A longtime African American friend of ours told us we were being too cautious, but when a man was shot down after a high-speed chase with the police on the street where Joe's friend lived, it settled the question.

What I hadn't expected was to find myself worrying about the safety of Joe's friends in *our* neighborhood. We live in what middle-income San Franciscans consider one of the last affordable areas, a topsy-turvy mix of mostly aging bohemians, Latins, gays, lesbians, and white starter-house families. It is separated from one of the poorest, most gang-dominated neighborhoods in the city by one traffic-clogged boulevard that leads to the freeway. Like a Pied Piper, Precita Park sits on the dividing line, drawing together kids from both sides to play. Parents sit on the benches, watching their kids mingle but rarely mingling with one another. At dusk they retreat to their own side of the invisible line. At night we are connected by sirens: the people on our side of the line often awakened by wailing from the streets on the other side.

Our neighborhood is by no means sheltered or privileged. But when Joe started bringing new friends from the other side up to the house or even hanging outside with his black friends from school, I noticed the neighbors tense up. People on our block paused a while at their doorways before going inside, watching them. Someone always seemed to notice if one of the boys hopped the back fence to get a stray ball in a neighbor's yard. When the boys rang the doorbell of a female classmate a few blocks away, her neighbor called the police. The girl's white mother had a black boyfriend whom the neighbors were used to seeing around, but the sight of those boys climbing the stairs to her door on a Saturday afternoon alarmed them.

I doubt they even noticed Joe—they just saw a gang of kids who shouldn't be there. They saw the scariest people in America—black teenage boys. I realized that everywhere these kids went—up the street, downtown—they were being watched.

A few summers ago, as budding filmmakers, Joe and his white friends had rung doorbells in the neighborhood and run off, catching people's reactions in a video series they called

"Pranking and the Human Response," a kind of precursor to Ashton Kutcher's *Punk'd*. I knew that Joe and his new gang could never get away with something like that.

As I got to know the mothers of Joe's new friends, I saw that they had their own apprehensions about sending their kids into our neighborhood, new turf that might hold unfamiliar dangers on the street. And they worried about their kids hanging out with some white boy whose idea of fun might be their sons' trouble. "I was so relieved to find out that Joey was a nice boy," one mother, Charmaine,* admitted to me one day. "You know, these white kids are bringing drugs and sex into the schools."

Slowly, awkwardly (much more awkwardly than our sons, who by now called themselves "brothers"), we moved from polite to friendly, from talking through a rolled-down car window to coming in to chat. My new friends were mothers raising their kids alone, with little or no child support. Unlike me and my other friends—mostly atheists and agnostics—they spent long hours in church and believed strongly in the power of prayer. Two kids' fathers were doing hard time. One boy's father refused to pay child support to his mother, but said that if his son needed something, "he knows he can call me." Another boy's stepfather had just died of cancer, and his birth father lived across the country. "Sometimes I wonder, why is God doing this to me?" said his mom, a Latin American woman who was raising three children alone. "Then I realize, God is doing this to show me I have the strength to handle it."

Fall and winter of eighth grade in San Francisco are dominated by the hysteria of the high school application process. The stakes are high. Good public high schools are few, so many middle-income parents also apply to private schools they cannot afford, praying for scholarships or, like us, resigning themselves to taking

---

*The names of some people in this story have been changed to protect their privacy.

out loans to pay tuitions of up to $25,000 a year. In fact, many private school scholarships go to families with incomes of $100,000 or more.

The crumbling, leaky halls of even San Francisco's elite public high school, Lowell, can't compare with the calm, safe havens the private schools offer. We visited pricey schools that supplied each student with a brand-new laptop, plush libraries that rivaled those of my college, campus "communities" that promised small classes and study support. Though the schools talked a lot about diversity and had elaborate, ultra-sensitive ethnic pride clubs, they seemed to have just a sprinkling of light-skinned black students in the mix. One school had enough clout to have drawn an elderly Rosa Parks to campus for Martin Luther King, Jr.'s birthday to sing "We Shall Overcome" with the overwhelmingly white student body.

For thirteen-year-old kids, the application process is needlessly brutal—essays, interviews, tests, shadow visits, open houses, all while having to keep up their grades. For parents, it is obsessive. "This *is* my job," is the familiar refrain from stay-at-home mothers. One working mother I knew took a leave from her job to keep up with the rigid schedules and paperwork required.

I went through the process like a stand-in in a life that was no longer mine. Up until a year or two before, Joe would have had a good shot at one of the top schools. But now his grade-point average was wobbly and his extracurricular activities weak. He had mustered the energy to make an impressive film in which he asks a wide variety of people to define what it is that makes them who they are. But he closes it with a tribute to Tupac—a big point of contention in our house that can be explained only by the insanity that had overtaken us. My husband—newly enlightened after seeing the film *Tupac: Resurrection*—argued that it was Joe's artistic right to do so; I said that most admissions people know Tupac as just a thug who got himself killed, and it wasn't worth the risk. But we both warned Joe to check his ghetto walk and talk at the door when he visited the schools. We made him wear Polo shirts and khaki slacks with belts. We threatened him about his grades. We even tried to force him back into volunteer activities.

But Joe had his own volunteer project going.

We had put in an application at a new school whose mission was exciting: It promised to groom students for the twenty-first century with a curriculum that emphasized science, technology, ethics, and spirituality. Students would learn how to negotiate a "potentially troubling world" by studying world cultures and learning how to become "peacemakers," according to its literature. Acknowledging the central realities of diversity and community, the school would "mirror the rich mosaic of the San Francisco Bay Area, reaching across its wide spectrum of race, culture, and economic circumstances" to draw its student body. Joe had decided that this sounded like a great opportunity for his friend Devon.

Devon was a kid who could benefit desperately from the support that only a private school could provide—and he could contribute much to other students' understanding of the troubled world. His father was out of prison and pretty much out of the picture; his mother was struggling to support her children on a lot less than the cost of one year's tuition. Beneath his serious street face, Devon had an open sweetness and unabashed curiosity about the world. Though guarded and awkward when I first met him, he soon revealed a deep heart and optimism about the future. Although he struggled in school, he had not lost his motivation to learn. But he was walking a tightrope, and his academic experience and support in the next few years seemed vitally important.

The school's co-director of admissions, a charismatic young black man, appeared to be scouring the Bay Area seeking out underprivileged students like Devon. He had met Devon and liked him, and encouraged him and his mother to apply. They were thrilled. So Joe quietly took it upon himself to tutor Devon and help him with his application. Devon chose to write his application essay on his relationship to God. Joe edited it. The night before school tests, I could hear him on the phone with Devon:

"Okay, now no cheating. Who wrote the Declaration of Independence?" Late one evening, I heard him reassuring Devon, "You're going to get in." I kept in touch with the admissions co-director and Devon's mom, to keep the process rolling. And then I held my breath for all of us. I was proud of Joe's empathy and compassion, but I knew that his personal version of "community service" did not have the institutional stamp of validation that counted on school résumés.

While we middle-income parents of eighth-graders sweated through winter with our eyes on the high school prize, a tide of violence quietly began sweeping through the city. Thirteen African American teenage boys were killed during our children's eighth-grade year. A young man whose sisters had tried to save him from the street violence that had claimed his mother was shot. Three boys on their way to high school were killed in their car. A fifteen-year-old was gunned down leaving a YMCA dance. Another boy was mistaken for someone else and killed; his cousin was shot a week later, on the day of the boy's funeral. "Kids are dying right and left here," Devon's mother exclaimed to me one day.

The violence blew in across the city like afternoon fog off the ocean, settling deep into pockets of town—Lakeview, the Excelsior, Sunnydale, Hunter's Point—and leaving others clear and untouched. Some of the murders didn't even make it into the *San Francisco Chronicle*. None of the white, middle-class parents I knew talked about them. I wondered if they even knew about them. Would we have known had it not been for Joe's impassioned updates on the subject? If one of the shootings had happened at a middle-class public school, San Francisco parents would have mobilized around it immediately as a school safety issue. But these happened in the shadowy places on the other side of those invisible lines. These are the things that we know without knowing.

My new friend Charmaine, however, took each one to heart. Arriving at our house looking particularly weary one day to pick up her son, she told me how hopeless she had started to feel. She went to memorial services for boys she would never know, wrote notes to their parents. She treated them as if she knew them. She couldn't help but think about how hard someone had worked to raise them right, and how easily that care could be destroyed in the flick of a trigger finger.

In the end, Joe's new identity hurt him with the elite high schools and didn't help Devon either. Joe didn't get into any of the top private schools. Though he was accepted at the new school with the exciting mission, which was under-enrolled, Devon was not. The cost of a full scholarship was just too high, we heard; there were other kids with better grades, and his application had come in late. So it wasn't that they didn't think they could work with him. At least not officially. It was that it didn't seem worth it. Unlike Joe, Devon would not be free to reinvent himself.

"It's probably better that he didn't get in," said the mother of a white student who was admitted to a few private schools, thinking she was providing some consolation. "He'd be on the bottom of his class there, but at a public school he won't."

The new school could be *our* chance to get Joe out of the ghetto, however. For months, it had been our salvation, beaming like the neon one-way sign on a fundamentalist church, pointing the way back to our side of the invisible line. But a curious thing happened the day we went to the school orientation. Out of about four dozen students who had been accepted into the first class, only two were black. The smiling African American students pictured in so many photos in the brochure were a lie. Some of the bright new freshman faces even belonged to kids from wealthy suburbs with excellent public high schools. Like that of all the private schools we had seen, this school's vision seemed to reflect what white liberal parents would like to be true rather than the real truth, a fantasy that makes it easier for us to live with our choices.

One of the two black students there was a longtime friend of Joe's, a middle-class boy whose parents are both African, and who is being raised by his black African-born aunt and white American uncle. I knew that top colleges accept many more students from immigrant African or biracial families than they do lower-income children whose families have been in America for generations. But how could there be any hope for the future if high schools did that too? "They're looking for kids like him," Devon's mom told Joe, referring to the boy with African parents. "They're not looking for kids like my son."

"This school says they're preparing kids for the future," David whispered to me during the orientation, rolling his eyes. "This isn't what the future looks like—it's not even the present." In the end, we were just too uncomfortable there. We withdrew Joe's application. I realized then that all that time while we were thinking that Joe was moving off on his own, he had been moving us with him.

Fortunately, Joe had also been accepted to a fairly diverse public arts high school, where admission is based more on creative talent than on grades. But Devon literally slipped through the cracks of the public school system. While his mother pestered the school district and while the better public schools filled up, his application simply floated around for months like a plastic bag on the city's windblown streets. Finally, he was assigned to the lowest performing high school in the city—one of the lowest in the state—a troubled school that is also notorious for gang violence. After last year's shootings took two students' lives there, the school's principal was quoted as saying he expected that other students would not make it through summer to return to school in the fall. I asked Joe how Devon felt about his placement. "He's scared," Joe said.

On the afternoon of eighth-grade graduation, their last day of school together, I drove Joe and his friends back to our house for a sleepover. These could not be the goofy kids I had driven around all year, all braces and giant shoes, smelling of greasy onion rings mingled with boy sweat. With their slicked hair and suits, their cologne and corsages, they looked positively suave. I savored the sight of them in the rearview mirror. And for a moment that I knew wouldn't last, I imagined them like this ten years from now, all young professionals getting together downtown after work.

• • •

Summer is here again, an end and a beginning. Joe's bedroom now doubles as a sound studio. In the room where his growth is still penciled on a doorframe, my teenager has created a website to introduce the world to Bay Area rap. He brings kids up from the projects to record songs. He brings Devon over to make beats. He's still angry that Devon didn't get into that school, but he thinks his friend has a good future in rap. According to Tupac, Joe says, just as television news kept the horrors of the Vietnam War in front of America's eyes, rap keeps the inequities of life in our ears.

Street life has warmed up with the weather. Teenagers cruise by at night and pause at the corner, their basses sounding the thumping throb of nowhere to go. *Some people want us to go away,* sings the hip-hop group Frontline. *No, aint goin' nowhere, we here to stay.*

A stone's throw from that corner, a few summers before my diagnosis, an apparition appeared at the chapel of Ave O Maria Immacolata. The Virgin Mary, with cascading hair and flowing robes, showed herself to the faithful on the verdigris gable of the chapel's roof. She came only at night, enveloped in the scent of roses, and disappeared before the morning light. All summer long, carloads of the desperate and the curious quietly climbed the hill at night, where an altar of candles and flowers had been set up on the sidewalk. Though the parish priest warned that "intangible items" require a rigorous investigation before being recognized by the church, the faith of the parishioners was stronger than reason. It was said that in Mary's presence an "overwhelming spiritual sense" washed over their bodies like the holy waters of baptism.

The Virgin appeared two days before the murder of two teenage lovers who were shot while picnicking in Precita Park on a sunny day, kids who must have thought their lives stretched out ahead of them. The Virgin left at the end of summer, but other miracles followed in her wake. Most recently, it's been said that the hands of a teenage boy bled with a rose-scented oil, so much that the priest put it in a bowl and used it to bless those who attended the evening services.

It has been almost two years since my cancer treatments ended and nearly three years since my diagnosis. My hair is down to my shoulders, although the curl has never come back. Neither has the cancer, though. I'm in a new phase—the "survivor" phase. With breast cancer, you are a survivor unless the cancer comes back to kill you. So I live sometimes in a surreal dream of uncertainty, but uncertainty about the future isn't solely my domain.

At night before bed, I rub my hands and body with rose oil. Then, sometimes, I lie awake worrying about the future of Joe and Devon and all the boys who now fill our house. *They don't have a prayer,* the old saying goes. But then, I think, they do have prayers; prayers are something they have plenty of. They are living on teenage life force and their mamas' hard work and prayers. They're praying too, *prayin hard for better dayz.*

"Jesus Walks" is the name of Devon's favorite rap song this summer. *God show me the way because the devil's tryin a break me down.* The other night, when he was at our house, Devon wished me good night in a way my sons never would. "I'll pray for you, Camille," he said. I'll pray for you too, Devon, and for all the other boys with chunky medallions and falling-down pants who come to our house to rap their hard, silly, hopeful songs.

I have to tell you, I still hate rap. But just when I'm ready to ban it from our house forever, I hear a phrase from that vulnerable place in the rapper's steely heart: the sweet nostalgia for his mother's love. It's a love that is, well, like my sons' love for me—a tenderness and a sheltering that make me think of that day on the soccer field when Joe's fierce eyes told me he was with me in the fight for my life. As much as he's changing, that has stayed the same. "I love you, Mom," the super-cool voice croaks from his bedroom sometimes, just before he drops off to sleep. Then, quietly, waiting until he's at the edge of consciousness so he doesn't know, I brush his forehead with a kiss, a blessing, and savor that glow before the night exhales its darkness and the moment is gone.

Thirteen

Janet Fitch

The Americans sit at a table in León, Spain, when the evening at last takes the bite off the heat, watching the couples, arm in arm, strolling in a steady procession past the cafés and cathedral. The wife envies how they walk in step, speak quietly to one another, couples who may have known each other for twenty, forty, sixty years. She marvels at how they still walk close to one another, muster a conversation, when she and her husband have nothing left to say across the gap of a very small table.

Their daughter sprawls in the third chair. Thirteen years old, and for years she has watched the rocky ride of their problematic marriage. The older she gets, the more obvious it becomes that her mother and her father have nothing left between them. And they have grown less able to conceal it. Or perhaps feel less need to do so—their girl is older, understands more. Perhaps they are tired of pretending.

It is almost four weeks that they have traveled together, without a break, and they are separating further with each passing day, while the daughter, on the brink of adolescence, is separating from them both. The wife watches her child's new detachment with mingled regret and fascination. Just a few weeks ago this was a slouchy, baggy pants–and–T-shirted American girl. Suddenly her grungy off-spring is watching herself in the shop windows of Seville and Cordoba and Madrid, Barcelona and San Sebastian and Segovia.

And men, for the first time, are noticing her. Thirteen, but with a graceful body, her rippling dark hair twisted and clipped up, rather than tightly braided, as it is at home. Thirteen, but in Spain, she is wearing her clothes differently; she stands erect, walks with a new self-possession. This physical change is mirrored in the café by how she divorces herself from her parents as they sit, fuming in their isolation, their rage and despair. They are a couple of old people with their own problems.

On their return to America, the husband and the wife separate. The girl is not surprised. After what she has seen, she would have been surprised had they stayed together. The husband moves to a beachside town. The wife exhales. The yelling is over, the criticism, the second-guessing of every decision. She and the daughter sit across from each other at the dinner table. They are free now—to make decisions, to make mistakes, to collude, to negotiate, with respect. Free to grow into something neither of them can yet imagine.

She had been ready for her husband to leave for years. What she had not considered was how it would feel seeing her daughter pack her suitcase, her toothbrush, her teddy, and leave with him for the first time. She did not do one thing until her daughter returned on Sunday night. There were things to accomplish, a book to write, friends she could have called, relatives, errands, and chores, and yet, she did none of them. The shock—that she would lose not only her husband but also her daughter, at least part of the time—was something that had never entered her consciousness.

The separation, which had begun in Spain and which was naturally a part of her daughter's movement into adolescence, would not stop now.

She thinks, *half the world has gone through this,* but now it was her turn to discover what it meant to be a single mother, to construct a new life with her thirteen-year-old daughter. Thirteen. That is an important fact. Keep it in mind.

• • •

It occurs to her that she doesn't know how to do this—head a household, make a family when it is just the two of them. The husband provided most of the structure in their family life. Vacations, mealtimes, chores, homework. Now that it's just the two of them, how very fluid their world becomes. They don't know when to eat, what to eat, how casual it should be, when Thirteen should go to bed, do her homework. How clean to keep the house, how often a child of thirteen should be left alone in the evening.

She feels how lovely it is, absolutely liberating, this freedom to construct a life tailor-made for them alone. It will give them a chance to be absolutely themselves.

On the other hand, she has to admit that, as the weeks go on, the responsibility is a creeping anxiety. What does it mean if she goes out again, the third time this week? What does it mean to reheat last night's dinner, or to microwave something from Trader Joe's? How far can a family break down and still be a family? Is two a family?

But the months go by, and they find their rhythms. Spain is a lasting influence—they find they like to eat late, sometimes nine o'clock, even on school nights. But it's a real meal, cooked fresh and eaten together in the dining room. The woman discovers that just picking up whatever and eating on the run feels wrong. She knows that people do it all the time—it's the modern condition—but the lingering sense of dropping the ball infuses her with a subtle depression, which, somehow, is relieved when she cooks a decent meal and sits down to eat it with Thirteen, even if it is nine o'clock on a school night. It makes her feel like a mother taking care of a daughter, not two coyotes scrounging in an alley. Like they're still a family.

Thirteen goes to bed late now, too, as late as she needs to. She knows when she's tired. This is new too—the woman trusts her daughter to know how she feels. In Spain, both of them took sies-

tas and easily adjusted to the late nights, dinner at midnight, fla-
menco at two A.M., and now, it seems, Spain is still teaching them
what is possible.

Thirteen is frighteningly able, tremendously generous, matter-
of-fact in her adaptation to their new life. The woman is grateful,
but also worries about relying on this too much. Thirteen can
cook for herself if necessary; she can put herself to bed. She does
her homework on her own. She uses her spare time to write her
monthly 'zine, play the guitar, cut up and refashion her clothing,
make collages, or draw her cartoon strip.

But how much time alone is too much time? The woman
begins dating. She worries that she is taking advantage of
Thirteen's competence, her ability to use her time alone, her lack
of concern when her mother goes out. The woman keeps her cell
phone on, tries to stay in the neighborhood; she can be home in
five minutes. She asks Thirteen, "Is this too much? Would you
like me to stay home tonight?" "It's fine, Mom," Thirteen says,
with that thirteen-year-old exasperated sigh. But how much faith
to put in that?

Both the benefit and the trouble with their new life is that it's
all experimental. No one can tell her if this is all right. Neither of
them knows how the experiment will turn out. They can do what
they want, what works for them both, custom-made and newly
minted just for them. On the other hand, the woman worries that
what might seem all right now might not be good in the long run.
And how can she ever know?

She thinks about her marriage, whether they should have
separated earlier. But she knows, deep in her being, that she wouldn't
have left him any earlier. She has to admit to herself, she is a coward
and a shirker. She knows many women who are raising young children on their own, and doing a fabulous job of it. She considered
it—when Thirteen was two, when she was nine. But if she is honest,
she knows she couldn't have done it—worked full time, kept a roof
over their heads, dealt with the discipline and heavy interaction of

early childhood, and continued to write serious fiction. Suicide would have looked like an attractive option.

But at thirteen, her daughter has turned a corner. Her bat mitzvah, where she proclaimed, "Today I am an adult," was no big deal to Thirteen.

The woman, however, took it surprisingly to heart. In some fundamental way, she began to see her daughter as having come of age and capacity, more entitled to make decisions for herself, no longer a child. It doesn't seem odd to her in retrospect that this would be the year her husband and she would divorce.

Now that it's just her and Thirteen, it's so comfortable, so casual; she can see how easy it would be to move from a parent/child relationship into a sororal one. Best buddies. They could go shopping together, see movies, hang out, have their hair done, exchange clothing even. Like girlfriends.

But she has seen that kind of mother/daughter interaction at close range, and there seems something brutalizing in it, the mother using a child as a girlfriend instead of truly being a mother. "We do everything together," one such mother says with a giggle. The daughter is a horror—so angry she cannot follow a request or even eat the food she is served, the terror of birthday parties and school days—and the mother blames everyone but the child and herself.

Now, however, the woman can understand how it happens, how seductive it is—especially when Thirteen is so deliciously wise and fun. She makes an easy co-conspirator, she can be indoctrinated into the mother's point of view, she's companionable, yet the mother still calls the shots. Such an easy buffer against adult loneliness.

The woman knows she must resist this temptation, the monstrous ease of sliding into "just us girls." Thirteen has friends. She needs a mother. What is appropriate is the separation the woman first saw in Spain. Her job is to support that and encourage it, and remain the parental figure, a fixture with a dignity and weight and a center of gravity from whom Thirteen can push off into the world. The girl needs the woman to stay back and let her emerge into her own space and her own style. But at the same time, she still needs the woman to set boundaries, to know that she is still being held, even when they're making it up as they go along.

This is what the woman senses in the importance of the formality of dinnertime. Even if they could just as easily order a pizza and eat it in front of the TV. It would feed her daughter's body, but would it nourish her spirit, make her feel held? No, it would not.

The woman can't escape the irony and humor in dating again just as her daughter is beginning to look up and notice boys in the world. She feels under a tremendous obligation to do it right, to set a good example. She hates leaving her daughter alone at night to go out with a man, but at the same time she feels she's showing Thirteen that you can have a bad experience and move on and find joy and pleasure in life again; these things don't have to leave you bitter.

On the other hand, she doesn't want Thirteen to get to know her steady date too well, because she wants the freedom to end it if it becomes necessary. At the same time, she doesn't want her personal life to be mysterious either, leaving her daughter to worry and wonder what Mom is doing and who she's doing it with. So every time the man comes to pick her up, she asks Thirteen, "Do you want to meet him?"

For a month or so, the answer is no. The woman talks about him, casually, hoping to get Thirteen used to the idea that there is someone special, but someone not very different from her other friends. Finally, one evening, when the man comes to pick her up, and she asks Thirteen, "Do you want to meet him?" the girl shrugs. "I guess I can say hi."

The man comes in, shakes her daughter's hand, and gives her a CD he's made—The Clash and Joe Strummer's last; he has a Thirteen, too. And that is that. How simple it is, and yet big. Her mother is not her father's wife anymore. And she's not going out with Axl Rose or Pee Wee Herman.

At her age, the woman discovers, the men who date have kids, too. She meets the man's daughter—it's surprisingly easy, natural. His daughter is accustomed to this, meeting her father's dates. But she resists the idea of getting their kids together. She is reluctant to make mistakes. It seems a big step, too much. Her husband has a girlfriend now, and she learns he is planning for Thirteen to get together with the girlfriend's family on an upcoming ski trip. Thirteen admits she is dreading it. The woman suggests she tell her father; Thirteen doesn't have to do anything she finds uncomfortable. But she also makes a note to herself: *Don't rush the family thing.*

The woman and her steady have their first major conflict. She comes home dragging ass, and tells her daughter she thinks they are breaking up. Thirteen is wonderful and funny about the whole thing—talks to her as if she is one of her friends breaking up with another eighth-grader: "It's all right, Becky. You'll get over it, you'll see," she says in her perfect Keanu Reeves/Ted of San Dimas imitation. "You're a great girl. Look how much you've got to offer." It makes her laugh, but the woman has to pull herself together, pull herself back. *This is my child, not my girlfriend.* It isn't up to Thirteen to console her, even as Ted of San Dimas.

Such a fine line, though—she lives with Thirteen, the girl sees her ups and downs, she can't turn herself into an Easter Island statue. When the woman is bummed, Thirteen cares, she's sensitive, she wants to make it better. And yet the woman cannot lean on her. She recites it over and over as a mantra: *It's not a child's job to make a parent feel better, to make them take care of you. It's a child's God-given right* NOT *to care about your personal life.*

Thirteen is applying to high school. Of course, the school she likes best is an hour's commute from their house. Before, during her marriage, it would have been out of the question to move, to uproot the family so that one member could go to the school of her dreams. In fact, had the woman and her husband stayed together, Thirteen probably would not have been allowed to apply to this school. The family had a center of gravity then; it wasn't a traveling show.

But now it is just her and Thirteen. They could just pick up and move.

And there it is, the frightening rub of this new life.

She lives in a particularly congenial neighborhood, interlaced with friends, colleagues, neighbors, and many of them are, like her, work-at-home writers and artists; theirs are relationships she has nurtured for fifteen years. They drop in, have coffee, see one another at Trader Joe's, meet at parties, at the clubs. Where she lives has been part of her identity; it knits her life together, like the layer of fungus that holds together the forest floor. The idea of moving an hour away fills her with unnameable panic.

But she looks at Thirteen, back in her braids and baggy T-shirts— Spain's sartorial influence has faded somewhat—and is reminded how time-sensitive kids are, that they're a product with a short shelf-life. She feels the weight of her responsibility to this particular item. She has exactly four more years with Thirteen, to have some kind of impact, to help make her life most closely approximate what this growing person would like for herself, to help her unfold into the young woman it is possible for her to become.

So here it is again—the benefit and the difficulty of this kind of freedom. Whose needs get met, who takes priority? Thirteen has already been accepted into a school nearby, a good school, but perhaps not as sensational as the one across town. Anyone who has ever visited Los Angeles and attempted to drive between Silverlake and Santa Monica during morning rush hour understands that this is not something a sane person would even attempt four times a day.

Oh, she reasons with herself, she could make it work. Find someone who goes to UCLA or Santa Monica City College and pay him or her to drive. She could carpool, do the heinous thing three times a week. But having Thirteen over an hour away, staying away until seven or later each night, busy with school projects, developing a whole new set of friends whom she will never see—the whole idea makes her fretful and sleepless. She remembers her own adolescence, and how little her parents knew. For herself, she would not want Thirteen that far away, physically or emotionally.

So whose needs? Which need? Her need to be a good parent, or her pleasure at being part of a deeply satisfying community?

She prays that Thirteen is not accepted to the school of the distant commute, or ultimately decides on something closer in. But she finds it interesting to consider the possibility of the move, the way it is interesting to torment a decaying tooth. She has the opportunity to be the mother that her mother was not, did not know enough to be.

She thinks back on all the times she has been bewildered upon learning that one of her neighbors was moving to some suburb of the "better school." It had always upset her to hear of one more woman scuttling her own satisfaction to provide for someone else's. First, as a daughter, to be a good girl, to please the parent; then, as a mother, shortchanging herself for the children's sake. *And when is it going to be your turn?* she always wanted to ask.

Now she thinks of her own mother, a woman who has in later life emerged as the grandmother from heaven, but who, back in the day, considered a child's place secondary to the needs of the adults in the family. The urgency of livelihood. It never occurred to parents of that day to ask, "What is it you need from me?" "How can I help you?" Pressed for time and energy, they kept their heads down in the battle zone and soldiered on. If someone had suggested that a mother could do more to support her daughter's unfolding self, that mother would have stared in blank incomprehension.

The woman once wrote a book about a mother and a daughter, and in the process considered long and hard the question *What is it that makes a good mother?* As far as she could ascertain, it seemed to boil down to a fairly simple set of issues. A lousy mother was someone who looked at her kid and said,

"Here's who I want you to be" and "Here's what I'm going to give you." A good mother was the one who looked at her kid, really looked at her, and asked, "Who are you?" and "What do you need from me?"

How many children are ever really seen? How many, on the other hand, are given what their parents want to give them—things they need like an Inuit needs an icebox? Things that leave a child frustrated and furious, like getting the Christmas present that's just what the giver wanted. Violin lessons when a child is an artist. Restriction when she needs encouragement. Stoicism when she needs a soft shoulder. And how many future neuroses can be traced back to those misfires?

So why is it so bloody hard for mothers to turn to their own children and look them in the eye and say, "What do you need from me?"

Now the woman knows why: Because then you know, and have to respond. It might not be convenient. It might not be what you wanted to give.

She remembered something that happened when Thirteen was younger. She'd saved a box of books from her own childhood—the best-loved, treasured, and carefully preserved—for the time she would have her own daughter. She had just got to the best of them all—*King of the Wind* by Marguerite Henry—a book in which she had lived for several crucial years of her unhappy but imaginative childhood. She worshiped that book, she became that book.

But when she finally opened that cherished volume and began to read it aloud to her child, her daughter groaned and said, "Oh God, not another sad horse story."

What fury, what frustration—at having saved those books for some idealized child who would appreciate just how wonderful they were, and then, instead, having this real little kid who didn't like sad horse stories. That ungrateful brat, trampling the mother's cherished fantasies of sharing these books with an appreciative daughter, connecting the then with the now.

Fortunately, just as her temper began to erupt, she had one of those blessed moments—perhaps there *are* angels or ancestors who do come to our aid—when you step outside yourself and see the reality of that little person. She had a daughter who did not care for sad horse stories. She didn't need what her mother wanted to give her. She needed something else.

Thank God for *King of the Wind*. It had been worth saving after all.

What does Thirteen really need from her? Not a good book, not even a soft shoulder to cry on, not kiddie art classes or even the benefit of her often shaky wisdom. She needs her to ante up. She needs a mother willing to cross a city for her, a mother watching, listening. Willing to know.

There are only four more years that she will have Thirteen. The girl won't need her hair brushed, won't want to play stuffed animals. She won't even necessarily be aware of what it is she needs. But the clock is running. The woman knows, has known since Spain, that there is not much time left. There will be time to live exactly the way she would like, many years for that.

But as an artist, she knows as she has always known, that the pleasure of creation takes precedence over any of the more passive pleasures. With her own child, she is creating a work of passion, all the more exciting and terrifying because it is utterly improvised. That day, at the table in León, she had seen what she wanted: relationships that continued and replenished themselves, like the couples walking in the evening arm-in-arm. And when the separation that had begun with Thirteen in Spain is complete, this is perhaps the best that she can hope for—that the mistakes and the negotiations and the trials and the errors of these freelance years have resulted in a mutual respect that will only deepen with time. And that they will always be able to muster a conversation over their coffee cups in a small foreign town.

On Giving Hope

Mariane Pearl

The storm is over, and it feels as if the elements are coming back to their senses. Paris bathes in a soft spring light, and my father is taking me for a ride on one of his seven motorcycles. I pride myself on being a perfect passenger. I am only eight, so I cannot stretch my arms around my father's waist, but I grab his jacket and follow faithfully the curves of his body when he makes a turn. The roads are still wet, but soon the sun will warm us through our black leather suits.

The purpose of our expedition is to visit the tunnel of a subway station. More specifically, to see the layers of torn and peeling posters that remain on an advertisement panel. When we get to the Metro station, my father goes straight to the booth and buys two tickets, as if we are indeed visiting a museum. Inside, above the track, I see my father's discovery: a giant kaleidoscope of colors in an otherwise dark and unappealing tunnel. Whatever information these posters had to give, whatever pictures were once there, have been hollowed out, ripped off, and covered over and over again, leaving an arresting patchwork of half-formed images and vivid colors. It's a jumbled puzzle. But my father sees public art. "Amazing!" he cries with childlike enthusiasm.

• • •

My father is a scientist, an intellectual, an original. A man living counter-clockwise, sleeping in the daytime and working at night. Lately he has been inventing a new method to play bridge, one of his passions along with riding motorcycles. He does not have a job. Our family is running out of money.

I love my father but I hate being different from other kids at school who have working and functioning dads. I want him to come back from work in the evening, put on his slippers, and watch the news on TV. I want to climb onto his lap. I want him to ask my mother, "What's for dinner?" and to scold my older brother, Satchi, and me when we eat like little pigs.

My father has applied for an engineering job at a company that manufactures toothpaste. He has the right profile for the job, and my mother has optimistically bought him new clothing. He looks handsome in his three-piece suit, with his green eyes and curly blond hair, when we see him off for his interview. Three hours later, the doorbell rings and the three of us run to the door to greet him and congratulate ourselves on our new life. But when the door opens, my father is standing there gripping his attaché case as if it is his last grasp on his role as the head of our family. He is still handsome, but in his green eyes I see despair. He goes back to his room at the end of our three-room flat and stays there.

This is two years after the 1973 oil crisis. Our mother tells us about how countries in the Middle East had stopped exporting oil to France and other Western nations to punish them for their support of Israel and the Yom Kippur War. "People worldwide are losing their jobs," she says. I try to pretend I understand what on earth she is talking about and how this relates to my father not getting work at the toothpaste place. Meanwhile, we are living off the money my grandfather sends us. The more money my dad's dad sends, the more my own father loses his self-esteem.

Summer 1976, a year later. It's August but we haven't left Paris yet for vacation. On a sunny afternoon, my father summons me to his room. My father's room is forbidden territory, a sort of cavern where he reigns like a bear; even my mom doesn't sleep there. Sometimes she joins my father in his hideout, and we hear them, my brother and I, screaming at each other until late at night. "We weren't screaming at each other, kids," my mother tells us in the morning. "We were just talking about politics."

My father hasn't left his bed for the last few months. Apprehensive and shy, I open up the door into an impressive mess that is revealing of my father's personality. Old copies of *Le Monde* are scattered on the floor. Sheets of paper torn from a sketchpad are covered with small handwriting in black ink. Words are compacted, pressed against one another, hastily jotted down without space or punctuation, as if my father's hand could not keep pace with his head. There is a dirty plate on the floor.

My father's fingertips are yellowed by nicotine. He is lying on the unkempt bed, putting out cigarette butts on the floor between the bed frame and the wall. The smell of cold tobacco seems to leave him undisturbed.

"Sit down," he says, and I feel that this moment is solemn without knowing why. All he tells me, though, at least as I remember it, is that he finds me a bit overweight. And he makes me promise that when I grow up, I will go on a diet. I say, "Oui, Papa." I'd do anything to please him.

"Now that's a good girl," my father says and he extends his hand to caress my cheek. It is an unusual gesture. My father is not cold; he is just usually absent, half gone in a world without intimacy except with his own thoughts. Most of the time, physical contact seems to feel too real for him. His skin is rough, but there is an infinite sweetness in the way his hand lingers on my face while his green eyes penetrate my soul.

My brother is then called in. My father is usually stricter with him, and when Satchi closes the door behind himself, I am a little worried. He can't possibly put Satchi on a diet; he is much too skinny. What kind of promise will our father ask of him? Their visit is as short as ours was. When Satchi comes out, he seems intrigued but proud of this unexpected exchange, just as I am.

The next day, our mother tells us we are leaving for the south of France, where we will visit one of her women friends. The rest happens very fast. My mother, my brother, and I leave for Marseille. My brother and I are given color pens. My mother goes back to Paris almost immediately. What should she bring back for us, she wants to know. "Scrabble," says Satchi. "Bring back Daddy," I tell her. Four days later, she is back. She hasn't even stepped into the apartment where we are staying when I hear her say, "It's over, kids. Your daddy has died." My mother takes us to a bedroom and the three of us lie on a double bed. My face is wet with tears—mine and my brother's and my mother's run together in indefinable grief. We hold one another for a long time and fall asleep in the middle of the afternoon.

While we are sleeping, I dream about my father. It is foggy and he is boarding a plane. I see his back, but he doesn't turn around. He doesn't say goodbye. I see his curly head disappear into the belly of the plane and the fog closes in around it, removing any trace of him from my sight.

Satchi wants to go home, but there is no more home to go back to—at least not the same home. With the help of friends, my mom has already moved us. We return to Paris, to a new apartment. It is in the same building as the old one, but it is smaller, for just the three of us. There is no mysterious room at the end of the hall; there is no scent of cigarettes or scraps of scribbled paper.

"You know your father . . ." our mother begins, sighing. I am tempted to say, "No," but I don't. "The doctor had told him to quit taking sleeping pills, but he took them anyway and his heart couldn't stand it."

She would like to protect us from everything, our mother, even from our own destiny. We never see a coffin or any clue to tell us where our father's body is. We never go to the cemetery to visit his grave. We very rarely talk about him; he has disappeared in a fog, as in my dream. My father was here. He is here no longer. Life goes on, and imagination takes over. Over the years I piece him together like a human puzzle, tearing bits from my memory and pasting them on, piece by piece, to try to make the picture whole.

The father I create has curly hair. He often wears sandals and plays Cuban tunes on the guitar. He is a physicist, an engineer, Dutch, Jewish, a genius, a painter, a speaker of many languages, unfair with people weaker than he, a revolution's lover, absent-minded, asocial, good at playing bridge. He is depressed, he is charming. He is a kaleidoscope of colors and shapes that I twist and turn against the light to make a coherent image.

As I grow older, I look for him in other men. I feel betrayed by his sudden departure and the mystery of how and why he died. His memory is the source of a vague uneasiness built of guilt and distrust, an anxiety that I am learning to live with as I pursue the impossible quest of finding my father again in the men I meet. It is a painful process in which my childhood conflicts with the young woman I am trying to become.

Still, my mother doesn't like to speak about him. "It's behind," she says.

Eight years after his death, my dad will be the one to tell us the truth. It is fall, and our mother is out shopping. Satchi is sitting in the walk-in closet in our apartment, a small case full of documents open in front of him, going through some family archives. He opens a letter. Despite my mother's willed forgetting, I immediately recognize my father's scribbling; the memory of him consigning his nostalgia on torn-out pieces of paper comes back all at once. Satchi's hand shakes as he reads the letter, and he turns pale. It is a suicide note from my father, addressed to a psychiatrist friend whom we don't know.

My father wrote: "When one sees a mountain, one wants to climb to the top. But once you are there, it is only to discover that the mountain has disappeared, you don't see it anymore."

His words make as much sense to me as the subway art he took me to see long ago. What mountain? And what about us, his children?

When my mother comes back, she finds us still sitting on the floor, reading the note over and over, trying to decipher from its spare words all that is unwritten. "You had to find out, I guess," she says, almost with anger. Finally, she tells us that our father died alone in his hideout in our flat. He swallowed barbiturates. He knew our brief visits to him in his room that summer afternoon would be the last. My mother doesn't offer any explanation for keeping the truth from us for so long. And we have learned not to ask her too many questions about our dad.

Although I am now a teenager, I suddenly see that something in me has remained stuck in the little girl who learned of her father's death that day in Marseille. I feel pain but also a strange relief, as if I had known all along that he killed himself, an intuition never confirmed by words until then. After I've read his letter, at last I am able to start mourning him and accepting his death. Long overdue tears, unshed since the day I heard of his death, pour out of my eyes.

Until then my psychological survival had dictated that I remodel my father into an idealized, misunderstood, and romantic hero. Finding his letter allowed me to step into his reality, to begin scratching through the layers of silence for the truth.

From family friends, I learn that he had struggled with his identity all his life. He was born a Jew in Amsterdam, at the beginning of the Second World War. To escape the Nazis, he and his mother walked all the way to the south of France, where he was raised in a Jesuit college in Cassis. He did not know who his father was. It turned out that my dad's dad had sex with my grandmother only once. In fact, my grandfather told us years after my father's death: he had had sex with a woman only once in his life. He was homosexual and lived forty-five years with his male lover.

My grandfather pretended to be an uncle who showed up in my dad's childhood once in a while, always leaving behind money for him. But my father didn't like this man. He was forever hurt when he found out, at the age of fourteen, that this "uncle" was actually his biological father. Like Satchi and me, my father had been scarred by having the truth about his father hidden from him.

As my picture of my father fills in, my anger and incomprehension turn into understanding and even gratitude. I am able to give him back his humanity. I visit his solitudes, his anguishes. I learn how to love him and his existential doubts. My father becomes a real man, a man who knew great trauma and fear. Although at first I mistook him for a coward for having taken his own life, I now sense that he had actually tried his best to live the longest time possible. And having prolonged his life, he made the lives of his children possible.

I wish I had known all this earlier, even if discussions of suicide don't befit childhood. My mother thought secrecy would protect us from the shame of it. But when the memory of your father is erased, there is an impossible void to fill—it is as if half of you has been confiscated. Even a desperado father is still a father. With the truth, he became a person again, and I became an adult.

Twenty-three years after my father's death, the night before I am to be married, he appears to me for a second time in a dream. This time he is coming out of an airplane. This time the weather is magnificent. He has come to attend my wedding. My father looks young, tanned, happy, and relaxed. He takes me in his arms and we dive together into a swimming pool filled with turquoise water. Everyone in the dream is smiling and laughing. My future husband, Danny, is watching the scene with his quietly triumphant expression. It is the most beautiful dream I have ever had. And after I wake, I do not suffer from my father's absence again.

May 2001. It is the monsoon in Mumbai, India—the air so moist that my hand sticks to the leather arms of the chair where Danny is sitting next to me. My husband and I moved to India about a year before, when Danny became South Asia bureau chief for the *Wall Street Journal.* When I met Danny, I knew I was really in love for the first time. Danny didn't resemble my dad in any way, and I liked that. By then, I wasn't looking for a reflection of my pain or trying to fill a void. For the first time, I loved a man for who he was and not for what my father had failed to be.

Danny is crying over the novel he has been reading for a few days. A big tear drops on the page, distorting the printed letters in its tiny pond. The world outside is hushed; there is only the tapping of raindrops on the window and a few palm trees waving on the dirty playground across from our apartment. Inside our little shelter, I feel great tenderness for Danny and his capacity to lament over the misery of a fictional character.

We have been married for two years, and I know of Danny's desire to become a father. Unlike him, I have never known for certain if I wanted to have a child. My father's suicide has left me unsure: You couldn't tell if a father would just disappear. But then again, I never knew that I was going to love as hard as I love my husband.

My father's suicide note taught me that to live doesn't mean only to be alive. You have to have a sense of purpose that is stronger than whatever obstacles you find in your way, strong enough to carry you on to the next mountain and the next. So, when your turn comes to give birth to a child, you must do more than exercise a biological privilege. If you are to give birth, you must also give hope.

This night, when I have never felt closer to my husband, I ask him for the first and the only time, "Why do you want to have a child?"

"To continue," he answers without hesitation, "to perpetuate myself." I look at him, sitting at his handmade desk surrounded by newspaper clippings, files, and notebooks. He is opening the first bureau of the *Journal* in Mumbai, a daunting task that he faces with optimism and courage. I realize there is no need for me to think twice; I know I will have no problem giving hope to the child of such a man. I start dreaming of a little Danny running around.

A few weeks later, I give myself a home pregnancy test. When I see the results, I scream and run out of the bathroom, forgetting to put my underwear back on. Danny is alarmed. I rush into his arms: There is the beginning of a little us growing inside of me.

I am six months pregnant when my husband is kidnapped by Al Qaeda terrorists. We are living in Karachi. It is four months after the attacks on the World Trade Center, and most journalists covering South Asia have followed the story here, to Pakistan. It is no mystery that the country has links to Muslim fundamentalists and those who harbor them.

Danny is writing a story about the "shoe bomber," Richard Reid, whose attempt to blow up a flight from France to the United States was thwarted when airport authorities in Paris found explosives hidden in his shoe. Danny discovered that Reid had been taking orders from someone based in Karachi, and he was investigating the kind of support Reid had received from Pakistan. Danny thought he was meeting someone who would introduce him to a Muslim leader he wished to interview, but he was lured into a trap by a British-born Al Qaeda terrorist, Omar Sheikh, who led him to his captors.

When Danny is abducted, I spend every minute of the next five weeks in Karachi fighting his captors. I fight like I have never fought anyone—with all my might, using everything I have learned about life and death, love and faith. I put together an investigative team that for the first time ever unites journalists with Pakistani police and FBI agents in a rescue effort. I spend a week without sleep, searching Danny's computer for clues; I pour my emotional energy into supporting the task force, so no one will give up hope.

Inside myself, I go beyond fear to a place where the terrorists can't reach me or even separate Danny from me. In my heart, I know my husband is defying them as much as I am. I don't know whether we will both make it out alive, but I know our spiritual victory over those who have him is certain. Everywhere I go and in everything I do, our child is with me. It is already as if our three souls have merged into one.

•   •   •

I am thirty-four years old when I become a widow, two years younger than my mother was when my father took his own life. Danny's captors killed him. First they accused him of being a CIA agent and then a spy from Mossad, the Israeli intelligence agency. No one believed those claims—not even the terrorists, I learned later. But Danny didn't need to be guilty of anything for them to kill him; he just needed to be American or Jewish or part of whatever group the terrorists want to target with their hatred. They wanted to terrify Jews and Americans. So they took Danny's life, decapitating him on camera, hoping that television channels around the world would broadcast the tape of the murder.

Two months later, I am alone in the delivery room at the Maternité des Lilas, in Paris, the clinic Danny and I had chosen. For me, this moment is an intense encounter between life and death, with me between them. I am lying on the delivery table, silently addressing my two men—one unborn, the other dead. In the days that preceded the first tidal waves of labor announcing the baby's arrival, I stayed alone. I called it my "jihad." In Islam, the most honorable holy fight is the one a person leads within his- or herself. I know that by killing my husband, the terrorists expect to break my life, too, and that of my son. But I am fighting the holiest of fights, and I win. Giving birth to our baby is my ultimate act of anti-terrorism. I am perpetuating Danny. This is what I tell Danny as our son, Adam, finds his way out into the world.

Through the pain of childbirth and the time preceding it, I know that there is only one answer to those who killed Danny: life. That gives me the courage to deny the terrorists their goal. I write my beliefs down for myself:

They want to silence me; therefore I will speak out.
They want to kill joy in me; therefore I will laugh.
They want to paralyze me; therefore I will take action.
They want war; therefore I will fight for peace.
Someday I will pass these words on to my son.

Through this life-and-death struggle, Buddhism is my walking
stick. Buddhism teaches that life is about climbing mountains,
and that only by doing so can you embrace who you are. It also
acknowledges the endless cycle of life and death, and the connection of individuals beyond life and death.

So Danny dies, and Adam is born. When I first see Adam, his
eyes wide open, staring at me, I can immediately tell he has the
same self-confidence as his dad. We look at each other for a few
seconds and then we both cry. For me it is the cry of humanity triumphing over evil. Now I understand that there is something
between people who love each other that even death can't erase.
Maybe therein lies the definition of hope.

For the first time, I call our son by his name, Adam. "We should
call him Adam, after the first man," Danny had said. He wanted to
celebrate the many bloodlines that would define our son. From his
dad's side, Adam is one-quarter Iraqi and one-quarter Polish. From
me, he has Cuban and Dutch blood. He was born in France, conceived in India; his mother is French, and his dad was American.
Adam is the antithesis of the message perpetrated by fundamentalist
terrorists; he is the anti-clash of civilization.

In the last picture ever taken of Danny, a photo that traveled
the world in an instant on the Internet, he has a gun pointed at his
head and a smile on his face. While everyone around me looked at
the gun, I saw the smile. I smiled with him, and I cried.

Adam is almost two years old. He runs all over the place,
hates his diapers, and has the open beauty of angels. I like the
way he extends his arms to strangers. He wants to be picked up,
confident that whoever holds him will love him.

"What will you tell him?" people ask me constantly. Most of
the people asking this question feel so sad they can't even look at
Adam. But Adam puts his face right up into theirs, as if playfully
searching their souls. It's a look that reminds me of his father, a
glance both unapologetic and sweet.

"I have no choice but to tell him the truth," I say, because I
have learned that you cannot escape from your own story, no

matter how hard you try. My father tried very, very hard. My mother tried to keep the truth from my brother and me.

But which truth will I tell Adam? The one conveyed by terrorists who sent out the videotape of my husband's gruesome killing, in order to intimidate and paralyze the rest of us? In that case, Danny's life would be defined by the way he died. All his beliefs, ideals, and passion would have died with him, torn to bits and pieces, as the terrorists tried to do when they destroyed his body.

Or will I tell my son the truth Danny fought so hard to convey, the whole truth? If someone put a gun to your head and you had no doubt he would use it, would you smile? And if you smiled, what would it mean? Would you smile to your unborn child? What would that smile convey about how you lived your life and even how you believed you should die?

I believe that in Danny's courage at that crucial moment—to show that his captors could not destroy his soul—lies the future of our child. I will try to raise Adam to smile in the face of life as Danny smiled in the face of death. Each of our smiles is a blow to terrorism, just like Danny's smile, his last one.

Omar Sheikh, the terrorist who organized Danny's abduction, has a son a few months older than Adam. They will grow up in the world at the same time. I wonder what Omar Sheikh will tell his son. A few days before Adam's birth, Danny's father shared with me his thoughts: "The children of those murderers will come to admire pursuers of truth like Danny and will despise their fathers for their arrogance and cowardice."

Adam will never get to believe this is a perfect or even a safe world. He will know before others that you can encounter absolute evil. But he will also know you can defy it even in the worst circumstances. He will understand that you have to choose your truth and live up to it.

The French writer Michel de Montaigne wrote, "The great and glorious masterpiece of men is to live with a purpose." My father could not find a purpose and he lost himself in despair. Now I wish I could tell him that with each mountain you climb, you reach a new summit within yourself. My husband knew his purpose and he gave his life for it. Danny was silenced, but the whole world knows who he was and what he stood for.

"Our son is going to change the world," Danny predicted, in his happy and confident way. Adam sometimes looks at Danny's pictures and blows kisses to him. Unlike my mother, I have hung pictures of my child's father in his room, happy ones. And when the day comes for Adam to see the photos of his dad in captivity, I will not try to hide him from the truth. I will point at the last picture of Danny and I'll say to our son, "See that smile, baby? That smile is our soul." And I know Adam will understand. I can see it already in his smile.

Harry Potter and Divorce Among the Muggles

Constance Matthiessen

We were listening to a tape of the most recent Harry Potter volume, *Harry Potter and the Order of the Phoenix,* on the way back from the beach, my three children and I. It was late, and everyone was sunburned and sandy, stunned into peaceful silence. The car was warm and rapt, and no one said a word as we hurtled down the highway, over the Golden Gate Bridge and across the city to our house.

The house was a new home for us, just five minutes away from our old one. We had only just moved in: boxes were everywhere, and a painter was scheduled to come in the morning. This new house was smaller, with no parking and one bathroom instead of two. But the biggest difference, the one that none of us had yet gotten used to, was that David, my husband, was living in an apartment in another part of the city.

By then *Harry Potter and the Order of the Phoenix* had been out for several months, and we'd heard rumors that someone close to Harry dies in the book. My nine-year-old, Aidan, had even discovered who the victim was, having wheedled the name out of his cousin. I wouldn't let him tell, but he had been dropping heavy, persistent hints to his younger brother and me.

But none of us, not even Aidan, was prepared for the shock of

Sirius Black's death, and it hit hard that night in our dark little car. We reached home soon after Bellatrix Lestrange knocked Sirius down with a wand blow to the chest, and I couldn't find a parking place near the house. I finally found a spot a few blocks away, but couldn't face the walk up the hill, or the prospect of lugging the wet towels and swimming suits, the cooler with its grim picnic leftovers and sandy drinks.

So we all just sat there and listened as Jim Dale continued to spin out the story of Sirius's death and its aftermath. Harry Potter had trusted and adored Sirius: since his mother and father were both dead, Sirius was a substitute parent. And Harry's grief was compounded by guilt because, through a complicated series of circumstances, Sirius died trying to save Harry's life.

At that moment, I felt keenly the weight of my new single parent-hood. Both boys were fighting sleep, and getting anyone to help me carry the bags was going to be a struggle. Julia, my four-year-old, appeared to be asleep, and would either wake up and wail when I picked her up or remain in a dead-weighted slumber. Either way, she would have to be carried. The walk to the house would likely rouse all of them and then I'd have to coax three grumpy children into bed. I was the only grown-up, I was exhausted, and I was in charge.

David and I had decided to separate the previous fall, and over the last six months I'd marched us through the house sale (which took a tortuously long time), found us a new home, orchestrated the move, and packed up everything we owned. Finally we were settled—David and I in different houses at last—yet I'd never felt so unsettled in my life. Some days were wonder-ful: to be living in a house with no undertones of anger was an enormous relief. On those days, I was optimistic that David and I could be good co-parents—better apart, in fact, than we had been when we were together. I envisioned our becoming friends in the months and years to come, as we both went on to happier lives.

At other times, I looked at our little family, and the kids seemed ragged, the grown-ups flailing, and this new life appeared lonely and sad. Huddled in the car on that chilly autumn night—miles, it seemed, from home—our little family seemed simply broken.

The tape was finally over, and the tape machine clicked off. "Why did Sirius have to die?" Dylan wailed out of the silence.

"Now Harry has nobody," Julia said drowsily, not asleep after all. "Lord Voldemort killed his parents when he was just a little baby."

"We know that, Julia," Aidan said scornfully. He was sarcastic to all of us these days. "Mom? Hello? Are we going to sit here in the car all night?"

After we reached the house Aidan told me he wasn't tired, that he needed to do something before going to bed. Later, when the other two were asleep, I went to look for him. I found him at my desk, hunched over a piece of paper. He'd been doing a lot of drawing lately: mostly strange, freakish figures on skateboards, or elaborate underground tunnels filled with the same freakish figures, or freakish figures caught in battle. Aidan has red hair and freckles and the rakish good looks of a boy in a Norman Rockwell painting, but he suffers from monumental feelings and a passionate heart.

"How are you doing, Aidee?" I asked him now. I knew he was missing his dad. He shrugged.

"Tired?"

"I hate her," he said fiercely, drawing thick black lines on the piece of paper, scratching out his drawing. "Why did she make Sirius die?"

"Who, Bellatrix?"

"No, the author, J. K. Rowling. She's an idiot."

I ruffled his hair, feeling futile. At that moment I kind of hated J. K. Rowling myself. Couldn't she have left Harry his beloved godfather, since he'd lost everyone else? Didn't she realize that this year had been hard enough already?

He looked so sad, my little nine-year-old, so fierce and knobby-kneed and heartbroken, that I ventured a foolish, hopeful thought. "Maybe he isn't really dead. Maybe he'll come back in one of the next books."

Aidan snorted in disgust. "He's dead, Mom, totally dead. He's never coming back."

Later that night, after Aidan had fallen asleep, I sat for a while in the boys' bedroom, listening to their peaceful breathing. I was tired, but I knew I wouldn't be able to sleep. On the nights when I could fall asleep, I would be roused at some point by my worries. Another writer I'd learned to dread during that difficult period—far more than J. K. Rowling—was psychologist Judith Wallerstein, whose warnings about the effects of divorce on children are the stuff of every parent's nightmares.

Wallerstein has spent years following the children of divorce and reporting on their lives in the years after their parents split up. Her conclusion, reiterated in her most recent book on the subject, *The Unexpected Legacy of Divorce*, is that these children carry the scars of their experience well into adulthood.

Wallerstein's most wrenching message is that parents *should* stay together for the sake of the children. It is in fact not true, she insists, that children are happier when their parents are happier. She writes, "Many adults who are trapped in very unhappy marriages would be surprised to learn that their children are relatively content. They don't care if Mom and Dad sleep in different beds as long as the family is together."

Julia, my youngest, clearly felt that way. Particularly in the beginning, she had a hard time going back and forth from my house to David's. One day, when we were driving through a dreary San Francisco fog, she said, "Mama? I think you and Daddy are both going to be sad until you get back together."

"I *am* sad that we aren't together," I said, fumbling for the right thing to say. "I think that Dad is too. But we seem to have trouble getting along when we are together. We make each other really angry. So, for now, this seems to be better for everyone."

Julia thought for a moment, then suggested practically, "I know what to do. If Dad says something you don't like, just pretend you didn't hear."

Most days, I could stand up to Wallerstein, and make the case that I was doing the right thing. At night, however, she prodded me awake, and I was defenseless. If she is right, then divorce becomes a Hobbesian choice between one's child's happiness and one's own.

And as a cautionary tale, Wallerstein's message doesn't allow for happy endings. She gives parents advice for how to make divorce easier for children, but makes it obvious that she doesn't think there is any way to split without causing lasting damage.

Many people have challenged Wallerstein's conclusions, and her methodology continues to come under fire. Still, her message endures, probably because it hits a parental nerve. Divorce is not a fate any parent would choose for his or her child. It is not a future I ever imagined or hoped for—for my children or myself.

So, like every other divorced or divorcing parent I know, I find myself scrutinizing my children all the time, wondering if they are okay—and exactly what is okay? They ought to be sad, right? Their lives are being ripped in two. They have a right to be sad and angry and devastated. But how much is too much? What is normal, and will I recognize irreparable damage if I see it?

A few weeks after we'd told the children we were going to separate, Dylan and I were at a café together, while Julia was at dance class. I asked Dylan how he was feeling about the separation.

He was eating a cookie and playing with two little knight figures. The knights were jousting, periodically knocking each other to the floor. He shrugged, stopping the game for a minute. "Sad. Bad. *Really* bad."

I tried to respond as the parenting books advise, and made a noise that I hoped was sympathetic and encouraging.

"Are you and Dad going to get divorced?"

"We don't know, honey. We are going to try and work things out, but if we can't, then yes, we'll get divorced."

Dylan put his head down on the table. "That is *so* sad," he said. He kept his head there for a while as I stroked his hair. After a minute or so, he sat up again and resumed the jousting. I started to say something, and he said, "Mom, I don't want to talk about it anymore right now, if that's okay with you."

But after the separation actually happened, Dylan grew increasingly melancholy. He developed some minor physical problems that puzzled the pediatrician, and claimed to be tired all the time. One day, on the way home from school, he said wistfully, "If you were a bus or a car, you wouldn't have to worry about anything, because you wouldn't have a brain. Or if you were a rock."

"Do you have a lot of worries, Dylan?" I asked.

"Yes," he said simply.

"What do you worry about, honey?"

"I don't feel like telling you right now, Mom," he said wearily. "It's too long a list."

Of course, this is just the beginning of the rest of my life as a parent. I will wonder forever, I know. In the years to come I will ask myself, is that why she is failing in school? Is that why he is getting a divorce? Dropping out of college? Drinking too much? For the rest of my life, I will search for the roots of their disappointments and failures in the decision I am acting out now.

Six months have passed since the night we learned about Sirius's death. The new paint on the walls of our house already bears fingerprints, and the familiar clutter is seeping into every corner. The children are getting used to going back and forth between Mom's House and Dad's House, and even seem to enjoy the transitions. Their comings and goings—so wrenching at first—now have the quality of routine.

The children are settled happily into our new home, but Judith Wallerstein continues to wake me up—not every night, but often enough. In her books, she speaks with approval of couples who remained in unhappy marriages for the sake of their children. These couples, she says, "struggled with all the problems that beset modern marriage—infidelity, depression, sexual boredom, loneliness, rejection. Few problems went away as time wore on, but that's not what mattered most to these adults. Given their shared affection and concern for their children, they made parenting their number-one priority. As one woman explained, 'There are two relationships in this marriage. He admires me as a wonderful mother. As a wife, I bore him in every possible way. But our children are wonderful and that's what counts.'"

I try to imagine what life must be like for these people. I envision hushed rooms, heavy drapes, the quiet shutting of doors. The rooms are dark, the colors muted. Only when the children come home do the curtains fly open, and light and color and noise flood the rooms. How do they trudge through every day, not to mention holidays and family vacations? And it may be true that very small children don't notice if their parents are unhappy, but those small children are going to become preteens, teens, and young adults.

In the end, Judith Wallerstein and J. K. Rowling, these two women who loomed so large during the early days of my separation, have completely opposing ideas about what children understand, and how much they can bear.

Many parents I know criticize Rowling for including so much evil and death in books intended for children. Harry Potter's world is not a safe one, and the adults in that world, when they are not evil, are often powerless to protect him. Rowling, once a single mother herself, does not shield her readers from the dark side of life. And I think this is why children love her books so much. Children sense at a very early age that dark forces exist, that bad things happen, and people often do not live happily ever after. They know these things without fully understanding them, and efforts by adults to keep such knowledge from them only give their fears more power. Like other great children's authors, from C. S. Lewis to Roald Dahl to Philip Pullman, Rowling deals directly with these fears, and allows children to wrestle with them on the pages of her books.

Judith Wallerstein, on the other hand, encourages parents to create a fairy tale for children; to keep the nuclear family together, no matter how much duct tape and Krazy Glue it takes to do so. But anyone who has experienced the exquisite misery of a failed relationship could never recommend it as an environment for children.

It has been a hard year for my children, and they show scars. But are they worse off than they would have been had we stayed together?

I'll never know for sure.

• • •

Aidan is right of course: Sirius probably won't ever come back to life. But recently the children were listening to *Harry Potter and the Order of the Phoenix* for the second time, and we all noticed something we hadn't before. On first reading, the shock and sadness of Sirius's death obscured the fact that the book has a rather happy ending. It is not a fairy-tale ending: Harry Potter is never going to live happily ever after. But at the end of volume five, J. K. Rowling gives Harry something very precious nonetheless.

In the final scene, Harry is heading home for summer vacation on the Hogwarts train. Since his parents' death, "home" for Harry has been with his Aunt Petunia and Uncle Vernon and their son, Dudley—a family of Muggles who have always treated Harry atrociously. He dreads the summer ahead and the prospect of his aunt and uncle's small-minded cruelty, his cousin's cloddish bullying.

As the Hogwarts train pulls into the station, the Dursley family is there to meet Harry, but another group is present to greet him as well. It is a motley assemblage that waits for him there on the platform: his friend Ron Weasley's parents; a wise and kindly werewolf named Remus Lupin; Mad-Eye Moody, a veteran wizard; and Tonks, a flamboyant young witch. It turns out that they have come to help Harry. They confront the Dursley family right there at the train station, warning that if Harry is mistreated in any way, the family will have to answer to them.

This warning infuriates Uncle Vernon, but the strange and powerful group frightens him, so after some spluttering, he falls silent. Harry is overcome with gratitude for the support of these friends, and so the book ends: "He somehow could not find words to tell them what it meant to him, to see them all ranged there, on his side. Instead he smiled, raised a hand in farewell, turned around, and led the way out of the station toward the sunlit street, with Uncle Vernon, Aunt Petunia, and Dudley hurrying along in his wake."

Harry may have lost his godfather as well as his parents, but it is clear that he still has a refuge in this world—and that refuge is not with his blood relations, the Dursleys. Harry has a different configuration of family, but it is a family nevertheless.

This is what I wish for my children: a sense of belonging in the world, whether their parents are together or not. David and I are trying to build a friendly relationship. Beyond us, the children have a broad constellation of family and friends who care about them, too. It's not perfect, not the nuclear family they were born into, or the happy ending they might have asked for. But maybe it is enough.

When David and I first separated, Dylan would often cry after David dropped him off. When I asked him what was wrong, he always said the same thing: "I miss Dad when I'm with you, and I miss you when I am with Dad." This became his mantra for the separation, a simple, eloquent expression of all that he'd lost, all that he would never have again.

The other day, I asked Dylan how he feels about having two houses.

"I like having two houses," he responded, pondering. "I like your house best when I'm with you, and Dad's house best when I'm with him. But I still miss you both."

Escape from the Devil's Playground

Ariel Gore

I want to take a road trip. I need to see dysfunctional America rushing past our tinted windows instead of taking root in my daughter's adolescent mind. If we move fast enough, maybe we'll be safe. If I pull her from her new world—from her school yard of glares and flipped hair, from her cheerleading squad rooting for players in a game I don't understand, from the windowless mall that consumes her youth, from her phone line, from her laptop Internet and instant-messaging hookup—maybe then I can save her from the parts of this culture I loathe; from the parts of this culture that cause self-loathing.

I want to run away. I need to feel like I can be a mother again. I need to feel like I can be myself again. When was I last myself? At twelve, before adolescent apprehension and uncertainty crashed over my head like a grand blue gray and white-foam Pacific wave? At nineteen, when I had a kid and traded teenage angst for welfare mama drama? At thirty-one, when I finally felt like I'd settled into self-acceptance, weird neuroses and all? My daughter was twelve, then. Adolescent apprehension and uncertainty hadn't yet crashed over her.

I need to get the hell out of here—away from the eyes of whoever it is we're worried will see us when we're seen.

"Oh my God, can you believe what she's wearing?" They whisper just loud enough for the wearer to hear.

"No way!"

"Mom, can you walk a few yards behind me?" my daughter pleads. "Can you drop me off a block from school?" And: "When my friends come over here, don't say anything, okay?"

Okay. I want to allow my girl-woman her space. But suddenly I feel like a secret, like something to be hidden away, silenced.

"Are you ashamed of me?" I want to know.

A blush. "No. Of course not. It's just . . ." she trails off.

My heart sinks. Here I'd imagined myself to be this tall, independent, and self-assured mama-woman. Who knew how easily I could be pushed off my platform shoes?

Eighth-grade self-consciousness is contagious. It's the opposite of hereditary—I'm catching it from my kid. I think: *My hair doesn't look right. I'm getting fat. I'm queer and I need to get back in the closet. I can't believe I'm wearing this sweatshirt.* And: *When did our little red car start to look like such a junkyard relic?* I was so proud of it when we bought it. Off the lot. Not new, exactly, but it smelled like new, and that's what matters in a car. The smell. My girl-child was proud then, too. Our own car. Over were our weekly roadside breakdown rituals. But now the thing is dented. Now it makes weird noises. And now it's white-streaked bird shat-upon because I parked it under the cherry tree.

"Mom! Why'd you park it under the cherry tree?"

Why, indeed?

Our own car. Now my girl-woman counts the days until she can get *her* own.

She wants me to hide my tattoos: "They're soooo nineties, Mom." She wants me to dress like her friends' mothers: pleated pants, pressed sweaters, and comfortable shoes instead of frayed jeans, faded tank tops, and platform flip-flops. And: "Mom? Make sure SHE isn't in the car when you pick me up from school, okay?"

Who is SHE? SHE is my girlfriend. SHE has been living with us for three years in a town where people talk about such things—not in a hating, homophobic way, exactly, but in a neo-liberal, "aren't we diverse because we have queer friends" kind of a way. Everyone knows. But this month we're pretending it's a big secret.

"Are you ashamed of us?" I ask.

A blush. "No. Of course not. It's just . . ." she trails off.

My daughter wears miniskirts with tight, off-the-shoulder Ts, retro-eighties pumps.

"I can't believe you let her dress that way," my sister admonishes.

I feel defensive even though I don't recall *our* mother having had any control over the ripped T-shirts, purple dye jobs, and combat boots of our youth.

For Easter, we rented a documentary about Amish teenagers who are allowed out into "the world" when they hit sixteen. *The Devil's Playground*, it's called. Amish tradition and religion hold that a kid has to be allowed to experience mainstream American life before making the choice to "join the church" of his or her childhood. Some of the kids go to a dozen raves, then return home to start their adult lives. A few embark on promising futures outside the church; they learn to drive, go to college. Others become meth dealers in southern Florida.

I wonder if *this* is what's going on right now. Does my girl-woman have to check out mainstream America—complete with mother-hating values and homophobia—in order to find her own way? I wonder if it is more or less embarrassing to have me for a mother or to have a couple of long-haired parents who dress like pilgrims and take a horse and buggy into town. I wonder what future my girl-woman will choose. Will she become a meth dealer in southern Florida? Weirder things have happened. Will she ever come back to our church? What is our church? The church of the little red car?

Safety in motion. I don't want to wait for her to make up her mind. I want to kidnap her myself. We could drive to the coast. We could get all the way to New Orleans or Mexico City. We could follow winding roads up into the wilderness. If a mother acts a fool but there's no one unrelated there to see her, is she still a fool?

In the car, I know where my girl-woman is. In the car, she has almost no choice but to listen to me. In the car, I imagine I can protect her, imagine I am in control, imagine we can outrun the devil at our heels.

Here's the irony: most days, my girl-woman doesn't dislike me. She doesn't wish me dead, gone, or disappeared. And perhaps that's part of the problem. If she hated me, maybe she wouldn't care so much if THEY liked me. Who are THEY? The teasers, the bullies. "The Stupid People," she calls them.

"Why do you care what The Stupid People think?"

"God, Mom."

"No. Really. I want to know. Why don't you just tell The Stupid People to grow up and get a life?"

"But, Mom! No one will talk *to* me if The Stupid People are talking *about* me."

Oh, right. I brace myself as old familiar mother guilt rushes in. What was I thinking, bringing a precious baby girl into a world I knew was run by The Stupid People?

"Being embarrassed by your parents, that's something everyone has to go through," my daughter wrote in a recent essay. So she knows—*intellectually*, anyway—that she's not alone. That it's not just me.

And I know, too—*intellectually*, anyway—that this new shame is nothing personal. It's developmental. It's a right of passage. It's the way things are supposed to be. My girl-child spent years looking up to me like I was the queen of cool. She strained her neck. I taught her my values, my fashion sense, my politics. I published a 'zine called *Hip Mama*; she published a 'zine called *Love and Death in Fifth Grade*. I took her to protests; she led the Radical Women's contingent of the Dyke March in San Francisco. She loved me irrationally. Now that we see eye to eye, she sees through me. I'm just a dorky human mama-woman, it turns out; I'm the bumbling wizard behind the curtain.

My power has been a farce.

What she doesn't know is that The Stupid People's power is an even bigger farce. I try to warn her, but she just rolls her eyes. "God, Mom."

I might be telling her the truth, but why should she believe me? I lied about Santa Claus. I lied about the Easter Bunny. And I lied when I pretended she was right to think I was "all that."

I want to be able to step back now, let my girl-woman out into the devil's playground, if that's where she might find her own values, her own fashion sense, her own politics. But this whole letting-go thing is bumming me out.

Please God, I pray, *keep her safe out there.*

I'm not the mother-of-a-teenager I meant to be. When I thought forward to these years, I saw myself so well adjusted: easy to talk to, the owner of the "safe" house where all the kids would hang out. At the very least, I imagined I'd be quiet and knowing, calm and rational. But most days I'm flailing around, flawed, clueless, irrational. No wonder she's embarrassed. I have to bite my tongue to keep from saying the most inane things. Some days I don't bite fast enough. The things that go through my head! The things I actually come out with! "I work my ass off so you can dress like a rich girl, and this is how you think you can behave!?" I actually said that.

I've always hated those dads in the movies who come out with shit like that. Shit like: "Not as long as you live under *my* roof, young lady!"

I never thought I'd catch myself dead feeling the same way, morphing into some authoritarian freak. For one thing, that's a *dad's* job. Mom is just supposed to sit home and worry, which I do plenty of, but it's this other set of emotions that's caught me off guard.

I'm angry. I'm bitter. I overreact and underreact at seemingly random intervals. I'm hurt when she thinks I'm a loser. I take the teenage angst personally. I have made a life out of speaking my truth about motherhood and have, at the same time, insisted that I would never define myself *only* as a mother. Now I have to admit that motherhood has gotten the better of me.

The night I woke up at three A.M. and—like Miss Clavel in the *Madeline* books—turned on the light and said "something is not right," I went rushing down the hall to her room and found her . . . *gone*. Every CNN-nurtured maternal fear I'd ever had swelled and burned in me until—after I got off the phone with 911 and every friend of hers I knew—I collapsed onto the floor and had to admit that along with all my fears for her safety there was this: *If anything happens to her, my life is meaningless.* All my feminist talk about being a woman first and a mother second has been nice, but it's been a lie. A nice lie. Because when it comes down to it, I would take a bullet for her in a heartbeat. And if I didn't jump fast enough, I would consider myself a failure. Not a failure at motherhood, but a failure at life. I wish it weren't so, I hope I'll grow out of it or make peace with it, but somewhere in me I believe that her survival is my sole life's mission. Maybe it's just biological. An irrepressible instinct to ensure the continuation of the species. But it's too much to carry. And it's too much to put on a kid. When she finally got home—six A.M. in the back of a cop car—I was so relieved to see her, I banshee-raged at her like she herself had kidnapped my baby. Which, come to think of it, I guess she had. But just when she needs me to be stable and rational, I'm falling into my most dreaded stereotypes: the over-protective mother, the under-responsive mother, the mood-swing mother. Worst of all, because my girl-child is so humiliated by me that I have limited contact with her friends and her friends' mothers, I am convinced that I am the only mother in history to be pushed over the edge by early adolescence.

Most of my friends don't have teenagers yet. Or their kids are entirely theoretical. "I would never raise a child in America," they tell me. Or, "That's why it's so important to have open communication."

Gee, thank you.

Sure, I read books. I talk to mom friends who live far away now. I've done my research. I know—*intellectually*, anyway—that this is the way it goes. But that knowledge doesn't change the way I feel: Alone, afraid, overwhelmed, pissed-off, self-absorbed, and guilty for being so damn self-absorbed.

Your kid needs you now, I mutter like some stupid daily affirmation. *Get over yourself and be the grown-up.*

Some days it works. Some days I have it all together or I pull it all together. Some days I'm calm and collected. But some days I am one seriously messed-up, whacked-out, control-freak mother, and the only solution I can think of is to pack ten sandwiches and my baby girl into our little red car—and drive.

Boys! Give Me Boys!

Jennifer Allen

Sunday—husband's working, sitter's off. It's you, all alone with the three of them, your three young sons, running you ragged in a burning barefoot marathon on a treadmill set on HIGH-SPEED PANIC. Its hot rubber mat jerks you back so fast you fall flat on your face. You feel like a cartoon character, flattened out into one dimension, as you are dragged—feet, legs, belly, chest, neck, head—backward, through this machine that sucks you in and spits you out all day long. You may wonder aloud, *Hey, how do you stop this crazy thing?* Wonder all you want, no one is listening—they're all boys, remember? You talk to yourself from a second-person stance, but you cannot help it, can you? Because when you are the mom of three little boys, who has time for me, myself, or I?

Certainly not you, not now. Right now, you have a six-year-old in a Tae Kwon Do uniform wiggling his top tooth loose with his tongue. You have a three-year-old in an inflatable Hulk costume making farting sounds. You have a six-month-old in a swollen diaper standing in the stroller and chewing on the straps of what was once your favorite and finest Italian silk bra. You have all of them all around you: the sole, freak female in the house, sitting on the potty, pleading, "Can I please, please, have some privacy, please?"

Your boys, these sons, think they have a right to your body

morning, noon, and night. If you lock them out of the bathroom, they will panic, shriek, shrill, and cry—as if you have locked them out of your very heart. They will kick the door, thrust themselves against it, and then rattle the doorknob, yelling, "Mommy, Mommy, Mom!" You mean mommy, you, how dare you try to insert a tampon all by your lonesome self on the potty at dawn when one of them needs you to pull the tooth from his mouth, another needs his Hulk costume zipped up, and the other needs his back rubbed NOW! "Did you hear us, Mom? Mom, Mommy, NOW!"

You tell them you hear them. You tell them, "I'm sorry, I can't right now," and the two older ones reply, "I'm sorry, I can't right now." And when you ask them, "Are you mocking me?" they yell (so loud the baby yelps), "Are you mocking me? Are you mocking me? Are you mocking me?" So you do what you must—and quickly. You insert, wipe, and wash. You apply peach-blossom lip gloss to ward off that pale post-partum menstrual look you have when you are passing clots the size of your liver, and when coffee and Advil and an occasional free-floating handstand cannot keep your cheeks rosy and glowing and girlish looking all day long. You open the door, check on the tooth, you zip up the Hulk, you give the baby a big peach-blossom kiss on the nog, and off you go, out of the bathroom and into the hall.

Each one grabs hold of the sides of the stroller, which is moving so slowly and awkwardly across the sticky carpet that you accidentally bang the baby's head on the door heading into the bedroom and he cries. He's got a big welt near your lipstick kiss. You tear off your sleep shirt and then your nursing bra and hand it to him, and he is immediately contented, calmed, chewing on Mommy's all-night-long-night-sweats smell. You then undress entirely because you refuse to be a mom who is still wearing pajamas in the yard in the bright morning suburban California sun. They close in around you and gawk and gasp and gape as you slip off your night drawers. There you are—naked, nude, undone. And there they are—staring at your dicklessness. You try to change the scenery by swiftly slipping into your rather stylish and mentally uplifting boy-short undies and matching halter bra, and saying, "Isn't this a pretty color?" But no amount of pastel can distract them from the fact that you are clearly, physically, not one of them.

You are certain the baby is eyeing this new halter bra and thinking, "Why has she kept that one from me?" The other two remain in pure boyhood shock, with their hands down their pants and that ten-thousand-mile-away stare you've seen thousands of times on boys and grown men alike. "Do you have to go to the bathroom?" you ask, and they quickly remove their hands from their pants. Sure, they see you like this nearly every day, but today they ask you, "What is *that*?"

So you must come up with an answer, a word, a name. "It's a ki-ki," you say, and it actually sounds logical because "ki-ki" rhymes with "pee-pee." Then you immediately regret this coinage for such a significant item of future personal exchange. Because you know that you have dreams of taking them all to Hawaii one day, and you already dread sitting in a restaurant and hearing the commentary when they read the menu and the list of things that begin with "kiki"—kiki burgers, kiki dogs, kiki pie. "Ki-ki?" they say, and you say nothing because what more is there to say? Enough has already been seen, revealed, in you, the first female vision they have ever laid eyes on.

And now your own questions begin: Are my breasts big enough? Are my thighs thick enough? Surely my waist is narrow enough? Am I, in total, womanly enough to be the standard bearer of sexuality for all their long lives ahead of them? Thankfully, your self-conscious and overly psychological questions become completely inane when they both scream and squeeze their penises and say, "A ki-ki, ew, ew, I don't want one of those!" And then, and only then, will they leave you. They will charge out of the house and onto the grassy front yard for a quick Hulk/Tae Kwon Do wrestling match, while loudly informing the entire neighborhood—jogging by, walking dogs, trimming lawns—"Mommy has a ki-ki! Mommy has a ki-ki! Mommy has a ki-ki!"

Look at them, united. The world makes sense to them now: They have a pee-pee and you have a ki-ki. Now it's a game—boys versus girl. You're the visiting team and you're already Out. They charge back into the house. They both push the baby in the stroller, and the baby drops your nursing bra and its frayed elastic strap gets caught in the stroller wheels and you don't even try to save it because it's served you long enough and well enough through these three sons. The boys forge on, pushing the baby into the bedroom they all share, and the Hulk shuts the door. You stand there for a moment, noticing all the crayon marks and snot stains, and are about to get some Clorox to clean it all up when the Tae Kwon Do Master opens the door and puts up a sign that reads NO GRILS and NO MOMS and then slams the door shut. Sure, you feel a little hurt, but you get over it. You must. These boys, they will break your heart if you let them. These boys, your sons, they will love you one instant and hate you the next. Why? Because you're their *mom*, the love of their life and the bane of their existence. And if you're going to stand there and wipe tears from your eyes because they've locked you out, well, then you're missing out on some serious self-serving quiet time.

So you head to the kitchen, where else? You make coffee. You drink coffee. You think, *Hmm, this is actually quite pleasant to be a girl, locked out.* You even read an article that has been sitting on the kitchen counter since before the baby was born. You read it backward, last sentence to first sentence, because you are certain you will be interrupted any second and you'd hate to miss the ending. This doesn't seem odd to you. Your days flow backward. You wake wishing the day would end; you go to sleep wishing you could start the day over. When you finish reading the article, you think, *My God, I have accomplished more than I could have ever hoped for on a Sunday, home alone, with the boys.* You pour another cup of coffee.

But then, suddenly, you stop. It occurs to you that it is a bit too peaceful in the house. It occurs to you that if it's peaceful, something is definitely up, meaning: something is definitely going down. You put the coffee down and ask yourself, *Do you dare interrupt? Do you dare peek in?* This is typical mother-of-three-sons behavior—you are constantly second-guessing decisions you have yet to even make. You reason, *Why bother them? No one's crying.* Surely if there was a problem, you would be the first to know, right? But then you remember, oh do you remember, that you are the responsible one here—remember?

You run to their room, kick the door open, and see the cost of your quiet time. The Tae Kwon Do Master is standing on a folding-chair, about to add his final touch—a ghoulish Halloween mask that leaks blood-colored goop—onto a pile of boy treasures stacked as high as your head: Battlebots, Power Rangers, Curious George, Hot Wheels, Hulk hands, Peter Pan and his sword, a battery-operated fire engine, a vibrating crane, a gyrating dump truck, an entire Mutant Ninja Training Academy attached to an entire Alien Space Lab, soccer trophies, T-ball trophies, Tae Kwon Do trophies, Mancala, a chipped ukulele, a rusty harmonica, an electric xylophone, several glow-in-the-dark dinosaur bones, a singular hand-painted ceramic tarantula, and a very buff and extremely naked G.I. Joe seated in his Jeep. When the boys see that you see what they have done, The Tae Kwon Do Master smiles sheepishly and hands you the Halloween mask. The Hulk says, "Look, Mommy, is that cool?" And the baby leans his big head so thrillingly far out of the stroller that the stroller appears about to tip when the Hulk announces, "Mom, Mommy, Mom, I have to make a boom!" You tell the Hulk to go ahead, make a boom, and he says, "Please, please, please, Mom, Mommy, Mom, help me!" And before you can tell the Master to clean up his chromosomal-XY mess, he declares, "Mommy, I have to make a boom, too!"

So now they are in a hair-pulling, foot-tripping, butt-kicking race to the toilet, and there seems to be blood involved. Is it yours? You pull down your pants. You check. No, it's theirs or, actually, it's the Master's, you discern after you pry them apart, and Hulk falls and hits his head on the side of the porcelain tub, and the baby spits up a shred of your bra, and the Master is now sobbing, blood drooling out of his mouth, "Mommy, Mama, Mom, he knocked my tooth out!" The Hulk stops and immediately enters into a litany of apologies. "Saw-ree, saw-ree, saw-ree," the Hulk says, and he allows his big brother to sit on the potty before him, and you think, *Well, there is some brotherly love here after all.* A bit of compassion, you think, as you watch the pooping Master gargle bloody spit into the palm of your hand. And the Hulk patiently waits his turn, sitting on the Winnie the Poo step stool and pointing at the baby, who has that red-faced WHAT IS HAPPENING TO ME, MOM? look that signals his poop is also on its way.

It's a pooping party, and you're the star. You are the star who is needed right now because this is a crucial moment in these boys' daily psycho-emotional lives. After boys poop, they hate to flush it down. They want to study their accomplishment. They need Mom to do so, too. They need Mom to approve of it, Mom to admire it, Mom to wave it good-bye, *bye-bye boom*, as it swirls down the whirlpool pot. And after it is all gone, they are terrified to wash it off their hands. They want to keep it with them all day long—just like men who will keep the after-sex musk on them all day as a kind of secret they share with their bodies, themselves. With boys, you have to bribe them into washing their hands after using the potty. You offer them bubble gum, candy, even cash prizes. And when you start doling out the treats, it starts another fight. Who got purple? Who got red? Who got a nickel, a penny, a dime? And as you watch the baby watching the escalation of yet another fight, surely thinking that this behavior is something to aspire to one day, you cannot help but ask yourself, *My God, does any of this really surprise you?*

Because admit it. You had three big football-playing brothers and a Super Bowl coach for a father, didn't you? You even named your three boys after football players your father once coached—Master Roman, after NFL MVP quarterback Roman Gabriel; Hulk Deacon after head-slapping defensive end Deacon Jones; baby Anton Lamar after six-foot-seven, 260-pound defensive end Lamar Lundy. You grew up in a cauldron of testosterone and even thought that someday *you* would make a fine NFL quarterback, if only given the chance. And if anyone ever even mentioned the notion of you giving birth to kids, you said, "Boys! Give me boys!" Come on, you *wanted* three boys. You said it yourself: "I think three boys would be fun." You said, "Better boys than girls. Boys are *easy*." You thought you had this boy thing down. You thought you'd seen it all—on the field and off. Shin bones broken in half; limp arms dangling from separated shoulders; skulls cracked on sprinkler heads; collarbones snapped; barfing head concussions; bodies hurled through sliding-glass doors, off of tall stucco walls, and, once, down a cliff. Hadn't you seen every catastrophic boy scenario ever played out on the face of the planet?

Apparently not, because now you get to see it all over again in a more intimate version with your very own sons. See the "na-na na-na-na" fights, the "you can't catch me" fights, and the never-ending "it's mine" fights. See them fight over rocks, shells, and straws. Fights over who can pee fastest, longest, sloppiest. Fights over who can burp, fart, and yell the loudest. Fights over washrags, snot rags, and dust rags. And then there are the fights over Mom: who can kiss Mom the most, who can pick Mom more flowers, who can hug Mom the hardest, who can draw Mom the greatest crayon drawing. Who can tell Mom the most, "You're the best mommy in the whole world." Those fights no one wins, except maybe you, drenched in hand-torn flowers, crayon colorings and purple Popsicle-lipped kisses. Still, so many, too many fights, and you wonder, *My God, how did this gender ever become world leaders?* So many fights, you think, *My God, I must be doing something wrong.* So many fights you find yourself—in parks, grocery stores, and school parking lots—frantically searching out and stopping other haggard, lean mothers of three sons to ask them, "Please tell, do yours fight?" And you are actually happy to hear painful stories about bones breaking, noses bleeding, teeth falling out. So, as you regard this hormonal freak show that has become your daily life, you remind yourself, *This is normal; this is natural.* Because, for a girl, anything normal or natural is good, Mother Nature-y and organic, and thus somehow not in need of immediate repair. And for that, you thank God.

You thank God a lot. Thank God you have healthy sons. Thank God you can swear like a lineman, yell like a lineman, and have the pain threshold of a lineman too. Because this last baby boy—whom you have now strolled out onto the back patio along with his brothers to watch the swimming pool–noodle fight in the driveway—he weighed ten pounds, eight ounces at birth. No C-section, no drugs, not a single stitch. The hitch? For forty days and forty nights, you could not take a single step without your hands gripped as tightly as possible on a squeaky old-folks walker. That's right. A walker. You walked with a walker and listened to the crunching of your own cartilage with every single step because the big boy baby had actually refigured the shape of your entire pelvic skeletal structure, so that the hip bones were not really connected to the butt bones anymore. And your sons, what did they do? They looked at you with mouths open, eyebrows arched—complete compassion—before asking you, as you slow-motioned yourself from one chair to the next, "Mom, Mommy, Mom, do you want to wrestle now?" And so, several months later, you sure as all thank God that you can now walk and sneeze and laugh and run without having to reach down between your legs nearly every second to wonder, *Holy Jesus, did my ki-ki just fall out?*

So you need to "put it all in perspective," as your mom tells you when you give her a 911 dinnertime call. Mom is so wise. She's eighty-one, fit, and clinically deaf. She's always said she went deaf from doing too many high-dives as a kid. But now you know the truth. You know she went deaf as a survival mechanism while raising three sons. When you call her, you can barely hear her because the boys are having a high-pitched shrieking contest in the driveway and the baby is practicing his laugh track. When you tell her that you feel like you are running barefoot on a treadmill set on HIGH-SPEED PANIC, she says, "Are you having your period? They're boys. What do you expect?" Then she says, "Wooden spoons. Why do you think I gave you those three wooden spoons for Christmas? How do you think I raised your brothers? They survived, didn't they?"

Back to your brothers, fine grown men with children of their own. Sure, they used to call your mom "a dog," "the maid," and a "stupid, selfish mother," but they all grew up, grew out of it, and love her today, don't they? And when she now tells them, "I love you," they reply, "It's your job." And don't you know that somewhere in the subtext of "it's your job" is a whole lot of love? So, when you break up another one of your boys' fights—this one over a bucket of wet mud—and have to hose them down like dogs, and they are shaking and cold and cowering in your arms as you dry them off, try to recall your mother's advice: "Look, try to enjoy this. Don't be in such a rush. Look at me, I have plenty of time, plenty of time alone now to think by myself—and believe me, it's not very much fun."

So, please, please, try to have a little fun, will you? It's a strapped-in, hang-on, long haul of a rollercoaster ride, and there's no need to shout or panic or cry. When it's all over, you'll be shaking, weak-kneed, and winded, and you'll say, "Hey, that wasn't so bad. Let's do that again!" But by then it will be too late.

GAME OVER. TILT. Time to go to bed. And you'll be oh, so very, very sad.

You can feel it coming on every night. After the bathroom-flooding baths, the pillow fights, and the jumping on beds. After the reading of the *Little Engine That Could* and the singing of the "Twinkle, Twinkle, Little Fart" song. After the sun has gone down and the mill you have been frantically treading on seems finally to slow down. After they have said their prayers and thanked God for everybody and everything. When the day is nearly done, and the house smells like a kennel, and there is spit-up in your hair, you cannot help but feel, not relieved nor necessarily accomplished, but sort of sad.

Tucked in their space-ship sheets, in the glow of their lava lamp–lit room, they still need you. The Hulk clutches his Peter Pan sword; the Master, his stuffed basset hound; and the baby, you. The Hulk twirls a strand of your hair and asks, "Mom, Mommy, Mom, even when we're mad at each other we love each other, right?" The Master puts his tooth under his pillow and asks, "Mama, can I kiss you?" The baby buries his head into your neck. You peek under the bed for monsters. You check the guardrails. You turn on every light in the room. You try to remove all the fears these little boys feel as the night grows darker. You give them their last "don't leave me, don't let me go, Mommy" hug. You pet their heads, tell them, "I love you, see you in the morning."

Soon they will be asleep. Then the tooth fairy will come. In time, they will be men. Someday "you" will become "I" again. And one day, when you tell them that you love them, they will tell you, "It's your job, Mom," and you will thank them.

For now, you wipe the sweat from their brows. You give them one last kiss. One last long hug.

"Sweet dreams," you whisper. "Hold on tight. Tomorrow's another ride."

Why I Can Never Go Back to the French Laundry

Jean Hanff Korelitz

You don't have to be a certified gourmet to know about the French Laundry. Unless your culinary skills are limited to the "Fast Cook" button on your microwave and the only thing you've ever watched on the Food Network was that live-from–Las Vegas competitive eating nausea fest *The Glutton Bowl*, you've probably managed to hear about it. It's that restaurant in the Napa Valley? That temple to the art of cuisine? The French Laundry is the home turf of Thomas Keller, a chef so wildly gifted that he brought even *Kitchen Confidential*'s verbally diarrhetic Anthony Bourdain to a state of stunned silence. Informed opinion holds that it's the best restaurant in America right now (although, since Keller opened Per Se in Manhattan last year, he might have knocked himself off his own pedestal).

I went to the French Laundry once, a few years ago, but I can never go back. The prospect is too humiliating to contemplate, and besides, somewhere in an office on the premises, my name is probably included on a list of not-to-be-readmitted miscreants: "Arrived an hour and a half late. Departed in the middle of the dinner."

You don't just turn up for dinner at the French Laundry, and you don't just call for a reservation, either. You phone precisely two months in advance of your hoped-for appointment, beginning at ten A.M. Don't be late, or you won't have a prayer of getting a table. I knew this, so when I started planning a family trip to Napa Valley four years ago, I circled the appropriate day on my calendar and picked up the phone at 1:00 P.M. on the dot, eastern standard time. After twenty minutes of hitting the redial button, I had my reservation: dinner for two on a Thursday night in March, eight o'clock. I phoned my husband in triumph. No sweat!

My next call was to Madrona Manor in Healdsburg, the inn we had already booked. I needed some help finding a babysitter for our two children, seven years and ten months old, and the inn referred me to a local agency. Because I am not a litigious person, I will not tell you the name of the woman I spoke to at that agency. But because I am not a very forgiving person either, I will henceforth refer to her as Miss Medea, of Medea Nanny Services. "No problem!" said Miss Medea. A babysitter would come to our inn at seven o'clock, in plenty of time to get the children settled before we headed to the French Laundry, a forty-five-minute drive away. I will admit to feeling somewhat smug at my handling of the arrangements. A little forward planning, that was the ticket! There was no reason we couldn't have a pleasant family holiday, spend quality time bonding with our children in the Petrified Forest and on healthful walks in the vineyards, and still enjoy a romantic, world-class dinner, à deux.

Arrogance, thy name is mother.

We drove north from San Francisco on the first day of our wine country vacation, picking up a light picnic lunch in Oakville—we were saving ourselves for dinner—and eating it up on a hill overlooking the gorgeous Napa Valley. We spent a few hours at the Niebaum-Coppola Winery, where you can ogle Vito Corleone's desk from *The Godfather,* and toddled our son around the manicured grounds. Then we got back in the car and headed west through the hills.

As we neared Highway 101, our next landmark, I might have noted the first omen of what was to come. Our hotel in

Healdsburg was north on 101, but Petaluma was south, and with my children snoozing in the back seat, I started to think about Petaluma. Not the Petaluma where Ronald Reagan's 1984 "It's Morning in America" commercials were filmed—their visions of flag-raising grandpas and smiling blond children hoodwinking voters into thinking all was swell on the home front. Not the Petaluma where I had once ordered eco-friendly cloth diapers from Biobottoms, a homegrown, earth-mother outfit whose catalog showed a United Nations of happy babies. But the Petaluma of twelve-year-old Polly Klaas, who in 1993 was snatched from her own slumber party, violated, traumatized, and murdered. Polly Klaas's mother had worked for Biobottoms, I recalled now. A few months after Polly's abduction, I started to get angry about all those frolicking babies in the catalog, and I wrote to the company: Why hadn't they said anything? Why had there been no expression of condolence to their own employee? Parenthood wasn't all lovely babies skipping around in (dry) cloth diapers, after all; it was also the horrible vulnerability of our children to the evil people with whom they shared the world—even in a pretty town like Petaluma, where the babies romped and it was Morning in America.

We arrived at the inn and got settled in a small cottage on the grounds. We set up the port-a-crib in the bedroom, unloaded the books and toys and rattles for our toddler, and then, like good, responsible parents with a hot date later in the evening, we took the kids to get some dinner in the inn's dining room, then brought them back to the cottage to be bathed and changed and readied for bed. We got dressed ourselves, for dinner at the best restaurant in the country. I headed down to the main part of the inn to wait for our capable representative of Medea Nanny Services.

I waited in vain.

With less than an hour left before our dinner reservation, I phoned Miss Medea. No answer. I paced and fretted and waited, then phoned again. No answer. Finally, my phone rang. Miss Medea had picked up my panicky messages. "Oh yes," she said cheerily. "Your babysitter is on the way."

"Good," I snapped. Our babysitter might be on the way, but she was already fifteen minutes late. Even if we left right then, we probably wouldn't make it on time.

Ten more minutes passed.

My phone rang again. Our babysitter, Miss Medea informed me, had been in a traffic accident. A fender bender. She had turned around and gone home. But fear not! Another babysitter had been dispatched. She would arrive within the half hour.

I don't wish to give the impression that I take car accidents lightly. Neither do I tend to naturally assume that what I am being told is a total, cooked-up, bald-faced LIE by a woman who has quite clearly forgotten all about the fact that I had hired her to provide a babysitter, so you may believe that my first impulse was to express regret for the trouble my intended babysitter had met on her innocent way to the inn that evening, and then relief that another, equally capable babysitter was even at that moment speeding (safely, of course) in my direction. My second impulse, however, was to scream bloody murder. But I needed a babysitter. "Fine," I snapped. "I'm waiting."

All this time I had been running back and forth from the inn lobby to the cottage, reporting on the developing situation to my husband, absorbing his frustration even as my own was building, peeling my cranky, ready-for-sleep toddler off my best dress, then running back to the lobby to wait for the still-absent babysitter. All this time, too, I had been eyeing the teenage daughter of a woman who was doing some decorative painting in one of the inn parlors. The mother, a groovy chick in coveralls with a long braid, was up on a ladder, sponging some historically correct hue onto the old plaster walls. The daughter was sitting cross-legged on the floor, her head in a biology textbook. As the clock ticked toward 7:45, my longing, my blatant hunger for this girl grew unbearable.

"Have you ever done any babysitting?" I asked her.

"Ooh, I love to babysit!" she told me.

Reader, I hired her.

Taking her swiftly back to the cottage, I explained that it

would be only until the real babysitter arrived, and just as well, since the girl's mother intended to knock off work in an hour or so. I hurriedly introduced the teenager to my daughter, my son, and my husband, showed her the lay of the land (uncovered outlets— bad! special blankie—good!) and tore out of there with my husband. The innkeeper had provided us with handwritten directions to the French Laundry, complete with now much-needed short-cuts. We dashed to the car.

Setting off from Healdsburg by the back roads, we had the land-marks, the road names—it was all in black and white on the sheet of paper in my hand. The innkeeper had kindly phoned the French Laundry to explain our lateness. We were fine. We were golden.

We were lost. I knew we were lost when I noticed that we were heading north on Route 101. *Still with the Route 101!* I thought, vaguely. But why were we going north? Wasn't the restaurant to the south and east of Healdsburg? Only then I noticed a sign for Ukiah, and slipped into another of my frantic, ominous reveries.

Ukiah, as any student of American depravity will likely recognize, was the place where, in 1980, a once-kidnapped boy led a newly kidnapped boy into a local police station and announced that he didn't remember his own real surname, but he thought his first name was Steven. He was, in fact, Steven Stayner, who had been abducted eight years earlier at the age of seven and subjected to years of torture by his kidnapper, Kenneth Parnell. A few days earlier, Parnell had kidnapped a new little boy. Steven saved him by bringing him to the police. Parnell got a pathetic five-year prison sentence; after his release, he was arrested on a charge of attempting to purchase a four-year-old. Steven Stayner was killed in a hit-and-run accident as a young adult. In 1999, Steven's brother, Cary, murdered a mother and two teenage girls in a Yosemite National Park lodge, where he was a handyman. He later confessed to a fourth murder and probably committed a fifth. Those poor parents, I was thinking, as that Ukiah sign whipped past.

"Honey," I said to my husband, "we're going the wrong way."

It was well after eight o'clock now. The bell had long tolled for our French Laundry reservation, and though we were speeding north, our evening was officially headed south. Of course we had just hurtled past an exit. Of course the next exit was eight miles up the road. By the time we reached it, got off the highway, and reversed our direction, we were a further half hour late and at least an hour's drive from the restaurant. We barely spoke to each other as we sped through the moonlit vineyards, with their strange, twisted scarecrows of crucified vines. I was furious at the innkeeper, whose useless directions were now clutched in my wet fist. When, after forty-five minutes of driving, we passed a sign that read: HEALDSBURG 6 MILES, I nearly howled in frustration.

My cell phone, which hailed from New Jersey, didn't work in the rural valleys of northern California, naturally. As we threaded our way southeast, I pressed "Send" unsuccessfully, again and again. When we at last approached a town, my husband pulled over and I raced to a phone booth. The innkeeper answered. The babysitter, she told me, had arrived. The teenager had gone home with her mother. And yes, she would call the restaurant. All was well.

"All is well," I told my husband.

We drove south through the entire Napa Valley: St. Helena, Rutherford, Oakville, where our carefree picnic lunch now felt impossibly distant. And finally to Yountville, where beckoned a beautiful, beautiful sign for the French Laundry restaurant. We were an hour and a half late, ragged and tense and utterly depleted. We raced inside.

They couldn't have been kinder. The maître d' seemed, actually, happy to see us and brushed aside my profuse apologies. He led us to a table for two upstairs and brought us a great unfolding accordion of a menu. Then he left us to ourselves.

Inside, all was muted and serene. The tables hummed with delighted men and women, each and every one of them in the midst of one of the most memorable meals of their lives. The room was elegant, and the smells were divine. The menus in our hands promised mind-bending things, never before contemplated combinations of foods, or simple preparations that stood every chance of being the single best roast chicken or poached fish we would ever eat. There was, in short, nothing now to prevent our having the evening we had set out to have months before.

Except that there was. Oh, there was, there was, even if, for those first few moments, as we sat looking at the menu, looking around at our fellow dining fortunates, savoring the fact that *We were here! We were at the French Laundry!,* I somehow failed to see it. Gradually, though, inevitably, the speck of unease that had been flickering inside me from the moment I ran out of Madrona Manor, nearly two hours earlier, became first irksome, then overwhelming. I was finding it difficult to catch my breath. I was finding it nearly impossible to think about food. The waitress approached our table to lead us through the labyrinth of the menu—the courses were many and the guidelines of the prix fixe bill of fare complex. Somewhere in that pretty, understated building in glorious Napa Valley, Thomas Keller was waiting on pins and needles to know our wishes, so that he could personally prepare our dinner. I tried to listen to her: soup and appetizer and recommended wines, fish course and meat course and cheese course, and beyond to pastry Nirvana. My heart was pounding. I couldn't quite focus on what she was saying. I had the strangest sensation of an egg breaking over my head, but the egg was full of acid, and the acid swept instantly through my skin and rampaged through my bloodstream. The past two and a half hours of worry and speed, and the utter, cataclysmic dimensions of my crime— yes, my crime—all converged in my pounding head. Where were my children? Who was with them? Were they safe? Would I ever see them again?

How could I have done it? How could I have left them like that? In the care of a person I had never even laid eyes on?

"You know," I heard myself say, "I think we're really just going to order a main course. We have to get back to our hotel."

My husband looked at me, incredulous.

The waitress seemed puzzled. Perhaps it was only her very good training that prevented her from saying what she was actually thinking. "I'm not sure you understand," she told me. "This is a prix fixe menu. Here," she said helpfully. "If you're short of time, I recommend the five-course dinner, rather than the nine-course dinner."

Five courses? I thought, my heart thrumming wildly. *Nine courses?* I calculated frantically. We wouldn't be out of there till 11:30 at the earliest, then another forty-five minutes to get home— if, that is, we didn't get lost again. And we had left the kids . . . when? 7:45? And I had no idea whom they were with.

"Okay," I said numbly. I started naming dishes. I have no idea how I chose them. I had absolutely no appetite.

After my husband had placed his order, I got up from the table.

"I'm just going to phone the inn," I said.

"Why?" my husband asked.

"Well, you know," I said carefully, "I haven't actually talked to that babysitter."

I took my phone downstairs and stepped outside. My call, incredibly, went through. It rang at the front desk of Madrona Manor. After six rings, an answering machine picked up. I checked my watch. It was almost ten o'clock. Of course the woman at the desk would have retired for the night. Our little cottage had no direct line. Whoever was in there with my children, I couldn't reach them. I went back inside.

Our first course arrived. I stared at it. I couldn't remember what it was supposed to be. It was very green. It sat on an elegant white plate like a little green sculpture. It tasted like the glue on the flap of an envelope.

"I have to go to the bathroom," I told my husband. He nodded, glumly. I went to the bathroom, locked the door behind me, and took out my phone to call the inn again. It rang and rang, then the same friendly recorded voice invited me to leave a message. I didn't want to leave a message. I wanted to talk to whoever was with my kids. I wanted to say: *Who are you?* and *Have you ever abducted, raped, or murdered a child?* and *How do I know I can trust you?*

But what right had I to ask? What kind of mother would just

run off and leave her children like that, with a stranger whose name she didn't even know? I wanted to weep, not return to my five-course dinner.

I went back to the table.

"Are you all right?" my husband asked.

"Sure!" I told him.

That was virtually our only dinner conversation.

The next course arrived. It was brown. I took a bite. It, too, tasted like the glue on the flap of an envelope.

The waitress came over. "Are you not enjoying the food?" she asked worriedly.

"I have a babysitter problem," I told her. "It's nothing."

She asked if she could get me something else. The check, I wanted to say, but I just shook my head.

"I'll be right back," I told my husband.

"Don't call the inn again," he said through gritted teeth.

"Oh, no, no," I said gaily. "Just have to pee."

I went to the bathroom, sat on the toilet, and phoned the inn. No one answered. My stomach was in knots. I mashed the phone to my ear with a clammy hand, hating the innkeeper, hating Miss Medea of Medea Nanny Services, mostly hating myself. I would have given anything at all to fly up out of the beautifully appointed toilet on the second floor of the French Laundry and over the nighttime hills dividing the Napa and Sonoma Valleys and down into the little sitting room of our cottage at Madrona Manor.

Failing that, I wanted to rend my garments and howl.

I returned to the table, trying to smile.

"I told you not to phone," my husband said.

The waitress materialized at our table. "I wanted to let you know," she said sweetly, "that our chef is aware of your situation."

This statement had the effect of a bucket of cold water thrown on the already sober evening. *Thomas Keller, the greatest chef in America, was aware of our situation?*

She brought the third course. I didn't even attempt my customary bite. I knew it would taste like the glue on the flap of an envelope. Everything would taste like the glue on the flap of an envelope until I could see my children again and know they were safe. We sat there in total silence as the gourmands all around us ate and drank and murmured appreciatively about what they were eating and drinking. Every table was happy, celebratory, except for ours. A rain cloud hung over ours. A rain cloud of acid rain. My husband, as if sensing the game was over, stopped trying to eat his dinner, too. My hands were shaking. I thought: *So this is what a panic attack feels like.* I had often taken the term in vain. *I'm having a panic attack!* I would joke. But about what? A missed deadline? A missed train? Now I knew what I had been joking about, and it was nothing to joke about. Every ounce of my remaining strength was required to keep myself from bursting into tears.

Suddenly, the maître d' was standing beside us. "Do you need to leave?" he asked us quietly.

"Yes!" I said. I nearly hugged him. I leapt to my feet. My husband followed me downstairs. I paid the bill, only vaguely noticing that they had charged us a fraction of what our complete meal would have cost. Then we were outside.

We drove back in bleak silence, north and west through the valley of vineyards to Healdsburg, and finally up the rustic drive to the inn. Door to door, the journey took us precisely forty-five minutes. When we pulled up at our cottage, the light was on in the sitting room. I flung open the door. A grandmotherly woman was sitting on the couch. She wore a gold crucifix and was reading a Danielle Steel novel.

"My," she said, surprised to see us. "You're home early!" The children were both asleep in the bedroom.

We can never leave them again, I told my husband after the babysitter had gone. I was sitting in an armchair, exhausted and incidentally famished. *Never, never, never.* I might have dodged a bullet this time, but that was utterly undeserved. What had I done, after all? I had consigned my children to the unknown. I had not shown care. I had failed to take that necessary moment when you look into the eyes of the person who proposes to be responsible for them and ask yourself: *Is this an axe murderer?* And for what? A dinner reservation?

I had no trouble gleaning the pertinent lesson, and my guilt drove it mightily home: no appointment, no reservation, no curtain is important enough for me to leave my children before I feel, if not *safe*, then safe *enough*. Though I have indeed left my children in the care of other babysitters many, many times since that horrible night, I have never repeated the mistake I made when I flew out the door of Madrona Manor, bound, however indirectly, for Yountville.

You may come to my door, and I will greet you warmly. I will shake your hand and introduce you to the kids, and show you around and give you my contact numbers. I will tell you what time they go to bed and what they should eat for dinner. I will ask you about yourself, your family, your Social Studies paper due on Thursday. But the truth is, I don't care much what time they go to bed or what they eat for dinner, and I don't care at all about your Social Studies paper. What I care about is looking at you and listening for anything that gives me pause, sizing you up in the starkest possible terms: *Are you sane? Are you evil? Are the children afraid of you? Am I afraid of you?* This will take only a moment. This won't hurt a bit. Just look me in the eye and then—and only then—I'll know if it's all right for me to go.

There's No Being Sad Here

Denise Minor

Max places the box on my head, and his laughter is muffled by the cardboard as it slides down to my shoulders. All is darkness except for the narrow rectangle of light coming through the hole on the bottom. I turn the box slightly so that I can look out of the opening at him.

"I see you," I say.

Max moves closer to peer in, and our faces are only inches apart. I suddenly feel like my insides are liquid—my boy is looking straight into my eyes for the first time since he was a baby. But he can't see me through the dark hole. I am certain. If he could, he would turn away because the eye contact would be unbearable for him.

These warm, brown eyes, I am convinced at the moment, must be the most beautiful eyes that have ever graced a child's face. They turn down softly at the ends, like the eyes of those huge-headed children in paintings that were popular in the 1970s.

I hear my breath echoing lightly off the insides of the box. My heart is pounding. I want this to last for a long time. I want to sit here through the dinner hour, through bath time, and well into the night. I want to make up for all the moments of looking-in-eyes that we should have had during his seven years on this earth, but that we never had because Max is autistic.

Max pulls the box off of my head and puts it on his own. "I see you," he says.

I should keep playing this game with him, should respond with words that make him laugh. But all I can do is sit on my living room floor with my chest rising up and down to accompany my quick breathing. This—this full minute of looking into Max's eyes—is the best moment I have ever stolen from autism.

Stand up. Have someone you know stand facing you with her toes almost touching yours. Now look into her eyes. That is what it feels like for my son to make what the rest of the world considers normal eye contact.

Autism is my enemy, and I am a cunning warrior. By day, I am a respectable general with ribbons on my chest and a cell phone on my belt. I use my sword to draw battle plans in the dirt for my dealings with the school district's special education administrators. I wage the good fight of a mother who attends meetings, reads the latest reports on autism treatments, and drives to three different towns for Max's speech therapy, social skills therapy, and Relationship Development Intervention. Through my bullhorn, I marshal and cajole the efforts of friends, therapists, and teachers. Also by day, I teach Spanish at the University of California at Davis, and am completing a Ph.D. in Spanish linguistics.

But by night, I am a guerilla fighter. I am a thief in fatigues with a face painted green. It is my secret battle whose only beneficiary is me. I silently steal from autism what I believe is rightfully mine—the moments, the feelings, the experiences that would have been part of my life if this neurological disorder had not taken hold of my son's brain. The beauty of my strategy is that I relinquish nothing of the satisfaction that comes from raising both of my children exactly as they are.

It began more than four years ago, not long after experts told me that my youngest son was not, as I had believed, a quirky and introverted daydreamer, but rather a child with "high functioning" autism. The depression that engulfed me was swift and deep. But through the pain, I researched and wrote letters, read and visited experts. At night sometimes I would lie down on the bed next to Max as he was sleeping. I would kiss him lightly, pull him close, and feel comforted, for some reason, by telling myself, *This moment is the same. This moment of kissing my sleeping son is exactly the way it would have been if he had never gotten autism.*

My stealth expanded from there. After a year in an intensive behavioral program that included rehearsing proper behavior in various scenarios, Max became an expert at, among other things, going to the doctor. When his regular Kaiser doctor was not available for illness visits, we would take an appointment with the first available practitioner.

"Take off your shirt. Now, this is going to feel a little cold," the doctor would say more often than not as he or she placed the stethoscope on Max's chest.

"Good job. Breathe deeply. Again. Okay. Now open your mouth and say, 'ahhhh.'"

Max's compliance was perfect. I would watch the doctor carefully for any signs of recognition that something was different about my boy.

"Now I'm going to look in your ears." Max would turn his head to allow the otoscope to be stuck inside. Sometimes he would mumble something like ". . . potatoes in there," and the doctor would laugh.

Then the doctor would turn to me and explain what appeared to be the problem and send us off. Four or five times the doctor didn't expect a word from Max and didn't appear to notice that something was unique about this child.

In the waiting room, I would always get down on one knee and place my cheek against Max's cheek. He seemed to understand best when I said things softly right next to his ear.

"Good job going to the doctor, little buddy," I'd say.

Max, staring blankly ahead, would say, "Good job, Max."

Another moment stolen from autism.

Language sounds and looks to me like a dance. Or, I should say, numerous dances. I blame my years of studying linguistics for having altered so drastically my perception of simple conversations between humans. I used to think that words simply conveyed information, but now I see the surface information as merely a ruse for interaction that is, in most cases, more like a dance that binds us as humans. We learn the steps very young. In the beginning, they are simple and repetitive:

"Wha' that?"

"It's a car."

"Wha' that?"

"It's a girl."

Question, answer. Question, answer. One, two. One, two. But the steps get more complicated as a child grows.

"Hello, how are you, little friend?"

"Fine, thanks, how are you?"

Greeting, question, term of endearment. Answer, courtesy, question. One, two, shuffle. Three, hop, four. They expand from these simple duets to complex productions that serve us for mating, wielding power, arguing, aligning ourselves with others, and raising our children.

Some couples prefer a simple two-step. More dramatic pairs like the tango. My women friends and I enjoy immensely the circle contra dance. Many professors and trial lawyers thrive on solo performances. Whichever our preference, we need these interactions, and we need to perform these steps, in order to be part of a community.

For Max, the dances are very difficult. He recognizes that there are steps and he wants to join in. But mostly he's relegated to standing on the sidelines observing and clapping his hands to the rhythm. Occasionally he tries the most simple moves, and because of his sweet nature, he can sometimes gain a partner.

In the beginning, Max spoke in what I thought of as metaphors. He had a large number of packaged phrases (most of which were parts of songs or nursery rhymes) that he used to get his point across. When he wanted to get in the bathtub with me, he would say, "Little pig, little pig, let me come in." When he fell down and cried, he would sing, "Ashes, ashes, we all fall down." When he was hungry, he would ask me, "You want a sandwich?" When he was sleepy, he would say, "You want to lie down with your mommy?"

After his diagnosis, I learned he was speaking in "echolalia." Young autistic children echo back what they have heard because their brains are not yet capable of creating syntax. When he was three years old, Max's language expanded to simple phrases, many of which showed that he saw more than was apparent. One warm day, he walked circles around me, pointing down at my painted red toenails. "You got, you got," he searched for words, "you got your ladybugs."

On another day, when we arrived at his grandparents' apartment in San Francisco, he stared at their ornate red Persian carpet for a few moments, then said to them, "You got your spaghetti."

Once, his father was bent in front of him waiting for a response to a question with his eyebrows lifted high. "You got, you got," Max said, "you got your birds." He touched Alex's forehead, and there I saw that the creases created by his lifted eyebrows looked like flying seagulls.

Get in your car. Drive to a highway that winds and tunnels through a mountain range. Turn on the radio. Find a station that is clear for short stretches, then fades to static and muffled voices from another station, then returns clear as a bell. Listen carefully for a long while. That is how most language sounds to my son.

The world is sending Max many signals, and he is constantly trying to interpret them. Animals send messages when they look at him. The trees are trying to tell him something when the wind blows their branches. But for Max, the most crucial messages come from signs. His favorites are icons with a line or an X drawn through them to indicate that an activity is prohibited. No food or drink. No bicycles. No Rollerblades. He seems to thrill at the idea that something is not allowed, and that he is *not* doing at the moment whatever is prohibited.

For about a year, going places was difficult because Max wanted me to read every sign. When he started to read, I thought my burden would be lessened. But now that he can read, it has somehow become my responsibility to figure out what these signs are prohibiting. "What you can't do there?" he asks after sounding out the words.

At first, I would try to reason with him, tell him that the sign was simply, for example, directions for how to get to the baseball field. "What you can't do there?" he would ask again, his voice beginning to tremble.

So, I began to get inventive and say things like, "Those are the directions to the baseball field and you *cannot* play soccer over there."

He would smile and look at me. "That's right," he'd say. "No playing soccer there."

One evening we arrived at In-N-Out Burger for a healthy hamburger and fries dinner. As we walked from the parking lot to the front door, Max looked up at two palm trees in front of the restaurant that crossed at the midpoint to form a giant *X* with green fringe at the top.

"What you can't do here?" Max asked, pointing at the trees.

I thought for just a moment. "You can't eat fresh fruits and vegetables here. Only fried foods."

This answer did not satisfy. "What you can't do here?" he asked again.

"No eating fresh fruits and veggies here, like lettuce and carrots and oranges and apples."

Max brightened. "No eating apples here!"

"That's right buddy. But we can have some French fries."

Inside, we ordered our usuals and waited for a table. Max played with the sticker game that the cashier had given him. When the food came, we ate silently. He brushed my forearm softly with his fingers. I responded by running a French fry along his forearm. Max giggled and did the same to me. As we were leaving, I realized we hadn't spoken a word.

Out in front, the sky was dark on one side but purple and orange behind the palm trees. It looked like a tropical sunset right here in the desert of Sacramento Valley. Max paused to look up at his giant X wearing two green wigs and said, "No eating apples here." We walked to the car holding hands.

Max may be a wallflower at the language dance, but my older son, Nathan, is a virtuoso. A fifth-grade Alvin Ailey in braces. A pint-sized Merce Cunningham with freckles. It's not that his syntax is more complicated or his vocabulary larger than that of any other eleven-year-old. It's not that his classroom compositions are anything other than average. If they were, I might picture him as a young Mikhail Barishnikov.

But what Nathan can do is harness words in conversation to capture abstractions, express doubts, or create a vivid picture in the listener's mind. And he has always been inclined to talk about life's most important questions.

It was this way even when he was very young. One cloudy afternoon, when we lived in San Francisco, four-year-old Nathan asked from the car's backseat: "What's the name of those guys in outer space?"

"What do you mean?" I responded.

"You know, those guys. They live in outer space, and they made the world and all the things in it."

I was puzzled, but I took a stab at it. "Do you mean God?"

"Yeah, that's them. Why did they do that?"

We sat at a stoplight and I stared at his reflection in the rearview mirror, wondering whether I should comment on the plural deity remark or go straight for an understandable answer. I chose the latter.

"So that people and animals could live their lives and sometimes be happy."

I continued to watch his face in the mirror to see if the answer was satisfactory. He nodded just as the light turned green, and I exhaled in relief. But I had a premonition that I would be faced with many difficult questions in the future.

• • •

Nathan and I stood outside a theater last week, enjoying the warm evening air for a few minutes before going inside to get a seat for the movie. As usual, he brought up an important topic abruptly and with no warning.

"How much of Max's autism will all this therapy get rid of?" he asked.

I considered explaining that "get rid of" wasn't really our aim, that "function at his highest ability" was a better way to phrase it, but I decided not to correct him because I knew what he meant.

"I don't know. I just know it makes a difference," I said.

"Because if he still talks like this when he grows up," Nathan continued, "that will *not* be good. I mean, he's just as smart as normal kids in some ways, but he just can't show it with the way he talks. He remembers everything, and he figures out problems. And he's a pretty good reader. He just can't communicate very well and he acts weird sometimes."

I nodded.

"But one thing's for sure: He's going to get married," he added.

"Why do you say that?"

"Because girls have always liked him. They think he's good looking."

It was true that some girls have really liked him. It began in nursery school. Each morning as we walked up the pathway to the school, one would have thought a young Elvis was arriving because of the chorus of, "Max! It's Max!" coming from the five little girls waiting at the window for him. Many of his days there began with a group hug followed by an argument among the five over who would play with him first.

Nathan looked away from me. "No girls thought I was good looking when I was his age," he said.

This took me aback. I had never before realized that, in Nathan's eyes, Max could be considered a worthy rival.

"You're just as handsome as your brother. Anyway, that's not why girls like him. I think it's because he's different," I said.

Nathan looked me in the eyes for a moment, then nodded. "He's not like other boys."

We stood quietly for a few minutes, then walked into the theater.

• • •

Davis is a bicycle town. There are about sixty thousand people living here with about the same number of bicycles. The bike is held in such reverence that developers and city engineers must put in parks and bike paths before building new neighborhoods.

It stands to reason, then, that in a town like this, learning to ride a bicycle is a rite of passage. For some children, the skill is gained before entering kindergarten. For most, it happens between kindergarten and first grade. There are a few stragglers with training wheels still on their bikes during first and even second grade. They usually travel the less-frequented paths with their families and pedal behind bushes to avoid being spotted by approaching acquaintances. On rare occasions, I see a big kid riding a bike with training wheels, and I usually assume the child has some type of disability.

I was afraid that this would be Max's future. He has problems with coordination and balance, and he had no desire to have his training wheels removed. But then I got word that Dr. Dick was coming to town.

Richard Klein, a retired mechanical engineering professor from the University of Illinois at Champaign-Urbana, travels to various regions of the United States with about a dozen contraptions he has invented in his retirement. Professor Klein decided to turn his attention to creating something that would help disabled children, and what he ended up creating were variations on the bicycle. Some have enormous tires in front, others have rolling cylinders where there used to be tires. What these contraptions do is slowly accustom a child to gaining balance while pedaling on increasingly less stable vehicles. I was told that the feat could sometimes be accomplished in as little as one week, the length of Klein's bicycle camp. I signed Max up.

Day one: Max started on a bike with wide, gently sloping rollers. He moved through three different levels in two hours. Day two: Max flew through the various stages of cylinders and, by the afternoon's end, was riding the most difficult bike with rollers. Day three: Max began with rollers and quickly graduated to the two-wheeler with a fat wheel in front. He fell off and went back to riding the one with rollers. Day four: Max rode around the gymnasium twice on a bike with small cylinders and then, with the help of one of Dr. Dick's aides, took off on a regular two-wheeler. I was ecstatic! This changed everything—we could really go places together. And Max would be able to do something just as well as other kids his age.

That night, Alex took the training wheels off the old red bicycle that had been handed down to Max from Nathan and that had served Max well for two years. Max was reluctant, but we convinced him to try it. He got started pedaling, then put his feet down and fell over. He refused to get on again after that and kept saying, "It's too big."

The next evening we tried again, with the same result. Then Alex said, "Max, you're right. This bike is too big. We need to get you another one."

The red-and-black Schwinn Falcon that came from the back of Alex's truck the next day was enough to make any boy's heart pitter-patter. Max walked around it and asked a few times, "This is mine?" Then Alex got on one knee and said, "Max, this is your new bike. It doesn't work with training wheels."

We took it across the street, parked it on the bike path, and said nothing more. Alex and Nathan started playing basketball. I picked grass and watched. Max circled the shiny two-wheeler, then stood looking up at the trees. He circled it again, then stopped to really stare. The black paint on the frame shone from the fine glitter in it. The racing stripes and the word *Falcon* were in red. The patent-leather seat had silver adornments on the sides. Finally Max said in a small voice directed at no one, "Can I ride it?"

With one hand on the seat and another on the handlebars, I ran alongside him as he pedaled, and then I . . . let go. And he kept going! I jumped on my own bike and followed, laughing out loud.

Now we go on many bike rides together, sometimes all the way downtown. Max usually leads, and Nathan follows him. ("It's okay, Mom. Always being first is little-kid stuff.") Sometimes Alex and I follow, but often I pull up the rear alone. As we breeze through the tunnels, past farmlands and through the parks, I sometimes catch myself grinning. Anyone seeing me, I am sure, must think I'm strange. But how could they know the importance of this triumph over autism? How could they understand that this was *exactly* how this moment would have been?

In fourth grade, Nathan wanted to know if Spanish was spoken in Africa. I said, "no" and got out a globe to show him the countries where it was spoken. I told him about howler monkeys on the Mayan ruins in Guatemala and about octopus fishing in Mexico. He asked many questions.

"I'd love to travel far away with you some day. We'd have a great time," I told him. "But maybe we'd better do it before you're in high school."

"Why?"

"Because you'll be a teenager, and teenagers don't usually like to hang out with their parents."

Nathan's mouth opened. One eyebrow shot up and the other moved down—his incredulous look. "Why would I ever not want to be with you?"

I laughed and resisted the urge to hug him. ("Mom, you *know* I am not cuddly.")

"Don't worry," I said. "That's what happens to most teenagers."

The next month, after his birthday dinner, Nathan blew out the candles on his cake.

"What did you wish for?" I asked.

"I can't tell!" The incredulous look again. "It wouldn't come true."

"That's a myth," I answered. "Telling can't stop it from coming true. Please! You know how much I love to know wishes."

Nathan leaned close, as if saying it softly would reduce the no-telling jinx. "I wished I'd never become the kind of teenager who doesn't want to be with his mom."

This time I did not resist the urge to hug him, and I almost made a joke about tape recording what he had just said so we could listen to it together in future times of need. But as I looked into his dark eyes, almost replicas of my own from childhood, I decided not to do anything to diminish the importance of what he had just said. It may have been Nathan's birthday, but he had just handed me the best gift I'd had in years.

Go to the library. Find the oldest cassette tape package they have for learning a foreign language and check it out. Best would be something recorded in the 1960s, with lessons developed around memorizing pieces of dialogue that were written by non-native speakers. Study the tapes until they are committed to memory. Go to a country where this language is spoken and find a store that sells something you want. Now go into the store and try to talk to the person behind the counter using your splices of dialogue.

Say, "Good afternoon. I have just arrived from America. If you please, I am interested in purchasing some deodorant."

The dark eyes of the owner stare at your face, then slowly move down to your hands and back up to your face. His mouth opens and he says something unintelligible. In fact, it sounds like nothing at all from your tapes. If you had an interpreter there, she would tell you he had said something comparable to: "Whaddya want?"

Repeat yourself. "Good afternoon. I have just arrived from America. If you please, I am interested in purchasing some deodorant." Improvise now, to see if it helps. "He got some?"

There is an expression on the man's face that you don't know how to interpret, but it makes your palms sweat. He says something in a loud voice and gestures with both of his hands. Was that a threat? Was he pointing to a store down the street? If his voice had been replaced right now with the voice from the tape recordings, you still would not understand him. Your ears have turned off.

Abandon the interaction. Slip outside and stand in the shade breathing deeply, trying to regain your composure. Decide to limit your interactions from now on to the employees that speak English at the hotel where you are staying.

This is what it is like for my son to talk to strangers.

The pain didn't go away. About a year after Max's diagnosis, I began to assume that, little by little, the pain would diminish until it finally disappeared. I imagined coming to a time when I would acknowledge Max's autism matter-of-factly, just as I acknowledged that he had a sweet, plump stomach and an excellent sense of rhythm.

But instead of disappearing, the pain merely dulled. It settled in like arthritis or a chronic back problem, and I suppose I will just have to live with it. I find that the pain is worse when he talks nonsense, throws a tantrum or is rejected by a group of children. I find that the pain is eased, and sometimes not even noticeable, by good times I spend with both of my boys. Those days are like Ben-Gay on aching vertebrae.

This is how I reunite with my sons after a long day out of town.

"Mom!" yells Nathan as I walk in the door. He gives me a quick, dry hug that leaves an echo of bone on bone. "Wait till you see what I downloaded for my Sims game. Come on." He runs off to his bedroom.

"Mommy!" Max mimics his brother and runs toward me. He gives me a soft hug that lasts a couple of seconds and leaves an echo of flesh on flesh.

"Hey, little buddy," I say as he pulls away. "What did you do with Daddy today?" Max turns his head away from me and walks to the edge of the living room. I follow him and try to get one more small hug, but he runs off to the kitchen.

"Ma-ax," Alex says in the voice he uses to talk Max into things. "Aren't you going to tell Mommy what we did today?"

Max moves farther away. I decide to give him time. I go to Nathan's room and lie on his bed on my side, with my head propped up in my left hand. Nathan is waiting for the download, and as he waits he paces in front of me. He decides to bring up a topic that I gather has been on his mind.

"What are your favorite animals?" he asks.

"Animals? I have to say more than one?"

He nods, and I have the feeling that he would like to hurry to the part where he gets to tell me his favorite animals.

I think for a moment, then respond, "I'd have to say horses and dogs."

Nathan pauses in his pacing, considers my answer, then nods again. I imagine a voice in his head has said: *Just as I thought.*

Max comes into the room carrying a stack of board books, some of his favorites, which are balanced between his hands and his chin.

"Do you know what my favorite animals are?" Nathan asks. "The swordfish and the chinchilla."

Max dumps the books on the bed at my feet.

"Swordfish?" I ask. "Can you even call that an animal?"

Nathan ignores the second question. "Yeah, you know, they have those long and pointed spears on their faces, like a weapon. And they have that really cool fin coming out of their backs. It looks kind of like a fan."

Max takes *The Mitten* by Jan Brett and places it under my left ankle. *Dinosaur Roar* by Paul and Henrietta Stickland goes under my left thigh.

"Secondly," Nathan continues. "I like chinchillas."

"Chinchillas?" I respond. "What the heck are they?"

David Kirk's *Miss Spider's New Car* goes under my left elbow. *The Icky Bug* by Jerry Pallotta slides under my ribs.

"Well, the body shape," Nathan pauses to draw a breath, "the body is similar to a guinea pig's but has a hump on the back like a rabbit. The nose is like a guinea pig's—you know, it curves and then goes flat."

Max crawls behind me and imitates my body pose, with his head resting in his left hand. "Its back feet are kind of like a rabbit's, except shorter," Nathan continues. "My first glimpse of a chinchilla's tail made me think that it was a line with a fuzzy ball at the end. But now I think that the tail is something that varies on different chinchillas."

Max's right arm comes around my torso and his small hand rubs my stomach. And then it comes, muffled through my cotton T-shirt, a kiss in the middle of my spine.

Nathan stops pacing and turns to face me. He holds his palms open with fingers spread slightly apart. "Do you know what I'm saying? Can you imagine what it looks like?" he asks.

"Oh yes," I nod. "I can picture it in my mind."

I dream that my friends and their children show up at our front door. Their kids are carrying boom boxes, giant water guns, and games. I realize it is Christmas day. I look in our living room, and there is a pile of toys for Max. For Nathan, there are only a few CDs. He smiles and nods to the children as they show him their toys, but he avoids looking at my eyes.

Some stores are still open, I tell myself. I grab my purse and step quietly out the back door. I am going to buy a bicycle for Nathan, and I must return with it before the sun goes down.

What does a friendship look like with very little conversation? Maybe it looks like Max and Breanna.

Breanna joined Max's first grade class in February last year. She had just moved from Sacramento into the new low-income housing complex down the street from us. I volunteered to help with reading every week at school, and I clearly remember the morning I met her. She was tall and sturdy. Everything about her seemed large—her blue eyes, her lips, her cheeks, her hands. She was wearing a too-small spaghetti-strap T-shirt on a cold day and too-large shoes with one-inch heels.

"Breanna, you're supposed to be reading," I said when she came to my station and sat scratching the paint off of a pencil.

"I read that book yesterday. I've read them all. I am really *bored* of these books," she said and slid one across the table at me. Level 24, it said on the back. The only child in class that I had heard read at that level was the daughter of a surgeon and a woman with a Ph.D. in English.

"You've read this?" I said, then slid it back to her. "Prove it."

Breanna exhaled and looked at the ceiling, as if her patience were wearing thin, and opened the book. "Once upon a time, in China, there was a man who had three grown-up sons. They all lived in the same farmhouse because that was the Chinese way," Breanna began, and continued for three pages. "Enough?" she asked and, without waiting for an answer, slammed the book shut and slid it across the table to me.

Smart girl, I thought. Rude and smart.

Two weeks later, I showed up to bring Max's lunch box as the kids were heading out to lunch. Max and Breanna were standing together in line, she about three inches taller. Breanna's arm was resting on Max's shoulder and her head was tilted back with a defiant look on her face. Max's arm was around her waist and he was looking at the ground with a tentative smile. I knew he was happy.

"When did this start?" I asked Max's classroom aide.

"On Monday," she replied. "They're inseparable."

Now, a year later, we still walk home together on many days. Breanna often carries a 2003 Day Planner with not a word written in it but with unused makeup brushes stuffed into its rings. On cool days she drags behind her a beige adult trench coat, which she likes to fling at flying insects. Because of her constant lies, conversation is usually interesting.

One day as we crossed the street, she reported, "I had to beat up everybody in my class today."

"Everybody?" I asked.

"Except for three kids. There wasn't time. The bell rang."

"Yeah," I nodded. "Recess is just too short."

Another afternoon at one of our regular tree-climbing stops, Breanna announced, "I went to tree-climbing camp last summer."

She and Max were balancing on a branch, she in a denim miniskirt and the customary heeled shoes. Her black tights sported two large holes that had originally been at the knees but had drifted down to her shins. The crotch of the tights hung only a few inches above her knees.

"Really? What kinds of things did you learn at the camp?" I asked.

"You know, how to climb trees in dresses. Stuff like that."

"Did they also teach you how to climb in heels?"

Breanna scanned my face to determine if I was joking. My expression must have passed muster.

"Yeah," she nodded. "We learned that."

"The things a girl has to know," I said, shaking my head.

On some afternoons, I carry Breanna's trench coat and Day Planner and Max's backpack as they walk along with arms wrapped around each other. She sings some teenage song that I don't know and pauses at the refrain to kiss Max a few times on the cheek. When the song is done, they usually run to the park to roll down the hill or push each other on the spinner.

I stroll slowly and chuckle to myself over this victory won single-handedly by my small, brown-eyed companion-in-arms. Other kids might arrange play dates and sleepovers, or head off to soccer practice with a group of friends after school. But my son walks home with the smartest (possibly) and the toughest (definitely) girl in all of second grade at Montgomery Elementary School.

There are many moments with Max that are wonderful simply because of the way he is, and I know autism plays a part in making him that way. He is very sensuous and loves, for instance, the touch of wind on his skin. Once, on a windy afternoon, I watched him standing on a small hill, his eyes half-closed, with his fingers outstretched to feel the moving air. Then, to my delight, he lifted his shirt so he could feel the wind on his stomach as well. Max can also be very affectionate. He knows how to melt into a hug and linger over a soft kiss to the cheek in a way that makes me feel limp. One morning, after a particularly sweet hug and a few seconds with his head resting in the crook of my neck, Max smiled and said, "We're loving . . . each to the other." I laughed and replied, "You got that right, little buddy."

I imagine this will end sometime soon—certainly before adolescence. But maybe not completely. I've seen the same easy affection between an autistic teenager who lives in town and his mother. One afternoon I picked up Max from speech therapy, and in the waiting room was the beautiful blond boy whom I had often observed chatting with the receptionist. I guessed, because of his mannerisms and speech patterns, that he was on the autistic spectrum. On this day, he was standing next to his mother (at least three inches taller than she was) and gently caressing her hair as she talked to the therapist. On a Saturday not long afterward, I spotted the boy and his mother at the farmer's market walking and holding hands.

If that woman had a magic wand, I wondered, and could erase autism from her son's mind and history, and instead have a gorgeous, sullen teenager walking six feet behind her because it is uncool to hang with Mom, would she do it? In a flash she would, I told myself, not so much for herself, but for her boy and his future. But then I reconsidered. I don't know her, and maybe she likes the life she and her son lead just the way it is. Maybe she wouldn't trade walking in the sunshine in the marketplace holding hands with a boy who loves her very much for anything in the world.

I watched the mother and son pass, and imagined myself in her place, heavier and grayer than I am now, with my dark-haired teenage boy holding my hand. Ahead of us I imagined Alex, his eyebrows and goatee no longer salt-and-pepper but gray and white. His hands are in his pockets, just like those of the handsome man walking next to him—a grown-up Nathan home from college.

Will this almost-grown Max walking with me be in high

school? Will he have close friends? A job? Will he be planning to move out on his own, or will Alex and I be preparing for the upcoming decades with the three of us adults living together? As Alex and I grow old, will Nathan need to step up to the plate to take responsibility for his brother? And will there come a time when I no longer look for the places where my life intersects with a life that doesn't even exist, when I can stay peacefully and gratefully in this life, just as I hope both of my sons will do with their time on earth? It will probably be a decade before I have the answers to these questions, but until then I will think about them often, for they are among the most essential questions of my life.

A catalog arrives in the mail from a company that runs training seminars for parents and educators of children with autism. On the catalog's cover is a photo of three smiling children of different ages. I assume they are kids with autism.

"What's this say?" Max asks, pointing to the title.

"Future Horizons," I answer, then decide to grab the opportunity to talk about something we have only recently begun to name.

"See these kids? They have autism, just like you."

Max purses his lips and tilts his head back. He brings his hand up to his brows, as if he were shielding them from the sun. It's a gesture he often does when he tries not to cry.

"Nathan has autism?" he asks.

"No. Nathan doesn't have autism."

"You have autism?"

I pause for a moment. "Yeah. I have a little bit of autism. I think in pictures. So do you."

Max brightens. "Yes. Mommy and Max have autism."

"Look, Max. Look at these children," I say and turn the magazine toward him. "They're smiling."

"How do they feel?" Max looks directly at my eyes, then looks at the wall to wait for my answer.

"They're happy. They have autism, and it's okay."

Max runs his hand over the glossy cover, then looks back to my face.

"There's no being sad here."

"That's right, little buddy," I say and move my cheek to his, partly from habit and partly to hide the watery eyes that belie my words. "There's no being sad here."

Was He Black or White?

Cecelie S. Berry

A few years ago, my sons and I were having dinner when Sam, who was then eight years old, told us about Dominick, a second-grade classmate known for his disruptive antics. When the Spanish teacher's back was turned, Dominick would rise and canter about the classroom, twirling an invisible lasso above his head. A God-fearing child, he punctuated the close of the circle with a rip-roaring "Hallelujah!" My six-year-old, Spenser, and I fell out laughing as Sam mimicked Dominick's escapades. When the laughter died down, a termite-sized query gnawed at me, so I asked, "Is Dominick black or white?"

Silence. Sam and Spenser looked at each other, a tacit conference. They were closing ranks and taking arms.

"What difference does it make?" Sam asked.

"It doesn't make any difference. I just want to know," I replied.

"But everybody's the same. So it doesn't matter." Spenser now.

"I'm just curious."

"Why're you curious?" Sam asked.

"Because I want to know." Great storm clouds thundered across their shared gaze: *Mommy is a racist.*

"I just want to be able to picture what was happening, that's all. Now, was he white or black?"

They crossed their arms. I crossed my legs. The stir-fry curdled. Everybody pushed back from the table.

I drew the ace card: "I'm your mother. Tell me now."

Even as the conversation unfolded, I knew that it would change us. It was a turning point in the compass of our relationship: a black mother and her children having careless fun, and then the issue of race spins us clockwise or counter—I'm still not sure which. That night, I stumbled upon the mores of a new generation that believed—they didn't just say it, *they believed*—that race didn't matter. My children's utter faith in this impressed me. They exhibited unwavering conviction and—warming to a mother's heart, if contrary to my will—they were fierce allies, utterly united. They fought me (me!) for an ideal world where they were ultimately human, and race was simply not worth mentioning.

I had discovered the vast new territory of their idealism, as unspoiled and fertile as the Americas must have been to explorers of yore. Appraising that Xanadu, I stuck my flag of racial awareness deep and declared it mine. Is my influence civilizing or am I—a black woman, the earth's earth mother—just another conquering barbarian? I wonder still.

Sam, ever loyal to his mother, gave in. "He was black."

That's what I thought.

"You see?" I said brightly. "It's really no big deal." I shrugged elaborately, but I could see they didn't believe me. One of the veils from behind which we mothers appear so perfect had slipped away that evening. They saw me a mite more clearly as a flawed and perhaps even dangerous person.

Look, we all do it, don't we? We take note of who does what and what color they are, comparing them to what we know and expect, sizing them up to our understanding of their kind, the world. My sons felt that the mere mention of race poised one, teetering, on the slippery slope to bigotry. I did not agree. It's human nature to form some lexicon for understanding other people, and race—a sociological construct, not a scientific term—has traditionally been one. We use it to help us get a handle on the situation, to think we know whom we're dealing with.

It is how we behave when our attitudes and expectations go

unmet—when the person standing before us has defied the rules that supposedly define his or her group—that tests us. It is the line of demarcation between how much we are trying to understand the world and how much we are trying to make it conform to our understanding.

When a white workman I called to fix a broken pane of glass arrives and rings our bell, he stares angrily at me for answering the door. He did not expect me. He has taken note of what is on the news, what he has heard and observed. He thought black people were in the ghetto and laid claim to an assumption that he is not entitled to but made him more at home in the world.

Nobody takes note of race more than we African Americans. A particularly gruesome crime occurs—the killing rampage of the "D.C. sniper," for instance. The tacit but almost universal assumption among blacks was that the sniper must be white "'cause we don't roll like that." The idea that blacks were less prone to this kind of crime made us feel safer, even morally one-up to whites. When the sniper turned out to be black, we found ourselves more vulnerable to the idea that we, too, can produce and be victimized by serial killers.

African Americans feel the loss of these assumptions acutely. Our habits and cultural predilections have traditionally been our fortress, where we could feel at ease in a hostile land. To preserve that sense of security, we can be merciless enforcers of the rules: Our speech, dress, interests are expected to conform to the topography of "blackness" as we know it. In my mid-twenties, I attended the family reunion of a black friend and when asked how I wanted my steak prepared, I requested it medium rare. "Oooooh," a woman ejaculated, a sirenlike noise assuring that all eyes would turn in our direction. "Only white folks like their meat rare. We black folks like our meat well done."

My life has been incalculably altered by the fact of race. I am not angry about it; being born black in 1961 to educated, ambitious, and committed parents, I led a life that was in many ways charmed. I was poised to take advantage of the movements—civil rights, women's liberation, affirmative action—that provided opportunities my ancestors had dared not dream of. From the beginning, I sensed that it would be my generation's challenge to fully tame the wilderness of race, to build a "settlement" for blacks in America where we could *completely* embrace ourselves. That step taken, we could stand as equals and embrace others regardless of their skin color. It is a journey that generations before me initiated and one that I continue now as a mother. Having taken up those reins, I have turned often for direction from the map my parents drew for me, veering from it as needed.

My parents, who bore the burdens of growing up in segregation, raised us according to the exacting gaze of the white eyeball. They knew that to get ahead, we would have to be fluent in classical music, ballet, everything in the European tradition—to show white America we knew what counted. Fervent integrationists, my parents resembled most ambitious black people of the Greatest Generation. They resented, feared, and always distrusted whites, but noted that the rare black person crowned as worthy was the anti-black, so they poured us into that mold. There were costs in many families. Nightmarish, secret costs: "too dark" siblings being marginalized; the very light ones passing into oblivion as they passed for white. And always, no matter what your shade, there was the pressure to conceal your interest in "black" things: tap dancing, basketball, gospel music.

The pressure to assimilate mounted after we moved from a street of respectable, middle-class Negroes in Cleveland to the predominantly white, affluent suburb of Shaker Heights in 1971. We lived in the center of town, so far from the vast majority of black families that we often felt like exiles in a strange, lovely Siberia. I suppose that is why, on Sundays, my dad would often listen to black gospel music on the radio. It was, in part, the black church and the influence of black music that enabled him to rise from being a poor foster child to a successful internist. While he and Mother knew we had to move up—and urged us to adopt the "white" interests and mannerisms and friends to do so—my dad quietly resented that certain "black" things would necessarily be jettisoned along the way: gospel music and a whole array of high-cholesterol foods among them. That music—like the smell of chitlins cooking—sent us kids diving under pillows. The sound molested us, leaving echoes of guilt and confusion. It made us *uncomfortable*. The more uncomfortable we were, the louder Dad played it.

One day—I might have been fourteen then—a screaming fight broke out between my father and mother because Dad was play-ing gospel music so loud that it seemed our white neighbors (a Cleveland Clinic doctor, a law firm partner) could hear. Mother marched downstairs, snapped off the radio, and cursed Dad out in tones so voluble, I couldn't help but wonder why it didn't con-cern her that the neighbors might hear *that*. Eventually, Dad stopped listening to gospel music. Eventually, he stopped coming home. He had a life we children knew very little about—one that included a "blackness" my mother despised and was determined, not altogether without cause, to banish from our lives.

Truthfully, I don't think my parents ever felt completely com-fortable with or even fully recognized the complex duality of our lives, or the toll that never fitting into either world would take on us children. They had tried to give us a better life and were con-fused by our flailing, identity struggles and discontent. Who and what was responsible for our unhappiness remains a source of division in our family even now. There was then and remains today only one gospel song to which we collectively knew all the words, and sang and danced to with abandon every Saturday night. It was "Movin' On Up," the theme to *The Jeffersons*.

As an adolescent in Shaker Heights, I tried to plot some middle ground between excelling like the white kids and being accepted—or at least left alone—by the black kids. At that time, there was no such Promised Land. So I conceived of my survival as a game: the Race Game. You pick up a card, a behavior or circumstance is described, you have to guess the race of the individuals involved.

Sometimes I played for fun; sometimes I played as if my life depended upon it. White people often refer to the "race card," the excuse that blacks supposedly hold at the ready to explain away our failures. But for my generation, the first to embark upon the brave new world of integration, the Race Game was much more complex: an obstacle course, as intricate as chess, more exhausting than Monopoly.

Playing the game, I used my experience to guess not just who was what but how those people might think, feel, react. To hear the silent subtext, anticipate the racial insult that comes seemingly out of nowhere to hijack you, hold you back, put you in your place. Sometimes I still find myself playing it, though I also long for what is instinctive to my children: the freedom to take someone, anyone, at face value.

One day, in junior high school, I hear a group of students enter the school library—cursing, bellowing, cackling—and I don't even have to peek between the stacks to know: They are black. They won't linger here, but while they do, I stay hidden.

Years later, in my thirties, I am in a boutique on the Upper East Side of New York, and the well-heeled shop ladies are discussing some missing stock: ankle bracelets, cute erasers, kitschy stuff. I bristle, expecting an accusation. The owner senses this and explains with an indulgent laugh, "This time of year the girls from such-and-so academy come in and take things, a springtime ritual of the senior class." I don't have to wonder: These girls are white and rich. The offense that I had anticipated did not come, and the owner knew to explain the situation: move ahead one step. But because these girls are privileged and white, their crime will be dismissed as a prank: move one step back.

That incident recalled a family discussion about race in my own childhood, when my sisters, who were attending the Hathaway Brown School for Girls in the early 1970s, came home with a similar story. They were slightly breathless and impressed with the exploits of the white girls—their friends—who regularly shoplifted at local pharmacies. My parents, astonished by the idea that shoplifting was an amusing pastime and frightened that my sisters were impressed with it, launched into a harangue on how we could not—should never even *consider*—doing what they did. We were angry at their tirade, an anger that would magnify through the years as we attended schools with well-to-do whites only to be reminded that we did not have their privileges, their safety net, their freedom. Our parents would continue to insist, often at the point where we were our most daring or inventive, to take note of how differently things can be interpreted when color is involved—their message *aim high* always diluted by the warning *but don't forget that you're black*. It was enough to radicalize many black children like us into the very militancy that our opportunities were supposed to render moot.

This is the part of the game that feels like Russian roulette: participate, work hard, move up, but act too much like everyone else and you risk losing everything. My husband, who was also educated in private schools and colleges, tells me that in the corporation where he now works, black people do not feel they have the same latitude as their white co-workers to read the newspaper half the day or "work from home." He is ever mindful of the way standards may unexpectedly shift when it comes to him, to us.

When I met him in law school, he was an artful tactician of pleasantness, managing to get along with everyone—black or white, radical or conservative. But after years in the corporate world, I have seen him develop a rigid, potent suspicion and an impatience with the children's belief that they are no different from anyone else. When our son Spenser wanted to be in the same class as his best friend, Seth (who is white), with a teacher his father and I know to be a racist (though white parents think she is superb), I was astonished when his father exploded, "What works for Seth will not work for you!" Spenser appealed to me with tear-filled eyes.

"You must trust us," I sighed. "We know the score." By the end of the year, Spenser's encounters with the teacher at school were enough to make him glad he wasn't in her class. He came around to our way of seeing things. You cannot win the game with your eyes shut.

• • •

Of course, times are mostly better now, so are we wrong to pass down this sensitivity to our children—so ready, willing, and able to greet all with open arms? Am I, mired forever in racialized thinking, dragging Sam and Spenser down with me? If I am on the side of caution, do I err? Will we all ever get beyond race if we don't stop making so much of it? Isn't there room for reckless idealism? If the Dominick of Sam's long-ago story had been white, I would have disapproved, but laughingly, part of me admiring the spirit—and envying the freedom—that it takes to be an irrepressible cutup. But because he was black, Dominick's bad behavior raised the ante and my antennae. I was less amused, more cautious, afraid for him and my sons and all the black boys who are too quickly discarded as trouble. As my parents had with me, I wanted Dominick to march boldly into the world, but not to take too many liberties, not to go too far.

I've decided that a rigid, unedifying color blindness cannot reign in my house. It is by taking note of race and all that accompanies it—the assumptions, the stereotypes flying to and fro like flaming arrows—that we can achieve a transcendental compassion, a unifying respect for the power of experience. People are people, there's no doubt about it, but you have to understand why things are the way they are. Not to take note of race or, more important, discuss it, would leave my sons in the dark. They must know where they stand and what to look out for, welcoming the surprise of those who reject the rules attached to skin color because to cleave to them would frustrate their inner truth. Luckily for my children, those rules are eroding, but they will endure if not consciously challenged.

Now twelve, Sam attends a summer camp for the academically gifted. He asks me, "Why are so many of these kids Asian and Indian?" The first time he asked, I ducked the question, not wanting to deal with all that it dredged up—the unpleasant racial competitiveness (*we* were here long before *them*), the bitterness of the black bourgeoisie toward blacks who, for myriad reasons, languish. But the second time he asked, I knew he wanted an answer, and why not? I have taught him to take note, and the exercise does not end with the observation. So I said, "In Asian and Indian cultures, learning has always been an activity for the elite and revered, and in America they know it is the key to upward mobility. For African American slaves, it could mean death, and until my generation, many blacks considered education worthless, since blacks were excluded from most gainful employment. Even today, higher education can have the effect of isolating many blacks from their community, leaving them to exist on the margins of a white society that is not yet fully inclusive." We talk and talk about the cultural differences, values and attitudes that are inculcated over time and passed down to one generation from the next. And the talking continues.

The years since our conversation about the unruly Dominick have fermented deeper queries, ones that I also struggled with while growing up, playing the Race Game. Who does what and why? And, most critically: Where do I fit in?

The last question is the toughest to answer. Are you going to cling to the status quo, internalize the stereotypes and traditions? To be "truly black," will you avoid sushi, decline steak tartare? Or, because they symbolize the "non-black," dine on them until you are nauseated? To racially deny or neuter oneself, even to get ahead, exacts too high a price. I have searched for some compromise that embraces the reality of race but that challenges it too; one that leaves my children and me free to pursue a personal dimension but that sustains a keen political awareness of who we are, where we come from, and why.

I despised my parents for their mixed messages, the sleight of hand that always left us looking for the kernel of who we were under the shell of who we would never be. But now I appreciate that born of my parents' insistence on "white" things came a sense of new possibilities for me (proving, I suppose, the bromide that what doesn't kill you makes you stronger). Without their passionate, demanding myopia, I don't think I could have seen that I didn't have to wear the straightjacket of my color. Even as I sputtered and floundered in synchronized swimming and ran half-heartedly across the tennis court, I grew more confident in my determination that I didn't have to cast myself according to "script": to be a bump-dancing, loud-talking, finger-snapping black girl. If I could endure the unavoidable discomfort, the never fitting in or measuring up, I could go anyplace, learn anything, pick and choose from a constellation of behaviors and interests. I was free to explore my own way to becoming me.

For a while in college, I slipped and slid between an angry, brittle exclusion of white folks and a keen desire to find in my black compatriots—smart kids who, in private schools and tony suburbs, were often lonely like me—a sense of racial and personal unity. But I grew uneasy when my roommates, bourgeois black girls from nice homes, joined a black pride organization that required them to do penance for their light skin and privilege. It seemed plain crazy when they complied with the demands of the grand poo-bah to shave their "damnable" processed hair to "make up for" their tawny skin and privileged backgrounds. I believed that the people who ran this group were angry and disen-franchised. They were manipulating my roommates not because they were believers in black power, but because they were jealous and insecure. I had noted that even with whites out of the equa-tion, the issue of race still dogged us: What was "black enough"? Who was "black enough"?

I slowly emerged from the cocoon we black students had cre-ated for ourselves in the misguided belief that we'd be safe from prejudicial judgments. I moved into a different suite and began talking to white students again. In time I realized that many peo-ple could teach me about who I was, and with that knowledge I shaped my future. To exclude anyone along the way would be to limit my own journey.

In the end, it was at Harvard, ironically, that I enjoyed being black more than I had since I was a child in Cleveland. I had fun—lots of heartfelt and genuine fun, with Donna Summer, Aretha Franklin, Sister Sledge, and Parliament Funkadelic providing a background beat. I tap-danced in my clogs across the Yard without guilt or embarrassment. I even grew to like gospel music, thanks to Kuumba, the black gospel choir. And from white students—some friends, some passing acquaintances—I learned about people I'd never heard of: Otis Redding and Stan Getz. I took quiet pride in the fact that nobody quite *got* me, but *I* was gradually getting me.

Dealing with race—experimenting and exploring it, embracing and rejecting it, playing with it, parsing it—turned it into so much more than a game. That was my adolescent way of experiencing my dilemma, of coping with the feeling that I had to manipulate people to see me the way I wanted them to in order to matter, to succeed. The Race Game was a necessary stage, a kind of puberty in itself. But my journey with race has, in adulthood and certainly with motherhood, eclipsed the metaphor of gamesmanship. It has helped me achieve something larger and far more important. My race has expanded the contours of my world and myself. My journey is inextricable from my race, and my race will be bound always to the journey. They are one. That, I think, is the way it's supposed to be.

My understanding of my parents, which grew with time and the forgiveness of one's parents that accompanies it, are gifts that I hope that Sam and Spenser will offer me. If I am wrong, and race doesn't matter to the extent that we should banish it forever from our conversation, I hope they'll understand why I thought it did. But for now, we routinely integrate race into our discussions. What I care about most is that these discussions are honest. Race doesn't determine the way my children see people—I am proud that they continue to give everyone a chance—but it is too potent to pretend it doesn't influence situations or alter lives. To grapple with it makes us better. My children and I don't always agree on what is racist, and they are free to say when the mere mention of the issue feels knee-jerk or inauthentic. When it is irresponsible not to discuss it, we face it together.

I have taught my children to note that other people—white or black—may think that being black means acting this way or that, but it doesn't have to mean that to them. I have exposed them to many things and have allowed them to embrace what they love. They have discovered that they prefer playing basketball to tennis or swimming, and that is fine with me.

I have dealt in the palindrome that race is involved in everything, but not everything is attributable to race. My theory is this: To realize how some people are likely to see you is an essential step to discovering and defending who you really are. I believe that I am, then, less a colonizer of my boys' impressionable minds than a tour guide to the world as it is, and it has been my job, in these formative years, to point out the major attractions, the time-wasting distractions, on the trip. Race is so many things along the way: a distorted fun-house mirror of misperception and depravity, a monument of cruelty and oppression. One must be familiar with the signposts of one's heritage—to measure the progress made, avoid the mistakes of the past, and, ultimately, move to higher ground.

So I stand by my flag of racial awareness—an obstacle to progress some might argue, but perhaps I point the way. In either case, history cannot condemn me because, in the final analysis, I am a mother and I have only the best intentions.

Motherlove

Ayelet Waldman

The mothers' group is an omnipresent feature of the landscape of contemporary American parenting. Like the baby wipe and the ExerSaucer, it is a fairly recent invention that seems by its very ubiquity to have acquired an institutional authority, even an inevitability, like the yearly Pap smear or attendance at a decent four-year college. A woman joins a mothers' group for many reasons—to make friends with other mothers with babies of more or less the same age, to have a reason to get dressed and brush her teeth, to share tales of sleep-deprivation woes. All good and rational motives, and all nonsense. I have been in many mothers' groups—Mommy and Me, Gymboree, Second-Time Moms—and each time, within three minutes, the conversation invariably comes around to the topic of primary interest: how often mommy feels compelled to put out. Everyone wants to be reassured that no one else is having sex either. These are women who, for the most part, are comfortable with their bodies, consider themselves sexual beings, know their way around a clitoris, and, while they may not have ever successfully found it themselves, are willing at least to credit the existence of the G-spot. These are even women who, by and large, love their husbands or partners.* Still, almost none of them is having any sex at all.

---

* I live in Berkeley, a place where some people are married, some are not; some people are heterosexual, some are not. Most women in my mothers' groups are married to men, but others are married to or in long-term relationships

There is general agreement about the reasons for this bed death. There are the easy answers: they are exhausted; it still hurts, even months after giving birth; they are so physically *available* to their babies—nursing them, carrying them, stroking them, touching them—how could they bear to be physically available to anyone else? But the real reason, or at least the most profound, difficult reason for this lack of sex, is that their passion has been refocused. Instead of concentrating their ardor on their husbands, they concentrate it on their babies. Where once their husbands were the center of their passionate universes, there is now a new sun, a new source of light in whose orbit they revolve. Their desire for this usurper is not carnal, not sexual, but it *is* sensual and lustful, and it has entirely replaced the erotic longing they once felt for their husbands. Libido, as they once knew it, is gone, and in its place is all-consuming maternal desire. There is absolute unanimity on this topic, and instant reassurance.

Except, that is, from me.

I am the only woman in Mommy and Me who is getting laid. This could give me a sense of smug well-being. I could sit in the room and gloat over my wonderful marriage. I could even use the opportunity to fantasize about my gorgeous husband, whose broad shoulders, long, curly hair, strong back, plump lips, high-arched feet, and full, round bottom still, twelve years after we first met, make my toes curl with desire. I could think about how our sex life—always vital, even torrid—is more exciting and imaginative now than it was when we first met. I could check my watch to see if I have time to stop at Good Vibrations to pick up a tube of lubricant and see if they have any exciting new toys—you can bet I would be the only woman in *that* store pushing a baby stroller. I could even

with women. I'm going to go ahead and risk offending people by using the word *husband* in this essay. First of all, it's too awkward to keep repeating "husband or partner," but more important, most of the lesbian couples I know seem not to get as worked up about the lack of sex in their relationships. This isn't true across the board, but it's true enough that it makes me think that there is something to the notion that men care more about sex, generally, than women do. Before you, dear reader, set my hair on fire, allow me to put this notion aside and explore it in some other essay.

gaze pityingly at the other mothers in the group, wishing that they too could experience a love as deep and profound as my own.

But I don't. I am far too busy worrying about what's wrong with me. Why, of all the women in the room, am I the only one who has not made the erotic transition a good mother is supposed to make? Why am I the only one incapable of placing her children at the center of her passionate universe? Why am I the only one who does not concentrate her sensual abandon on her babies instead of her husband? What is the matter with me?

When my first daughter was born my husband held her in his hands, her face peering from underneath a pink acrylic hospital hat, her mouth a round O of surprise at having been tugged from the wound of my incised abdomen. His face softened and got all bleary, the way it does when we make love, right after he comes, or when we are driving together in the car and he grabs my hand in his, saying, "Give me the hand," and kisses my fingers. He turned to me and said, "My God, she's so beautiful." Or something like that. Something tender and loving. Something trite.

I unwrapped the baby from her blankets. She was average sized, with long, thin fingers and a random assortment of toes. Her eyes were close set and she had her father's hooked nose. It looked better on him.

She was not beautiful. She was not even especially pretty. She looked like a newborn baby, red and scrawny, blotchy-faced and mewling. I don't remember what I said to my husband. In fact, I remember very little of my Percocet- and Vicodin-fogged first few days of motherhood. I remember someone calling and squealing, "Aren't you just completely in *love*?" and of course I was. Just not with my baby.

I do love her. But I'm not *in love* with her. Nor with her two brothers or sister. Yes, I have four children. Four children with whom I spend a good part of every day—dressing them, bathing them, combing and curling their hair, reading to them, sitting with them while they do their homework, holding them while they weep their tragic tears, cheering them on at their soccer games and violin recitals, volunteering at their schools, cleaning up their vomit and changing their diapers, smelling their sour and delicious baby smells and squeezing their soft and pliant, bony and spiky little bodies. But I'm not in love with any of them. I am in love with my husband. It is his face that inspires in me paroxysms of infatuated devotion. *His* is the beauty on which I insist, perhaps as inaccurately as he did on our daughter's. If a good mother is one who loves her child more than anyone else in the world, if a good mother is someone who would sacrifice anyone else to save her child then, unlike those other women in Mommy and Me, I am not a good mother. I am in fact quite the opposite. I am that most abominable thing—a bad mother.

I love my husband more than I love my children.

Perhaps because I am a writer, perhaps because I am a neurotic Jewish girl, perhaps because I come from a long line of hypochondriacs, I often engage in the amusing pastime known as God Forbid. What if, God forbid, there were another Holocaust, say, and my family and I were forced into cattle cars and sent off to concentration camps? What if, God forbid, my husband were on an airplane blown up by suicide bombers? What if, God forbid, a sexual predator were to snatch one of my children? God forbid. I imagine what it would feel like to lose one or even all of my children. I imagine myself consumed, destroyed by the pain. I would pine for my child, think about nothing else. And yet, in these imaginings, there is always a future beyond the child's death. Because if I were to lose one of my children, God forbid, even if I lost *all* my children, God forbid, I would still have *him*. I would still have my husband; he is what matters most. But my imagination simply fails me when I try to picture a future beyond my husband's death. Of course I would have to live. I have four children, a dog, a mortgage, books to write, parents to support in their old age. But my life would be over. I can imagine no joy without my husband. I can imagine no color in a world without him. All would be gray and then it would be over. *The world could show nothing to me,* to quote Brian Wilson, *so what good would living do me?*

I don't think the other mothers sitting around the circle in Mommy and Me feel this way. I'm sure they would be absolutely devastated if they found themselves widowed; of course they would. But any one of them would sacrifice anything and everything, including their husbands, for their children. Because they are all good mothers.

Why am I the only bad mother in the room?* Can it be my husband's fault? Perhaps he just inspires more complete adoration than other husbands. He cooks, he cleans, he cares for the children at least 50 percent of the time. If the most erotic form of foreplay to a mother of a small child is, as I've heard some women claim, loading the dishwasher or sweeping the floor, then he's a master of titillation. He is utterly unfazed by spending a day or even a week alone with four children. He buys me lavish, thoughtful presents that are always in the most impeccable taste. He's handsome, brilliant, and successful. But he's also scatter-brained, antisocial, and occasionally arrogant. He is a bad dancer and he knows far too much about Klingon politics and the lyrics to Yes songs. He's not that much better than other men, at least not enough to cause such a categorical change in my behavior. The fault must be my own.

I am trying to think back, to remember those first days and weeks after giving birth. I know that my sexual longing for my husband took a while to return. In the period immediately after the babies were born I did not want to make love. I did not want any genital contact. I did not want an orgasm. I did not even want to cuddle. I recall feeling on occasion that if my husband's hand had accidentally brushed against my breast while reaching for the saltshaker, I would have sawed it off with the butter knife. Even

---

* Okay, I know I'm probably not the *only* one, but it feels as if I am, and if there are others like me, we're all so intensely ashamed of ourselves that we're not making eye contact, let alone confessing our misplaced devotion to the group.

now I am not always in the mood. I am a working mother. There are many evenings when I am exhausted. By the time the children go to bed, I am as drained as any mother who has spent her day making lunches, driving carpool, building LEGO castles, shopping for the precisely correct soccer cleat, and writing 1,500 words of a novel due at the end of the month. I am also, with consequences potentially fatal to a sex life, a compulsive reader. My only hobby is reading. I would rather read a novel than do most anything else in the entire world. Put together fatigue and bookwormishness, and you could have a situation in which nobody ever gets laid. Except that when I catch a glimpse of my husband from the corner of my eye—his smooth, round shoulders, his bright blue eyes through the magnification of his reading glasses, the curls of hair on his chest—I fold over the page of my novel.

I think sometimes that I really am alone in this obsession with my spouse. Sometimes I think even my own husband does not feel as I do. He loves the children the way a mother is supposed to love her children. He has put them at the center of his world. He has concentrated his passion, his devotion on them. But he is a man, and thus possesses a strong libido. Having found something to usurp me as the sun of his universe does not mean he wants to make love to me any less. He can revolve around *them* and still fuck *me* every night.

And yet, he says I'm wrong. He says he loves me as I love him. Every couple of years we escape from the children for a few days and take ecstasy together. We pop the pills, strip off our clothes, and wait for the waves to start washing over us. MDMA is an experience about which it is difficult to write without sounding like a banal disciple of Timothy Leary. A combination truth serum and love potion, it transports us back in time, to the moment we first realized we loved each other, but with all the ease and fluency of mutual experience that a dozen years together bring. For somewhere between four and six hours, my husband and I talk about our love. We talk about the intensity of our devotion, about how much we love each other's bodies and brains, about the things that make us happy in our marriage. We talk about how exciting it is to work side by side, how eagerly we await each other's homecomings when we are apart. We talk about how remarkable it is that we love the same movies and food, how wonderful it is that our interests and skills are so complementary—I am good at managing the business of the house, he loves to cook and play with the children; I am better at plotting, no one line edits as well as he does. We talk about how lucky we are that we agree on the basic values of parenting and family life.

During the course of these meandering and exhilarating conversations, we touch each other, we start to make love, we stop. MDMA is a long and languid tangle of lovemaking—physical, mental, and especially verbal. The fucking part is definitely subsumed to the talking, but each complements and stimulates the other. Hours later, when the immediate effects of the drug have ebbed away, we are always left with the residue of a metaphor—a ship, a solar system—one we will refer to over the next two years to remind ourselves and one another of the truth we have rediscovered about our relationship.

When he takes MDMA my husband says that we, he and I, are the core of what he cherishes, that the children are satellites, beloved but tangential. He says this under the influence of a drug that makes it difficult to lie, and thus I must believe him, despite the fact that he seems entirely unperturbed by loving me like this. He feels no guilt. Loving me more than his children does not bother him. It does not make him feel like a bad father. He does not feel like I do. He does not feel that loving me more than he loves them is a kind of infidelity.

And neither, I suppose, should I. I should not use that wretched and vile phrase "bad mother." At the very least, I should give myself a break; I should allow that, if nothing else, I am good *enough*. Do I really believe that just because a mother would rather sleep with her child nestled in her arms than with her husband between her legs that she is a better mother than I? I don't know. I'm not sure. I do know this: When I look around the room at the other mothers in the group, I know that I would not change places with any of them. I would not give up the all-consuming passion I feel for my husband, even if by doing so I would make myself a better mother. It would be wonderful if some learned sociologist published a definitive study that established, once and for all, that children from marriages where the parents are desperately, ardently in love, where the parents love each other more than they love the children, are more successful, happier, live longer and healthier lives than children whose mothers focus their desires and passions on them. But even in the likely event that this study is not forthcoming, even in the event that I face a day of reckoning, that my children, God forbid, become heroin addicts or, God forbid, are unable to form decent attachments and wander from one miserable and unsatisfying relationship to another, or, God forbid, replace love with a bitter and all-consuming religious fervor, even if any of these things or, God forbid, others too awful even to imagine befall them, I cannot regret that when I look at my husband I still feel the same quickening of desire that I felt twelve years ago when I saw him for the first time, standing in the lobby of my apartment building on Fourteenth Street in New York City, a bouquet of purple irises in his hands.

And if my children resent having been moons rather than the sun? If they berate me for not having loved them enough? If they call me a bad mother?

I will tell them that I wish for them a love like I have for their father. I will tell them that they are my children, and they deserve both to love and be loved like that. I will tell them to settle for nothing less than what they saw when they looked at me, looking at him.

Immaculate Conception

Fufkin Vollmayer

My mother was a single mother, in the same way that my grandmothers were single mothers: All had left difficult marriages and raised their children on their own, without much help. My lineage is deadbeat dads and then some. My father—a violent, often inebriated man—refused to pay child support and hid his assets when he moved to another state. I grew up hearing Mom begin sentences about him with "that alcoholic son-of-a-bitch, your father . . ."

My father may have been Dennis Hopper, but my mother's parental role model was Joan Crawford. She put on a great face to the public and had a fabulous sense of humor, but her most consistent role behind closed doors was that of a vengeful bully. Today I rarely drive down Arguello Boulevard in San Francisco without thinking of the time my mother's car swerved into the oncoming lane of traffic because she was so busy hitting me.

That was the scenario I grew up with—relentless fighting from my parents because my father ignored all court orders and refused to pay for anything, and not much tenderness left over for my brother or me. So I knew I never wanted to do what my mother did: marry, divorce, and then become the sole provider. And my brother's remark, "I hated not having a man around," only confirmed this. But when I collided head-on with the huge billboard of forty, I realized that I could be a single parent or not a parent at all. Like a forensic investigator, I kept muttering to myself, "How did this happen?"

How *did* this happen? I am not a lesbian. Nor do I hate men. I just couldn't seem to get it right—find the right guy at the right time who also wanted to settle down and have a family. Through my thirties I went to engagement parties, weddings, and then the inevitable baby showers. I tried blind dates, the personals, even saying "yes" when I got hit on at work. The Peter Pan refrain was always the same: not ready, not sure, not now. Only in San Francisco, where there is an endless buffet of lifestyle choices— even micro-niches of choices—can children be categorized as just another lifestyle issue. Take the vegan computer programmer who wanted children and an open marriage. Or the nonprofit administrator who said, "Let's revisit this in two years." By the time I turned forty, I'd had enough of ambivalent men and was tired of waiting.

I probably could have held out a little longer, but for what? One of my friends had waited for it all to fall into place—the right guy, marriage—but then the baby didn't come. By the age of forty-four she was clinically depressed from failed fertility treatments and a husband who wouldn't consider adoption. Twenty thousand dollars later, she got pregnant via in vitro fertilization using a donor egg. But I couldn't imagine facing all the medical procedures, much less the astronomical bills.

I knew women who were single mothers, of course, but I always saw them through the eyes of myself growing up. "A single mother isn't really a family," I thought. Then one day when I ran into my friend Linda, I suddenly saw her not for what she lacked but for what she had. She was a thirty-nine-year-old attorney—smart and capable—and had conceived her daughter with a gay male friend. She had deliberately created her own happy family.

Linda invited me to a meeting of a national group she belonged to, Single Mothers by Choice. I went with some trepidation. I thought I'd meet incarnations of my own mother, women who were struggling and stressed out. I braced myself for what I thought would be a long morning of discouraging, teary stories.

Instead, as the women introduced themselves, I discovered that they were women like me; professionally competent, educated women in their late thirties and early forties. And they weren't discussing men, but rather the usual gripes associated with working parents—discipline, affordable childcare, and the endless cycle of childhood illnesses. In the middle of the circle was the happy chaos of a dozen heaving, drooling toddlers. Here was the face of a new kind of family, headed by a single parent who was tired but basically happy.

I left the meeting feeling elated one minute, wiping away tears the next. I was happy because I had discovered a different universe of women who had deliberately chosen to start families on their own. Then I'd sob because I realized that for the last five years I'd never had a backup plan. I wasn't on Plan B; I was on Plan F, for failure. Plan L, for no luck here.

I was a working journalist and had taken on faith those goofy notions that you could have most of it, if not "it all": a full-time career, plus marriage, plus children, plus time for yourself. But I was wrong. A demanding career and perhaps my unwillingness to settle had brought me to this. So it would be by default, this solo parenting, because all the other possibilities had quietly left and gone home. Yet, thanks to the women at the meeting, my point of reference shifted: I could look to them instead of to my own experience growing up. Lone motherhood was not the ideal choice, but maybe it was the best choice I had now.

And so it began. I needed more money and a less demanding schedule, so I joined the dot-com boom. Every day I went to work as a writer and researcher for a multinational software company, but my real job became getting pregnant as quickly and as cheaply as possible. I scrolled down sperm bank screens, reading men's profiles, looking for the perfect guy whom I would never meet. I read donors' personal essays, looked at childhood pictures, pondered their stated reasons for doing this. Every once in a while it would get to me—here I was choosing the father of my child on the basis of genetic profiles and the information that these men were willing to disclose about themselves. (Would anyone ever admit to a mentally ill relative?) Maybe a handwriting analyst or astrologer would have had more insight into who these men were.

Then I'd go back to work. Did I want the Jewish systems analyst whose hobbies included cooking and ecotourism or the mixed-race grad student who golfed? I decided no on mental illness or substance abuse, yes on brains and, owing to the history of melanoma in my northern European stock, a plus for brown skin.

I finally narrowed it down to the Pakistani physicist completing his Ph.D. and the Mexican MBA student who played guitar. Urdu not being a language I speak, I chose the Mexican donor. Even in the pre-9/11 world, traveling to the Indian subcontinent to introduce my kids to their heritage didn't seem that easy. But I do speak Spanish, have traveled extensively in Mexico, and have Mexican friends. Besides, I'm terrible with money and numbers, so the MBA student seemed to be, well, the right guy for me. Or at least for my children.

Every choice has its sacrifices, and this choice had a big one. The price of bargaining for better genes was forfeiting my child's right to ever know his or her father. Like most children conceived through donor insemination, mine would almost surely want to have that option. But only one sperm bank in the world guarantees it, and because these donors are the most sought after, the waiting lists are long—too long for someone my age, I thought.

Occasionally I wondered about the real motivations of these donors. I assumed that mine was selling sperm to help pay for graduate school. I wondered what his family thought, or if they even knew. Someday, if he has a family of his own or doesn't, will this decision come back to haunt him? My friend Mark donated sperm years ago and learned from the sperm bank that his vials had produced at least one child. He's over fifty, single, and doesn't have children of his own, yet he says he has no interest in learning about his progeny.

But my curiosity about the donor was supplanted by a staggering fact. The policy of my sperm bank is to discontinue using a donor when either twenty to thirty individuals have purchased vials of his sperm or a total of eighty vials have been sold. I got dizzy doing the math. Theoretically, my child could have a couple of dozen half siblings out there who don't know each other. So it wasn't just the donor who was anonymous; it was the siblings as well. Then I was jolted out of my ponderings by the stark reality that, hey, I'm not even pregnant yet, by a donor or anyone else.

Nothing about donor insemination is left to chance. If you are paying thousands of dollars to get pregnant using frozen sperm or other assisted reproductive technology, you have to narrow down ovulation to within twenty-four hours. Like most of modern life, it's a process that involves tracking, planning, scheduling.

I got absolutely wistful for decidedly unsafe sex. What had ever happened to the beery kiss and fumbling fuck, along with all the other vagaries of my misspent youth? All those mornings I woke up to the blurry handheld camera of my life, looked at the snoring heap next to me, and wondered, "Animal, vegetable, or mineral?" It used to be that if the cervical cap snapped off or the condom broke, I panicked. Monthly menstruation was not a curse, but a blessing. Rejoice, girlfriend, rejoice. You are not pregnant.

Fast forward to me at forty: Monitoring and measuring my body, day in and day out. Charting my luteinizing hormone surge, body temperature, and menses as if they were the stock market on a rally or decline: up, down; up, down. It was so weird and clinical and lonely. Suffice it to say, the only person looking at my vagina at that point was me. Like some kind of gynecological Shiva, I managed to injure myself one day inserting a speculum with one hand while holding a mirror and flashlight in the other, trying to decipher the exact texture of my cervical mucus.

After months of military-like preparation, however, I was finally ready to launch the field operation. I had three hours to drive to Silicon Valley, pick up nitrogen tanks with the frozen vials, and arrive back in San Francisco in time for my insemination. On the hour-drive back, I got caught in traffic and the storage tank fell over as I slammed on the brakes. Nitrous oxide curled up like a big ball of burning incense in the backseat.

I made it to the hospital frazzled and panicked. I went to my room. After decades trying to not get pregnant, there I was, legs in the stirrups, cold steel speculum ratcheting an opening into my cervix as I waited for the type of syringe used to impregnate cows to knock me up. A midwife had advised me to replicate the actual physical act as much as possible. Right. It was just me and my vibrator and a buzzing backdrop of fluorescent lights.

But at that point, I'd have done anything to get pregnant. For months I had not let dairy, sugar, or wheat touch my lips. I chanted to hippo-shaped goddesses and even entertained the possibility of fertility drugs. So why not stand on my head, as some advised? Gravity has very little to do with getting pregnant, but since fertility is part voodoo, I went upside down against the door. Unfortunately, the nurse opened it, knocking me down and damaging my sciatic nerve.

Somehow it all worked. I got pregnant. Mission accomplished. I should have been ecstatic, right? I was—except buyer's remorse kept creeping into my thoughts. Was there some ideal candidate out there whom I'd overlooked in my haste? Should I have gone with the Ph.D. instead of the MBA? Wasn't it more important for my child to have a predilection for ecotourism than for guitar? I finally realized there is no perfect donor.

One thing about single women who become pregnant: Everyone seems to think it's their business. While heterosexual married couples can conceive through IVF or even use a surrogate mother, no one's the wiser. It's only if you are a single woman that the spotlight shines on the biology of your family. People want the details. I learned to fend off questions about being unmarried and pregnant with vague statements like "The dad is not really in the picture." Adding to the circus was my mother, chiming in to enhance my fears and hormone-induced emotional maelstrom. "After how you grew up," she demanded, "why are you doing this?"

And then I had my baby. And all of the grief and struggle—

the expense, the void of no father, the hemorrhoids, my mother's rage—they all just disappeared within days of beholding my perfect little child, Joaquin.

Nine months later, against all good advice, I got pregnant again. The reproductive endocrinologist who was sure that I'd have to do IVF and a lot of embryo hatching was aghast, along with most of my friends. But I felt that if I couldn't give my son a father, I could at least give him a full sibling. With the very last vial from my donor, I got pregnant with Javier. I am one of the luckiest women I know.

Now Joaquin is three and Javier is one and a half. What's it like? Difficult. Really difficult. Often it feels that I just trudge through the fog of my own comatose state doing all the requisite caretaking. First they get sick, then I get sick, and then my work performance suffers. Actually, my work suffers a lot. Tending to the nightly needs of small children starts to resemble the fate of American POWs during the Korean War—insomnia as a special form of torture.

Shoppers step aside when they see me coming down the grocery aisle. "You've definitely got your work cut out for you," they giggle. I have to agree. There isn't a day that goes by that my thought bubble doesn't go up with the caption: *This caretaker needs caretaking.*

I look at the nuclear families at the playground—the mom-and-pop families who go on vacations and cook dinner together—and I wonder, do they know how lucky they are? I want average; it just looks so good from here. Maybe especially because I never had it.

So, shortly after Javier's birth, I forced myself to get back out there. Out there dating, that is. I wrote a banner for my online personal ad that read, BABE WITH BABES-IN-ARMS SEEKS A FELLA. When a friend read that, she gasped and warned me about sex offenders circling in cyberspace who troll the lines for single moms to get access to their children. While I did not have any pedophiles respond, any worries I had about keeping up my end of the conversation were rather premature. I did hear from a man who wistfully shared his lactation fantasies. What he wanted was a latter-day wet nurse centerfold à la Anna Nicole Smith—lots of bosom to go around.

Then, as if there were not enough excretions oozing out of infant orifices into my life every day, I heard from a man interested in diapers. Not an e-mail from a guy in Depends sitting in his wheelchair at the convalescent home, but sort of a regression fantasist. He mentioned that he was part of a group that had "poo parties," where the guests walk around in dirty diapers. Efforts to toilet train my toddler being hit and miss, I declined. (Ah, the Internet—always there to provide an online "community" for all interests.)

In all honesty, now I'm not really sure what I want. Yes, I'd love to have had a better past. But the future? Dating and even marriage won't guarantee a simple or happy ending. Marriage is a leap of faith: That it will work. That it will last. That if it doesn't, some superior court judge won't suck money out of my kids' future in the form of alimony payments to my ex-husband. And I suspect that the demands of small children are so intense that they strain even the best marriages. As much as I yearn for a partner, for someone to love me and to enjoy my children as much as I do, I've seen enough modern marriages to know I'd probably be doing pretty much the same thing I am now—most of the work. I'd assume all the responsibility and resent a spouse who didn't help out enough.

Many of the single mothers I know are cautious or ambivalent about marriage for those reasons. They're still interested in romantic relationships, but not necessarily in tying the knot. At the single-parenting classes I've attended, I've seen a huge divide between the divorcées and those of us who have chosen this path. Many divorced women seem to have a harder time of it. Whatever the reasons for their frustration, they have something I don't—animosity toward someone they'll have an ongoing relationship with for another eighteen years. I'm occasionally sad, even lonely, but I'm not aggravated by a divorce settlement embedded with all the constantly shifting variables of child support, custody, and visitation.

That was my mother's situation. She was a single mother who

worked full time and battled the Goliath of indifferent judges, along with an ex-husband who shirked all of his responsibility for his children. I definitely have an advantage over her that way. I have more maturity and money than my mother did—I was twelve years older than she, with savings in the bank, when I had my first child.

But I see that my mother and I were different for another reason. My mother should not have had children. She was just a bad parent, irrespective of her marital status. She had all this drive and rage, and nowhere to put it. Had she come of age in the 1970s rather than in the 1950s, she would have gone on to run a large company instead of a family.

Many of my friends say they forgave their mothers once they had children. "Oh, this is what it's like," they realize. "This is how bone-crushingly hard it is." I wish I could say I felt that way, but I don't. My mother died from a respiratory disorder just ten days before my second son was born. But not before she had raged at me for my decision to have children, hissing that I'd not only ruined my life, but would probably ruin my sons' too. She died before I had a chance to prove her wrong.

So here I am, at a historical moment, on the cusp of a huge demographic change. One hundred years ago, I'd have remained a spinster. Fifty years ago, if single and pregnant, I probably would have given my child up for adoption. Now, along with gays and lesbians and others, I'm a pioneer in the creation of the "alternative family." What a relief, really, that there is a new name for it, not like the sad term of my youth, "broken home."

But I'm starting to feel less like a cultural phenomenon and more like just another mom, Joaquin and Javier's mom. I am head over heels about my children. I gaze at them in a way that I have never looked at any man I've adored—with complete love. Compared with work and status, I've come to think that parenting is vastly underrated. My only regret, really, is that I waited so long.

Thin, Blonde, and Drunk

Kristen Taylor

Two weeks after my daughter was born, we planned a trip from our home in Los Angeles to New York. We were going to visit Grandpa upstate, then spend a couple of days in the city with my sister-in-law. Capping off the trip was the New Year's Eve black-tie wedding of our dear friends Sarah and Billy, in SoHo. This may have been their wedding, but it felt like they were throwing the party for me. Who could dream of a better first night out without the baby?

I had three wishes for that New Year's Eve: to be thin, blonde, and drunk. Twenty-five pounds had to go, my grown-in roots had to be lightened, and after ten months without alcohol, I very much wanted a drink. Or eight.

Our trip was six weeks away. My first wish denied? You've probably already guessed: drinking. At the first whisper of a proper grown-up New Year's Eve, I had pushed the "breastfeeding = sobriety" equation out of my conscious mind. Then a couple of weeks later, my father-in-law asked if it was okay for me to join everyone in a champagne toast, and I remembered that the baby and I were still very much physically connected. If I did drink, there was always the option of "pumping and dumping" the tainted milk. But planning debauchery to such a degree does a number on my party mood, and I resolved myself to staying dry.

My second wish denied: being thin. Who can lose twenty-five

pounds in six weeks? That doesn't even work in real life, much less in sleep-deprived/nursing-sixteen-times-a-day/uterus-can't-shrink-that-fast post-partum life. For those first eight weeks I ate everything in sight, and then stuck my hands into the backs of cabinets for the food I couldn't see, and ate that too. My weight barely budged.

But I *was* blonde. When my mother came to town, I took the opportunity to hit the salon and get reacquainted with my lovely hairdresser. In 1995 Los Angeles, it was impossible to leave any hair joint without looking like one of the *Friends*, but never mind—my hair was finally streaked vertically rather than horizontally.

New Year's Eve arrived, and my husband and I got dressed— he in his tux and I in a gold satin number that slipped over my head. The dress's bias cut hid my pooch rather well, I thought. My strapless bra hid the massive nursing pads well enough. We were on our way.

Everything was dandy for the first four hours or so. The ceremony was lovely, and the guests ambled over to a hot new restaurant for a fantastic dinner and dancing afterward. Things got a little uncomfortable around hour five. My breasts, which were used to almost hourly emptying, were all dressed up with no place to go. I was looking like an R. Crumb girl, and the word *granite* kept popping into my head. My milk was letting down like crazy, so I had to keep peeking surreptitiously at my chest to make sure that the nursing pads were holding up. Worrying about leaky milk stains will truly ruin a festive attitude. So will intense pain. I had no choice: I was going to have to express some milk. But the breast pump hadn't fit into my evening bag. Could I do it by hand as I had read in the books?

I let myself into the single-stall bathroom and locked the door. Then I remembered that this particular dress didn't have any buttons. Or zippers. Or Velcro. I had to take the whole thing off over my head and hang it on the door hook. The strapless bra had to come off, too. I stood over the bathroom sink wearing pantyhose and high heels, trying to express milk by hand.

They say that when you want to encourage the "let down" reflex, you should be relaxed and calm. Thinking about the baby helps, apparently. Unfortunately, all I could think about was how good the lock was on that door and how many people were lined up on the other side of it, knocking every couple of minutes. And what would they think I had been doing in there when I finally got out fifteen minutes later? "There goes that coke-head new mom." "Hope she quit while she was pregnant, so her kid isn't a drug-addled bundle of blown nerves." I couldn't exactly tell the next person in line, "I had to take off all of my clothes and express breast milk into the sink. Sorry it took so long." I couldn't even explain it to anyone in the room but my husband, because we happened to be the first of our friends to have kids. No one else would have gotten it.

I didn't express more than a few dribbles of milk, even when I tried again an hour later. The extra nursing pads I had packed were soaked because my milk let down just fine whenever I wasn't standing naked in the bathroom. We were going to have to cut out of there and get back uptown to that baby soon. I was just about to make our excuses to the bride and groom when my friend Adam provided me with all the excuse I needed in the form of a full glass of champagne down the front of my dress.

"Whoops, we really should be going. Happy New Year, everyone!"

Later we asked Adam to be our baby's godfather.

The next morning, New Year's Day, I was struck by a migraine that must have been triggered by all that backed-up milk. As I nursed my baby and tried very hard not to move my head, I was a little miffed that I had all of the hangover but none of the booze. Now that my children are older, drinking isn't such a big deal (though I do try to avoid hangovers), and my goals have less to do with the physical changes brought on by mother-hood and more to do with how mental the children make me. By next New Year's Eve, I hope to be present-minded, patient, and up to date on the checkbook. Mothers always dream big.

Fight Club

Rahna Reiko Rizzuto

I am sitting at my desk when the fight begins. Outside my window, a man is screaming, "You want to take me to court, take me to court!" I hear the words, let them float in the shallow end of my brain as I wait for a response; I wade through the ripples of before to see if there was a screech of brakes or the dull tin-can crunch of someone pulling out into traffic at the wrong time. I live on a bus route in Brooklyn, across from the storage yard for a hardware store, cattycorner to a submarine sandwich shop that attracts double-parked police cars like they were bees, and directly above a clinic that dispatches two private ambulances, but only in the middle of the night. Street noise—whether threats or a boomeranging bass that rattles the ice in my glass—has to be a real contender to make me look out the window.

What I am reading, on my computer in my improvised office, is a custody agreement for my children: entirely extralegal; fraught with bold letters, red letters, asterisks, and parentheses. We have passed it back and forth, my husband and I, questioning, amplifying, rejecting, and not yet taking the actions we are negotiating because no lawyer has seen it. If this is not par for a New York divorce, it is for mine: we have no legal "grounds" except for having spent the last two years unable to speak to each other without sarcasm and pain eating into at least the edges of our words (and too often choosing the words themselves, words that we would never, I am sure, have formed if our conscious minds had not been knocked out already, TKO'd or at least on the ropes and whimpering), and so, in the strange configuration of New York law, since we have not yet behaved so badly that one of us can take the other to court to sue for a divorce, we have to work together to draft a formal separation agreement and then live under it for a year. We have started and stopped this process more than once, and have now begun it again with the good of our children, with their well-being, as a center-piece, because they are the closest thing we still have to a common interest.

It has been two years, and still they ask me, lying on my lap, heads on my heartbeat, *Mommy, why don't you live with us any-more?* They listen for the hollow drop behind the face of the answer.

Your daddy and I don't get along anymore. We fight too much.

What is that answer? What is any answer? I am scrolling through the agreement on my screen, looking for it: watching Christmas run by, and vacations, graduation, questions of risk, of who decides in an emergency and what constitutes one, of when a new spouse gets as much priority as the used one. These were the things that were important to us, about which we are now fight-ing, and our new mediator may throw them out the window (where the shouting is still going on—"Call the cops then. Go ahead. I dare you!"—still with no audible response), because they are things that cannot be set in legal stone. We have written them because we want them set; we want to be correct and also to have some protection against the pain that still lashes at us, especially after weekends when one of us has had hours on end with the children to introduce wildcards and realign bonds. We want the law to keep us safe, unflayed; my husband wants closure, he wants judgments handed down—right and wrong, with wrong banished—and I have condemned him for wanting the end and the answers so badly that they don't have to be the right ones, but at this moment, I, too, would give anything to have an answer.

The answers I am seeking are not the same as my children's are. Mine are more numerous, and less heartbreaking.

Your daddy and I don't love each other anymore.

How bad is that to say to a child? How true but terrifying to a young mind who must surely be certain that the same thing could happen to him? If there can be, in this world, the decision not to love, and if it can happen to the two people whom he loves the most, then what hope is there for the child to find love and keep it? Of all the answers to their question, this loss of love is surely the worst one. But right now, if someone handed me these words and told me that they would release us, I would speak them.

Yesterday my husband and I fought again. It was entirely unintentional and exactly what we always do, except that, this time, things blew apart. I walked in bleeding; I think we both did—it is the chronic consequence of being too long separated without being truly separate—and I came out stunned. And now, as I try to decipher the latest annotations to this custody agreement, I am afraid of the ugly things we said, of the lawyers and locksmiths and restraining orders that were born in our "conversation." Of the threats that *I* made, hearing them at the same moment that he did, then hearing his response. I couldn't believe that someone would say those things, would push me so far off the path that I had hoped to chart for my life, let alone say them in a voice that sounded just like mine. There are promises that we make to ourselves—that we will remain who we are and not turn into the people on TV—and these are the promises that we break. I don't know how we can climb down off the peak of fear and anger that we raised yesterday. And so I have come back to our last relic of semi-agreement, to mourn. There is finally a response to the voice outside my window. It is a woman, yelling in Spanish. I don't understand Spanish, so I go into the kitchen to stretch my shoulders and get something to drink.

I am the one who left. The calculus will never be quite that clear, but it is true, a fact: I am the one who moved out of the house, and I chose to give my husband custody—to create, instead, my own equation between "undivided attention" and "part time mother" and "life on my own terms." And so, when I give my son a small medallion and explain to him that the figure on it is his guardian angel, who will be with him always and who can see into his heart, I am also the one who cannot breathe when he hugs me and asks sadly: *Can she see that I miss my Mommy?* I am haunted by the image of my son graduating from college, his tender chin shot through with a man's hair, with me, and his father, and my replacement at his side. What will she have been there for that I missed and what will I have given my son instead, and will it be enough? Divorce is hell on grownups; how do we make it work for children? And when you are the bad guys, fighting in court over—what? Whose pocket the children's money should be in? How well a woman should know their father before my children are crawling into bed with them on Sunday morning?—how do you look at yourself in the mirror and like what you see?

These are the questions that I carry, the ones that come back with me from the kitchen, as I hear the man in the street yelling, and the woman yelling back, and the man saying in English, "Let him decide then."

I don't even have to go to the window. Standing at my desk, I can see out clearly, down to the sidewalk immediately below, where the man and the woman are fighting. Between them, there is a young boy, about six or seven. He is crying, not touching either adult, and as I watch, he sits down flat on the concrete as they both look at him.

The man is screaming: "Let him decide who he wants to go with." The woman responds, and the man says, "I can take him. Who do you want to go with? I'll take him. Who do you want to take you? Her or me?"

I have started to cry, framed behind glass about ten feet above them. The boy answers, and the man explodes.

"You don't understand, do you? She left you. Don't you get it? She abandoned you." He grabs the boy's arm and yanks him standing. "Get out of here, bitch. You aren't even supposed to be anywhere near him. Get out of here now or I'm gonna call the cops."

She yells back, but her voice is getting fainter. *Cops* is the last word I hear him utter, and then all three of them are gone.

I am sobbing in my chair; the distinction between me and them has collapsed. I cannot breathe and I cannot identify myself on the telephone clearly enough to call anyone for help. Not for the boy—he is gone, and though I could have been downstairs to save him in a matter of seconds, it never occurred to me. I am the one who needs help. I have made too many promises that I did not keep, and I need someone to wrap me in loving arms and make a promise for me: that I will never be so weak that I will find myself ripping my children limb from limb in my own pain.

I love my children. It is not enough. It never has been.

Read to us, Mommy, they say to me, and then they curl, one under each arm, still young enough to rest their heads where they can cover one ear and hear my voice muffled through my ribcage, much as it must have sounded before they were born. This is not what I intended for them when I had them—these scattered nights and weekends when we can sink together into the book that I loved as a child, which I can now share with them before I send them home—and I will not allow it to be the sum of what I can offer. I am more than the number of hours I spend with them, and if I have chosen not to live with them and their father, I can still be a mother: I can find a way down from this saw-toothed peak for them, keep this out of court and in a place where my husband and I both have a better chance of remembering who we are.

One small promise at a time, *that* I can give, fulfilled at the same instant when I make it so that it will not be lost: I page through the custody agreement to find the point of contention that means the most to their father, the one I hate more than all the others and thought I would perish on the spot before I allowed—and I agree to it. I want to reread, to hedge; I want to condition, but I cannot afford it. This is for me, this is for them. This is what I can give to my children: the custody agreement in the queue; the arrow pressing the button "Send."

Chaos Theory

Mary Morris

It is a Tuesday morning and my daughter is heading out the door. She has showered, preened, put on her Urban Decay makeup, properly gelled her hair. She's wearing a cute little skull-cap, various baubles, dangling earrings, layers of T-shirts, her pants slung low.

But her bed isn't made. Her drawers and closet are left open. Her floor is strewn with homework assignments to be completed later, thongs that the dog will walk around with all day, scribbled notes to herself, textbooks, a collection of stuffed pigs thrown haphazardly around the room. The phone, removed from its base, rings somewhere beneath a pile of clothes.

In the bathroom nothing has a cap. Moisturizer, toothpaste, acne medicine ooze onto the counter. And then there is the hair. My daughter has a head of thick auburn hair that can only make one think of chestnut mares racing through open fields. When she showers, she takes the strands that come out and attaches them to the bathroom wall. She does this, she explains, to prevent them from going down the drain. I spend my showers trying to decipher some message encoded within. I see dolphins, ancient roads, my daughter's dreams.

I grit my teeth and kiss her good-bye. I tell her I love her. In another era, another moment in time, I would have picked a fight. Or worse, I would have spent an hour or so cleaning up before I settled down to my own work. Instead, as soon as she leaves, I shut the door to her room. I put the cap on the toothpaste. I locate the phone.

This, of course, is a classic teenage M.O., except to me it is something else. It is chaos—the nonlinear dynamic system with which I must cope. It is my Achilles' heel. The stumbling block down the dusty road to martyrdom. The thing I was put on this planet to overcome.

Once upon a time, before the life I am now living began, my goal was simple: I wanted to have everything put away and in its place. I even had fantasies of this. The Hold Everything catalog was my idea of heaven. In some ways it still is. Kate and I know this. Just last year I received a refrigerator magnet in my Christmas stocking. It featured a fifties housewife with her head on a pillow. The caption reads, "I dreamed my whole house was clean."

I identified. Never mind that I was a cliché on a refrigerator magnet. I wanted to have all my papers filed, books in alphabetical order, photos in albums, spices labeled and on a rack. I wanted archives, a Dewey decimal home. It shouldn't be so hard to achieve. In fact, before I had a child it even seemed an attainable, if not admirable, goal.

I lived my life at right angles, and by that I mean I created piles of bills, books, work, pencils, erasers. Whatever I needed had to be neatly stacked. No one could move these piles except me. The dirty secret is that I wasn't *really* neat because drawers were full of broken earrings, scarves bought in marketplaces around the world that I'd never wrapped around my neck, shoes worn to the soles. I had no mind for throwing out; for the decision-making that entails. But I needed a sense of external order, at least, on the surface of things. It was a solution to ordering the mess I was inside—the swirling mass I could never straighten up.

I wasn't always this way. As a little girl, I wallowed in disarray. My room looked as if a bomb had gone off. Those expensive clothes my parents bought me never found a hanger. They were unceremoniously dumped onto my spare bed. My assorted collections of rocks and insects, jars of caterpillars, books and dolls were scattered around. It looked as if I was moving.

Once my father picked me up at a girlfriend's house and he came upstairs. He stood in that girl's room, staring at her shelves, admiring all her dolls carefully displayed. In the car home he asked why I couldn't keep my dolls on their shelves, neatly dressed and combed, and I replied, "Because my dolls are having more fun."

But fun was a concept that would soon drift away. I didn't grow up in a household that was fun. What I grew up in would come to terrify me. My childhood was a minefield that I navigated with mixed results. My father could easily have been the official spokesperson for Worst-Case Scenarios. It was rare that an ordinary household object did not pose a serious threat. A pencil, a kitchen knife, a drinking glass could all somehow become the instruments of my demise. If I walked with a sharpened pencil, I risked tripping over some unseen object and stabbing myself in the eye. Kitchen knives could be mysteriously launched. A glass could fly out of your hand and smash into your skull.

The problem was that these things not only incited my father's worry, they also set off his rage. In the language of fairy tales, the house was booby-trapped and he was the dragon, lurking behind its doors, ready to catch us off guard. I recall the way he looked when one of these rages came over him. A handsome man whom people compared to Cary Grant, with dark skin and dark eyes, but when he went into his rages, it seemed as if those eyes were lit with a fire from within. His words flew out of his mouth like flames.

His paranoia about the physical world translated itself into the social order. At any moment one could fall from grace. Table manners apparently insured against such a fate. There was a list a mile long: about how bread was to be broken, pieces chewed, soup sipped, cutlery put on the edges of plates once eating was done. I had to get into the habit of being a lady. Perfection was a kind of norm. Children, as we know, are not very good at perfection. They are snotty, dirty little beasts. They are reluctant to fit the mold.

My mother was not immune to my father's extremes, though she had her own version. If his had to do with how I behaved, hers focused around how I looked. It wasn't quite JonBenet, but it was close. My dresses had to be just right, my hems just so. Outfits had to match. Everything had to be neatly pressed and sewn.

An afternoon comes to mind. It is spring and the weather is nice. There is a smell of cut grass, fresh blossoms. I am perhaps twelve or thirteen, and I've been given some cash. Sixty dollars—I remember the amount. My mother came into my room and said I needed some clothes. "Go to Fell's and pick out some things."

I can still see myself perfectly. I'm riding my bike into town. I go to Fell's and try on matching sets—shorts and shirts. I try them on, one after the other. I have never been given so much freedom. I find it exhilarating, standing before the mirror, turning from side to side. I like a lemony yellow short set, another in pale blue. Then there is one that seems a little bright—fuchsia or crimson. I take it as well.

I pedal home, my purchases in my bike basket. I pedal fast, eager to show my mother. She is waiting for me when I return. "Oh, let's see what you got. Try them on."

I do. We go upstairs. I try them on one after the other. "I don't think yellow is your color," she says. The blue outfit is too tight, the fuchsia too bright. In the end she decides they're not right. "No," she shakes her head. "I don't think so."

Inside I begin to seethe. I rage. But I keep my anger under wraps. If what I felt inside is volcanic, I manage to keep it capped. Of course I want to be loved for who I really am, but if that isn't possible, I can compete. I learned well from my parents' wacky rules and perfectionist goals. If my inner life was the equivalent of a garbage dump or a seedy alleyway, my outer world was going to be museum quality. Papers in neat stacks, clothes put away. No clutter, no debris. I knew the best way to get from A to B. I knew the best table in a restaurant. In other words, I became a control freak—a rather accomplished one, I must say. I was a big success at living alone.

Then I had a child.

I had my daughter because I couldn't not have her. I had her because I was looking at forty and got pregnant with my partner of five years—a professor of international law. When I asked him if he wanted to "make it legal" and he replied, "Legal in what sense?" I knew I'd be going it alone.

I had her on my own, as they say. The right decision, but I had no idea what I was getting myself into. I was quite literally clueless. But I planned carefully, carved out a space for my daughter in my well-ordered life. I had a deadline of four essays for the *New York Times* all due in the week before Kate was due. This would be no problem. I'd get my work done and then I'd have my baby.

My water broke on a cold winter's night. It had been snowing all the previous day and my back ached. I went to the park and made snow angels. I lay there, a beached whale, wondering what I was doing lying in the snow. That night I couldn't sleep. Sleep had been eluding me for weeks, to such an extent that my downstairs neighbor asked me what was wrong. When I told her I wasn't sleeping, she said, "The baby's coming now."

She came three weeks early and I wasn't prepared. The shock took me completely unaware. Briefly, I contemplated returning her as if she were something I'd picked up at Bloomingdale's. "That's not your color," I could hear my mother say. "Let's take it back." But the first six months were a cinch. I wrapped her up in a blanket and she rested beside me as I worked. She would gaze up at the sky. One afternoon I curled up beside her to see what she was seeing. I saw clouds rolling by.

This is going to be easy, I told myself. I'll get a lot done. Then she started to move. She moved everywhere: under beds, into drawers, near electric sockets. Of course, children by definition bring mess. Once, before I had Kate, my cousin came over with her twins. I made them spaghetti and they threw it all over my house. I begged them to leave. No splotchy fingerprints for me.

But Kate brought chaos with her wherever she went. She ate sand. She jabbed her thumbs into the shells of living snails. She pulled whatever was in her reach off the shelves. To dress Kate, I had to sit on her. She hated being dressed, hated putting clothes on.

She resisted me. Fought back. I was astonished at the strength in less than twenty pounds. Was this a pit bull I'd given birth to? At a time when I neared single parent exhaustion and collapse, I met Larry at a writer's conference. Kate wasn't with me. After a week of what became friendlier and friendlier exchanges, I told him that I had a toddler and she would be arriving on Sunday with my mother. Without batting an eye, Larry said, "What time do we have to pick them up?"

The first moment Larry saw Kate, she dashed off the Jetway, through the airport terminal, and was heading for the revolving doors. My mother stood dumbfounded, bags in her hands, as Larry ran after the fleeing child. They began a game, this stranger and my child, racing here and there.

I was amazed at his ability to play. He could roll around on the floor with her for hours. He could be a horse. He could squeeze his body into the narrowest of spaces, just to come jumping out while she feigned surprise. I was too busy rinsing out her dresses, wiping tables clean. But entropy was winning and my energy depleting. I couldn't keep up with the mess.

Larry and I got married. One night, when Kate was three years old and I was multitasking—paying some bills, trying to make dinner before Larry got home—Kate asked me to be a gorilla. Sure, I can be a gorilla. I began jumping around, scratching my hands under my arms while stirring a pot and rinsing the dishes. She looked at me, dejected. "I want you to be an upstairs gorilla, not a downstairs gorilla."

An upstairs gorilla.

She wanted me to stop what I was doing—to leave the dishes in the sink and the meal half-prepared before my husband got home. But I wanted to straighten up; I had to get things done. Why couldn't I be a downstairs gorilla? I want to know. We began to argue about this. I knew this was stupid. I was arguing with a three-year-old, but the fact is, I have trouble being an upstairs gorilla. I have trouble allowing disorder, letting tasks go unfinished. I tried to stop what I was doing and go upstairs, jump up and down. I tried to let debris accumulate, let chaos reign. But my mind was elsewhere. Did I turn off that pot? Who paid the electric bill?

One Sunday we had somewhere to go that must have been important. As we were about to leave, I went upstairs and found that Kate had made a funhouse out of my scarves—the ones I'd purchased on a million journeys and never once wrapped around my head. My room was a cross between a harem and an obstacle course, and she had created elaborate rules for crawling through, which I was expected to follow. This was unbearable to me. I dismantled the funhouse, then spent an hour folding every scarf, putting them back into the drawer.

I tried to remember my dolls that once had fun. But somehow I'd taken all the disappointment and anger I'd ever felt and found a place for it, tucked away neatly on an upper shelf where no one could reach it. Not even me.

Then one night it happens. It is late and Kate won't go to bed. She has to have one more story, one more song. There is always one more thing. The house is in disarray, her room is a mess. I have failed as an upstairs gorilla. I have lost the battle of the scarves. And now I have a child who challenges my sense of order and timing. She won't sleep. She won't leave me alone.

"Go to your bed," I tell her the third or fourth time she reappears at my door.

"I don't want to," she says.

I am staring at the book I want to read. "Go to bed," I say once more.

"No," she says. "I want you."

And then I yell. I roar. I order her to bed. I can hear her in her room whimpering. I race in and grab her by the shoulders. I shake her and shout. I scream things at her that make no sense. I tell her she is selfish. (She is four years old.) I tell her she is wearing me out; I can't take it anymore. Then she looks at me, sobbing, straight in the eye, and seems older than her little years as she says, "You scare me."

I stand there as if nailed to the floor. A bolt goes through me. Call it an awakening, an epiphany. I stop, pull away. I remember how my father's rages terrified me. How he screamed about a light left on, a dish in the sink. How afraid he was of taking the wrong road or being in a restaurant where the soup wasn't hot. And how frightened we were of him.

I walk out of her room. I shut the door. Never again, I tell myself. That's it.

I begin small. I allow stuffed animals to stay on the floor. I stop inviting over the one friend she doesn't like—the girl who will spend the better part of a playdate cleaning Kate's room. I stop making elaborate meals, and while making dinner, I allow myself to be enticed away. "Mommy, be a snake and I'll be a frog escaping." Sure, I can do that. Snake, frog. So what if dinner is late? I get on my belly. I learn to slither and crawl, not unlike a baby, I think, as Kate hops away. I can do this, I think. I'm even good at it.

I let little messes go. I give in to entropy. It's a law of physics, after all; a close cousin to chaos, I'm sure. And it always wins anyway. Systems come apart. I'm going to try and go with this flow. Kate is ready for kindergarten, and we go looking at schools. I like one a lot until I hear the teacher say to a kid who has just finished a drawing, "That's a nice drawing, Mickey. Now put all the crayons away. And remember, the blue doesn't go here."

No control-freak teachers for my child. Been there, done that. Let her put that blue crayon where the red one goes. I let her bite off bigger pieces than are humanly possible to eat. She will learn what she can and cannot chew. She will know if she needs to wear a jacket or not. I evoke Buddha's definition of health: to eat when you are hungry and sleep when you are tired. I'm going with Zen.

At night I ask her to help me with dinner. When I was growing up, my mother shouted up at me every night, "Mary, make the salad." It was not a request but an order, one I was loath to follow. For years, as an adult, I couldn't bring myself to make a salad. I try a different approach with Kate. I say, "Okay, here's what we need to do. We have to set the table, feed the animals, and make the stir-fry." She opts to do the stir-fry. She chops the vegetables. Ginger, scallions, mushrooms. In a few years she will become a fairly accomplished cook.

After dinner we luxuriate in baths and I comb and braid her hair. One day Kate shows me a picture from a magazine. She announces that she wants to cut off her rich, thick, almost red hair; to wear overalls and become a tomboy. She is perhaps eight or nine. I am, well, looking at fifty. I have great plans for my little girl and that hair. There is a closet full of dresses, boxes of ribbons and barrettes.

For weeks I try to find reasons why she can't cut her hair. Then I hope she'll just forget about it, but she doesn't. "I want short hair," she says, holding the picture in my face. Late one night I run this by Larry.

"She wants to cut off her hair."

"It's her hair," he says.

We go to the beauty shop and Kate sits on the phone books from New York City's biggest boroughs. How can she make such a big decision when she's so small? Then I remember all the decisions that were made for me. I've brought a plastic bag, and as that lush, red hair cascades to the ground, I crawl on the floor, scooping her thick curls into the bag, which I still keep in a drawer.

But the situation grows complex. Kate is barred from a women's washroom in a restaurant in Florida. In Alaska, when we have a run-in with a state trooper, he refers to Kate repeatedly as "son." "So, son . . ." I am walking down the street with a friend I hold dear and I tell her I am being tested. My daughter won't put a dress on. She's cut off her hair. People think she's a boy.

And my friend says, "One day Kate will look in the mirror and know she's a knockout. Until then, let her be her own person. And pick your battles. . . ."

Pick my battles—that was good advice. And of course my friend was right.

"Okay, Kate, so you're going to go to so-and-so's party in jeans and a T-shirt. In that tie-dye shirt you made at summer camp." The hair stays short. I grit my teeth. I make a decision then and there: She will be her own person. I will not run her life the way other people ran mine. I give up on the shoulds and shouldn'ts, on curfews and punishments. Our message to her becomes clear: The only thing that matters is truth and trust. She'll be admonished only for a lie.

In school she picks her own courses, her own friends. She decides when she's ready to go to bed. We set limits but no strict rules. In fourth grade she wants to walk to school on her own. I make her a deal. There is a payphone at the entrance to the school. I go and get a roll of quarters. "Here's what you do," I tell her. "Every day when you get to school, put a quarter in that phone. Let it ring once so I know you're safe, then hang up, and you keep the quarter. If you don't call, I'll be on my way to school."

That year she has candy money in her pocket and I never have to chase her down.

She grows older. The hair grows back. We go shopping at Urban Outfitters and, with background techno music blaring, I let her pick out weird T-shirts with silver sequins and name brands emblazoned across the chest, jeans with rips on the butt. (I don't even say, "Let's buy a cheap pair of jeans and you can rip the butt yourself.")

But she's still a little girl—barely ten. I still tuck her in. One night I've just read to her and given her a backrub, and she turns to me and says, "Mommy, I love you more than anything in the world."

"Really?" I say, my heart beating hard in my chest. "How come?"

"'Cuz you let me be what I want to be."

"Oh yeah," I say, my throat constricting. "Well, that's all I wanted for you, really. Nothing more."

I place a kiss on her brow. I close the door behind me. Tears run down my face. Okay, that's it. I did it.

Recently my daughter, who will soon be graduating from high school, applied to become a peer counselor in her school, giving guidance to entering freshmen. She was asked to name her strengths and weaknesses. "My weakness," she wrote, "is that I am a sloth." She described the lazy sloth, munching mangoes in its tree. It only comes down once a week to go to the bathroom.

That, of course, is not my child at all, but we laughed over the description. My life is another minefield now, different from the one I grew up with—one of dirty laundry I must tiptoe over, a parrot who tosses her food on the floor, a kitchen of dishes in the sink. The signs of people eating, sleeping, in a hurry, with too many things to do and not enough time to do it all. I revel in the mess. One day soon my house will be neat again, and oh how I will miss it.

Are Hunters Born or Made?

Ana Castillo

I was in the kitchen one late afternoon last summer when my son stopped by. Actually, he was moving back home.

The first year of college I had put him in the dorm. (That sounds as if I had him incarcerated. The truth is that I had suggested, in no uncertain terms, that he stay in a dorm.) Never mind that the university he chose is exactly two blocks from the high school he attended, and both schools are exactly five quick "L" train stops away from our place. It was time, his mother felt, for him to take the next step toward independence. His and mine. Just like when I weaned him from the bottle and potty trained him right after his second birthday. Now we do it, *Mi'jo. Y ya.*

You might say it has always been a matter of unilateral decision-making in our family of two. "Such a feminist having to raise a boy!" was the customary response to my status as a mother, as if there were a secret feminist agenda to procreate a race of Amazons. This was not true, of course. I raised my son much the same way that I would have raised a daughter, conscious not to fall into gender stereotypes. You monitor TV programs, reading materials, music, activities, and playmates.

While he was growing up I took writing residencies around the country. At the end of one school year and in receipt of a letter inviting me to join the faculty of some department in a university across the country, off we went. Mama packed, made arrangements, a trail of furnishings and personal belongings left in storage rentals strewn along the way; I sold and bought things as needed. I found new schools, encouraged friendships, signed him up for a basketball team at a boys club in one town, sent him off to basketball camp in another, taught him to ride a bike at five, drive at sixteen, slow dance, shave, do his own laundry from the age of twelve, and, once, when he broke my French espresso pot while doing the dinner dishes with an attitude, I made him pay for it then and there. He never broke anything again.

We managed. He grew up; he's got about six inches on me now. In high school he lived in his bedroom. He never ate. I was certain that my gaunt, dark—in mood as well as in pallor—child had been bitten by a vampire. But even vampires need to learn independence. He took this particular stage with him to the freshman dorm.

He didn't care for the dorm that freshman year. He came home, he said, to shower. Apparently he didn't like sleeping in the dorm much either: more often than not when I'd get up and walk past his old bedroom, I'd find the blankets on the bed making a much bigger, or more specifically, longer lump than *Mi'jo*'s little Boston terrier, who still slept there, possibly could.

What my son really wanted was his own apartment.

"That's why I am putting you through college," was the usual course of our brief exchanges that year. This way—or more precisely, *my* way—someday, with the right credentials, he'd get a job, and thereby support himself. Then he could afford his own place.

Nevertheless, the following autumn, at the start of his second year of college, he found a roommate with a job. They got an apartment in a neighborhood that I wish I could say would have caused any parent to worry—but then so would the neighborhood we have lived in for nearly seven years. Unlike the roommate's mother, who immediately set herself to the task of redoing her son's vacant bedroom in her own house and turning it into a sewing room for herself, I kind of lapsed into a period of domestic confusion. What now?

He'd left behind his bedroom furniture, taking only the bed, as well as a spare dresser and futon that had been in the guest room. During the following school year both my son's former bedroom and the semi-plundered guest room remained in a perpetual state of suspension, the absence of their defining accoutrements giving the term "empty nest" literal meaning in my home.

Even the little dog, with its year-round shorthaired shedding, had moved out. (Actually, the dog's departure had been upon my own insistence. One more opportunity for my son to learn responsibility, I believed.)

We had been separated many times during my son's lifetime. His father had maintained *Mi'jo* during all of his vacations and holidays. Weeks had passed during his childhood when I received no return phone calls.

But of course, this was different.

Have I mentioned yet that I teach at the same university my son attends?

He avoids my office. But not those of my fellow colleagues, from whom he'll take classes or to whom he'll look for guidance, at least with regard to his education. So I knew some things about his life during that second year. Meanwhile, with each rare visit home, he showed increasing signs of intentional disregard for the hygiene and other regimens strictly enforced during his upbringing—even commonsense rules like wearing gloves in mid-winter in Chicago—so that one night he ended up in an emergency room with frostbitten hands. Most grating to a mother or to any reasonable, mature individual, he continued to refine his contrariness toward any and all opinions and advice I offered.

His junior year of college was coming up, and he was moving back in. I made it look like it was his idea. That is, once his roommate announced he couldn't keep up with the rent and go to school, while my son, a full-time student, had a mother living all of a fifteen-minute train ride from campus, I did not have to point out the obvious.

Instead, I kept quiet. If the truth be known, I was starting to get used to prancing around in my *pantaletas* and skinny tees in the morning, once spring came and the gloom of a long, lonely winter was past me. Not that I didn't miss my boy. The Good Son, that is—the one with the jagged front tooth and traces of baby fat around the middle and the Buster Brown haircut; the one with a forgiving nature who never understood why the girl cousin who was exactly his age (as well as size and weight) was so free with the back of her hand. He had no more wanted to give his girl cousin the back of his hand in return (which was his father's advice on the telephone) than he wanted to receive one from her, or from anybody.

He had always been and, I assumed, would always be sensitive to others. We had never taken to yelling at home. He learned early on to respect my privacy and my property, as I always did his. For example, he would never have gone into my purse for lunch money. Instead, he would bring the bag to me, as he had been taught, so that I could dole out the dough. He grew up without paramilitary toys. (Prohibition of such gifts elicited some consternation on the part of the male family members, who obviously feared that the boy would miss an important aspect of his macho development.) Because I refused to pay for any toy with an implicit political dimension so counter to mine—meanwhile aware that out-and-out denial on my part would render my son an adolescent outcast—he had to buy his own PlayStation, which he got used from some other kid in a later stage of puberty.

He was, as I said, a person who was naturally sensitive, guided further toward being respectful, an independent thinker, responsible. Still, I noticed. It happened subtly: my son's definite and undeniable enlistment on The Other Side.

Not that he just became a man—a natural process—but he became one to the fullest extent of the sociological and traditional meaning of gender. How and when it happened exactly I cannot say. But by the time my son, about to start his third year in college, was moving back home, he had definitely become a guy, a dude of the highest rank. Public Enemy Number One for any girl looking for a steady beau and believing that in my sensitive, introspective son she might have found him. By the time it became clear that he had all the requisite traits to allow him full lifetime membership into Guyness, she'd realize she was in mined territory.

When a woman gets together with a man, she has to work with what's there, in terms of the taming process. But when she has issued him forth from her own womb, wrapped him in swaddling clothes, and waded down the river with him to find a place to raise him away from the Pharisees, a place where he might learn to value the gentler and more nurturing culture of women, where household chores are an equal division of labor, where men always put the toilet seat down, brush their teeth before coming to bed (if not take a shower), and not only listen with marked interest to their companion after the perfunctory question, "How was your day?" but actually care, she does not expect ever to stand in her kitchen and hear the following proclamation: "Oh yeah, no doubt about it. I'm a hunter."

My son was talking about the urban preying of the so-called "groomed male" on the opposite sex.

The specifics were the following and I put them to you, reader, now: Should I not have been somewhat wide-eyed and speechless, at least momentarily, in response?

As I said, there we were, in the kitchen, when he shared with me how the girl he was "kicking it with" lately had stopped talking to him. We had been away for a weekend—one of those "family trips" on which I had successfully coerced my son into accompanying me to an event related to my public life. During this particular weekend he had intentionally not notified the girl he was seeing of his whereabouts. "I wasn't that interested in her, I guess," he admitted.

Ah. To have had the vantage point of a nineteen-year-old guy's honesty when I was a girl! How many hours on the phone with my girlfriends would that have spared me? "I thought you liked her!" I said, remembering the conversation when he said how beautifully she played the cello, the same instrument he had studied in high school. They seemed to have something in common, at least.

"I like her all right," he said, standing next to me like a poplar tree. (I got over the height disparity in relation to power dynamics between us when he was twelve and had passed me by. It took a few months, but I was determined.)

You can't push. You can't say too much. You mustn't show your eagerness to right their world, to fight off the dragons, to show them that the thirty years you have on them is worth something even if you lived those years way back in the Garden of Eden. I went about my business. All ears, I relentlessly wiped the counter like an obsessive-compulsive. I may have begun to whistle a little tune to really feign only the most casual interest in his big, fat, mysterious, juicy life outside the paltry world of my half-abandoned and orderly apartment.

He shrugged his bony shoulders. "I just wasn't into her, you know? Once she showed she was interested."

The blood left my brain. Would I faint or grab the nearest blunt instrument at this news, which was in such opposition to all the feminist principles I had ever tried to instill in him? Not by words. Not by lesson plans. I never said, "This is what a decent guy does and this is what a jerk does." Not outright. Not even to other members of the male gender when within his hearing range. Still one hopes, against the monolithic onslaught of society, that a mother gets her message across on an impressionable young mind.

Stay calm, I told myself, rubbing the sides of my pulsing temples.

"You getting a headache?" he asked.

"You mean to say," I asked, "that it's all about the thrill of the chase or else you lose interest?"

He nodded. Proudly. Confidently. Standing there with his hip-hop baggy pants and paint-stained hands from nocturnal graffiti activities, T-shirt with photos of Che, Subcomandante Marcos, and Malcolm X, with block letters underneath reading: WE ARE NOT A MINORITY.

"In other words"—I needed to paraphrase what he'd just confirmed to give myself a little time to absorb it—"if a girl goes after you, you are automatically not interested in her on principle."

"Oh, without a doubt. I'm a hunter."

"Okay, Bambi," I said. "As you go off to join the thundering herd, what do you expect from the girl now? You blew her off. You were rude. What do you want from her anyway?

People say my son has my eyes. They are very dark. When he was a child, after someone made such an observation, he'd answer, not quite comprehending but already defiant, "No, I don't. I have my own eyes." I don't know about mine, but his get even darker when he gets pensive, like a mood ring, with black raven eyebrow wings-in-flight above them, set against the wind.

"I'd still like us to be friends," he said, sounding a tad remorseful, this confession maybe something he wouldn't admit to his crew. "I mean, it's awkward when we run into each other now. It would be nice to talk like we used to at least."

I don't think we ever discuss our sons losing their virginity the way the world observes the loss of sexual innocence in a girl. But I suspect I know at what point in his life and with whom it happened in the case of my son.

How quickly we learn, after that first rush of carnal passion, that sex isn't everything. He was going on twenty soon, on the autumn solstice; his teenage years about to disperse like countless memory motes floating around him for the rest of his life. To plague him. To cheer him in more complex times, perhaps, with their simplicity.

"So why don't you talk to her about it?" I asked.

"Whenever I see her, she's with her girlfriends and ignores me," he said. Perhaps as much as she knew, now, that he was a hunter, she knew she needed the protection of her pack.

"Call her then, *Mi'jo*," I urged. "Ask her to meet you somewhere for a cup of coffee so that you can explain things to her. More than anything, bottom line, women want to be respected as people. They're not pillage."

In the next few seconds, as this simple statement began to sink in and the racket of innumerable influences from all around that had been delivering the very opposite message was pushed aside, at least for the present, the black thunderbolts of his expressive eyebrows relaxed, as if a storm had just passed. His slightly slanted eyes brightened. He pulled out his cell phone, went to the living room to call her, and left a message. He was all smiles when he came back into the kitchen.

Now I remember what we were doing that day in the kitchen. We were having tacos, the kind we Mexicans enjoy, especially on Sunday—where you get meat already cooked at your local *carnicería* and you put each taco together yourself. A warm corn tortilla, chunks of *carnitas* or *barbacoa*, add on *salsita*, sour cream and avocado slices—it's a cholesterol fest for the arteries. For some reason, both *Mi'jo* and I insist on eating standing up, just like at the taco stands in Mexico.

"You're great, Mom. I'm so glad I talked it over with you." He grinned, reaching for a tortilla to start on another taco, thereby proving to me that he hadn't been bitten by a vampire after all.

"It's what a mother lives for." I smiled back, although, for sure, once he moved back in I would miss the prancing around in the last summer days in my undies, like Jill Clayburgh in *An Unmarried Woman*. But, then, there is no such thing as an "unmothered woman," which doesn't even make sense. Or maybe it could, if you really gave it some deep thought and were open to the concept. But not for me. Any feminist of my day worth her salt knows: The re-evolution starts with one man at a time.

Wolves at the Door

Karin L. Stanford

My grandmother's house always smelled of gingerbread. After the spicy scent made its escape from the kitchen, it ran wild and seeped into anything that would hold its sweetness—the curtains, the couch, the sheets and pillowcases. Even the paint on the walls was soaked with it. Entering my grandmother's house was like walking into a fairy tale, full of magic and music, safety and promise. My grandmother's house was a place where little girls could wear bright red coats and ribbons tied in bows at the ends of their pigtails, a place where the wolves would not enter, where the world could be kept at bay. My grandmother's house was, if nothing else, a refuge.

Inside the comfort and protection of my grandmother's house there was a beauty that I claimed—or perhaps it claimed me. When I was in my grandmother's presence, I was told that I was beautiful, that I was talented, that not only would I grow up to be successful but I would also marry a wonderful, sensitive, and successful man. My husband would shield me from harm and pain; he would take care of our family's financial and emotional needs. We would have wonderful children. "Are you sure about that?" I would ask my grandmother, trying to mask my doubt and insecurity with playfulness.

"Yes, Karin, I am sure," my grandmother would always say as she pulled me into her embrace, into her challenge to prevail.

"You're gonna make us all proud." And during those times I dared to believe, if only for a few precious moments, that she was right, that I could be anything—whoever or whatever I chose to be.

But outside of all that—outside of the house, the fairy tale, the dream—there was another reality: a world of joblessness and hopelessness, of broken-down, dilapidated schools and drunken men on street corners. It was a truth that belonged to the world, not to me, but I felt forced to own it. I was an ordinary black girl living in South Central Los Angeles, a place where fantasies of glass slippers and princes, piggies who went to market, bread crumbs and hot porridge could not survive for long. I was not special and, chances were, my life would never be charmed. I was—and most likely would always remain—a nobody.

But I became somebody. Several experiences during my childhood inspired a tremendous sense of belonging in me. I grew up in the late 1960s and early 1970s in the eye of a mighty storm. I lived in the center of a city whose residents spoke their minds, a city in the midst of a moment in history—one plagued by fights for civil rights and inner-city rebellion. It was a time when black people in America were struggling to attain a new level of pride and dignity. Images of strong race women were commonplace in my neighborhood. Storefront windows, magazines, and newspapers, and the walls of neighbors' home were adorned with images of activists such as Angela Davis, Elaine Brown, and Kathleen Cleaver.

I was raised in a family of women who were determined to see me succeed. In 1944 my grandparents had moved their family from Mississippi to California in search of a better life. My mother and aunts established their careers early as beauticians, grocery store checkers, and secretaries—the kinds of careers that were available to black women during the civil rights era. They demonstrated a strong work ethic for my siblings, cousins, and me, but they also understood the importance of community involvement. My grandmother volunteered her home as a polling station for local and national elections. Our entire family helped prepare her home for those special days. I have fond memories of watching the voters line up to cast their ballots, of greeting our guests and playing with the children who accompanied their parents.

I wanted so desperately to emulate my elders and those strong race women I had come to admire. I was the first person in my family to get a college degree. I went on to earn a Ph.D. in political science, and my dissertation was published as a book.

I became a college professor. Then one year, while on sabbatical, I went to work in Washington, D.C., for an African American leader who had become an inspiration in my life. He championed the causes of the oppressed and advocated tolerance between the races. Our work was intellectually stimulating and professionally exciting. We had so much in common. I admired him, and he respected me. Our work relationship turned into friendship, then a romantic partnership, with the trappings of the enchanting fairy tales my grandmother had once described to me.

But my life was not a fairy tale. My Prince Charming was not single, and I was his employee. He assured me that his marriage was nontraditional. And in the myopic world of Washington politics, our "open secret" was quite common. Our colleagues, friends, and even some of his family members knew of our relationship. Still, I was not totally comfortable with it.

My discomfort was soon overshadowed by a more critical event in my life—I was diagnosed with breast cancer at age thirty-five. As a young African American woman, I knew that my prognosis was not good. Breast cancer is usually more aggressive in younger women, and even with equal care, African Americans are more likely to die from it than women of any other race.

Throughout my treatment, I was dazed and often depressed about the unexpected turn my life had taken. Although several family members traveled to be at my side, it was difficult to live so far away from home. But through the surgery, chemotherapy, and radiation, I was never alone—my partner was always physically and spiritually with me. As I struggled for my life, I temporarily cast aside my reservations about our relationship and counted on his support. I know that cancer destroys some relationships, but ours only grew stronger.

My treatments were successful, and my cancer went into remission. But then I was faced with another potential loss that cancer and chemotherapy can bring on: infertility. I had always hoped to become a mother, but I was told to bury that hope, to place it in my past. Even if my body returned to its regular hormonal rhythms, pregnancy could trigger a recurrence of cancer. Though I mourned the fact that I might never have a child of my own, I felt lucky just to have my own life. I didn't want to tempt fate.

It seemed, however, that I had already done so. I discovered in August 1998 that, against all odds, I was pregnant.

My doctor advised me to terminate the pregnancy. I understood all the reasons why—all the scientific evidence, the facts, and the figures. He was most concerned that the increase in estrogen that accompanies pregnancy might lead to a return of the cancer, and possibly death. But what I understood most was that I had been given a chance, one chance, to have a child. Yes, there was a risk that the cancer would return; there was also a possibility that it would not.

"If you have this baby," my doctor warned, "you might not be here in five years."

"That's true," I told him. "But even if I don't have it, I might not be here in five years." So I decided to take the chance.

At first, I did not tell my partner about the life forming inside of me. I was afraid that the revelation, if made public, could damage his reputation and political ambitions. I broke off our relationship and told him that I was carrying someone else's child. But he knew the truth and the reasons for my secrecy. Given his family and professional obligations, I never had grand expectations of him, but I was gratified when he pledged to face his responsibility to stand by our child and me. My focus was on keeping my daughter and myself alive through the pregnancy and birth, but I was comforted that we would not be alone.

Publicly, the birth of our daughter, Ashley, was shrouded in secrecy, but behind closed doors, we felt the same joy and pride that other parents do when their child smiles or learns to talk and walk. We had the perfect baby. And despite the unconventional nature of our situation, we were determined to raise an emotionally healthy child. She had an attentive mother and father. She would grow up knowing that she was loved and cared for by *both* her parents. Someday later we would tell her why we could not marry, at least not then.

No matter how we tried to make our home as solid as brick, in the end it was a house of straw. Following up on a rumor, a national tabloid learned about our daughter. Reporters smelling scandal began calling me and showing up on my lawn.

My partner made a public statement acknowledging that he was Ashley's father. Coming at a time when President Bill Clinton was being crucified for lying about his affair with a White House intern, my partner was praised by the media for his honesty. Then he quietly bowed out of public life for a while to "spend time with his family" and "revive his spirits."

Suddenly, I was at the center of a mighty storm, one that was purely destructive. My life was torn from its roots, heaved about, and came crashing down in pieces. My partner's withdrawal from political life left me alone to answer publicly for our relationship. I was attacked by friends, strangers, and the black press without mercy, my only moral support coming from a few close friends and my family. I turned for spiritual help to a friend who was also a pastor, but instead he publicly accused me of "setting up" my now ex-partner. Black religious leaders and congregations prayed for him and his "family," but not for our daughter and me. Apparently, we didn't merit any spiritual help.

The black media requested interviews with him, his family members, and our colleagues, but did not speak to me, choosing instead to label me a political stalker. While the black press ignored me, the tabloids couldn't get enough of me: They offered me hundreds of thousands of dollars to share the secrets of our lives together. Though I refused them all—our daughter's life was not for sale—the black establishment called me a gold digger and an opportunist.

I soon realized that in one fell swoop I had joined the pantheon of women who—in the process of living, loving, and carrying out their lives—become seen in the black community as pariahs, women scorned, fatal attractions preying on the lives of famous black men.

Consider the case of Anita Hill, the bright young academic star who worked for Clarence Thomas when he was a federal judge and encountered a familiar brand of patriarchal control. Having no choice but to testify during Thomas's Supreme Court nomination hearings about his sexual impropriety on the job, she carried out her duty with grace and dignity. Nonetheless, Hill was excoriated in the press for having dared to challenge a black man's career ambitions.

Likewise, when heavyweight boxing champion Mike Tyson was accused of raping Desiree Washington, a former Miss Teenage Black America, he was protected by black community leaders. Never mind that Tyson's violent temper and abusive behavior were well known; his former wife, Robin Givens, had accused him of battery on a national news program. But just as Givens had been criticized for "going public" about her husband's abuse and chastised for "gold digging," Washington was demonized for charging Tyson with rape.

The sympathy received by O. J. Simpson after he was accused of murdering his ex-wife, Nicole, the white mother of two of his children, also shows how commonplace woman-bashing has become within the black community. Although race became the subtext for Simpson's trial, among black people gender was also an important issue. It was not unusual in private conversations to hear Nicole Simpson referred to as an opportunist who deserved her fate because she had, after all, married O. J. for his money.

Another outrageous instance occurred in the summer of 2002, when R&B singer R. Kelly was charged with twenty-one counts of child pornography for videotaping sex acts with a minor. Although Kelly clearly had a predilection for underage women—at twenty-seven, he had married the fifteen-year-old singer Aaliyah—black supporters of Kelly called the teenager a "slut" and hurled other insults at her at the pre-trial hearing. Two years later, Kelly was nominated for an NAACP Image Award and invited by the Congressional Black Caucus Spouses to perform at its annual benefit concert.

The list goes on, unfortunately now with my own name upon it. Despite my attempt to become the quintessential race woman— despite the fact that my life's work had revolved around advocating for economic, political, and social justice for minority people—I was suddenly antithetical to all black interests. I became the scapegoat in an orchestrated effort to protect a black male, and part of that protection involved destroying my credibility. Those who sought to discredit me, attempted thieves of my humanity, were skillful. Their goal was to mute my voice, for fear of what I might say. And like so many black women before me, I found myself wondering, Am I not worthy of respect, protection, and support?

I was stunned by the fury from those who had no vested interest in my life. Whether the choice I made was right or wrong, it was a personal matter—how could my professional future and political life hinge on it? Yet overnight, the person whom I had worked so hard to become had been erased. Again, I was a nobody. Even my colleagues thought *I* needed to pay a price for *my* transgressions. A high-level position promised to me by the Democratic National Committee was delicately revoked. I was also quietly vetted out of all party activities. Colleagues who once considered my political and policy advice an asset refused to return my calls. At one point I found myself a single mother, unemployed, and with no real prospects for work. I became fully aware of how black women, no matter what their commitment, are liabilities in the world of black power—a world in which black men receive unquestioned loyalty despite their sometimes unconscionable actions.

When the news media ran its headlines, spreading false statements and innuendo, I did not run to pick up my pen. When the national tabloids and black press called me an opportunist, a wanton woman, I did not answer by sending them photocopies of my various degrees and hard-earned curriculum vitae. Nor did I hit the streets when black radio and talk show hosts accused me of trying to bring a good man down, to break yet another one of our people's icons of success.

I was silent because I was shocked and frightened and had a feeling that my efforts would not make a difference. Other than family members and close friends, who would listen? Who would hear me? Who would care? In part, I was afraid that by engaging in public confrontations, I would continue to hurt the people I loved. I was especially concerned about protecting my daughter from being caught in media crossfire. But I was also concerned about protecting her relationship with her father—as a cancer survivor, I needed to know that no matter what happened, that would remain intact.

Perhaps somewhere deep inside me, I also believed the declarations that I was "a nobody." In truth, I was not totally surprised by the treatment I received. Intuitively, I knew that sexism in the black community was stubbornly entrenched, though I was encouraged early on to ignore it. Like most young black women, I learned that it was our job to take care of ourselves while helping our black men succeed. We were urged to shield them from the mainstream's genocidal bullet of bigotry—period. Nobody ever sat us down and told us this directly, at least not in my home. Nobody said, "Black women, your job is to stay behind black men, not eclipse them." But it was understood. It was a piece of knowledge that was handed down quietly, like an old pair of jeans or a picture quilt that tells a family saga.

In retrospect, I had always known subconsciously that those black female activists with big Afros did not always receive the respect their hard work warranted. I also knew the unspoken truth: that black women suffer disproportionately from abuse, battery, rape, assault, and lack of physical and financial child support. Contrary to the prevailing myth that black men endure the brunt of racism, black women suffer from the triple jeopardy of racism, classism, and sexism.

Black women have been complicit in maintaining this status

quo. Surely for fear of being ostracized and left unmarried, we have been slow to critique the system that leaves us marginalized and often on our own. Years of being called "Jezebel," "sapphire," "controlling matriarch," and "emasculator" have silenced us, even when we are confronted with physical assault or sexual harassment.

Looking back, I can see clearly my own collusion with this unspoken code. I now realize that my initial attempt to lie about my pregnancy was a reflex, based on cultural expectations. Drummed into my head by those who knew of our relationship were phrases such as, "Unlike white women, black women don't tell." My bifurcated childhood experiences, growing up in a harsh reality with fairy tale expectations, haunted me. I had pretended to reside in a world of gender equality, of black male and female camaraderie, that did not always exist. Although my partner did not attempt to protect my good name, I rushed to protect his. I realize now that I was upholding the idea that his reputation was more important than raising a child in truth.

Being a mother has emboldened me. It took a while, but now I realize that my silence will not resolve the problem of sexism and gender bias within the black community. My silence, my capitulation, is a poor example for my daughter. To be silenced is one thing; to silence yourself is quite another. Now, in the words of John Edgar Wideman, I feel compelled to do "the disruptive duty of . . . bearing witness." I hope that my words and example, and my support of other women who are stepping out of the shadows, will provide my daughter with courage and a candid understanding of the challenges she will face.

Sexism within the black community has not gone totally unchallenged. Ntozake Shange's 1976 choreopoem, *for colored girls who have considered suicide / when the rainbow is enuf*, and Alice Walker's Pulitzer Prize–winning *Color Purple*, which was turned into a film by Steven Spielberg, both took on the issue of sexism in the black community. (And both provoked protest among blacks, who picketed stage performances of Shange's work and admonished Walker and Spielberg for presenting black men in such a negative light.) Other feminist writers such as bell hooks and Patricia Hill Collins—as well as black male intellectuals such as Michael E. Dyson, Manning Marble, and Cornel West—have continued to speak out for change in consciousness as well as public policy.

Even so, these are difficult times for black women and girls. We live in a society and community that happily sacrifices our well-being for the success of black men and boys. Female degradation has become almost a staple of black youth pop culture: It is not uncommon to turn on a rap song and hear about "bitches" and "'ho's" or see images of girls and women in various states of subjugation in hip-hop videos.

It is no wonder that keen-eyed writer and anthropologist Zora Neale Hurston, in her 1937 novel *Their Eyes Were Watching God*, called the black woman "de mule uh de world" because she seemed to carry all the burdens of her race. What's surprising is that black women continue to bear most of these burdens. To be black and female right here and right now is to be standing at the threshold of a freedom we have yet to win—for ourselves or our daughters.

My daughter, Ashley, is now five years old. She is beautiful, inquisitive, smart, and mischievous. Ashley's most defining features are her vivacious laugh and her smile. Like other children, her simple questions about the nature of life are as complicated as the makings of a space station.

Although her father had originally caved in to the pressure to disassociate himself from our daughter, he has resumed a relationship with her. Ashley understands that our family life is different, but she knows she is cherished by both her mom and dad. She is truly a happy child.

At some point, however, our daughter will inevitably pick up a newspaper that calls her mother a "mistress" or "paramour." She will also discover that she has no relationship with some members of her father's family. Someday she will question why the fury of her community was hurled at her mother after her birth by people who would never be part of her life.

When those days come, I will not presume to speak for her

father, who can speak for his own actions. But I will have a conversation with her about the circumstances of her birth. I will tell my daughter that I acknowledge the view held by many that my relationship with her father was wrong, but for me it was a loving relationship that produced a wonderful baby girl. I will tell her that her birth was a miracle. I will tell her that she comes from a long line of strong women—women who gave me a sense of power and belonging.

My grandmother is now ninety years old. Although she suffers from Alzheimer's disease, her eyes still smile when I greet her, and they have a special sparkle when she sees Ashley. "You are such a pretty little girl," my grandmother says to her, and sometimes I feel that they communicate in an unspoken language. My daughter will not have the chance to know my grandmother in the same way that I did, but I will pass on to her those stories that my grandmother told me. I will teach her that fairy tales belong in storybooks, but that heartfelt dreams, despite surprising twists and turns, are always worth reaching for.

I will also tell her stories of what a *real* little girl could grow up to be: a somebody, a race woman, and a feminist. I will tell her that the choices I made stem from the belief that women should have all the opportunities available to men, even the opportunity to make mistakes. I will talk to her about how my grandmother, mother, and other women worked hard to instill in me a sense of independence and personal strength. And I will tell her that they succeeded.

Mothers Just Like Us

Debra Ollivier

Over a decade ago I married a Frenchman and moved overseas. Our oldest child spent his early toddler years in a public nursery school in Paris. Like many French citizens I took for granted a social infrastructure of family support so extensive and cherished by the French that any threat to its well-being sent millions to the streets in protest, virtually paralyzing the nation. Beyond free public nursery schools and long-term education, this infrastructure includes numerous affordable day-care options, national health-care plans, pediatricians who still make house calls, and a lavish amount of vacation time that allows parents to have a life, not just make a living.

During those early French days I'd visit Los Angeles and marvel at the army of Latina nannies tending to this white-collar oasis: the Guatemalan with her long braid pushing a Dylan or an Ashley in an ergonomic stroller. The Salvadoran doing laundry; bringing order and shiny surfaces to the chaos of the *patrona*'s world. I was reminded of a peculiar antebellum era of landed gentry. Comfortably rooted in a French system that instead of paying lip service to family values actually underwrote them, it was easy for me to scoff at mothers who toted their nannies around like accessories. And then a curious thing happened: Shortly after my second child was born I inherited a house in California, moved back to the States, and became, for all intents and purposes, one of those mothers.

Full disclosure: I grew up in Los Angeles with two latchkey siblings, a single working mother, and a live-in Mexican woman named Maria. But Maria was as much a "nanny" as she was Mary Poppins. Back then she was called a housekeeper. What strange spin on the onerous job of caretaking has brought us the word *nanny*, with its primly aristocratic overtones? Did the word emerge to mitigate the extent to which nannies have become indentured to us? For the only difference I could note in the decades since Maria was in our life is that the nanny has become a more pervasive fixture among American families. Even the at-home mom seems to need her these days, not necessarily to spend more time with her kids but, ironically, to spend more precious time away from them. As we outsource the chaos that comes with children, the nanny provides priceless relief, filling in the gaps cleaved out not only by our own parenting anxieties, but also by the black holes created where our public institutions have failed us.

These observations hit me with a particular vengeance when we moved into our house in a quiet suburban American neighborhood. I found myself with a two-income family, a husband who worked overseas, and a paucity of child-care options, each as problematic as the next. Barely settled back in the States, with the social benefits of France far behind me, I realized that I needed, quite simply, a nanny.

But where to begin? I could transform a spare bedroom into a new living space, with cable TV and five Hispanic channels (TelemundoLA, Alegria y Movimiento) but I was still clueless: How much should you pay your nanny? What about vacation time? Or sick days? Does she eat dinner with the family every night? What constitutes a full working day? When does it begin? Or end? Surprisingly, no clear-cut answers emerged—just a vast gray zone of conflicting views capped on one end by the mother who earnestly tried to bring the nanny into the family dynamic and, on the other end, by the mother who operated from a position of distrust. "Nannies talk among themselves," said one neighbor. "If you pay more, you set a precedent. Word gets out. Then we all have to defend our pay scales. Start low, cut your losses. Those are the unspoken rules of the game." Of course the rules of the game were not only unspoken; they also seemed largely unwritten. Because despite various books on the subject, no one seemed to have read the literature. In this frontier of domestic help there appeared to be no ultimate constitution, no code of ethics. It was every woman for herself. Which might explain why what seemed antebellum from the outside, suddenly seemed more Wild West from the inside.

I decided to accord my future nanny the rights she'd have if the politics of exile weren't working against her: Two weeks of vacation time, sick days, national holidays, and a Christmas bonus. It was wildly extravagant for us, but somehow the idea of striking a bargain with someone who would care for the most precious beings in my life seemed base to the point of repugnancy. Equally pressing was the notion that a well-paid nanny is a happy nanny—one who, presumably, will pass that happiness on to my children. I had only to put out a quick word. Within days, count-less job-seeking Latina women were at my disposal. I met Marta and, one week later, she moved in with her blue gym bag and her *Libro Catolico de Oraciones.*

Marta's first day: My kids clamored to the door to meet this person who would become a new presence in our lives. We'd already looked on a map, found the tiny slice of land tucked under Mexico called Belize. "Can you get there on a spaceship?" my son asked. When the bell rang we opened the door, and there was Marta: short dark hair, pink sweater, faded jeans. She stepped forward and opened her arms with a slightly awkward air. My kids stood close to me, a bit wary at first. There was a moment of curious anticipation—a breath held, a second of mutual scrutiny. Then, slowly, with all their big-hearted innocence, my children walked into Marta's arms.

I showed Marta around the house, tried to elaborate on her duties. It was a colossal process in part because I hadn't even articulated them myself. Where some mothers are consummate masters of their domestic universe, others, like myself, are bush-whackers living in a forest with a life of its own. So what kind of expectations to set up here? How many times should she vacuum the floor or clean out the fridge? But as Marta followed me through the wilderness of our home, it was the psychological landscape that loomed larger, the inarticulated world of this communal space we now shared. Because while I hadn't decided how much Pine-Sol to use (in large measure because I simply didn't care), I also hadn't defined in explicit fashion the rules of parenting. Aside from a few basics, when it came to raising my kids I still vacillated between the more straightforward French approach and the onslaught of parenting dogma that assailed the American parent. So where, in this vast playing field, would my parenting end and hers pick up?

Life together began with a tentative play at pretending that this forced intimacy was natural. Are we roommates? Family members? Employee/employer? My kids, with their immeasurable acceptance of the abstruse, helped us out. "Marta, did you know that Jupiter is made of gas?" my son asked at the breakfast table. Marta smiled back. "Oh yes," she said. "Of course." Not to be upstaged, my daughter declared, "Piggies eat clouds. Did you know that, Marta? In France they eat clouds." Marta put her fork down. She looked genuinely impressed. Perhaps they *do* eat clouds in France.

When my son Max began kindergarten, Marta lavished her attention on my daughter, Celeste, doing things I'd never had the time or skill to do: She spent fifteen minutes working Celeste's hair into complex braids or multitiered ponytails that stayed remarkably in place. She sorted through piles of clothes to find things that were frilly and feminine. "Why do you dress her like a boy?" she asked when I'd throw a generic T-shirt on Celeste. "You must dress her pretty." Every morning, as I bid farewell to my well-dressed, well-coiffed daughter, I was a mother divided: part of me had already mentally departed, my mind focused on the pressures and distractions of my job. Meanwhile, Marta seemed unfettered in this way. She was free to focus all of her energies exclusively on my daughter, because my daughter *was* her job. I tried to ignore a certain inchoate emotion that I couldn't quite place. It was a vague emotion, fuzzy but not warm. Later I would realize: that emotion was jealousy.

In this sisterhood of mothers with nannies that I had unwittingly joined, mutual grievances were shared and a sort of homespun, do-it-yourself legislation was constantly in flux. "Why should I pay my nanny when *I* go on vacation?" asked one. "My nanny needs back surgery and has no health insurance. What happens if I don't pay for it?" asked another. Among the talk, one horror story inevitably emerged that set off a tsunami of paranoia. A child drowned in a pool while his nanny looked on. It was her fault because, as one woman put it, "the nanny didn't know how to swim." I found out that Marta didn't know how to swim either and, wondering what else she might not know how to do, I immediately enrolled her in a Spanish CPR course. It was an ironic gesture because I'd never taken one myself, and God forbid I should have to, say, perform the Heimlich maneuver. But Marta was now spending more time with my daughter than I did (a sobering reality), so what if Celeste plummeted down a cliff? Or got burned? Or needed mouth-to-mouth?

However, CPR, so I was told, was the least of my worries. Because while a surface wound could always be dressed—a skinned knee, a broken bone—an emotional one lasts forever. And it was here that the NannyCam asserted itself—that wireless hidden camera with 2.4-Ghz video transmitter and receiver stuffed inside a fluffy teddy bear. Never mind the suspicions that a nanny might steal, lift, or somehow lick the frosting off our hardwon cakes. "I caught my nanny screaming at Cindy. I fired her on the spot and got a NannyCam," said a neighbor. When I asked what she thought of this egregious infringement of privacy she replied, "What's more important, your nanny's privacy or your child's well-being?" Familiar prime-time horror stories of abuse and abductions floated in the ether here. But when does simple discipline—a stern voice, a time-out—turn into actual abuse? (In France, a little slap on the rump will raise eyebrows only if those brows belong to Americans.) And what mother left to care for toddlers and clean house for eight hours a day (or more) wouldn't scream from time to time, let alone pull her own hair out?

Oblivious to the irony, we shuttle to parenting workshops to figure it all out while the nanny stays home with the kids. And perched in a crib there is the NannyCam, a mechanical eye patrolling a static corner of the nanny's world. Meanwhile, the nannies get the big picture of *our* lives. Marta, who'd joined a sisterhood of her own in our neighborhood, came home with stories from the front: tales from the nanny who worked in the messy "piggy house." Or the place where they had "those bad videos" (she shook her head: porn). There were the hair-raising fights, the piles of dirty underwear, an unlocked gun found in a dresser. I was intrigued by the dirty little world behind the closed doors in this preternaturally calm suburb where we lived. And then I wondered: what does Marta tell other nannies about us? After all, she was exposed to it all: the intimacy of a rumpled sheet mangle after a love tryst, the domestic spats.

But what unsettled me most was not that Marta was witness to the private inner life of our home—it was the growing intimacy that she shared with my daughter. One night I returned late from a meeting. It was one of my favorite moments—the dreamy joy of coming home, the look of angelic repose on my children's faces. I tiptoed into my daughter's room, where a mobile of bright fish slowly turned. But when I pulled down the sheet for a silent goodnight kiss, there was Marta, her face nestled against my daughter's as they curled into one another, both asleep. Though I'd fallen asleep countless times putting Celeste to bed, I was vexed by the image. For Marta and Celeste were clearly a duo now, partaking in their daily routine of outings, meals, naps—moments of joy and disgruntlement, the stuff of life. Here was a web of emotional exchanges that the NannyCam could not pick up: invisible bonds that for many mothers are the hidden source of deeply charged and complex emotions. For to see these growing bonds between nanny and child is to experience the silent confirmation that a mother's role has potentially been usurped: her role as the child's one and only mother, the one who should be tucking the kids into bed at night, the one who should be doing the disciplining. Perhaps that's why the nanny exercising normal discipline becomes unacceptable to a mother.

It was in this context that I had implicitly asked Marta to love my child as she would love her own. And she rose to the task with an almost swooning attachment to my daughter. So why shouldn't my daughter love her back? Let her exercise her own heart muscle, I thought. Let her learn to spread her love around. Still, there was lingering discomfort. Possessive mother, guilty conscience. I roused Marta awake. "Sorry, Marta. It's late." She woke, bleary eyed, and shuffled into her room.

By now Marta was fully entrenched in our lives. I was part of this community of white women shuttling nannies who stood at bus stops and gas stations, wearing Salvation Army parkas, waiting for *la patrona* to pull up in her big car. I'd grown used to the luxuries of a nanny as well: the conflagration of messes that were instantly cleaned up, the beds made, countless gestures and chores that I was spared, that would have weighed me down immeasurably. One day, nearly a year into her job, I stumbled on a photo of Marta from her early days and was shocked to see how much younger she looked. She had clearly aged while taking care of my kids—new lines on her face that were meant for my face, the toll of this life. Meanwhile, we continued to live together, waking up and falling asleep at the same hour. Over the months I noticed that we were even menstruating at the same time, aloft on the same jet streams of pheromones. And yet our worlds would never really meet. On the day the World Trade Center collapsed, I stood at the TV and beckoned Marta to watch. She stood beside me with her broom in hand, taking it all in. After a while she seemed restless. "Where is that?" she asked.

That evening, like every night after her bath, Marta spoke with her husband, whom she saw on weekends. She sometimes talked for hours, and I wondered what on earth she could possibly have to say after a long, repetitious day of caretaking. And then I'd feel shame. Because, of course, beyond the walls of my home, this woman had a life. They all had lives. One day my friend opened the medicine cabinet in the bathroom that her nanny, Ana, shared with her children and found a bottle of herbal aphrodisiac. "Oh my God," my friend exclaimed. "Ana has a sex life!" Yes, they all have sex lives, we discover, and different sexual credos as well. Marta did not approve when my son ran around naked, his little *zakette* flopping around. Likewise, she thought it was insolent to let Celeste go to bed without underwear. "Marta, it's not healthy to wear underwear to bed," I said. "You don't go to bed with underwear yourself." To which she looked at me, a bit perplexed. "Of course I do." That night I dreamt that I came home unexpectedly in the middle of the day. I walked into the bathroom and there, in the bathtub, my son and Marta were making love. Marta looked at me, horrified. "Oh my God," she cried out. And the dream ended. The next morning I could barely look her in the eye.

Like kids who are surprised to discover their teachers outside the classroom ("What are you doing *here?*" my son asked when we bumped into his kindergarten teacher at a supermarket one day), we're surprised to see our nannies in their own personal habitat. In fact, we rarely do. But my daughter was now supremely interested in doing so. "Can I go to Marta's apartment?" she asked. "Please?" I am loath to admit that my first response was conflicted. If I let my daughter spend time with Marta at her home on weekends, would I shift the emotional barometer in Marta's favor, give her too much power, too much latitude? But the implications of not letting Celeste see Marta's world were just as inglorious: my daughter, growing up in a lily-white world, with private patrol cars, suburban values, and no clue as to how the "other half" lives.

How the other half lives. I had a glimpse once, nearly forty years ago, of the place where Martas and Marias come from. It was the sixties. My mother, in a gesture of immense goodwill and naïveté, was determined to help our housekeeper, Maria—not as her employer, but as a mother. And so she told my two siblings and me to pack our duffel bags and get ready for a trip. With no papers and no husband, Maria stayed behind while we boarded a Greyhound bus and journeyed into the heart of Mexico, to bring Maria's children back to the States.

Somehow my mother found them, a little boy and a girl. Here's what I remember: One room divided by a shower curtain. Neighbors living in discarded appliance boxes. A dusty, corn-yellow sky in a sad place of troubling Otherness. Preparations were made in a flurry of movement and muffled Spanish. The same Greyhound bus retraced its road northbound a few days later. We were now a family, an ad hoc family of five. After an interminable night drive, North America beckoned just over the horizon. Freedom—and *mama*—was just a stone's throw away. But once we were in Tijuana, two border police greeted my mother and her five children: three white faces, two dark faces. *Who are you? The mother? Of all these children? Where is the father? Where are their papers?*

What was she thinking? My mother was a bad liar. Confronted with these basic questions, she couldn't improvise her way out of her own best intentions gone awry, nor could she cross the tremendous divide between her world and Maria's. Overwhelmed with remorse, she realized that the doors to freedom that had opened just a crack were now being irrevocably shut. The girl, in a paroxysm of grief, broke down. Her brother was stoic; the good graces of simple people prevailed. The bus driver assured my mother that he would get Maria's children back home. The border police didn't press charges. When we said good-bye, the little boy was holding his sister, who had collapsed in his arms. "It will be okay," my mother heard him repeat over and over to his sister. "It will be okay. It will be okay." He was all of seven or eight years old. Decades later, the emotional resonance of that moment still haunts my mother. "I'll never know if I did the right thing," she said.

• • •

"Mommy, Marta lives far away," my daughter said. "She lives very, very, very far away." This was true. I had dropped Marta off at her place on weekends but had never met her entire family. On her dresser in our home the faces of her two children were framed: her son standing in a colorful but shabby living room, her daughter in a blue satin dress posing for her Sweet Sixteen. They were both being brought up by sisters or aunts thousands of miles away, and Marta had not seen them in six years. I could not imagine the economic hardships that had compelled her to leave them, never mind the emotional ones she now had to shoulder. I probed only tentatively, protected by our language barrier, because I was certain that the truth would be too painful.

So how could I reproach her when other mothers commented that she was not "bubbly" enough? How could I bother her when she stared out the window at times, introspective and brooding? Could I blame her if there was a transference of love from her children to mine? For she had become like a second mother to Celeste, responded to her with effusive affection, indulged her with candies and tortillas despite my protestations. "It is good when little girls become *gordita*," she said. But I didn't want my daughter to become a *little fatty*. I was aware of a contemptible sentiment, but there it was: I adored Marta for her effusive love, but I was wary of our worlds overlapping. Conversely, I was aware of Marta's quiet disapproval of me—of my need to establish boundaries, to define certain limits as my children grew. "My daughter slept in my bed until she was ten years old," Marta said. "What is wrong with that?" I didn't answer. Instead, I asked her to lock her bedroom so that Celeste would not run into her bed if she woke up at night. If anything, I wanted her running into *my* bed.

"Can I go to Marta's house? Can I?" my daughter continued to ask. "One day," I said. But one day we traveled to a different place. It was the dinner hour, and Celeste was having a tantrum, with all the fiery histrionics of a two-year-old on a rampage. She threw her food across the kitchen. I spoke to her in a sharp voice; Mommy was clearly not happy. She ran out of the kitchen and headed for Marta's room. Before I could grab her, Marta had scooped her up. *"Chickie-tita,"* she said. *"Mama-linda."* She stroked her hair. "What is wrong with my baby?" Celeste hung onto Marta with a defiant look as if to say, *Come and get me.* And that is precisely what I did. "Marta," I said. "Give Celeste to me." Celeste wrapped her legs harder around Marta, then strained past her at the lure of the TV. Marta held Celeste and did not move. "Marta," I repeated. "Give me Celeste." And in that fleeting moment Marta did the one thing she should never have done: She did not give my child back to me.

And so we were finally at this place: a pinnacle where the slippery slope of love and power divided us, the ground zero of our true distrust and suspicion. All of the sociocultural complexities behind our relationship fell away, and what was left was a weighted sense of loss and displaced motherhood. I had implicitly asked Marta to love my child like her own but never to cross that invisible line. But she did. Could I reproach her for that as well? I was unsettled by the need to reassert my role as both mother and employer. Later we spoke at length and found a truce, but something had definitively shifted. There was distrust on both sides now: not only mine of Marta, but Marta's of me. For what mother makes her child cry like that? What mother does not immediately and unconditionally console? What mother, by extension, dresses her girl in boys' shorts or lets her kids run around naked? Perhaps, underneath it all, there was also the unconscious questioning of our mutual predicament, in all its cruel and relentless irony. For what mother lets her children be raised by other people? And the answer is: mothers just like us.

The ensuing days were strained. I felt like I'd ripped out a little piece of Marta's heart, and this sadness moved me to do something I'm loath to admit: One day I went into her room and rummaged through her affairs. Why was I here? Was I trying to understand Marta in some way? Or get closer to her? There was her faded blue purse. A small phone book with numbers written with curious childlike precision. A half-used tube of Ben-Gay (a reminder that caretaking is backbreaking work). I pulled open the drawer of her bedside table, and there was her *Libro Catolico de Oraciones*. I noticed that Marta had underlined several verses in red. I don't read Spanish well, but I got the drift: the prayers, the yearning for salvation and God-like intervention. This was such a different world from mine, a world of painful crowns of thorns, flaming red hearts, resurrections. I imagined Marta at night, exhausted after a long day cleaning house and watching Celeste. With her Bible and her Ben-Gay, she was praying for a better life.

I didn't know if she would get this better life. But inevitably the time came: Celeste was rapidly approaching preschool age and soon, I would no longer need Marta's services. I dreaded the moment, for I'd grown to care deeply for this woman—even the confrontations and the strain had become a source of connection between us. But now there was the queer sensation that she was already fading into memory even as she stood in front of me; that she was already moving into that oneiric place where all Martas and Marias and Anas went—dark-skinned women and mothers who shepherd our children through some of the most pristine moments of their lives. I had my own memory of our house-keeper, Maria—a strange but faded confluence of images from the sixties: there was *Gilligan's Island*, Black Panthers, flower power . . . and Maria, ironing, chasing us through a messy house. What had ever happened to Maria? Did she ever reunite with her children, whose lives were marked by that effusive and naïve American *patrona* so long ago? And what would happen to Marta? What would Celeste remember of her as Marta slowly dissipated from the urgency of the moment?

Six months after she stopped working for us as a live-in nanny, Marta still comes by to clean our house. When she crosses paths with Celeste en route to preschool they are overjoyed to see each other. Paradoxically, a new closeness has developed between the two of us in the absence of our live-in relationship, with all its emotional gray zones. Marta has still not found a new full-time job and she worries. She needs the money: Her son in Belize has health problems. Her daughter, who was accepted to medical school in Juarez, is pregnant. Now Marta wonders—and the irony does not escape her: Who will take care of my daughter's child? Who will take care of my grandchild? Meanwhile, she continues to look for new work and does lots of housecleaning. One woman gave her a handwritten list of instructions broken down in great detail. Marta showed it to me: *Toilet bowls, tubs, showers, and sinks in bathrooms must be scrubbed with Clorox prior to use of antibacterial deodorizer. Floors mopped with Lysol kitchen cleaner and Clorox used on counters, stovetop, refrigerator, and all cabinetry prior to use of appliance cleaner. Iron sheets and towels in addition to designated clothing.* Marta sighed. "It's a lot of work." "Yes," I said, "but at least you know exactly what you're getting yourself into." She smiled as if it were consolation, though we both knew that it was not.

Iranian Revelation

Katherine Whitney

I was six months pregnant with our second child when Farhad and I finally got married. Technically we'd been married for seven years, but this was our religious wedding, uniting us as Muslim husband and wife, and the necessary first step of a journey to visit Farhad's family in Iran. As Farhad's Muslim wife, I was entitled to an Iranian passport, which would facilitate my travel in Iran. Without it, the authorities wouldn't recognize us as married. Bound by the laws that segregate unrelated men and women, Farhad and I couldn't even stay in the same hotel room.

Our original wedding was on a bluff overlooking Tomales Bay, California. We created an untraditional wedding ceremony "from whole cloth," as the saying goes, writing our own vows and commissioning a rendition of *The Owl and the Pussycat* for violin and double bass. Overwhelmed by nuptial details, Farhad let his mother direct the Iranian portion of the wedding. Guity and her friends prepared the *Sofreh-ye Aghd*: a satin cloth laid out with candles, eggs, flowers, and sweets. During the ceremony they held a silk canopy over our heads while our guests rubbed pillars of sugar above it to ensure sweetness in our marriage. And Farhad's sister Nasie surreptitiously instructed my sister to sew a few stitches into the canopy, a tradition that symbolizes sewing shut the lips of my future mother-in-law.

Following that ceremony, however, there was little Iranian flavor to our daily lives. It wasn't until we became parents that I began to wonder what of my husband's Iranian heritage would be passed on to our children. We gave them Iranian names, but would they speak Farsi, or be familiar with Iranian folktales? And who would teach them? It was beyond my scope, but it didn't seem important to Farhad. When it came time for "family sharing" at Leyla's preschool, I dragged Farhad in to present *Noruz*, the Iranian New Year. I had researched the holiday on the Internet and printed out pictures for the kids to color in. However, it took us a few years to transition from presenting *Noruz* at school to celebrating it at home. As Leyla got older and more captivated by ritual and tradition—and more curious about what it meant to be Iranian—our *Noruz* celebrations became more elaborate. But it was also clear that if we were going to observe *Noruz* or anything else Iranian, I was going to have to organize it. Farhad, seemingly indifferent to his heritage, had left the mining of his culture to me.

Farhad left Iran when he was just sixteen, sent to the U.S. by his parents in 1979 to escape the revolution. From his perspective it was a great adventure, liberating him from a protected childhood. Once here, he focused on blending in as best he could. When I met him in college, he was barely distinguishable from his young male counterparts—a smart, funny, basketball fan with only a slight foreign mystique about him. And even though I'd known him thirteen years by the time we got married, I knew next to nothing about his Iranian past. He rarely mentioned it. Instead, after Nasie moved to the Bay Area and we'd spent more time with her family and friends, I realized how *un*-Iranian he was. Nasie's friends marveled at his nontraditional, enthusiastic parenting style and his renowned abilities in the kitchen—"such great *pad thai*," they'd whisper to me, eyes wide.

Slowly, over time, the Iranian touches in our family life expanded beyond *Noruz*. Farhad served up pomegranate margaritas to our dinner guests and created his own version of the traditional *noon panir sabsi* appetizer, adding olives, dates, and nuts to the bread, cheese, and greens. Authenticity was less important than providing a tasty conversational gambit at parties, especially in a city where people are almost competing to be the most ethnic. But aside from adding to the multicultural demographics at Leyla's school, I still wasn't sure what our children would gain from their Iranian bloodline. Would an interesting cuisine be all they absorbed of the culture? Would they feel cheated out of half of their heritage someday? Or would they just want to be thoroughly American, as their father had seemed to become?

Now, with our son's imminent arrival and the pressure mounting for us to make good on our promise to visit his parents, it was time for Farhad to assume his Iranian mantle in earnest and get us married. After scouring the Iranian Yellow Pages, he found someone who would perform the ceremony. We drove with two friends—our witnesses, Fran and Arlene—to our appointment with Mehri, a smartly dressed woman who welcomed us into her small apartment.

Mehri began with counseling for the infidel. Sitting beside me on a couch, she looked me in the eye and informed me that I must give up allegiance to my Christian god. I stared back at her and nodded. I must become a devotee of Allah and subscribe to the teachings of the prophet Mohammed. Again I nodded, somehow maintaining eye contact. She knew I was lying. This was a marriage of convenience. I just wanted to sleep in the same hotel room with my husband.

After my drive-through Persian Pre-Cana, Mehri put Farhad on the spot. "What are you going to give your wife?" she demanded. Farhad, unfamiliar with the Persian custom of giving a special wedding gift to his bride, stared at her blankly. "You must give her a present," she insisted. "What about jewelry?"

"I've already given her a lot of jewelry," Farhad sputtered. At this point Fran and Arlene chimed in, indignant that Farhad would try to shirk his culturally mandated responsibilities. He reluctantly suggested that he would buy me something. But Mehri demanded details—she was writing them into our marriage contract. "Gold?" she asked. "Diamonds?" Farhad was as vague as she'd let him be, and we got on with the ceremony. In the end she handed us a tacky certificate with a border of dot-matrix hearts, encased in a blue plastic folder. This hardly seemed a substantial foundation for my new citizenship, or my now official status as an Iranian wife in good standing.

Two years into our Muslim union, I had seen no signs of wrath from Allah. Nor had I seen any significant jewelry, gold or otherwise. And we still hadn't applied for our Iranian passports. But our son, Kian, was sixteen months old, and the pressure to visit Iran had intensified. We made a plan to take the kids in September of 2003, after the initial crisis of the Iraq war had settled down.

Despite years of cultivated apathy, Farhad was excited about taking the kids to see where he'd grown up. I was excited too, and curious. I wondered if the kids would be fascinated or bored, and whether the close-knit Iranian family would be cozy and welcoming or overpowering. Would Farhad come back with a renewed interest in the culture that he would want to share with Leyla and Kian? I was also wary about playing the Iranian wife, concerned about the unclear cultural expectations for an American mother of half-Iranian children. When I first met Farhad's family, Farhad and I had been a couple for only a short time. And although I made great efforts to be warm and courteous—nodding and smiling as people chatted in Farsi all around me—it wasn't enough. Farhad could tell me only after the fact that I'd been perceived as cold and passive. Since then I've evolved in their eyes from the American girlfriend (whose loyalty to their son/brother/cousin was reflexively questioned) to a devoted wife and mother. I've won Guity over—sending pictures of her grandchildren and writing long letters detailing our daily life. Nonetheless, I knew that I would need to be on my best behavior in Iran for the sake of my husband and to set an example for my thoroughly American children. But meeting the standards of conduct in Iran would be a challenge, and I wasn't sure how much direction I would get from Farhad, even now.

Preparation for our journey continued with pictures for our new passports. In compliance with Islamic law, I covered my head with a large paisley shawl I'd dug out of a drawer, and smiled for the camera. Leyla, then six, dressed up in a leopard print velour ensemble, brushed her hair, and smiled widely. Even Kian, held up against the wall in his jammies, presented a happy face. Then we enlisted Nasie's help. She rejected my passport picture, which revealed my hair and neck. So I pulled a black turtleneck partially on so that only my face was showing. In the final picture, I looked grim and repressed. Perfect.

Once we'd completed the paperwork, it didn't take long for our new passports to arrive. And before we knew it, September was upon us. The usual flurry of back-to-school mania was magnified by preparations for our trip. In the midst of all this, Farhad assumed an altered state. He often departs for his business trips before he actually leaves the house, his mind far away from home as he gathers and packs his things. But this time it was different: maybe it was the prospect of bringing his new family to his old home, or the pressure of having to buy gifts for everyone we would encounter in Iran—from his parents and other relatives to the man who waters the pomegranate trees in his father's orchard. His father had sent a lengthy list with requests for items he can't get in Iran: disease-resistant tomato seeds, Phillips' Milk of Magnesia, and human insulin "to be kept cold throughout the journey." Recognizing that this was not my husband and that the normal ground rules no longer applied, I adopted a "yes, dear" attitude that I suspected I'd have to maintain until we were home from Iran.

Nasie, veteran of many trips back home, came by one day with two huge rolling suitcases. Once these were filled to the brim with gifts and requested items I dragged them to the front hall where they sat, a huge hulking presence. I could barely lift them, but they were mine to carry for the first leg of our journey, along with my own luggage and the two kids. Farhad, traveling ahead of us to Paris, didn't want to be burdened with extra luggage on his business trip. After I pressed him, he agreed to take one of the huge bags, but joked, "You're a second-class citizen, baby, get used to it!" I wondered how much this would be true in the weeks to come.

Driving Farhad to the airport the next day, happy at having been relieved of one of the suitcases, I was back in "yes, dear" mode until Farhad mused, "You know, last time Nasie came back from Iran, she was by herself with *five* huge suitcases and two children. And one kid had diarrhea." Resisting the urge to slam on the brakes and throw him and his luggage onto the side of the highway, I replied through gritted teeth, "If I had no choice but to carry fifteen suitcases and two vomiting children with me to meet you in Paris I certainly *could*. However, I was hoping you'd be happy to help me out." I dropped him and his luggage at the curb and parked the car. When I met up with him in the terminal, Farhad apologized, back to his normal self again for the few minutes before he passed through security.

Still in America, I was already between two cultures, balancing both the familiar responsibilities of an American working mother and the unfamiliar assignment of Iranian wife. I spent my last precious afternoons driving around in search of the remaining items for Dr. Farzaneh. In addition to his list, I had myriad lists of my own: the list of things I had to do before leaving for three weeks, like informing my clients I'd be gone and getting keys to the house sitter; the list of toys and food that would keep my kids entertained and emotionally stable during the long plane trips; and the list of clothing I'd need to buy to comply with the Islamic dress code and still remain somewhat cool and comfortable. September is extremely hot in Iran, and according to Islamic law I would be required to cover my hair, shoulders, arms, legs, and ankles and conceal the shape of my body. All females over the age of nine must wear a *hejab*, or head scarf, a baggy trench coat, and trousers. I'd received no direction from Farhad in this area, and now he was gone. So I bought baggy linen pants and a linen overcoat—things I'd never wear at home— and hoped for the best.

Predictably, the solo-parented flight to Paris was long and hellish, thanks to my screaming, writhing, kicking toddler. The next morning, in Paris, reunited with my husband, I folded my Western clothes and packed them, along with my American passport, deep in my suitcase. I put on the baggy linen pants and stuffed the jacket and paisley scarf in my carry-on bag. Though Nasie had rejected this scarf for my passport picture, Farhad had assured me that it would be fine in Iran: the rules in the street are less strict than for a passport. "That picture was going deep into the belly of the beast," he explained. But at the airport, I looked around self-consciously at the Iranian women milling about the airline counter. There was a wide range of dress, from sophisticated Parisian pantsuits to black *chadors*—the all-encompassing head and body covering worn by traditional Muslim women. I felt like a peasant in my baggy linen trousers. Perhaps I should have worn more tailored pants instead. Were *any* other women wearing sandals? And when did I need to put my scarf on? Farhad didn't know.

The closer we got to the gate, the more homogenous the crowd became, and the more the kids and I stood out. Even if my clothes had been more in line with what the Iranian women were wearing, my bright blue eyes would have given me away. The kids' eyes are brown like their father's, but their light hair betrayed their mixed blood, especially Leyla's wavy, strawberry blond corona.

When we landed in Tehran, the women around me slipped on their scarves. Theirs were small and sheer, nothing like my heavy, woolen shawl. I struggled to get it on and keep it from slipping while carrying Kian and my bag off the plane. A man commented to Farhad in Farsi, "How can you possibly explain to a foreigner what we ask them to do in our country?"

In the crowded airport lobby we looked for Guity, who had traveled to Tehran from Farhad's family home in the southern city of Shiraz to meet us. I spotted her and smiled—I hadn't seen her since Leyla was a newborn. She stared blankly at first, not recognizing me with my head covered. Then she reached out her arms, laughing and crying at the same time.

As Guity dried her tears, Kian sprinted away from us across the lobby. I caught up to him just as he ran through the door to the outside. When I tried to re-enter the airport, I was stopped by an armed guard. At first I panicked—I had no money, no identification, and I couldn't speak the language; I wasn't even sure that

Farhad knew where I was. It turned out that I'd tried to go in through the men's entrance. The guard pointed to the women's entrance, draped with black curtains to hide the goings-on from the eyes of men. Inside, berobed women checked the contents of my pockets and waved a metal-detecting wand over us before allowing us to pass.

Accompanying Guity were Afsaneh and Mastoneh, her sister Parvoneh's daughters, whom I'd looked forward to meeting for some time. These smart, independent, lively women had embraced me from afar despite never having met me, sending friendly e-mails and reaching out to their only American cousin. It was after midnight local time when we arrived at Parvoneh's apartment. She had converted her bedroom into a barracks for us, with mattresses extending from wall to wall. Exhausted and giddy, we stumbled into bed. "This is what I love about Iranians," Farhad said to me as we lay in the dark, trying to calm our over-tired children. "They come meet us at the airport in the middle of the night, and then give up their bedroom." I took note of what he said, thinking it would be only the first of many things he would reveal to me.

The next day, Afsaneh brought me a light silk scarf to replace my woolen shawl. Smaller and nearly sheer, it was much better in the heat, and I was grateful to finally get some sartorial assistance. I remembered a newspaper article I'd read about a woman who owns an Iranian delicatessen near San Francisco. Around *Noruz*, she told the reporter, she reaches out to the American wives of Iranian men who wander into her shop unsure how to prepare for this important holiday, looking for guidance they don't get at home. My Iranian husband had brought me here, but like the shopkeeper, the women would help me fit in.

Warm, generous, and patient, the cousins took a day off work to drive us around the city and show us the sights. After dinner we piled into their mother's ancient Toyota and drove to the cooler hills of northern Tehran. Although Farhad had tried to prepare us for the chaos of Iranian traffic, the reality was terrifying. Cars zigzagged across the road, ignoring the painted lines dividing traffic into lanes, refusing to stop at the lights. Leyla was at once nervous and intrigued by the lack of seat belts. "Why don't you have seat belts?" she asked Afsaneh, who was driving down the middle of two lanes of traffic. "We have too many seat belts already in this society," Afsaneh obliquely replied.

We parked the car and walked up a trail lined with cafés, kebab shops, and drink stalls, where crowds of people were out walking and socializing in the cooler evening air. Traditionally dressed women clad head to toe in black robes mixed with younger women pushing the limits of the dress code in cropped pants and remarkably tight trench coats. Their scarves sat far back on their heads, merely a nod to the law, though Afsaneh took pains to adjust mine over the nape of my neck.

We left the next day for Shiraz, where we were greeted at the airport by an entourage: Dr. Farzaneh, the paterfamilias; his sister; her husband; as well as the family driver and his son. I began my campaign of relentless cheerfulness, good manners, and grace and embraced everyone.

We arrived hot and sweaty at the Farzanehs' home. At the end of a quiet, narrow, dead-end alley off the busy main road, a tall wooden door opened onto a beautiful garden courtyard. Invisible from the street, it was an oasis of tall green trees, running water, and flowering plants. We women removed our scarves and all of us sat outside to drink *secanjebeen*—a refreshing drink of mint and shaved cucumber. The sun had set, and the evening was cooling down. The plants had just been watered, giving off the scent of fresh dirt. In the calm stillness, Kian ran around merrily and Leyla, despite being totally excluded from the conversation going on around her in Farsi, tried really hard to be polite. Later, when the suitcases had been unpacked and the gifts doled out, she glided from room to room with a shawl tied around her head, deep into make believe.

Our days in Shiraz were leisurely and languid, slowed by the heat and the baby. I tried to let go of my itch to get out and see more of the country and instead to just enjoy being in Iran, hanging around the house, making modest excursions, watching the kids connect with their grandparents.

As a toddler just learning to talk, Kian's experience was sensory and social, just as it would have been at home. He loved his low sleigh bed that had once been Farhad's, so shiny with fresh paint that it looked new. For Kian, it was like being in a little boat. He could get himself in but not out, lifting himself up on his arms as high as he could and then, using his belly as a fulcrum, tipping forward, planting his face on the sheets, feet flailing in the air. Each morning he woke and cried, "Mamani! Mamani, come!" Guity played peek-a-boo through the curtains and then took him downstairs, leaving the rest of us to sleep a little longer. Outside in the garden Kian would cheerfully greet Dr. Farzaneh, kissing him on the cheek. One morning he climbed into his stroller and stretched out his hand, beckoning his grandfather. "Bia, Baba, bia," he said. Baba rose stiffly from his chair and pushed the stroller slowly around the garden, with Kian looking very smug. "You make me young," Dr. Farzaneh told him, beaming.

Leyla was utterly entranced by the nuances of Iranian life, which fueled her already rich, passionate imagination. One afternoon I sat alone in a seldom-used sitting room. Though the sun was still high in the sky, it was a little dark inside, and a breeze played with the sheer white curtain at the open window. Leyla flitted into the room talking to herself, sprawling on the overstuffed velvet chairs. She lifted up the cover of a glass dish filled with sweets, slipped a treat into her pocket, and flitted out, barely aware that I was there.

Another day we visited the tomb of the poet Saadi, which Farhad had loved visiting when he was young. Leyla stood before a reflecting pool, staring at the coins on the bottom glinting in the sun. "If I had a coin I know what wish I would make," she said, "that Iranian culture would be free." Taking three coins from Farhad she made three wishes, keeping the other two secret.

We descended into the underground teahouse to see the fish pond beneath the domed tile ceiling. Leyla leaned over the tiled barrier to look at the fish and Farhad smiled, watching his daughter do the same thing he'd done as a child. But in the close quarters of the teahouse, Leyla got self conscious. "Everybody's staring at me because of my stupid red hair," she whispered. I told her that their curiosity was kind, not hostile. "It makes my face turn red," she replied, longing to blend in with the other Iranian children.

After lunch one afternoon, Guity, Farhad, and I sat together in the kitchen drinking tea. Guity was taking a rare break from her routine of managing the house; she spoke English for my benefit even though it was tiring for her. As she and Farhad told stories of their accomplished and eccentric family, I saw a different side to my husband. He was calm, happy, and reflective—more relaxed than I'd ever seen him. Was the shift in his behavior because of the warmth and comfort of unconditional maternal love? Or was Iran, and his childhood home, the one place in the world where Farhad was truly comfortable? I realized this was the first time I'd seen him in his native country, at home.

Thanks to the barriers of language and cultural understanding, most of the time I was unaware of what was going on around me: where we were trying to go, what time we were supposed to be there, and who was waiting for us. Yes, I was insecure in my role as an Iranian wife and mother; I wasn't juggling clients against soccer practices or maneuvering my work around the babysitter's availability. I'd forsaken both control and responsibility, but instead of feeling excluded, I felt oddly liberated.

Farhad glided seamlessly between English and Farsi, forgetting what language he was speaking and unaware that I didn't understand half of what he was saying. If I was in the room, he assumed I heard him say to his mom (in Farsi) that we would be ready to go to the bazaar or the museum or the restaurant in ten minutes. Then he would become confused and irritated when I didn't jump up and get ready. "We've been trying to get out of here all morning," Farhad would complain. Until that point I would be unaware that we were trying to do anything besides hang out in the garden playing with trucks. I would round up shoes, diapers, water, and snacks, put on my frock and scarf, gather the kids, and get in the car. There I would sit in the heat, conserving energy by not talking, my lack of Farsi all the more convenient. I was so hot in my overcoat and scarf that, despite the glaring sun, I finally abandoned my sunglasses because they just slipped down my sweaty nose.

Official government slogans proclaim that "the *chador* is a woman's freedom." Though clearly propaganda, there was an ironic truth to it, at least for a while. Aside from the discomfort of wearing so many layers in the heat, I found my prescriptive Iranian wardrobe unexpectedly freeing as well. I wore the same linen overcoat every time we went out. My floppy linen pants were basically cool and comfortable and did a remarkable job of hiding the dirt. Confined by the law, I was not responsible for, nor was I judged by, my appearance. But then again I was only a visitor—I hadn't been forced to cover myself for the past two decades.

One afternoon Guity dressed in formal black for the funeral of a twenty-year-old boy who had been struck down while crossing the street. She cursed the regime that demanded that she wear a long black trench coat, black stockings, and a black scarf in the oppressive heat. As Guity got dressed, Leyla sat on her bed mesmerized by a basket of scarves, pulling out one after another, holding them up to the light, tying them under her chin, listening to our every word. "When it ends, I will take these scarves out into the garden and set them on fire," Guity declared. "Oh, no," Leyla cried. "Send them to me!"

Eager to spend some time alone with her grandchildren, Guity urged us to do some traveling on our own. So Farhad and I left the kids and went for an overnight to Esphahan, one of the finest cities in the Islamic world. With Farhad the happiest and most relaxed I'd ever seen him, I looked forward to being a couple again, even if only for twenty-four hours. And I was eager to see more of Iran through his eyes, without the children's needs distracting my attention. Yet, as we walked down the aisle of the packed plane, I felt acutely self conscious, and instinctively I reached for my kids—who of course were not there. Until that moment my universal identity as a mother had mitigated my foreignness. I felt suddenly naked without the protective cloak of motherhood.

Arriving in jewel-like Esphahan, we had dinner under the stars, surrounded by fountains in the magnificent, romantic courtyard garden of our elegant hotel. After dinner we walked to the beautiful *Pol-e Si-o-Seh*, or Bridge of Thirty-three Arches. Descending the stairs to the riverbank, we went under the bridge onto a patio extending over the water. A cool wind blew, and we sat with our backs to the bridge, looking over the water and the city beyond. The dank, swampy smells of the river mixed with sweet smoke of water pipes. The tea was warm and I drank too much of it, not wanting to censor my experience in any way.

For a snapshot in time we were ourselves again, a couple in easy sync, traveling and having an adventure in a foreign land. As we strolled in and out of the shops in the city's expansive bazaar the next day, Farhad began haggling, teasing, and bonding with the shopkeepers. He was in his element: connecting with people, hearing their stories, joking around—the charming, curious guy I'd married. And yet I was seeing another side of him as well, just as I had in his mother's kitchen: that of an Iranian man in Iran, reveling in a lifetime of cultural understanding. While Farhad talked and talked, I wandered around each tiny shop, looking at every last item. I longed to move on together; as fascinated as I was to see my husband in this new light, I was also eager to linger in our intimate experience of the city, to understand more of what I was finding so indefinably Iranian before we had to head back to Shiraz. The afternoon was closing in on us and we were running out of time, but I wasn't in control.

On the plane back to Shiraz, Farhad basked in the memory of the bazaar. Stories of his childhood bubbled up: how his mother, charming and warm, once sat with a tailor through hours of conversation and innumerable cups of tea before walking out with a pair of pants at the price she'd wanted. Or about an old restaurant in the Shiraz bazaar where the waiters wore traditional baggy pants, felt hats, and colorful sashes, and how magical it was to see the dust floating in the beams of sunlight streaming through holes in the walls. I was grateful for the stories. But they heightened my sense of missing out on the richest facets of our trip.

Near the end of our visit we accompanied Farhad's aunt Mahine to the mosque where his paternal grandparents are buried. In keeping with the rigid dress code required in religious places, I was ordered to put on socks, shoes (no sandals today), a scarf, overcoat and, on top of all that, a *chador*. Mahine sent Farhad back into the house to get a more formal long-sleeved shirt. This was the first time he'd had to wear anything other than a T-shirt the whole time we'd been in Iran. Although men are not allowed to wear shorts, their wardrobe is otherwise not strictly controlled.

"Aaaaaah," he grumbled as he struggled to pull the shirt on over his T-shirt. We were out of the car and in front of the mosque. "Be thankful you don't have to wear a *chador*," I mumbled under my breath. "It's not that bad," he replied. I wanted to remind him that his mother had wanted to burn her scarves in the garden. But as a "good Iranian wife," I felt I couldn't complain. I had begun to feel stifled: I'd been grinning and bearing a lot, and because I hadn't spoken up, Farhad assumed I was as happy as he was.

As we walked toward the mosque, it was all I could do to move forward without becoming completely unraveled. These Muslims clerics clearly fear the power of women. Why else would they tie them up in robes, scarves, *chadors*, and long skirts and send them out in the heat? How could anyone fight back when they were doing all they could to grasp fields of cloth around their middle and keep their damn hair from showing? The *chador* is a ridiculous contraption, meant to be draped over the head, then gathered up in each arm, swept across the front of the body, and secured under an armpit. With any luck, one arm will be free. The whole operation is destined to fail, which is why even the most devout, experienced Islamic woman is constantly adjusting and

readjusting the layers of fabric binding her. I was fairly compe-
tently draped when I left the house, but getting into and out of the
car had undone me. Each time I tugged the *chador* forward, the
head scarf underneath slipped farther and farther back. Unsure of
the consequences of taking it all off and starting over, an action
that would expose my hair in public, I clutched the *chador* under
my chin in desperation to preserve my modesty.

We entered the mosque through separate doors. A man wearing thick white woolen gloves took our shoes and stuffed them
into a little cubby. A high wall separated the women's section
from the rest of the mosque. In this small alcove, women in black
robes lounged about on the floor and leaned back against elaborate mirror-tiled walls. Some held babies. Others leaned forward
to pray, ignoring the toddlers who climbed all over them.

Mahine said a prayer, and I stood awkwardly beside her,
wishing I were invisible. There were no foreigners inside, and
everyone stared at me. When Mahine was finished we walked
through an opening in the wall, out into the arched and mirrored
space of the greater mosque. Farhad stood there in his socks,
waiting for us. In the center of the great open space was a large
tomb covered with thousands of mirrored tiles. People—mostly
men but some women—walked up to the tomb, ran their fingertips over the pressed metal decoration, touched their lips to it,
and put their foreheads against it to pray. Mahine ordered Farhad
to say a prayer, and he stood awkwardly next to the tomb, making minimal contact with his fingertips. We walked to an adjacent
wall. "This is where my father is buried," Mahine said to me. She
prayed for several minutes. Farhad stood still, looking down at
the ground. I looked around at the incredible architecture and
tried to keep my *chador* on. We walked over to a corner of the
mosque. Against the wall was a bookcase containing tattered
copies of the Koran. "This is where my mother is buried,"
Mahine said. There was no obvious indication of either tomb,
though given my ignorance of religious symbols and inability to
read the language, I might have been missing clues. In that holy,
spiritual place all I could think about were my slipping scarves.

• • •

On our way home to California, we stopped once again in Tehran to see Parvoneh, Afsaneh, and Mastoneh. In the presence of these gregarious women, I felt a renewed energy. The cousins included me with ease, translating the gist of conversations as they unfolded. This was so jarringly different from what had transpired in Shiraz and Esphahan that my resentment began to surface. Not that I had expected full translation of every nuanced detail. There were many times in Shiraz when I was content to be excluded. But this new wave of hospitality reminded me that my feeling slighted had not been just a matter of being left out of the conversation. My husband had been inattentive to me. After so many years with Farhad, I knew that this was in accordance with Iran's culture of hospitality toward others; the comfort of one's self, and by extension one's family, is considered last. Special attention is reserved for guests and outsiders. For the most part I'd become used to this. But during those last days in Tehran, I realized the frustrating irony that Farhad had neither helped me fit in nor granted me outsider status. With the cousins giving me special guest treatment in Tehran, my husband's neglect grated on me.

Late one afternoon we took a walk to do some last-minute shopping. I followed Farhad and Mastoneh down a busy road— the sky getting darker, the sidewalk more and more broken up, the crowds around us thicker—until we got to a massive, congested traffic circle. Leyla slithered here and there, unafraid of the cars and unfazed at the prospect of being separated from us. Kian rode on Farhad's shoulders, and I tried to keep Leyla safe while pushing the empty stroller over potholes and up and down steps. I finally declared, "I really don't like it here." I'd hit a wall. It was hot, crowded, dirty, and I wanted out.

We ducked into a shop, where Leyla, eager to take home something that was typically Iranian, found a small kilim she liked—though it didn't compare to a seven-hundred-dollar tapestry of an Iranian princess she had hoped to buy earlier in the trip. While Farhad paid, she turned to me to say, "This doesn't mean that I don't still want to get a tapestry like the one we saw in the Shiraz bazaar." I summoned all my reserves of patience, taking her chin gently in my hand to tell her, "When someone is giving you a present it is unbecoming to start talking about something else you want." I wondered remotely if the same rule should apply to me, too. Now, at the end of our trip, I struggled to contain my irritation. Her behavior was understandable given her age and the difficulty of traveling. But my greatest urge was to yell, "Just get over it!" even as I felt I couldn't.

When I finally got Farhad alone, I boiled over. He was surprised and a little disappointed that I was so upset. He wanted me to be happy just to be in Iran, absorbing the culture and basking in the foreignness of it all. But I was cut off from so much, I told him, and he hadn't done much to help me. Just as Farhad shifted easily between Farsi and English, he took for granted how effortlessly he moved between the two cultures that were both part of him. I, though, had only my Americanness to rely on. "What can I do?" he asked. I couldn't even articulate what I wanted because I didn't know myself. The truth was that I hadn't had a terrible time. It had mostly been very interesting, if mysterious, and having the kids connect with all of the extended Iranian family had been incredibly gratifying. But the liberation I felt earlier in not having any responsibility had morphed into frustration with my lack of freedom to do anything for myself or on my own, being reduced to a dependence so opposite my life at home.

I wanted to be a woman in America again, not his wife in Iran. After I spilled all this, Farhad was empathetic and appreciative. "You've been great," he told me and hugged me tight. "I love that you kissed my father every morning, and took care of the kids. You've been such a good sport and so easygoing. I haven't had to worry about you." I felt worlds better. His acknowledgment and appreciation of my efforts dissolved my aggravation. My husband, the one I'd known before this trip, was back.

Suddenly, it seemed, we were at the airport again, and it was time to say good-bye. Guity wept as we cleared security and walked up the stairs to our flight. Leyla, overcome with emotion, ran back down the stairs to give her one last hug.

The good-bye in Shiraz had been just as emotional. Out in the garden, Dr. Farzaneh held a Koran over the heads of the children and said a prayer for a safe journey. At his request, Kian kissed the book while I had tried to fight back tears. When Firoozeh, the housekeeper, threw water and rose petals out the door toward the car to ensure our safe return, I broke up completely. Having lost all composure, I climbed into the car and hugged Kian close on my lap. Before he pulled away, the driver gently told Farhad to remind me to cover my head.

After about a month at home, most things had returned to normal. Leyla's celebrity at school had faded; her "My Trip to Iran" shelf had been replaced by curriculum material on bones. Kian had turned two and refused to wear anything but corduroys. Farhad had resumed his hectic travel schedule and American ways. But I resisted slipping too easily into my old routine. The trip to Iran lingered in my consciousness as I picked up my life where I had left it.

Walking Leyla to school one day we saw a paper bag on the sidewalk labeled FREE BOOKS. Inside, in a coincidence that could only be attributed to fate, I found Geraldine Brooks's *Nine Parts of Desire*, a book about "the hidden world of Islamic women." I devoured Brooks's book and headed to the library for more. I searched out books by Iranian women, laying my life alongside theirs, observing the dramatic differences and subtle similarities. Their stories filled in gaps left by Farhad, and gave context to my experiences—both in Iran and at home.

I was struck by one woman's description of her extended family "that loops around and around itself, never letting anyone be alone." This was Farhad's family—the one that enveloped him as a child, the one he had turned his back on as a young man. This family is woven into his very being, despite his attempts to struggle free. For their part, they never entirely cut him loose, and they

have looped me in as well. It began long before our Muslim marriage; it started at our first wedding, when the Iranian women
sheltered us under the silk cloth. Unknowingly, then, I inherited
the woman's work common in so many cultures: that of interpret-
ing and creating family traditions—some that were not mine to
start with. Rather than cutting me off from the wisdom of my
mother-in-law, my sister's stitches bound me more closely to
Farhad's family and his culture.

I realize now that our trip to Iran completed my initiation
into that culture. It is mine as well, whether I wanted it or not.
Like my daughter struggling to be satisfied with her gifts from the
bazaar, I have been given something I must learn to love.

Understanding that culture and weaving it into my family's
life—and into mine as a mother and a wife—is something that
will come over time, from an accumulation of details. I've come
to understand that those little Iranian elements in our lives that
previously seemed so inconsequential—from Farhad's customized
Persian appetizers to Guity's hand-knit sweaters that Leyla wears
so proudly to school—are each uniquely important, like the individual threads in a tapestry.

Our family tapestry will always be a hybrid, one with an
Iranian warp and an American weft, woven from the fabric of our
family life: my opinionated half-Iranian toddler obsessed with
corduroys; my whimsical half-American daughter, wrapped in her
grandmother's scarves; my husband, so thoroughly Iranian
beneath a patchwork of American mannerisms, and me, an
American mother finding my way in foreign terrain. I, too, will
wander into the Iranian delicatessen, wondering what sweets to
buy for *Noruz*. And I will drag the family along to pick out the
perfect fir tree in early December. At some point I will hand over
our family's unfinished weaving to my children, with all its complicated threads. It will be theirs, then, to interpret, to pick apart,
to reweave, and to embroider with details of their own.

Survivor

Andrea Lawson Gray

We were finally doing everything we had dreamed of doing to our house. We had put a fresh coat of pastel paints inside and out. Big, beautiful slabs of dark green granite were being laid for the kitchen counters, in place of the old tile that had always trapped grime in its grout. Now it would be a kitchen to really cook in, with its Viking stove and sleek new appliances. My office, along with that of my two assistants, was being turned into the master bedroom suite I had always envisioned, complete with French doors, a new duvet, and luxurious throw pillows of every size and coordinated print. The room of my daughter, Cienna, would have cottage-white furniture and a fluffy pink quilt; my son Armand's room would have cowboy curtains and a toy train table. Getting the garden professionally landscaped was a finishing touch I had never had the time or the money to do.

We had come a long way in our eleven years in San Francisco. When we first moved to the city, we had big dreams, one child, and a one-bedroom furnished apartment. We shared a bath in the hallway with several other renters. I bathed our four-year-old, Andre, in it only after scouring the tub thoroughly. Most of the food in our tiny refrigerator was leftovers from the café I managed at the time. My husband, Chris, had just been officially declared disabled for a nervous system disorder, so I was going to be the breadwinner for our family.

With what limited help Chris was able to give, I established a small advertising agency in 1991. Seven years and two children later, we finally could afford to put down eighty thousand dollars in cash on a house. Of course, in order to afford the house, I had to be gone from it half the time, traveling on business more than a hundred thousand miles a year. While Chris took care of the kids during the week, I was often home only on weekends. How I ever had time to get pregnant, never mind to bear two children, I can't even remember now. I traveled with each baby until they were too old for free seats on the plane, nursing them in airports, hotel rooms, even business meetings.

I was the consummate working mother. I thought of writing an article entitled "You *Can* Do It All!" As the business grew, I created a home office and hired one assistant and then two. We earned enough to put our three children into elite private schools.

That it had taken until I was in my early forties to own a piece of the American Dream only made it that much sweeter. I never took what we had for granted. Every time I opened my double-door refrigerator—something that rental units almost never have—I was thrilled. I loved doing the back-to-school shopping, getting the kids ready with all new clothes, down to their shoes and back-packs. Every year at Christmas, I hid a mountain of presents—so many that when Andre was eight, he said, "Mommy, I know there's a Santa Claus, because you could never afford to buy us all these presents."

I shopped at midnight from catalogs and had organic produce delivered to our door; our dry cleaning was picked up by a French cleaner with valet service. I didn't have time to do the renovations on the house that Chris and I talked about, but I knew I would get to them soon enough. We talked about expanding the house so we would never have to move—creating a master bath and adding another bedroom so the kids would each have their own rooms.

During that time, some good friends, a well-established graphic designer and his wife, lost their sizable advertising agency and had to take their kids out of the French-American International School, which my boys also attended. This frightened me, but then my business was growing nicely every year. We always had several solid clients, among them a few Fortune 500 companies. We were winning awards, and I was being paid to write and speak in addition to my client work. Even when we lost a client, we immediately signed another.

That was until September 11, 2001. Our agency was the preeminent consulting firm for merchandise sourcing and product development for many of the nation's top mail-order catalogs. But after September 11, the work for consulting businesses like ours dropped off drastically. Between fear of public places and the dot-com bust, retail and catalog sales were hit hard.

I had this conviction that if I really threw myself into an endeavor, any endeavor, I could make it happen by sheer force of will. When at first we lost two clients (that, in and of itself, should have been a sign), then three and then another without signing anyone new, I adjusted. I let one assistant go. I renegotiated our long-distance and cell-phone contracts, and began traveling coach. Then I had to let my other assistant go. I started answering my own phone, opening my own mail, and paying, or at least trying to pay, my own bills. Then I stopped traveling at all. For four months I looked for any kind of work related to my field, but there was nothing.

I was too busy scrambling for work to see how far we had been falling, and how fast. By the time I looked around and realized that the world had changed—not just for us, but for many, many people—we were months behind on our mortgage, struggling to pay the car lease, and in debt up to our ears. Something had to give—and fast. As far as I was concerned, school was a priority; taking money from the kids' education was not an option. Slowly, sadly, it hit me that we had no choice but to sell the house.

When I brought this up to my husband, he couldn't even discuss it. So I just moved forward. I met with the realtors, recruited the painters, plowed through the piles of clutter in every corner. I hired "home stagers," who moved in prop furniture that made each room look like a glossy spread in a home décor magazine and advised me on other home improvements that would help bring in the best price in the competitive market for affordable homes.

So there I was—looking on as crews of painters, carpenters, and gardeners bustled around us, creating the ambiance of a well-lived family life. But as soon as the renovations were complete, we were to leave. To avoid foreclosure, we were selling our dream to someone else.

Not only that. We were literally down to our last dollar—the money for the home improvements was to come out of the escrow. The rest of the funds we cleared from the house sale would go toward paying off some of our debt. So, every way I could scrimp on the renovations, I did. To save money on painting, I went down to the local paint store, where anxious unemployed laborers, mostly from Mexico and Central America, mill around on the corner waiting for the next car or truck that might bring them a day's work. Being fluent in Spanish, I assembled a crew of four Latin men and bought the cheapest brushes, paints, and materials I could find. In four days, my house was painted. Little did I know then that this was something I would do many more times in the next few years.

I went into survival mode the day I realized we had to sell the house. Three years later, I wonder if I will ever come out. My husband collapsed under the emotional stress of the decision to sell and move, but with three kids, I did not have that option. Someone had to give them hope, strength, and dinner.

I found us a small rental house in a shabby neighborhood a few blocks off the freeway. I felt deflated when I turned the key to open the front door to that house. Every room was painted sallow "renter's white." The refrigerator hadn't been replaced in twenty years, and the controls on the old electric stove consisted of five little colored push buttons. The fence in the backyard was broken, and the linoleum in the kitchen was god-awful faux marble. I thought for a moment about the beautiful new terra-cotta tile in the kitchen of our old home and then shoved that picture out of my mind.

I had never felt so lonely in my life. Obviously, I couldn't cry to my husband because he was already coming unraveled. Certainly I couldn't let the kids see the disappointment on my face. If I called my friends or my mom, I knew they would just feel terrible for us, and couldn't do anything to help anyway. It was bad enough that I felt horrible. I didn't need to make anyone else feel worse. So, really and finally, I was alone—with my devastation and dozens of boxes to unpack.

I had no idea how I was going to pay the bills now that I had literally no business. I couldn't afford the long-distance phone calls, the computer hookups, the travel—all that was needed to keep a small business running long enough to get new clients. I couldn't even afford new business cards. And soon enough, I was to find out, I would not be able to afford the home phone line that gave me computer access to the Internet and e-mail, both indispensable to the professional life I had been living.

The people who had staged our home suggested that I might use my bilingualism to assemble a crew to paint the next home they were staging. Thus I became a painting contractor and house painter. I quickly learned the business from my crew, sometimes painting myself, even climbing scaffolding, something I had never expected to take up in my late forties. Because exterior painting is very seasonal, I also assembled a crew to clean houses, another service that often precedes a home sale. Again, with my fluent Spanish, which had become even more fluent, I gathered a ready team of Latin ladies, all experienced but unable to find regular work with their limited English. Thus I became a housecleaner. Suddenly I was dashing around giving job estimates, transporting the women and cleaning supplies to various jobs, buying paint, and looking for that next job. The work was my salvation, although it was also sporadic at best and not nearly lucrative enough to sustain a family in one of the most expensive cities in the nation.

As heartbreaking as it had been to lose our house, losing my career and my self-confidence was worse. I had to give up my identity in the white-collar world and all the trappings of success that went along with it. I returned my plush leased car to avoid repossession and bought an '86 station wagon with 250,000 miles on it. I sold my Armani suits to a second-hand shop—with all the stress, I had lost thirty-five pounds, so they didn't fit anyway.

Although I had always been outgoing, I could not bring myself to socialize. At first I was too shell-shocked at finding myself so alone, too busy trying not to feel a failure. Then I was just depressed. I was tired and sad, yes, but I also began to feel strangely out of place in the world, like one of the "illegals" in a Mexican rap song my painters played—*no soy de aci, ni soy de aja*, "not from here nor from there."

I was moving further and further away from having anything in common with the parents at the private schools my children still attended on partial scholarships. My children, too, felt the change—they had gone from being ordinary, high-achieving kids living a privileged life in an affluent, mixed-race family to being the poor black children at their exclusive private schools.

When one of my closest friends got married, I pulled myself together to attend her wedding reception. Now two sizes smaller, I borrowed a dress from one of my Latin cleaning ladies and tried to make myself look like the picture of success that people would expect to see. But I made the mistake of starting a conversation with a friend of the bride who was whining about how bored he was with his job, and it paid only $130,000 a year anyway. I could feel my eyes fill with tears. I left shortly after I arrived, feeling depressed and invisible.

Likewise, I couldn't face my former business associates, only to have to tell, once again, the sad story of the demise of our business. One of those colleagues had been among my closest friends; we had spent hours talking into the night about family, business ethics, our childhoods in New York. But as my fortunes took a different turn from hers, she became judgmental, telling me that it was my fault, and eventually bowing out of our friendship. I was reminded of the saying about walking a mile in someone else's shoes. What did she know about my life now?

The truth is, I now had more in common with the guys who painted for and with me and the women with whom I cleaned houses than I had with most of my former friends and associates. I learned about food stamps and Medi-Cal, about Catholic Charities and Jewish Family and Children's Services. I learned firsthand what it feels like to have the checker at Safeway look down on you when you pay for groceries with the food stamps "credit card." Though it is designed to look like a real credit card to save you that embarrassment, the checker at an upscale market near my sons' school was even less discreet, asking loudly, "So you're paying for that with food stamps?"

Like other poor people, I learned to be wary of the police. I had been stopped for a broken taillight that I couldn't afford to repair and issued a ticket requiring me to pay a fine of $160 if I didn't fix it. Well, if I couldn't afford to fix the taillight, how was I supposed to afford the fine? I was too busy trying to make my rent. So I missed my court appearance. Today, there is still a bench warrant out for me.

Our marriage began sagging under poverty's crush. When things had been good for us financially, Chris and I could get away with what, in retrospect, was a union laced together with threads. Without the distractions of vacations, dinners out, a social life, and travel, the bare bones of the marriage were exposed. And they clearly weren't enough, at least not from my perspective. I think Chris just gave up after we lost the house. But I couldn't give up, and I couldn't stand that he did. He was home most of the time, but you would not have known it for the minimal time he spent taking care of the children.

Andre was old enough to help out, but he had transferred to a more academically challenging high school in Marin. He had long dreamed of playing college basketball, and I wasn't going to let the burdens of our present life deprive him of his hopes for the future. He helped some at home, but he had a full load of homework, a fifty-mile round-trip commute to school every day, and basketball practice, which meant he didn't get home until nine or ten at night.

On the many occasions when I worked late at night to finish painting a house that had to be ready the next day, Chris let the younger kids get their own dinner, if they even remembered. Other times, I'd come home at ten to "What's for dinner, Mom?" And I always came home to a sink full of dishes, a dirty kitchen, and piles of dirty clothes. The less Chris did, the more I did, and the more resentful I became.

Our sad little house was bursting with the tension. One night, when I returned at bedtime to find that Armand and Cienna hadn't eaten dinner yet, Chris and I fought so hard that the children insisted they hadn't been hungry at all, so it was okay that Daddy hadn't fed them. In the meantime, Andre started to find more reasons to stay over at friends' houses, sometimes for the entire weekend.

This was breaking my heart and clearly my children's hearts as well. With all they were going through, I didn't feel that this was the time to file for divorce, and I didn't have any energy to devote to anger. So I decided to just let it go, to let everything Chris did or didn't do that I resented or worried about just slip away. I stopped counting on him for anything and started counting on the kids to take care of things when I worked late.

When I had my advertising business, I always had a housecleaner. It was all I could do to coerce the kids into picking up their rooms before she arrived. And I reasoned that their homework was more important. Now that I *was* a housecleaner, they would just have to do both. I taught my ten-year-old, Armand, how to cook dinners for himself and his little sister. When I went off to work on Saturdays and Sundays, I left the children with lists of chores that would have overwhelmed some housekeepers. I bought Armand a cell phone, and he began getting himself to basketball practice and home from school by bus. Sometimes he caught the bus to where I was working that day, so he could do some small task and earn a little pocket money. Ironically, he became the envy of the other fifth-graders in his private school, who longed for his freedom (but probably not the responsibilities that went with it).

Then one little act—originally an act of desperation—began to turn my life around. Even with the children's help, I had not been able to stay ahead of the chaos and the mess, and I couldn't have them growing up inside of it. So I started getting up before dawn to do an hour of chores before getting them out the door to school. I'd make myself a cup of chai tea and putter myself into an awakened state. I watched the sun come up while I did my chores. And suddenly it was as if the sunrise each morning was giving way to a sense of renewal inside me.

First, I started making my bed again every day. By now Chris was sleeping downstairs in his basement "office," which was as close to a legal separation as we could afford to get. So, upstairs, I had the whole big bed to myself. When I dragged my aching bones into the house late at night, I found real comfort in sinking down into the plumped-up pillows and crisp, smoothed sheets. Then I cut and colored my hair—myself, of course (fortunately, curly hair is very forgiving)—and found that, for the first time in my life, I looked great in jeans, the reward for working off all that weight worrying. I gave myself my first-ever pedicure and found myself admiring my pretty feet in a pair of open-toed shoes I had bought on a business trip to Florida a few years before.

Room by room, I started to fix up the house with found objects and my newfound conviction that I could turn our sad little rental into a comfortable home. Of course, I painted—mixing the odds and ends from various paint jobs to create a soft sage for my bedroom and a buttery yellow to warm up the walls of the rest of the house, all without spending a penny. I made a bedroom for Cienna in the tiny breakfast nook, fashioning a headboard from a purple ballet skirt. I scavenged rugs, lamps, even chairs from job sites where people were giving them away. What I didn't have, I bartered for.

I worked around the house's quirks and cracks to create a

cozy, eclectic home that reflects us, not the imaginary family in a stager's repertoire. In winter, we built fires in our fireplace from the free firewood the local lumberyard gives away. The younger kids thought it was a hoot to go down to the lumberyard to collect the wood. A regular family excursion!

For the first time I could see clearly what was really solid in my life. I discovered that there was nothing my two closest girlfriends wouldn't do to support me. If I needed to drop in just to "cry it out," they understood. When I asked if I could borrow a roll of toilet paper from one because I was just too tired to stop at the store on the way home, she saw through my excuse to the truth—that toilet paper is an expense food stamps don't cover—and sent me home with several rolls. Last year I cried when one of them delivered us a Thanksgiving turkey. The other paid my electric bill one month without asking or even telling me. I just knew that the disconnection notices had stopped coming. Who could ask for more? And how could anyone survive with less?

As strange as it may sound, I began to see the incredible richness of the life we now had. Instead of waiting, exhausted and desperate, for some light to shine at the end of a tunnel, I began to relish my journey and all its miracles, not the least of which were friendship and faith.

At night, I went to bed thanking God for every little miracle—that I had two wonderful friends, that my car was still running, that I had had two calls that day for possible jobs, that all the painters had shown up for work and no one was drunk or too hung over to paint, that I had almost all the rent money. That we had a home. That I had the energy to keep going and my kids were still in great schools—that was probably more important than anything else.

When you're broke, Christmas can be more melancholy than it is merry. A few days before Christmas last December, I lost a painting contract and all hope of paying my rent. So I gathered myself and went down to the welfare office, figuring that this was the time to get whatever government help was out there. It was raining, and there was only metered parking. I scrounged through every seat crack and pocket of my car for money for the meter and finally found enough change for an hour. An hour later, I went back in the rain and scrounged for some more change for another hour. An hour later, I did it again, and during that third hour of waiting, it was finally my turn.

First of all, the caseworker said, I had to come in with my husband, which I knew was not going to happen. Chris's pride was so damaged he couldn't even stand to drive to our old street to drop the kids off to play; there was no way he would be able to bring himself to the welfare office. But my caseworker said I could go through the application process anyway to determine how much in assistance we were eligible for. So I did. It was $237 a month. Prorated for the seven days of December that were left, it came to all of $55.30. I left in tears, mostly of frustration.

Was it pure coincidence that that same day I ran into an old friend who knew all about the Season of Sharing fund, which helps families with short-term financial emergencies pay their rent? With help from that group, I paid the rent and had a little cash left over to Christmas shop at garage sales and used-clothing stores.

That year I got one of the best presents I have ever received. On Christmas morning, Andre surprised us all with wrapped presents. I couldn't possibly imagine where he had gotten the money. It turns out he went to a used bookstore and bought everyone books, carefully selected and inscribed to inspire each of us.

I have begun to see that, despite all the uncertainty in my life, things always seem to work out, and this has become my mantra. This faith has given me the ability to get past the fear, the depression, and even the resentment at having to do this all alone. It's given me an optimism and humility that I pass on to my children, which helps them through their crises, at school and at home. I know this when Andre tells me that he does not need a backup plan if he doesn't get a basketball scholarship because "that's just not gonna happen, Mom." I know this when Armand cheerfully cleans his old sneakers and adds colorful new laces, but doesn't ask me for a new pair until his old ones have holes. I know this because, although my children are now the least privileged kids in their privileged schools, they don't complain about not getting to go to the mall or the movies, which their peers do weekly, with wads of their parents' cash. Andre just shrugs and says it's a good thing the kids in his suburban white high school don't know "what's fresh," so he doesn't really have to have the "freshest" new clothes.

I am not saying that they never complain. Armand has cried to me that his friends don't have to clean their whole house, just their rooms. Cienna, who is now seven, complains that she can't go to dance class every day after school, so she has to manage with once a week. But I have a great summer planned for all of them—scholarships to basketball camps, science and technology programs, and cooking school for Armand, whose experience cooking dinners convinced him he might want to be a chef. In my new state of mind, it never occurred to me that anyone would say "no," and so no one did. The children will even have trips to Colorado to climb and mountain bike, thanks to airline tickets paid for with what's left of the frequent flyer miles from my "other life."

And I'm happy to say that I have created a beautiful home for my family, something I never managed to do in our more affluent life. It's a place where I feel safe in my room; where I read, write, pray, and renew my spirit. It is a place where the kids can have friends over without embarrassment, where we can all come home and be glad we're there.

At Andre's exclusive Marin school, it is a tradition for the kids to get hotel rooms in San Francisco on prom night, so they don't have to drive home from the dance in the middle of the night. It would not occur to anyone there that some families may not be able to afford San Francisco's astronomical hotel rates. But we could not. So Andre and his girlfriend stayed here—in the home that he used to avoid—when all the other kids were in hotels. My ladies pitched in and we gave the place a top-to-bottom cleaning, even folding the toilet paper in the bathroom as they do in upscale hotels. And Andre and his girlfriend were genuinely happy to be here.

It is now the summer before Andre's senior year of high school, and he is a young man on fire. His grades last year earned him a full scholarship for next year. This summer he is washing windows and making enough money to pay for his clothes, dates, and even a basketball exposure camp, where he hopes he will get a shot at a college basketball scholarship. But even if he doesn't, he aced his SAT tests. So the future is looking bright. I have to laugh now when he argues with his girlfriend because his highest priorities are school and basketball. And I have to say that I don't believe any of this initiative would have surfaced had we still been comfortable financially.

I was reminded of this a few weeks ago when I went to a Fourth of July bash at the home of the friend whose wedding reception I had left in tears. More confident now, taking my life in stride, I had no problem figuring out what to wear or what to say when I got there. And I knew I looked great when Andre told me, "Wow, Mom, your arms are really cut!" My "buff" arms made me look like I spent hours in exclusive body-sculpting classes and personal training, although, of course, they were really from the hard work of housecleaning and painting.

Several of us got to talking about teenagers and their drive, or lack of it. You could say that I was once again out of place, but this time I didn't mind: Most of the parents complained that they can't motivate their teenagers to get off the couch, out of the house, or away from the PlayStation. One man's son, who went through thirteen years of top education at the French-American school, is flipping burgers instead of filling out college applications. My former friend—the one who blamed me for my business's failure—confessed that she and her husband had threatened to take away the driving privileges of their onetime soccer-star son if he didn't get a summer job, or at least go to soccer practice.

Listening to them talk, I thought, if I had to lose my shirt to have children who inspire me and amaze others with their self-reliance and drive, then our family has gained more than we've lost. Maybe I've paid for their bright future with my losses, but what mother wouldn't be happy to do that for her children?

Bald Single Mother
Does Not Seek Date

Christina Koenig

I must have spaced out again. Everyone in my support group was looking at me.

"Huh?" I asked. "What was the question?"

The well-meaning counselor looked at me, lips pursed. "I said, 'What will you tell someone when you start dating again? How will you break the news to him about your having had breast cancer?'"

"Oh, I'm not going to be dating anybody," I shrugged.

She had to be kidding. Me? Dating? A bald single mother with cancer? What a catch. After enduring what's known by us insiders as the slash, burn, and poisoning—surgery, radiation, chemotherapy, and hormonal therapy—the idea of ever dating again had not really entered my fuzzy chemo brain. In all sincerity, I was just happy to still be around and enchanted with my beautiful daughter, especially since I'd certainly be infertile for the rest of my days, however many were left. Dating? Not even on the radar screen.

Months ago, the night before my first chemo treatment, I had gone for a margarita at this tiny, out-of-the-way bar—my decadent, guilty pleasure. I had been to The Matchbox only a couple of times during the four years I'd lived in Chicago. When I had first moved to the city, I was on my own with a one-and-a-half-year-old. Since we lived in a completely different part of town and

I wasn't much of a bar person to begin with, I rarely got to The Matchbox. It was hard to reach by public transportation and convenient to nothing in my life. So only when the planets lined up right—when I drove to work that day and managed to have child care arranged—did I ever get there.

But when I did, it was great. The Matchbox is a wedge of brown brick that looks like a boxcar and bills itself as "Chicago's Most Intimate Bar." And they got that right: it is minuscule, with about fourteen stools. On the corner of Chicago, Milwaukee, and Ogden Avenues, in a no-man's-land near the expressway, it is also worlds away from the singles pickup scenes downtown.

Because of the close quarters, everyone talks to each other at The Matchbox. Carpenters, judges, cops, artists, poets—you never know who'll be sitting on the stool next to you. But nobody ever hit on me. I loved it. I really felt comfortable. And the margaritas are amazing: made with fresh limes and served up in a martini glass rimmed with extra-fine bar sugar and garnished with long, skinny twists of lemon and lime.

I thought it was fitting to go in for a ceremonial margarita before I had the first of six rounds of chemo the next morning. Sipping my second margarita, I leaned over to the bartender, Jay, and said "Hey, you won't see me for a while." Not that I was a regular anyway, he pointed out. Then I spilled my guts. I told him I had been diagnosed with breast cancer and had had surgery. The cancer had spread to my lymph nodes. The average woman who is diagnosed with breast cancer is in her sixties, and since I was thirty-nine years old, the cancer was considered more aggressive and would have to be treated aggressively. I was going to lose my long, straight, blonde hair.

I told him all about my sweet, beautiful daughter, then five years old. I showed him her photos, recounted for him that she understood my explanation about surgery to "get out the bad lump." But on the day before Thanksgiving, when I told her I was going to also have medicine to make sure no lumps ever came back—medicine so strong that it was going to make me throw up and my hair fall out—she screamed bloody murder. Then I told him about how the very next day, she pulled up her chair to the Thanksgiving dinner table and proudly announced to those gathered, "My mommy's going to have medicine that will . . ." and there she paused, eyes opening wider with wicked glee, "make her hair fall out!"

At the end of my sob story, I promised Jay that I would be back as soon as I could stomach one of his margaritas. I thanked him for his support and made a crack about joining a support group.

Fast forward through eleven months of chemo, radiation, exhaustion, depression, baldness, and, yes, support groups, I was finally ready to go back to The Matchbox for that promised libation.

The place looked comfortably the same. Crowded, only one stool open, and Jay was behind the bar. Would he even remember me and my story? I asked the guy sitting next to the empty stool if it was taken, and as he answered, "No," I felt a slightly unfamiliar jolt—he was handsome.

Suddenly I heard Jay exclaim, "Christina! How are you? Look at your hair! Nice crew cut! How was the chemo? How's your daughter? Let me get you your margarita!"

I pulled up my stool and spilled my guts once again to him. My daughter was six years old now, strong and beautiful and so composed through the whole ordeal. The chemo seemed to have worked, and I was getting back to the world.

As Jay went off to fix other drinks, I turned to the guy next to me. Damn, he was good looking, with a full head of short gray hair, a strong jaw, and blue eyes. I was surprised to find myself speculating on whether he was "taken." He was a lawyer, he said. When I asked what kind, he said "criminal." I told him I needed his card because I was the type to really get in trouble and would probably need his services in the near future. He laughed. He said he couldn't help hearing my story.

"Congratulations," he said. "Can I buy you a drink?"

I said, "No, I really don't think I should have another one of these." He looked a little disappointed. "But I am really hungry," I said. "Want to take me to dinner?" So he did.

I never did figure out how to tell a prospective date about my cancer—or "break the news," as the support group counselor put it. I never needed to.

The lawyer and I got married.

Natural Mother

Lisa Teasley

Imogen is born on a full-moon evening, late in June when the city is hot and empty. Skin the color of wheat, dimpled cheeks, and a crown of soft midnight curls, my tiny heroine goddess effortlessly carries her Shakespearean name. We thought she might make her regal entrance en route from SoHo to midtown Manhattan during the dizzyingly brief four-hour labor. I was fully dilated upon arrival at the hospital. To maintain calm as the nurse rushed me to the birthing room, despite my mother and husband's panicked breathing as they ran beside us, I visualized baby ducklings giddily pacing the corridors. In the birthing room, as I pushed I urged Imogen to squeeze out like toothpaste. She cooperated with alacrity, and as her head swiftly popped out, my husband excitedly exclaimed, "We can have another one!"

"Let's take care of this one first," the doctor barked.

"It's a girl, it's a girl, it's a girl!" my mother couldn't stop squealing.

And now here, lifeline still attached, Imogen lies on my tummy, knowingly looking up into my eyes, both of us in awe, at ease with our mutual recognition. Upon the doctor's command, my husband shyly cuts the umbilical cord, and I put Imogen to my breast. Throughout the entire physically trouble-free, no-hitch pregnancy, we had worn one another so well; now body to body, skin to skin, there couldn't be a more natural texture in the world. We are both ready for the second part of our journey—mother and daughter together in the outside world. We make a good first attempt at breast-feeding, neither of us discouraged that there isn't yet milk. When the nurse takes Imogen, my mother follows at her heels to watch her bathe, footprint, and bracelet our little girl.

A crowd of newborns has also arrived on this full-moon night, in keeping with the lunar cycle, the nurses say. They pack the hospital nursery, not one extra bassinet. Most of them are Puerto Rican and similar in coloring to Imogen. The nurses tease my mother that they won't lose our baby in the mix due to the dimples so identical to her grandmother's.

My mother is a Panamanian sweet caramel brown. I am African American earth sienna. My husband is blue-eyed, Caucasian light beige. Imogen's godfather is Iranian, the color of natural bamboo, and when he arrives with white roses, he holds her in his arms, coos, describing to her how she resembles his baby sister. When re-swaddled and placed back in the hospital bassinet next to my bed, she fights to get the mitts off her fists to wipe her own navy glass eyes, her fitful expression like childhood pictures of my husband's feisty, scrappy, tow-headed brother. Of course, this is something that thrills any mother—seeing your own best world reflected in your infant's face.

In the morning, when my husband, mother, and I take her home, Imogen fills a fourth of her car seat, and remains a sleeping beauty duckling for an uninterrupted twenty-four hours. But I can't sleep myself for the excitement of seeing this new ravishing life, a real and true and perfect miniature person whom I hosted in my belly for nine months. I lie on the bed with her and stare at her the entire night and morning through. Over and over, my husband plays Springsteen ballads softly in the background, and all of us—my husband, mother, and I—share in the tremendous bliss. Tears stream continuously. How can I express the new infinity of my love?

On Imogen's seventh day, my mother returns home to Los Angeles, my husband back to work, and so we are alone together in public for the first time, my daughter and I, Imogen safely wrapped in a sling against my chest. We walk the few blocks from Sixth Avenue and Spring to Thompson and Prince for a pound of coffee. As I make my way toward the door, a girl of maybe twenty with a skin tone close to mine stops me at the sidewalk and asks earnestly with a Caribbean accent, "Excuse me, but where did you get your babysitting job?"

She can't be talking to me.

I hold my baby so closely in my sling, and everything about me sings. My shock is so fluid it is viral. How could anyone mistake us for anything but mother and child? Why should my dark skin and Imogen's light skin influence anyone to think otherwise? I don't hear myself tell the woman that I am my baby's mother. Maybe I say nothing. But her shoulders shrink in such a heartfelt apology that it could only be too apparent how much her comment crushes me.

My husband and I met at UCLA twelve years before Imogen was born. We courted two years before marrying, and he was well on his way to a career in the music business, while I pursued writing and painting alongside a string of jobs in journalism, music, and film. We moved every couple of years during the eight in greater Los Angeles, and though very emotionally supportive of each other, we weren't yet financially ready to start a family. When a new position in New York afforded him more opportunity— opportunity for me as well, we both assumed—we moved there in 1992, nevertheless with hesitation. I had always felt incompatible with the rat-race pace, and it seemed likely we would be swallowed by a culture of long hours at work.

Even so, when we left the less hectic, more home life–oriented West Coast, where interracial relationships and biracial or multiracial children seemed to be everywhere, neither of us was ready for the snobbery, hostility, and resentful stares we received when we held hands in New York. Incredulous of the second looks, the disapproving tight mouths, we never became accustomed to the insults. I was hurt by the white elderly lady who refused to use the stall after me in an uptown movie theater bathroom. During dinner with my husband and his parents—who were always openly affectionate with a daughter-in-law they had known for so many years—I was appalled by people staring at the four of us with the kind of disgust reserved for the sight of regurgitated food at the table.

All of it chipped away at me. I had arrived on the East Coast a boho—a colorfully dressed, wide-eyed, open person—and more and more I was losing myself to the dehumanizing responses I encountered.

The first time we discovered I was pregnant was when I began a slow miscarriage. The white female doctor we happened upon through our group insurance wrongly diagnosed a tubular pregnancy, and speaking directly to my husband rather than to me, said it was a miracle I had conceived at all given the amount of body hair and male hormones I carried. She then declared that I would most certainly need fertility drugs. Later, the radiologist assured me of the idiocy of this statement, and told me I was having a very natural miscarriage after so many years on the pill—a kind of dress rehearsal.

The radiologist was right. Two months later I was easily pregnant, and thought I'd found the right group of doctors. But by the second trimester, before each ob-gyn visit, I'd find myself hoping that it would be the African American of the group's three women doctors who would see me that day. Even though it was me on the table, *my* heart they listened to, *my* body they examined, the two white female doctors, just like the doctor who treated my miscarriage, addressed only my white husband, and rarely, if ever, looked me in the eye. It was as if I didn't exist, my person merely a mechanical object to be checked from time to time.

Friends in the city told me to look above people's heads in the streets when I walked. But that would have been to change the essence of who I am: As an artist and a writer, empathy is of the utmost importance, and I can achieve that only by observing everyone and everything around me. So I would sit or stand on the subway, maintaining connection to the lives going on around me, and in the process taking on other people's bad weather. I spent far too much time worrying about how others perceived me. I tried convincing myself that New York could be a kind of boot camp for tossing aside sensitivities, for toughening up. But in the emotionally fraught time of pregnancy, it was hard not to worry what kind of world I was bringing my child into. That worry then became a kind of mental slavery.

Out in the street, I was weighed down—not by the extra forty going on fifty pounds, but by the anxiety, ignorance, and turbulence of others. When I could no longer fit behind the wheel of my orange Karmann Ghia I sold it, keeping only the California plates propped on my desk. Gone, along with the car, seemed to be my pink coat, turquoise shoes, humor, optimism, and freedom. I wondered why I had grown doubtful of the kindness of any strangers. Only inside our home was I happily pregnant, exuberant over the heightened sensitivities of motherhood, celebratory of the new spirit inside me. When cabdrivers passed me by or tried taking off even as the exiting white passenger held the door for me, I fought back—I yelled, or complained to the taxi commission, where I won one discrimination case and still have another pending. But the fighting-back was getting to me, as well as to my husband.

I wished for the natural fatigue of an expectant mother. And as it became far too harrowing to consciously confront racism on an everyday basis, I finally elected to take positive action for the sake of the energy I was surrounding my baby with. I needed to be myself; I needed to become a more natural mother. Inside, my body was nearly bursting with richness, new life, and possibility; I needed to find a way to get my internal optimism to flower outward. Impulsively, I answered a choreographer's ad searching for pregnant dancers in the Urban Organic newsletter. Though not a professional dancer, I love music and love to move, and so, twice a week for two months, I rehearsed the "Pregnant Tango" with seven blooming women, our bellybuttons like headlights in our tight red costumes. There was an incomparable kind of joy in our hormonal, emotional exchange. We performed three nights, and I cried after each one, so delighted to have danced on stage with my child beaming proudly from inside my womb. I imagined that Imogen, like me, could relax and look forward to our relationship post-placenta.

With Imogen now outside in the world, and the woman's question about my "babysitting job" just the first of the many insults we encountered together, I find myself quickly losing that natural, contented gleam of new motherhood. Instead of the relaxed, open, and harmonious temperament I'd taken on during the Pregnant Tango dance period, I am back in hypervigilant mode, wary and brittle with the expectation of affronts. I coach myself on toughening up even more, for the three of us. I even deny myself the outrage that hitherto came as second nature to me in my reactions to injustice. Injustice, now, becomes standard in my head, in order to simply cope.

I see my husband snapping back at people, not so much from a position of vulnerability for himself, but as archetypal protector of wife and daughter. We get relief only from the relentless, wearing insults on the occasions we travel back to Los Angeles for visits. We don't have to hold our breath when someone leans over in line to get a closer look at Imogen. *What a beautiful baby you have! Oh, but I can see how she gets her looks from both of you,* a sweet older white woman says to us from over the cushy red booth at an L.A. restaurant. After almost a year of California respites since Imogen's birth, I believe we can escape the East Coast's grueling objectification in other places as well, and experience natural, unfretted, even festive times.

We could never feel sorry for ourselves with a helicopter waiting for us at Jamaica's Kingston airport. It is as if our feet could touch the treetops of the lush neon landscape; I fly with my eleven-month-old baby in arms, my husband on one side, pilot on the other, as we land on Golden Eye. What used to be Ian Fleming's estate is now the compound of my husband's boss, who has invited us to stay while he is away. With a choice of seven guesthouses, we are waited on hand and foot by a private staff, who take kindly to us. Of course, we choose the guesthouse with a front door opening onto the beach—spending days in the water, sand, and grass, our urban baby finally getting a taste of gorgeous nature. Imogen holds onto my leg, head back, her mouth open to the spray of the outside shower, all of us elated to be naked in the fresh air. She laughs, toddling after the hen and chickens, clapping her hands as they skedaddle from her. She kneels in the sand, building odd and royal monuments, making friends with roaming beach dogs and cats. The three of us sit in the shallow, quiet bath of the ocean in a ring-around-the-rosy. Self-consciousness, anxiety melt away.

Due to the sneaking paranoia that something could break this spell of easy familial reverie, we hardly ever leave the private property. And why would we want to go anywhere else? For one of the few times since the week of her birth, Imogen, my husband, and I are free to be in perfect sync. On the plane back to New York, luxuriously rested and mellowed to jelly, my guard is way down when the white American flight attendant hands my husband an American immigration and customs declaration for him and "his" child, while I, holding our baby, am handed a Jamaican immigration card without so much as a question. We tell ourselves it's back to the grind.

With the ever-increasing escapes, mostly thanks to my husband's work, Imogen is well traveled by her twentieth month. When the phone rings in a Miami hotel, I run to get it and she chases after me, tripping over a cursedly placed woven-straw chair that busts the gentle, narrow space between her eye and brow. We rush her to the emergency room, my baby bleeding in my arms, and the triage nurse asks if we know how to "contact the parents of this child." Neither of us can believe that she can't see the singular panic and concern that only a mother and father exude for their threatened baby. Do we not seem real and natural with her? An hour later, as the three male nurses hold our baby down to apply a butterfly bandage, the African American explains to the two Caucasians how one can tell from the curly hair and golden complexion that she is "mixed" and so, therefore, standing right here are the parents. My husband and I each have one of Imogen's hands in our own, and we share an unspoken moment of promise and strength. When the white male doctor arrives on the scene, he looks me in the eye as he speaks, and I'm grateful he understands we are human.

By the time I feel ready for a part-time nanny, extreme sensitivity becomes the main requirement. My husband and I go through disastrously awkward interviews with a string of prospective babysitters—three of them happen to be white NYU students—who look from me to my husband, wondering why, sometimes aloud, the exiting babysitter is doing the questioning. Finally we meet a warm, talkative, fortyish Puerto Rican who reminds me just a little of my Panamanian mother, and who immediately recognizes me as Imogen's mother. She is hired. I stay on one side of the loft writing, while the two of them read and play on the other side. After a few weeks of Monday, Wednesday, and Friday shifts from one to four P.M., I take notice that our babysitter is becoming more and more attached.

"Imogen looks so much like me that if I took her home to Jersey no one would know she wasn't mine," she says to me one day. Few statements could be more frightening in my frazzled, insecure psychological state. The frequency of my vulnerability—of not being recognized as Imogen's mother—has scared me away from ever letting her out of my sight. I've taken no chances. During the days, thus far, the babysitter hasn't been allowed to take my baby out of the house, and this rule continues through the length of her increasingly unreliable employment. She calls in sick at least once a week.

Two babysitters later, my paranoia ever increasing with the extreme violence, racism, and fear I'm feeling everywhere, our talk of leaving New York takes on paramount seriousness. Our current babysitter lives through the nightmare of losing her sister to murder—by her own boyfriend. Though our babysitter's horror could have happened anywhere, the everyday dehumanizing that I encounter on the street takes on a new, sickening depth.

Our life has not been shabby here: the SoHo loft above the fish restaurant is considered chichi by anyone who visits, restaurant mice included. Nevertheless, I have grown tired of the weekday view through my window—of lunch breaks on the grass island, all kids of color tracked for lesser achievement at the corner tech school. Lowered expectations. At the most basic, selfish level, I miss having my own car, a bubble of security to get my baby and myself to and from home rather than worrying about the time of night on the subway, the danger, the sense of threat, the dread of rain or snow when cabs are scarce and black people more easily avoided by the drivers. For these six New York years, strained by the glare of racism, I have become too hurt and intimidated to see or express my individuality, and conversely overly conscious of how my baby, my husband, and I are perceived. Though I stand five foot ten, I've made myself small. I am neither natural nor the best mother I could be, and through closer examination of it all, I need to shed the outer and inner judgments I feel. I crave the freedom I had in L.A., as well as a mother's delight in a world's recognition that Imogen is mine.

Imogen and I leave New York a month early while my husband wraps up his old position with the company for the new. Even the search for a preschool back home in Los Angeles is a delight. I can feel the ease in my neck, back, and voice. I had always been considered the type who smiles most of the time, and my face reclaims that easeful openness. When strangers approach us, I no longer feel my body tightening, preparing for the blows. I stand my full height and meet the world with optimism. The freedom I feel after our escape from New York isn't simply attributable to my car's turquoise paint job, or funky clothes. Maybe it isn't only geography. Los Angeles is far from utopia. I know my experience of racism and objectification on the East Coast isn't unique, just as my experience of simply being a member of the human race on the West Coast is something others still struggle with. (It well may be the case that if I were a Latina woman with a white husband and baby with skin fairer than my own, my experience in L.A. would be similar to what I felt in New York.) Even so, the difference for our family is as stark as black and white.

What has come to matter most to me—what always mattered most—is the way I relate with Imogen, now without the weight of what had become a kind of haunting. So many white Californians are quick to say, "How beautiful your daughter is!" California black people remark upon how closely, at two and a half years, Imogen resembles me. "She is a light-skinned version of you!" they exclaim. Imogen's self-assuredness becomes all the more apparent, all the more defined, as she surely feels how much more relaxed and natural I feel as her mother. One afternoon I get up to do a silly dance with an Austin Powers talking toy. Imogen does her best imitation of my steps and words. I call her Mini Me, and this becomes the nickname she most prefers for years—over Immi, Munchie, Piccolina, and Moe.

Of course she is not a miniature of me, and not one of the three of us would want her to be. Eight years old now, Imogen is a complete individual, proud of her Skate Rat fashion tastes, Hot Wheels car collection, woodworking pieces, new karate levels, stellar math and chess abilities, gifted academic placement, and incessant humor. Since we moved back to the West Coast six years ago, our family has had little or no struggle with "interracial" or "biracial" issues, only an annoyance with categories for race on school forms.

Now, out from under the thumb of any but the most minimal, ordinary irritations, we are seen just as we always imagined ourselves to be: a family, pure and simple. I am constantly inspired as Imogen blossoms into her ever-increasingly unique and brilliant self. And just as I never deny her self-expression, I don't deny my own.

No Blame

Rosellen Brown

Almost every time I take part in a "Q&A" after a reading, I hear a variation on this question, often presented in a plaintive voice filled with (what I take to be) trepidation for the future: "How did you manage to write after you had children?" No man has ever asked this. Nor have many women who are already mothers seemed to feel the need to inquire, unless out of sisterly curiosity; presumably they've either figured out what they needed to or they've resigned themselves to putting their writing aside, at least for now.

It is not a question I answer glibly—I am truly sympathetic to anyone who still has this challenge ahead of her—but I suspect that my experience may still come across as too facile or self-congratulatory. "No, I never stopped. I doubt I could have managed a novel, but fortunately I was writing poetry when my first daughter, Adina, was born and I discovered the advantages of the fragmentary way in which poems can be worked on. (Say I need a two-syllable word that means 'encourage.' I could spend the day trying out a cascade of words, filling in the blank. Plus she was a good napper.)" "I hired a high school girl who came to my house four afternoons a week." "After I made the bed, I did no housework until late afternoon, after my 'own' work was finished for the day. Who cares when the breakfast dishes are done?" "My husband defended my 'right to write' more zealously—that is, without self-doubt—than I did. Luckily, he knew he was marrying a writer (though of course he had no idea what that would mean)." "I had already published a bit, which made my writing easier to justify to myself and others (chiefly my mother . . .)" "I learned to use every spare minute. I was better at that when time was scarce than I am now." And so on. All these things are true, but they make those years sound too easy and unconflicted.

Picture this: About to deliver my second child, I have asked my hippie babysitter, who is devoted to such things—it is 1970— to throw the yarrow stalks that are used with the *I Ching* to divine the future. Coins can be used instead, but I am delighted that Laurie has access to the real thing. I am skeptical but curious: Will the particular arrangement of the dry stalks reveal the sex of my unborn child? (This is many years before ultrasound.) We sit opposite each other on the living room floor, and I fling the stalks down between us like pick-up sticks.

There is no easy way to describe this, but let me try: The *I Ching*, or *Book of Changes*, a three-thousand-year-old collection said to be one of the "Five Classics of Confucianism," presents its predictions through a three-stage process. This begins with more than seven hundred pages of arrangements called hexagrams, which are composed of six broken and unbroken lines in many permutations, each of which is meant to be a graphic representation of the order in which the little stalk piles lie after they are tossed. Each of these hexagrams is accompanied, in turn, by a lovely but cryptic paragraph of prose poetry said to foretell the future. The poems have evocative, mysterious names: "Treading (conduct)." "Darkening of the Light." "Biting Through." "Grace." They conceal even as they illuminate; they make the curious work hard at interpretation. ("Nine in the second place means: / There is food in the *ting*. / My comrades are envious, / But they cannot harm me. / Good fortune." "Nine in the third place means: / The handle of the *ting* is altered. / One is impeded in his way of life. / The fat of the pheasant is not eaten. / Once rain falls, remorse is spent. / Good fortune comes in the end.")

It does not matter, to dabblers like Laurie and me, that we don't know what a *ting* is. Something from the kitchen, we assume. More to the point, we recognize that before I cast the yarrow roots down, I will hold my destiny in my own hands. And then I will let it go.

I ask the *I Ching* whether my baby will be a boy or a girl. The "answer" to my question is almost a rebuke: It is a perfect balance of yin and yang, and discloses—happens or chooses to disclose?—nothing.

I am embarrassed at the idea that I have asked something impertinent. "All right," I say, "let's try this." I have been very worried that a second child will complicate, even put an end to, my writing. I have managed just fine with one, but what difficulties await me now that both my arms will be full?

This time the *I Ching* seems to smile on me. Understand that, although all the hexagrams suggest the proper—moral and pragmatic—way to act, some of the apparent subjects of those mysterious fortunes concern military matters, princely power, riches, shame. Which is to say, many seem only remotely connected with my particular urgencies. Laurie bends over the flung stalks, calculates their placement, finds the corresponding hexagrams and matches them up with their texts. Because of the particular way the stalks have fallen, leaning on one another, tipping this way and that, apparently I have produced a "change." I am owed not the usual one but two responses.

The two responses I am given are so appropriate and encouraging they bring tears to my eyes. The first reads: "THE TAMING POWER OF THE SMALL / Has success. / Dense clouds, no rain from our western region / . . . The wind drives across heaven." (Dense clouds indeed; it is February in Brooklyn.) And the second seems, without forcing, so relevant to my expectation that in a few weeks I will be nursing my baby and worrying about the possible loss of my writing, that it stuns me.

A devout rationalist, I do not really believe in the predictive power of any book, but, still, this pure voice seems to be speaking directly into my ear. "THE CORNERS OF THE MOUTH (PROVIDING NOURISHMENT). / Perseverance brings good fortune. / Pay heed to the providing of nourishment / And to what a man seeks / To fill his own mouth with." The prosy interpretation reads: "In bestowing care and nourishment, it is important that the right people should be taken care of and that we should attend to our own nourishment in the right way. . . . Nature nourishes all creatures . . . He who cultivates the superior parts of his nature is a superior man." Everyone alluded to in the *I Ching*—except the maidens who occasionally show up to be wed—is male, it goes without saying. But, as a creature about to give suck to a child, and who is concerned about attending to my own mental nourishment, this oracular directive is enough to make me swoon with relief.

A few weeks later I am indeed in the hospital, my beautiful little girl-baby, whom we have just named Elana, beside me in her plastic basinet when my husband brings me the galleys of my first published story—I have recently ventured into prose—and I correct them on the rolling bed table that has just accommodated my breakfast tray. I take it as an augury, the perfectly timed fulfillment of the *I Ching*'s promise—or was that a challenge? I am ready to write my own mini-*Ching* poem: "DARING. / There are many roads to the same destination / and better ones, perhaps, than you can yet imagine."

But of course, even the *I Ching* did not say it would be simple. Another picture: I am at the dining room table, typing out my handwritten day's work. Elana is at day care; Adina should be on the school bus on her way home from first grade. She is six.

Eager not to steal from our time together, I am always careful to pack away my writing when she's due at home—we live now very far from the road, down a wooded drive, so I can't hear the bus, but I certainly know what time it is, and I make sure to be ready for her return. But this particular day, I am in the middle of a paragraph and just need a bit more time when I hear her come up on the porch and in the front door.

"Give me a minute, honey," I call out to her. She stands in the arch between the living room and the dining room, where my pages are spread out around me on the table. "Sorry, Dina, you know I never do this. Just give me a second, okay? Take off your stuff." It's winter in New Hampshire; she's trammeled down with snowmobile suit (red, navy, and yellow, I remember it so well, and those clumsy, complicated boots with the felt liners). "There are milk and cookies on the table!" For which the Good Mother gestures her to the kitchen.

And she continues to stand beside the table, stubborn, silent, looking hard at me and my typewriter. Finally, guilty and exasperated—can't she cut me this much slack? I *never* do this!—I say, "Adina. *Please!*" To which she replies, shyly, "But I never get to see you *working.*"

It is thirty years later as I write this. Adina is, herself, a writer; after nine years as a film critic, she has come out of the dark and published a superb book of essays. If I were to ask whether she suffered for my occupation, and the concomitant *pre*-occupation that so often accompanied it, I dare to think she would only laugh.

As for the girl-baby who tamed my distraction with her power, I still cringe at the memory of her calling me from school when one of the class chaperones failed to show up to take her second grade to see—oh, what a clutter stays forever in our minds!—the dubious choice of a movie, *Pete's Dragon*. She knew that I was a reluctant class mother; I protected (and taught her to protect) my time the way violinists protect their hands, and so I remember all too vividly how tremulously she asked me if I could possibly—"Oh, Mom, please, could you just this once?!"—fill in for the missing mother and come along with them to Nashua for the afternoon. Of course there was no way I would say no. But it is the way her regret and apology and something almost like fear accompanied her entreaty that lives with me even now. (It didn't make it any easier that, because I was one of those mothers with too many opinions, she knew what I thought of her teacher's choice of movie!)

And yet, and yet . . . here is a fragment of a letter she sent to me when she had just started college and I was away at the MacDowell Colony, where artists of many kinds retreat for a long spell of uninterrupted work: "I guess I don't get very much opportunity to tell you how proud I am of you. . . .When people find out who you are, although none of them knows your work ('Nothing personal'), they are so impressed. Although I usually answer with 'She's just my mom!' (because you are just my mom, after all!) I realize how . . . wonderful your accomplishments are.

. . . I know you've been having trouble with this book. I hope your time at MacDowell is peaceful and productive. . . . You can give me your *completed* novel for my birthday. If you are pleased with it, it is the best present I can get."

Why is it, I wonder, that no one in those Q&As has ever asked if I think that having a mother deeply committed to work like mine—exceptionally solitary until (one prays) it becomes exceptionally public—might be useful to a child, might be a model of dedication against difficult odds, with an uncertain outcome and modest rewards. Instead, the questions always seem to suggest a zero-sum game. And for mothers with other kinds of jobs, with different issues (long commutes, awful bosses, inflexible hours, paper grading long into the night, too many hours in airports and hotels, or sheer gut exhaustion and aching feet), why must the assumption be that children derive nothing from their example? No one dares challenge those who have to work for the paycheck, but it seems that those who fulfill less visible, internal needs will always be suspect, no matter how many days we devote to "Take Your Child to Work." (Boys get equal time these days. And why not? When my brother was a child and someone asked him what his father did at work all day, he brought forth all he knew about the matter: "He grows whiskers.")

There is no moral to this story. No one knows, when she is grabbing that nap time to disappear from the *here and now* into her own imagination, that she will ever hear her daughter speak lovingly of her "accomplishments." No one can promise herself, acknowledging her frequent absence even when she is present, that she is not cheating herself as well as her child. But there is will and there is need, and somewhere in the equation I suppose there must be—there was for me, however blind—faith that things will balance out; that for every choice that I would do this thing I had to do, with a different passion than the one I felt for my child but a passion nonetheless, that somehow she would gain something from it, too. Burying that passion is no solution; its denial will be smoke that rises from an invisible fire.

Tillie Olsen, who so often allowed her family and political obligations to distract her from her writing, published an entire book about the *Silences* that eat up so many lives (mainly, though not solely, women's). In it she speaks of the need to become a "habituated" writer, so that the work habit is ingrained and one needn't face down fresh guilt and self-denial, not to mention rusty muscles, every time she feels the tug of words.

Something that saved me, I think, is what comes of being so "habituated" that by now it takes more discipline for me *not* to write than to get a long day's work done. Just as my husband always insisted that my work was as important as his, and that I had the right to assume for it whatever protection it needed, so I had to respect it sufficiently to indulge that narcissism that every artist must have at her core. But that is what creative ambition—reflexive and rarely lucrative—looks like. Disappearing into one-self seems just as disruptive of a family's equilibrium as walking out the door in the morning with a briefcase or a black bag.

So be it, I finally learned to say. It is what it is, and if it feels like a choice, then perhaps it is one that can be ignored. In the end, to use the most frequently repeated words in the *I Ching*—they recur and recur, like a tolling bell sounding across the centuries—"No blame. No blame."

A little poem from my book, *Cora Fry*, uttered by a character who is describing me:

I have a neighbor
who is always deep
in a book or two.

High tides of clutter
rise in her kitchen.

Which last longer, words,
words in her bent head,
or the clean spaces

between one perfect
dusting and the next?

Why I Left My Children

Mari Leonardo

As told to
Marina Pineda-Kamariotis
and Camille Peri

I came to the United States three years ago on a tourist visa and I never went home. I work cleaning houses and taking care of people who are sick, and sometimes I take care of children. But it has been very difficult for me to see children here. Every night I have looked for my own children when I go home, but they are not there. That's why I don't like to go home. I just want to be out, because when I go home I remember them. I look at their photos. I say to myself, I've lost three years with them.

My mother grew up in Guatemala, one of four children who lived with their mother on the streets. Sometimes they slept in the park and their mother would put newspapers over them for blankets. Sometimes they slept in the doorway of a restaurant, and the owner would throw water on them to wake them in the morning. My mother never went to school. Today, even though she has not been homeless for years since she came to the United States, she still looks for things on the streets to take home.

My mom experienced life and death on the streets. Her mother beat her. She had too much responsibility for a little girl.

One of her most vivid memories is of bathing her baby brother in a public *pila* when he slipped from her arms and died. My mother watched her mother suffer a horribly painful death of ovarian cancer. She had no medicine to ease her suffering because she was homeless and destitute.

At nine years old, my mother was an orphan with nowhere to live. She was hired by a woman to help around the house, but if she broke something while cleaning, the woman would beat her on the head. The woman had a daughter for whom she bought beautiful clothes, and my mother would think, "When I get paid, I'm going to buy a dress just like hers." Then my mother and her younger sister were taken in by another woman. They earned their keep by helping her care for and clean up after her five children. Eventually my aunt ended up a prostitute. She would hide if she saw my mother coming, because my mother would give her a physical beating to stop her from continuing that lifestyle. She died, probably of AIDS, when she was about thirty-five. We don't know where her body is.

My mother's other sister was sold to a couple by her mother before she died. My grandmother must have thought that at least one child would be taken care of. My mother never saw her again. It's been thirty-two years, and she is still trying to find her.

My mother moved to Guatemala City and met my father when she was about seventeen. She went to a movie with him and then just went home with him. She didn't have anywhere else to go. About a month later, a woman knocked at the door, claiming to be his wife. My mother was already pregnant with me. Although my mother was in love with him, my father put her on a bus to the country, where his sister was living, and he went back to his wife. After I was born, he showed up and demanded that my mother give me to him. His plan was to take me away from my mother to raise me as a servant to his wife. He said to my mom, "You are nothing and you have nothing, so the baby is mine." But my mother had something—she had me. That was all she had. She ran to a park and sat crying with me in her arms. A kind woman saw her. When my mother told her what happened, the woman took her into her home for several months.

When she was twenty, my mother got together with my step-father, and they had three children together. He was a hard worker, but she was too young to be married. She was not really in love; she was looking for security. She still wanted to go out to dances without him. They were physically abusive with each other. I remember one night when I was twelve years old, she scratched his face while defending herself from him, and he broke a bottle and came after her with it. I was right in the middle of it, and I just fainted.

Just as my stepfather beat her, my mother beat me. But only me, not my half-brothers or half-sisters. I think she saw my father in me—literally, because I guess I look very much like him. And she was emotionally abusive, too. When I was thirteen and she was resting in a hammock, I went to her and said, "I love you." She answered, "Get away. I don't want to see you." Then my sister went up to her and my mom took her in her arms.

After my mother and stepfather split up for good when I was fifteen, things got very hard. My stepfather gave us no financial support. My mother did housework for other people, but she earned very little, barely enough to pay for our school books. When we could eat, we did; when we couldn't, we didn't. We often went to school hungry. I had a friend who fed me sometimes so that my mom could feed my brothers and sisters. Although my mother was mean to me, I could see how she sacrificed herself for us. She was only thirty-two years old, with four children to take care of alone.

I was eighteen, working as a dental assistant to help support the family, when I met Ruben*. He worked on a melon farm, checking the fruit for disease. One day shortly after I met him, I got in a fight with my sister and hit her, and my mom told me to get out of the house. I called Ruben to tell him that I was leaving, going to Guatemala City to look for my stepfather. He said, "Pack your things. I'm going to come and get you." He told me he didn't want

*The names of some people in this story have been changed to protect their privacy.

me to take the wrong path, to end up a prostitute or a drunk in Guatemala City. He told me I could stay with him in his brother's home, and I decided to take the risk.

Ruben went overboard to treat me well. He pampered me, brought me treats. I felt gratitude for his support when I needed it most, and that gratitude turned into love. Although his family thought I was coarse, he said he didn't care. He said he wanted me to be the mother of his children. For the first time, I felt loved and cared for. We were married in 1987. I was eighteen years old.

Despite thinking I was not good enough for her son, my mother-in-law did offer us a place to stay. She had a large lot of land and a small home next to her house. After we moved there, Ruben told me to stay at home, saying that I couldn't leave the house. I thought this was strange, but I was in love and I did what he told me. In Guatemala, a married woman is expected to wait on her husband—cook, clean, wash the clothes, everything. But gradually he started to treat me differently. He became easily agitated with me. He started to say the things his family said—that I was base because I came from a poor family, and that I would bring him down. He said, "They were right. Why did I set my sights on you?" He also started to push me around physically. He would pull my ear or hair for no reason.

I gave birth to our first son, Eddie, a year after we were married. Soon after, his father demanded that I begin to work to show his family that I could help support our family. I had already started to learn beautician skills, so I went to work for Ruben's nephew, who had a beauty salon.

I will never forget the first time Ruben brutally attacked me. I was twenty-one years old. My son was two. My husband was not working at the time, so I worked from about eight A.M. until six P.M., then had to rush home to make dinner for him. I was late one evening and a co-worker gave me a ride on his motorcycle. Ruben was very jealous. He was waiting for me at the door with our son in his arms. I was happy to see my son, and I took him and started to go into the house. Ruben grabbed my hand, took me into our bedroom, locked the door, and grabbed our son from me. He threw our son on our bed. He started to kick my legs and then he threw me on the floor and started to forcibly undress me. Our son was crying and screaming for me. Ruben said that I was cheating on him and with this, he thrust his finger inside my vagina. This whole time I was screaming and crying. He stood up and put the point of his boot on my throat, and I started to choke. I thought I was going to die. I looked into his eyes and said to him, "Please take care of my child, and God bless you." He let up and I gulped for air. Then he left the room.

A few days later, I was in extreme pain and I began to hemorrhage. Ruben called the family doctor, who said that I had to be taken to the hospital. There, I found out that I had been pregnant and was experiencing a miscarriage. Ruben felt guilty and he asked for my forgiveness. He said that he would never hit me again. I forgave him.

Although he continued to have outbursts, he did get better, and I thought that the miscarriage had taught him a lesson. We had two more children, Sandra and Carlos. Ruben bought equipment for me to operate a beauty salon and built an extra room onto the house. Clients began to come, and soon my business was doing well. But I knew Ruben was going out at night with other women. He would become affectionate with me just to get me to go to bed with him. If I refused, he would accuse me of being with other men, perhaps my clients.

About four months after Carlos was born, Ruben and I had sexual relations. It was very painful for me. The doctor told me that I had contracted a venereal disease from Ruben and that we had to undergo treatment. Ruben denied the whole thing. He knew that it was painful for me to have sexual relations, but he forced himself on me anyway.

Things got very bad between us. Ruben would say awful things to me. He would say that I was a prostitute just like my mother. He laughed at my Caesarian scars and said that no one would find me attractive. He began to hit me harder. He punched me in the face, threw me against the wall. I think he might have permanently injured my nose, because the bridge of my nose still hurts to this day. He started to sodomize me, and eventually I couldn't even walk from the pain. I seriously considered taking my own life to end my misery, but then I would think about my children and that would stop me. So, even bruised and scratched, I continued to act as a dutiful wife. I would bring him food to bed, anything to keep him from hurting me. I began to think maybe I was doing something wrong and that I deserved this abusive treatment.

Once Ruben became very angry with me because he could not find a clean pair of socks to wear that evening to go out. He grabbed my hands and squeezed them very hard, until I could hear and feel my bones crack. I told him that I was going to check the patio but I had it in mind to escape from him. There was a ladder on the patio that led to the roof, and I climbed it to get away. As I was climbing, Ruben came out on the patio and yelled that if I didn't have socks for him, he would choke me with the thick shoelace that he had in his hand. He climbed the ladder after me. He caught my foot and I fought with him to get away. He let go of me, and I jumped onto my neighbor's roof. My neighbor was surprised to see me, but she gave me refuge for about half an hour when she saw how frightened I was. She talked to Ruben to try and calm him down.

When my neighbor left, Ruben warned me that I had better not go to the police or I would find out the consequences. Ruben's family has many connections to the police force and to the military in Guatemala. One of his brothers was a police officer; another was an artillerist who was considered a hero for infiltrating Sandinista camps and single-handedly killing many Sandinistas. Other brothers and his sister had worked on military bases. And his family had money. In Guatemala, if you have money, you can get away with anything. Ruben threatened me, "If you ever divorce me, I'll take the children away from you." I knew he had the money and the power to do that. I knew I could do nothing to stop him.

Once, he pulled me out of the car on a bridge. He leaned me over the railing. Below us, the river was rushing over large rocks.

He threatened to throw me off the bridge. I got on my knees and begged him to spare my life. Ruben said he was satisfied with my answer and let me go. We returned to the house and he acted as if nothing had happened. I then knew that my life was in his hands.

My mother had left the country shortly after I was married, before my husband started beating me. She left to make more money so that my brothers could go to school to get teaching credentials. She was undocumented, so she crossed the border into the United States with a group of other undocumented workers. My mother was so brave to do that—I would never have had the courage. She got to San Francisco and got a work permit and sent money back, and my brothers did become teachers. Later, they joined her in the United States.

When I would tell my mother on the phone about Ruben's abuse, she would cry. She encouraged me to come to the United States, too. She said, "Come here, and we'll figure something out."

Back in Guatemala, my sister, Carmen, took me to the police station to file a criminal complaint. I got the courage to finally denounce Ruben. The police officer told us this was a family problem and I had to go to family court for a judge to decide whether I could leave the household. I told the judge I just wanted to get away from Ruben and take the children with me. She saw my injuries. She issued a court order acknowledging the abuse, prohibiting Ruben from harming me or any of my family, and providing authority for the police to protect me. But she said the children would have to stay with Ruben or he would have grounds to accuse me of kidnapping them. If I took them, I could be put in jail!

I went back to Carmen's house and stayed for a few weeks. The children came to see me and told me that they wanted to stay with me. Then Ruben came over and said that if I didn't return the children to him, he would have me "disappeared" and he would tell the children I had run off with another man. I borrowed money from my family to hire an attorney for the divorce process, but it was all for nothing. Ruben refused to sign the divorce papers and said that he was going to make my life impossible. Without his consent, the judge had no choice but to close our case. But she and a court psychologist recommended that I leave the house immediately to get away from Ruben.

I had nowhere to go. I couldn't stay with my sister indefinitely. I didn't want to go back to the house because I knew what Ruben would do to me. I borrowed money from my sister and rented an apartment, but I lived in fear that Ruben would come after me or that I would encounter him on the street. Was Ruben really going to have me killed? Would he hurt my children if I did not return to him? Not too long after this, my son Eddie, who was nine years old, knocked on my door and I opened it for him. His father jumped out from nowhere and forced the door open. He locked it behind him and pushed me onto the sofa. He put his legs against mine to pin me down. He grabbed my blouse and shook me, yelling that I was a prostitute. My son begged me to return to the house to make his father stop hurting me.

We returned to the house, and my husband told me to feed the children. My children and I were so happy to see each other, but they and I knew that I would no longer be safe. Before Eddie fell asleep, I told him to ask his father for the key to get water from outside, and I planned to use the key to lock myself in the room that had been created for my beauty salon. My son gave me the key, and I locked myself in. This was the only way that I knew I could save myself from Ruben. I literally had to jail myself to be liberated from him.

I locked myself away from everything. I would open the door for my children only when Ruben was gone from the house. They would feed me. I was suffering from an episode of the herpes I'd contracted from Ruben, so I had to send my daughter to get medicine for me. Once, Ruben threatened to pump propane fumes into the room to poison me and get me out. Sandra heard this and called her brothers to save me. While their father was in the kitchen, the children came to the door and I opened it for them. Sandra yelled at her father that he would have to poison them too.

I stayed in my "jail" for a month. Ruben had plans to leave for Boston, where he had family. Before he left, he told me to stop acting "stupid" and to come to an agreement. He wanted me to join him in Boston and find work there, but first he said I could visit my mother in San Francisco. The children could stay with my sister Carmen while we were gone. I agreed. Since my children were everything to me, Ruben didn't question whether I would join him or return to Guatemala; he felt sure I would.

Once Ruben left, I was able to come out of my jail. I was so happy to be finally alone with my children, but it was only for a few days. I told them that I had only a little time with them because I was going to see my mother in San Francisco. We cried and cried, but I trusted God to take care of the children and me. I left for the United States in June of 2001. It broke my heart to go. I had never been separated from them before.

Once I joined my mother in San Francisco, I thought about my life with Ruben. I had already breathed freedom for those few days when he was gone from Guatemala and I was alone with my children. In San Francisco, I had family who would care for me and protect me. I called my children and told them that I was going to stay in the United States. It was the hardest thing I ever had to do. My children are my life. But they were supportive because they knew that my life was in danger if I stayed with Ruben any longer. My oldest son said, "I'd prefer that you leave us, go far away, than to have to bury you some day. And I don't want to make a mistake that I'll regret for the rest of my life." He was twelve years old at the time.

When I called Ruben to tell him that I wasn't going to return with him, he became very angry and said that he was not going to send any money to my sister for our children. He said that once he returned to Guatemala, he would take the children back and turn them against me. True to his word, he did not send any money. My family helped me send money for their food and support. And when he returned, he started saying terrible things about me to our children.

I had one moment of hope the following year. My son Eddie came to the United States. Briefly, I had dreams that his father would tire of having the children and send them to live with me. But my son told me that his father's plan was for him to persuade me to return to Guatemala. He told me that his father was bringing women to the house; that he would leave the children alone at night; that he had a new business, a bar where the men would get out of control; and that he had begun carrying a gun. I wanted my son to stay with me and I enrolled him in school, but he decided to return. He felt that he needed to protect his brother and sister from their father. When I dropped him off at the airport, I had to say good-bye in the parking lot because I didn't have legal status and could not risk going inside. My son told me not to cry or he wouldn't have the strength to go on with his journey. I sat in the car and held my tears. I was afraid I would never see him again. As he walked away, he kept turning around to blow kisses to me.

In the meantime, I learned that I didn't have to get Ruben's permission for a divorce if I divorced him while I was living in California. I wasn't sure if this would be my freedom or my death warrant. I was trembling and crying as I filled out the papers and filed them in court. I called Ruben, and he said he would not sign the papers. I told him that the U.S. laws were different and that I didn't need his permission to divorce him. He just laughed at me and he never returned the papers. The divorce went through and I was free.

Coming to this country, I realized that women have value. My immigration attorney suggested I go to Woman Inc., a place that provides therapy for women in domestic violence situations. I did, and that helped me to see that even I had worth. I then sought and was granted asylum.

It has been two years now since the divorce. I was abused by my husband for thirteen years, but I escaped from that life and I feel better. I live in my own apartment. I can give an opinion, I can make decisions for myself, I can work, and I decide where the money is going to go. I am finally in control of my own life.

I live near my mother, but I can't live with her. She is still abusive to me emotionally. When I came here to be with her, I never imagined that she would treat me this way. I thought she would be happy to have her daughter with her. Sometimes I feel like I never want to see her again, that I don't want to feel this heaviness inside anymore. But I know that she is not a bad person. I understand why she is the way she is because of what I've been through now.

Over the last two years, I have called my children often and tried to be a mother to them from here. I know they have not been doing as well in school. I know that Ruben has insulted them and said they are good for nothing and stupid like their mother. The kids have told me that they hate their father; they can't forget what he did to me—that is what they carry inside of them. They say, "What he's done to us has no name."

On the phone one day, my older son said to me, "I was feeling so lonely and I thought about you." I asked, "What did you think about?" And he said, "I remember when we were going to bed and you would kneel at our bedsides and bless each one of us. Now I kneel and pray to God to protect my mother. I miss your kisses, Mommy. But don't worry, I'm going to take care of my brother and my sister. And someday we're going to treat you like a queen."

My heart hurt so much. It has been only with the help of God that I have been able to endure this pain. My faith stopped me from taking my life, because I believe that only God can decide when I am to die. I have wanted to rest, but I suppose that God had another plan for me. I prayed that Ruben would find peace within himself. I prayed for the safety of my children. I prayed that one day I would see them again. It is my children who have given me the strength to stay here. I want to make a better life for them, to make sure they get a good education. My goal is to have my own house for them to live in here.

And now, that may happen soon. I spoke to my ex-husband recently by phone. He was jovial and joking, not the man who used to yell and threaten me. He has a new girlfriend. After all I went through, he now wants to make our divorce legal in Guatemala. He asked me, "Do you want the kids?" From his perspective, he's better off without them because they're a financial burden. I had always been the one who was responsible for the kids, watching over them, so for him, it will be just one less thing to do.

I got off the phone and I was shaking. Finally, everything I've waited for is coming my way. I immediately started sending money to my son to pay for the airline tickets for them to come in October. I'm worried about supporting them in this country that is so expensive. But I believe that God will help me and I will have work.

There isn't a night since I've been away from my children that I haven't asked God to watch over them. I've asked God, *When will my children be with me? What is the price I have to pay?* I guess the price has been the waiting for this beautiful moment. Before we hung up the phone, my son Eddie said, "Pretty soon we won't have kisses by telephone anymore, Mom. In October I'm going to give you real kisses."

Invisible Worlds

Nora Okja Keller

When my older daughter was three, she started visiting the "invisible world." Slipping into a seam of air, she'd enter this imaginary country where she was proclaimed queen.

"There are so many children there, Mama," my then only child would tell me, "so many friends."

Playing the ultimate hostess, she often invited these friends into her world and insisted that I treat them as family. "Don't forget to brush Asha's, Annie's, and Sarala's hair too," she'd say when I braided her hair. Or: "Aki just loves the way you read *Goodnight Moon*," she'd gush. "Will you read it to her again?"

On those days, I would hear my daughter tromping through the rooms of the house, providing the ambassadors from the invisible world with informational tours: "This is the bedroom, where dreams come from. . . . This is the bathroom, where doots comes from. . . . This is the refrigerator, where milk comes from." And always when they reached the kitchen, I would have to supply my daughter and her entourage with snacks—pouring not just one glass of milk, but three or four; offering cookies not just to the only child I could see, but to a gang of unseen ones as well.

"I'm like the Old Woman in the Shoe!" I wailed to my mother, only half-joking as I described the way my daughter talked to and about her invisible friends.

Instead of chuckling over my daughter's imagination, my mother scolded me: "I told you not to have so many kids!"

"But, but," I stammered, thinking my mother misunderstood. "They're not real kids!"

"So?" she scoffed. "The work is real, isn't it? Tell her to send them all home!"

But I was reluctant to take my mother's advice. Perhaps because I spend so much of my own time exploring the alternate universes provided by books, I wanted to indulge my own child, to nurture her own creations. "You go right on playing with your pretend friends," I told my daughter.

"Don't call them pretend!" my daughter chastised. "Just because you can't see them doesn't mean they're not real." And with little murmurs and coos, she turned to soothe her slighted friends' hurt feelings.

Five years later, my second daughter turned three. "Mama!" she yelled after an afternoon of playing in her older sister's bedroom. "I went to the invisible world carnival! And somebody came back with me!"

I squinted and nodded to the air next to her shoulder. "Hello," I said, ready to handle a new batch of imaginary playmates. "Nice to meet you."

My daughter laughed. "No, silly. My friend is here," she said, pointing behind her. "W is shy."

W, the invisible friend, just happens to love ice cream bars and Popsicles, Gummy Bears, and chocolate chip cookies—my little girl's favorite snacks. She also likes to color on walls and tables, doorways and couches; the walls of our house are adorned with hip-height, prehistoric-like paintings of stick people with bulbous heads. When I found the first rainbow-hued mural scrawled across my bathroom door, I took a deep breath and thought about how to reprimand my daughter in a way that was stern yet supportive of her emerging creativity.

"I love your artwork," I said, "but we do not scribble on the walls. Crayons go on paper."

My daughter took a deep, mother-type breath herself, then let it out in a long-suffering sigh. "That's what I told W," my daughter replied. "But she said they don't have paper in the 'visible world."

One day, W brought a gift from the invisible world. "Look, Mama," my daughter said, running toward me with her hands cupped. "It's foo, foo!"

"Food? Food?" I repeated and lifted the invisible offering from her hands. "Thank you!" I said and, smiling at her and where I thought W might be, popped the morsel into my mouth. I put on a big show: smacking my lips, closing my eyes as I chewed with relish and delight. I made loud gulping noises as I swallowed the imaginary snack.

I opened my eyes to see my daughter, stunned with horror, burst into tears. "Foo Foo!" she screamed.

"What's the matter?" I asked, patting her back, frantically scanning for spontaneous cuts or bruises. "Are you hurt? Tell me!"

My daughter wailed louder, and when I couldn't get her to calm down, I called for her older sister.

"What's she saying?" I asked, hoping she could interpret what had gone wrong. "All I did was eat some of her pretend food." Making another attempt to placate my grief-stricken daughter, I added a compliment: "And it was delicious." I rubbed my belly. "Mmmm-mmmm, good."

My older daughter gasped. "Mama! She's not saying, 'Food, food'; she's saying, 'Foo Foo'!"

"Foo Foo?" I repeated slowly, knowing something bad was coming.

"Foo Foo!" my younger daughter screamed.

"Foo Foo," my older daughter confirmed, "is W's puppy dog. I think it was a poodle."

I tried coughing Foo Foo back up. "There," I said, spitting into my hand and pretending to pet a soggy lump of regurgitated dog. "Good as new."

Both daughters shook their heads. Foo Foo was gone, never to return.

• • •

In the first few weeks after the alleged digestion of Foo Foo, when my daughters' grief was still palpable, I tried to resurrect him numerous times. Pointing into various corners, I claimed Foo Foo sightings. "There, he's back! I see him under the piano." I cocked my head and whispered, "I hear barking. . . . It's Foo Foo, behind the couch!"

"No," my baby would say each time. "He's gone forever. In your stomach."

Even now, months later, my daughters continue to reminisce about the demise of their invisible pet. The other night, the girls and I rented *Good Boy*, and after the movie about a dog and his boy was over, my younger daughter snuggled up to her older sister and sniffed, "Remember Foo Foo?"

"Yeah," my older daughter said, shaking her head slowly and sadly. "He was such a good dog."

My younger daughter turned her face up toward the ceiling and howled, "Why did Mom have to eat him!" I almost expected her to shake her fist at God and curse her fate.

"Oh, please!" I said, finally impatient with their ongoing drama. "You know that's not true!"

My older girl narrowed her eyes at me. "What's not true?" she growled. "Are you saying you think that Foo Foo was just pretend?"

"He was real! He was real!" my younger daughter cried.

"Of course he was—is!" I backpedaled. "I just meant it's not true I ate him." I whirled and pointed out the window. "Hey, there he goes now! Foo Foo just ran under the lanai chair!"

"No, he didn't!" My younger daughter fisted her hands on her hips and stamped her foot. "Don't try to trick us!"

My older daughter pursed her lips. "Mom," she said, "you shouldn't act like you see when it's obvious you don't. Only children see the invisible world. Only children really believe."

I looked at her, suddenly struck by how old she seemed. "Do you still see it? Do you still visit there?"

"Of course," she said.

Later that day, she came back to me, her journal in hand. "I'm writing down everything about the invisible world," she explained.

"May I read it?" I asked.

She shrugged, passing it to me, and this is what I read on the first page: "Some people believe in magic when they're kids and totally disbelieve it when they're grown up. I don't want that to happen to me. I don't want to stop seeing the invisible world. I don't want to stop believing in magic."

"Keep writing everything down," I told her, thinking that the journal will be a good way for her and her sister to remember what they saw and imagined at this age, that these memories themselves will one day provide another type of magic; hopefully, the words my daughter writes now will later remind her and her sister to keep believing in their own dreams and visions, even if—especially if—the rest of the world doesn't.

As for me, I still keep an eye out for Foo Foo, hoping to catch a true glimpse of him under the kitchen table as I cook dinner, between the bookshelves as I dust, behind the desk as I write, coaxing various imaginary characters onto the page, conjuring my own invisible worlds.

The Babysitters' Club

Ann Hulbert

For spring break my almost thirteen-year-old daughter
begged me to take her across town to help out with day care at
Martha's Table, which runs children's programs and a soup
kitchen in Washington, D.C. A seventh-grade service project with
school had introduced her to the Classroom A kids—three- and
four-year-olds—and she wanted to see them again. Needed to see
them: that was actually how she put it. Clare isn't a saint, but she
is adored by Zachary* (who looks, she told me, like a little football player). And she's the one who can get Terrell to go down for
his nap. ("I miss my mommy, I miss my mommy, I miss my
mommy," he chants as she pats his back.) Javier is her small
shadow, grateful for her efforts to speak rudimentary Spanish, the
only language he knows. Over the weekend, before her vacation
stint of child care was going to begin, she asked me more than
once, "Do you think they'll have forgotten me?"

I still remember Jane, the teenager who babysat for me and
my older brother and younger sister the summer I was seven. In
fact, if democracy had prevailed in our household, there would
have been a living memorial to her in our family: that fall, when a
new baby sister arrived, the three of us lobbied very hard to name

---

*The names of some people in this story have been changed to protect their
privacy.

her Jane. It strikes me now as an apt, if upside-down, tribute. The status we had just acquired, thanks to our "afterthought" baby, was something like what Jane enjoyed: she was in a sense a sibling caretaker. She wasn't a squabbling competitor (as we three older kids often were with one another), but she wasn't an adult authority figure, either—though I recall we were flustered, and fascinated, when she showed up one day with a boyfriend. Jane was the relevant future seen up close, and no gesture, expression, intonation, item of clothing—or, that day, bit of flirtation—went unnoticed. And yet Jane, whose energetic swagger I swear I could still recognize if I saw her on the street, had us convinced that she hadn't yet forgotten our language. She was still one of us, and we worshipped her.

The feeling was not awe, but a kind of highly charged enthrallment—altogether different from the honor and reverence that children are said to have felt for their parents once upon a time. It's more like the imaginative allegiance inspired by those magically young-at-heart nannies—Mary Poppins, even the Cat in the Hat—who have starred in children's favorite escapist literature for decades now. Yet it isn't quite that. Young babysitters aren't mother substitutes who usher their charges into an exotic realm, but who can be counted on to have them scrubbed and calm when the parents return. They're more like parent apprentices, nominally in charge but subliminally aware, as their charges are too (and so are their employers), that they're in less than complete control. Those fictional nanny figures, supervising fairy tale–like flights from the familiar, help sustain a sort of extended childhood. But girl (and more rarely boy) babysitters are testing their autonomy, teetering on the brink of maturity and encroaching on the edges of adulthood, with their charges in rapt (and sometimes unruly) tow.

Or at least that's my rather romantic memory of it, from both ends—as Jane's acolyte and, later, as a sought-after babysitter myself, caught up in the role of undercover agent in other families' lives. Paid to be an ally of children, which came naturally to me, I found myself well placed to spy, indirectly, on parents—

who, since they weren't mine, invited probing. Perusing book-shelves and even poking into drawers, I couldn't resist prowling once the kids were asleep. As penance of a sort for my snooping (my biggest finds were a diaphragm and a copy of *Fanny Hill*), I rarely indulged in the expected babysitter misbehavior. I didn't raid the refrigerator or tie up the telephone (not that parents back then ever called to "check in"—at least I certainly don't remem-ber it). I was a low-impact interloper.

I even made sure to look cheerfully clueless when my employers returned flushed and loud, and when the fathers who gallantly walked me home bumped into me more than a few times along the way. Little did they know what an expert I was at assessing states of parental inebriation, much less that I, an overly dutiful adolescent who was finding it hard to rebel, was busy ferreting out (or at any rate, fantasizing about) the dark side of domesticity. I was convinced I had intuited the true story of the trim tennis-playing mother who hired me for the meltdown hours of the day, 5:30 to 7:30 P.M. She came to the door all dressed in white and ready to play, but her real mission was elsewhere: a martini in the lounge area by the neigh-borhood's indoor courts, or was it adultery? (I wavered, wishing I knew more about her husband, a handsome preppie whose cologne-tinted scent wafted from his closet but who never got home from the office before I left.) Her kids hurtled toward me ready to play, too. The rumpus was wild, and as it got wilder, I started sweating along with them—seized with that radiating anxiety I could remember as a riled-up child myself. Who was in charge here? The adult-imposed order seemed fragile as I got the hot, damp bodies fed and bathed, but I also had a rare feeling: a sense of my own power.

Amid the bright lights and antiseptic smell at Martha's Table, Clare's child-care avocation makes my babysitting forays as a kid look amateurish and sheltered and yet also—like so much in the unregimented past of my adolescence—a little dangerous by cur-rent safety-conscious standards. Poison control, the rescue squad, even a phone number where parents could be reached: I have no memory of being equipped with an emergency list, and did infant CPR even exist? In the late 1960s and early 1970s, I was still doing much the same unmonitored, in-home tending that had flourished in my childhood during the 1950s, when the term "babysitter" first made it into the dictionary—only for me and my friends, the proto-parenting was happening against a backdrop of feminist and family turmoil that was headed who knew where.

For Clare, I'm struck by how the landscape has changed. Occasionally, she does have old-style neighborhood jobs, and she's a hit in part because having "big girl Clare" come is such an exciting departure from the usual round of grownup guardians (often the nanny network) that most parents I know use—so exciting, in fact, that two kids around the corner, when they learn that Clare's on for the evening, clamor to come over hours early to get her. But for the most part, like so much else in her life, from sports to playdates, babysitting for her has all but ceased to be an improvisational, unsupervised pursuit—a chance to write the rules for an afternoon or evening, to tyrannize and empathize on her own terms, to infiltrate another family, however briefly. There are no tipsy dads chauffeuring her, just her own familiar mother shuttling her to and fro.

So what is it, exactly, that draws a girl with a packed extracurricular schedule to the institutionalized, organized, adult-directed work she does across town, I've wondered? Not surprisingly, the Martha's Table staff welcomed Clare back for another week under the impression that she was polishing off some community service requirement or other: that is de rigueur on the résumés kids these days are busy burnishing well before the college crunch arrives (and it's what keeps Martha's Table going—waves of volunteers meeting assorted standards of do-goodism). "Don't forget to give us whatever paperwork you'd like us to fill out," the day-care director told us as we stopped by her office on the way out one afternoon. I would be lying if I said that I hadn't considered the possible future cachet of this highly presentable pastime of Clare's; I had even briefly wondered whether it might have occurred to my super-conscientious child, too. I wondered again that day as I paused to watch her through the glass-windowed door of Classroom A before collecting her in the nap-time lull. There she sat, studiously filing each kid's daily form (about meals, activities, behavior) in the right take-home bin—a day-care bureaucrat, worlds away from the undercover agent I'd imagined I was.

But I could tell from the utterly blank look Clare gave the director that the last thing on her mind was some take-home form attesting to *her* performance or, for that matter, any need to explain her presence there on her vacation. "See you tomorrow," she said in the cheerfully polite tone she's cultivated for conversing with adults, and left with me at her heels. I picked up some news on the way to the car. Zachary had acted up on the class walk that day, because Clare had been asked to hold two other kids' hands. Javier, she was pleased to report, had finally spoken up in circle time. My girl then sighed a little like a beleaguered mother, saying she was tired, and flicked on the radio as usual.

I guess I shouldn't have been surprised that when we got home she didn't want to curl up for a mother-daughter reading of *Jane Eyre*—the novel about a "raw school-girl governess" that had mesmerized me back when I was beginning my babysitting career. Even for my bookish daughter, that was carrying spring break enrichment too far. ("Family reading," which we used to squeeze in, lately makes her roll her eyes.) Together we'd gotten through poor orphan Jane's red room ordeals at the hands of the heartless Reed clan, and met Bessie, a raw unschooled nursemaid herself. Barely more than a child, Bessie was a capricious yet kindhearted source of comfort before Jane was cast out, first to the cruelest of "charitable" schools and then to "earn the dependent's crust among strangers."

From there I carried on alone, and rereading, I couldn't help wondering how much of Brontë's subversive portrait of unprotected childhood I had truly absorbed at twelve. Half waif, half wise witness left adrift in a bleak world, Jane had hovered over my rather gothic investigation of dark passions behind the doors of adulthood— but of course there had been no haunted attics or craggy, love-struck employers in my babysitting adventures. When Mr. Rochester sighed to Jane, "You Neophyte, that have not passed the porch of life, and are absolutely unacquainted with its mysteries," I think I remember feeling that she, and I, knew it was not so simple as her enamored "master" thought. In truth, though, I had barely peered into the vestibule of life. What Clare would have made of Brontë's insight into the brutal drama of dependency and thwarted intimacy, I realized I really had no idea.

And as I thought about it, I wasn't entirely disappointed that she put the book off. It had never struck me before how spooked some of my favorite writers have been by the spectacle of vigorous, virginal caretakers dispatched into the corrupt adult world—and if Clare wasn't yet drawn in by Brontë's ur-tale on the sexually charged theme, maybe so much the better. From anti–child labor crusades to latchkey-kid panic, irregular custodial arrangements for children have aroused alarm for more than a century—and inspired some haunting fiction. Literally haunting, if you think of Henry James's *The Turn of the Screw*, a very different story about a "young and pretty" governess and ill-fated orphans, in which who can say where innocence ends and depravity begins?

Compared with her friend James, and with Brontë, Edith Wharton was astutely satiric rather than gothic in her exploration of precocious—and precarious—nurture in *The Children* (1928), a book of hers I had belatedly stumbled on. Her title, it's immediately clear, applies not just to the wandering tribe of siblings at the center of the novel, but also to their elders—divorce-prone American parents too distracted to be bothered with the offspring produced by their convoluted (often trans-Atlantic) affairs. Wharton's fifteen-year-old "little mother," Judith, the eldest of eight, steps up as "playmate, mother and governess all in one; and the best of each in its way," joining Jane Eyre as a valiant survivor of adult negligence. "If children don't look after each other, who's going to do it for them?" she says as she shepherds her flock from crisis to crisis. "You can't expect parents to, when they don't know how to look after themselves." In the Brontë tradition,

Wharton plants a middle-aged male admirer at the heart of the story, drawn by Judith's uncanny blend of competence and innocence. Yet is he protector or predator? He's certainly no Mr. Rochester, and in the end Wharton doesn't hold out very promising prospects for a weary Judith and her juniors, forced to grow up too soon.

Even (or especially) in the family-focused 1950s, when the spectacle of young parents-in-training fit the postwar ideal of domesticity, Brontë's insight into the power of young interlopers to upset domestic harmony and hierarchy lived on as a literary theme. The scene of Francis Weed, swiftly kissed by the babysitter he's been lusting after as he drives her home, is so vividly lodged in my head that I'd almost swear I was an impressionable babysitter myself when I first read John Cheever's story "The Country Husband," which won the O. Henry Award in 1956 (the year I was born). But of course I must have been older, not least because I remember being struck by Cheever's prescience about suburban suffocation: he had diagnosed the male version of Friedan's problem that has no name.

Well before *The Feminine Mystique* (and before, as the story notes, divorce had come to his fictional Shady Hill), Cheever evoked a quietly disenchanted couple whose scripted routines get derailed by a night visitor—a sitter who is not "the old lady who usually stayed with the children" but a young girl, "frowning and beautiful." In the fable-like story, she offers the illusion of liberation: Francis is swept up in a passionate infatuation. But Cheever has frustration in store. Husband and wife briefly rebel against their daily rounds and roles, only to end up clinging to each other in childlike dependence. And the babysitter, catalyst though she is of glowing fantasies, is hemmed in herself. Saddled with a father who's "a terrible rummy," she has a jobless—and hapless—fiancé, who can't wait to marry and "have a large family."

Thank God I didn't hear of Robert Coover's "The Babysitter," which came out in 1969, when I was still a novice at the job. What a jolt the intervening decade had delivered: Cheever's wistful parable is reborn as a disorienting horror story.

In cross-cutting scenes of mounting mayhem, Coover lets every character's consciousness loose to spin out libidinal fantasies. As the TV flickers and jangles in the background and the phone keeps ringing, the suburban house fills up with the conflicting, converging urges that grip the babysitter's edgy boyfriend and his sinister buddy, the blubbery drunken father, the keyed-up kids and screaming baby, and the hormonally supercharged babysitter herself. Violence erupts, and Coover's surreal montage poses a disconcerting question: Is what's happening fantasy or not?

I didn't see the movie version of Coover's story when it appeared in 1995 either. (It's an adaptation, I gather, in the terrifying tradition of *When a Stranger Calls* of 1979, which popularized the chilling refrain, "Have you checked the children?") Back in the babysitting market by then, this time on the employer end, I knew enough to steer clear—and to expect getting more than my quota of sitter horror stories from the newspaper. In 1997, even dogged efforts to avoid bad childcare news (and isn't the most unnerved mother, and father, among us in fact perversely drawn to it?), were futile in the face of nightmares no novelist would dare invent. It was a Kennedy—one of RFK's sons, Michael—to emerge that spring as the ultimate dad-you-don't-trust-to-drive-the-babysitter-home. He'd begun a four-year affair with a family babysitter when she was fourteen, just the age of the Catholic girl two doors down from us who giggled irrepressibly (and ate voraciously) whenever she came over to watch our kids. A few months later came the murder trial of an eighteen-year-old British au pair, Louise Woodward, charged with shaking her infant charge to death—an anti–Mary Poppins drama that kept Americans riveted.

By these standards, Alice McDermott's novel of a couple of years ago about a fifteen-year-old star babysitter, *Child of My Heart*, hardly rates as shocking, I suppose. "If my husband tries to fuck you while I'm gone, don't be frightened. He's an old man, and he drinks. Chances are it will be brief": though those parting words, delivered by the mother who leaves her baby in young Theresa's care, ring harshly in the early 1960s setting of the story, of course I'd heard a lot worse. Still, with my then sixth grader beginning to get a few calls for nearby jobs, McDermott's novel struck me as particularly unsettling. Theresa's first-person reminiscence of one freighted summer of child care— a sort of portrait of the artist as a young babysitter—hit a nerve as my newly independent daughter headed out among strangers.

Here was a curiously lyrical summation of the long-standing fear, and allure, at the heart of the babysitting saga: the secret of family bonds isn't simply, or mostly, bliss and safety, but loss—of freedom, of control, even of innocent trust. It's a secret that adults generally try to keep from children, yet can't help betraying— certainly to adolescents intent on discovering it for themselves. McDermott's mellifluous delivery makes the message, if anything, seem more ominous—and timeless. Parents can behave like capricious children (that mother in the novel absconds to New York City for weeks, her artist husband is indeed horny and rummy, and every other adult is somehow adrift). Even model adolescents like Theresa are elusive, and transgressive, creatures. And vulnerable children are at the mercy of both. In McDermott's Long Island enclave, domestic responsibility has a way of deadening creativity and breeding cruelty. Yet it also inspires curiosity and empathy, and her babysitter narrator (a *Jane Eyre* fan) is a reminder that young interlopers in the lives of others can be busy honing their imaginative gifts.

So perhaps it was perverse of me to balk when Clare, then eleven, picked up McDermott's novel—the two lollipops on its cover made it look almost like preteen fare—when I'd just put it down. I knew the flap copy would draw my eager reader in. "Theresa is . . . a wonder with children and animals—but also a solitary soul already attuned to the paradoxes and compromises of adult life": it sounded almost like a profile of my girl, an uncanny analyst of character and, as it happened, a petless child devoted to dogs. What lay behind my protective urge, when I thought about it, wasn't a desire to cosset Clare or play censor, but the opposite. Let her launch her babysitting career on her own, without a writer's vision in her head—without yet more adult apprehension hedging her in.

After all, it isn't that I thought the mother's warning to Theresa would be all that jarring, even to a young reader like Clare. Inevitably, she's been steeped in PG-13 entertainment and has read her share of young adult "problem" literature drenched in family dysfunction. She's well armed with the latest enlightenment on such topics as sexual harassment, child abuse, date rape. (As for the actual deflowering scene, which is brief indeed, Judy Blume gets more graphic than that.) But that's precisely why I bothered to put away McDermott's book, a Brontë-inspired story shadowed not just by sex but by a child's death. Kids today have been reared on public warnings about endangered childhood, embattled parenthood, marital woes, harried households—a legacy not just of the fraught era of my adolescence but of decades of mounting alarm about the eroding home. What heartens me about my daughter's caretaking spirit is how undaunted, and unhaunted, she is.

Martha's Table is organized and supervised, but it's anything but familiar. Gentrification hasn't hit the neighborhood yet, and Clare, the private-school helper—she continued going once a week after spring break—doesn't exactly blend in with the regular staff. (I've meant to ask what she did on lunch break during that vacation week, since I doubt she parked herself at the hall table where the teachers eat and talk, often in Spanish.) Clare doesn't seem deterred by the hints she gets of dire family hardships. The children get fed breakfast because they might go without it otherwise, and some of the parents who pick them up look awfully young. I'm equally struck by how eager Clare is to be needed—to be helpful and, yes, powerful, able to maintain order and dispense comfort and guidance (and, in spare moments, sort papers). Isn't that what we need—kids who feel necessary? There's an irony at the heart of a century devoted to sequestering and protecting vulnerable children: we've all but eradicated the useful child. "Do you think they miss me?" Clare asks. "I miss them," she says.

I don't worry that she's emotionally overinvesting in the kids, or paving the way for a life of full-time domesticity: this is day care, and she's a girl with ambitions. She's thrilled to be the object of crushes among her charges, and she's doting in return, but she's also picked up a certain cool-headedness from the Classroom A teachers. They're matter-of-fact and pragmatic, the unsentimental style Jane Eyre favored yet knew might discomfit "persons who entertain solemn doctrines about the angelic nature of children, and the duty of those charged with their education to conceive for them an idolatrous devotion . . . ," doctrines Jane dismissed as "humbug." Clare is well aware that child care is not bliss. First hand, as a kid herself and as a babysitter, she's experienced her share of stress and injustice, and has had to deal with tedium and messes. Zachary mopes or gets mad when her attention is elsewhere, super-sensitive Brianna won't share, one weepy toddler from the younger class insists on being held, nonstop, out in the play yard (which irritates the other teachers, but Clare's still narrow hip is ever ready). Nap time is long but rarely peaceful, and one of the aides can be a little heartless.

I suppose I could worry when I stop to realize that my daughter owes not just her realism about little kids, but also her unusual enthusiasm for tending them, in no small part to a youthful babysitter I hired back when Clare was seven and my son was ten, someone they adored and admired: Lena was a teenage mother. As a Howard University junior, she headed over every day after school with her toddler in tow (and no father in sight). But I don't worry. Lena reminds me of the Jane of my youth—a charismatic figure (a great athlete, even) who immediately inspired worship— and Lena's daughter was the little sister I had never produced, despite Clare's pleas. Lena reigned over all three kids with a blend of rigor and vigor I couldn't begin to match, and then she graduated and went off to Teach for America. My daughter isn't the only one who will never forget her.

But will Clare's Classroom A kids remember her, she keeps asking? The four-year-olds, she suddenly realized after a long summer away, are heading off to kindergarten. But Zachary, as luck would have it, has a little brother who should be moving up. I don't think Clare will be moving on.

Ourselves, Carried Forward

Beth Kephart

I married a man who seduced me with stories about the shape and the smell of his youth. He'd spent time in a jungle, he said, and caught glimpses of witches. He'd surfed with the sharks and saved his brother from earthquakes. Even the marketplaces of my husband's past were mythic, and there were talking birds and flaming fighter jets; eruptions in the street; big spiders; a cave that led to a cavern that finally spiraled right down into the belly of the earth.

It takes nothing to listen to a man who tells stories; it takes something to believe in your own. I didn't. With every scene my husband resurrected, my past lost volume, rhythm, color. The birds didn't talk where I'd come from; they just clung to limbs and twittered. My backyard had a strawberry patch; jungles were for Tarzan. There were no bombs in the silver jets overhead, there were no sharks as big as surfboards at the shore, and witches hobbled near but once a year, when they traded their taunts for candy. There is little democracy when it comes to telling stories; the best stories always rule. The untold stories fade away, and memory goes flaccid.

I claimed as my right and my talent the present moment. The sun skewered on the horizon. The overwrought attitude of spring. The cool in a plank of shaded floorboard. The imminent heat of a hearth. Touch this. Hear this. Smell this. Know this. I was good at that, and that, as it so happens, is what motherhood requires: A capacity for being here now, in the company of a child. A talent for pointing the way toward wings and stars and snow. A faith in the transitory shimmer. We named things together, my son, Jeremy, and I. We figured out (a conspiracy) just what it was that we loved. And when things got hard—because things always do get hard—we defined what we were up against and did our best to solve it. My son wasn't asking for my childhood stories. My husband had already settled on who I was. If there was time at the end of those long mothering days, I did not spend it adding fractions of my past.

I was the memoirist who wrote little of her childhood. I was the wife who knew more about her husband's history than she could conjure of her own. I was the high school graduate who could not remember the name of her third-grade teacher, or her fifth, and I was also, all this time, the sister who grew up listening to her brother talk about moments that were, in her mind, indistinct, the color of old denim. All of which was just fine, I told myself, because I was living in the moment. I was alive, with a child.

I am not trying to suggest that my entire past had gone and vanished, nor am I undermining the inevitable ways the past will waggle forward. Someone from before will hunt you down with a treasure of a tale; it always happens. Someone will salvage an old photograph and present it to you in a frame. They will say, inevitably, *I remember you singing.* They will ask (an unexpected question), *Whatever happened to that shoe box?* And one afternoon, in winter, your brother will get a look on his face that suggests honeysuckle and lightning bugs, stars watched from the roof. My brother climbed trees when he was young; I am certain of this, this I remember. My sister made mud patties near the swing. I played kickball and ice skated and once, in sixth grade, I won all the blue ribbons on a sun-soaked Field Day and then again, during that very same year (but was it before or was it after Field Day?), I was doing my best with a science test when the teacher, whose name I still cannot remember, called me to her desk and said, *Your mother's car has been hit hard by a truck, but she's okay, don't worry. Go home. Be with her. Tell her we are sorry.* Walking home, running home, flying to my mother.

A splash of paint on a stretch of canvas. A jagged, blinding flash.

Everyone knows something about memory. Everyone knows what and how it is: episodic and aggrandizing, mischievous, iconic. It defines some waylaid part of us when we find our way back to it. When our lives start to shift, when the husband's tales are already told, when the son, that daily companion, is off increasingly on his own, then it is time for our own stories. "I'll see you, Mom," Jeremy had started saying (standing at the door in his leather jacket, headed down the street, toward his job). "See you." He'd grown taller than I'll ever be. He knew things I'll never know. He had his cache of secrets, a cluster of girls with whom he flirted, things that he alone had chosen to fight for or to love. The house felt emptier than it had in years, and in ways that I won't count or measure, I was keeping company with myself.

I wasn't sorry that my son was tall. I wasn't sorry that he understood himself, that he had his friends, that he knew precisely where he stood on politics, rap, religion, torn pants, movie plots, and girls. I wasn't sorry that when I looked up, into his face, I glimpsed more man than child. We had gone on a journey, my son and I, and now a new road spooled before him. What he had learned, I hoped, he'd hold to. Who he had been, I hoped, would become the stuff of his tales. I wasn't worried about losing my child. Jeremy is my son; he always will be. But in Jeremy's increasing absence—distance?—I was starting to think about the lost parts of me, about the rumors and the whispers of the self I'd left behind.

I remember you singing, someone had said. *You were eight or you were nine.*

I was there. I saw you win. I saw the ribbons in your hand.

Do you remember the honeysuckle? That big hedge, up near the field?

Do you remember those kittens that summer?
Do you remember the stars from the roof?
Do you remember Windjammer?

Who are we after the first long sprint of motherhood is through? What parts of our history do we return to ourselves when the days shift in shape and size and tempo? I hadn't been young for years and years. But I remembered the cat and the ribbons and the kittens and the hedge. I remembered, and for no other reason than that I found myself longing to. I remembered my mother's amber-lit sewing room and my father's long car and the grocery store where we Saturday shopped, its big, wide, briny vat of pickles. I remembered roller-skating on the basement floor and soaring high on the backyard swings and trying, desperately, to draw butterflies, to draw anything at all. I thought I could conquer the wings with symmetry, but my butterflies wouldn't fly, wouldn't perch. They were never more than pencil colors, but I was proud of them.

There were marathon games of Monopoly. There were miniature carnivals up the street; tadpoles in the nearby creek; splinters of mica in the dirt, which I found and polished and showcased. There was a mother and a father and a warm meal every night. There was a brother and a sister and a cat, a calico we called Colors. I called her Colors. I named our cat. I made such bold, unblinking declarations when I was younger than I am.

Somebody says so, and suddenly it's true: I am in the back of the car, behind my mother—my brother on the left, our sister between us. We are driving home from the beach on the last possible day of summer, and I have the soundtrack from *Windjammer* on my mind—those songs of the ports, those sounds of the cadets, that calypso, those melancholy ballads. "Kari Waits for Me," I sing, and my brother whistles harmony. "Don't Hurry Worry Me," I sing, and my mother sings the chorus. "Everybody Loves Saturday Night," I sing, and my brother, mother, father, sister sing along with me. We are in the car, coming home from two splendor weeks away. We are singing the songs of the sea. Do you remember *Windjammer*? Yes. The music lives. I remember.

I was a sun-spotted, unruly-haired girl long ago. I vacationed at the seashore and lived on a cul-de-sac street, beneath skies that hosted strictly friendly planes. I stayed outdoors, whenever I could, looking up and out at things. I sat down every evening to a family meal and played kickball late on summer nights and hiked through the snow in winter. I had, I am trying to say, the very sort of childhood that I have attempted—intuitively, quietly, perhaps old-fashionedly, never perfectly—to shape for and yield to my son. For haven't we sat down to family meals, most every night? Haven't we gone hiking in the snow? Haven't we sung our own favorite seafaring songs, when driving home, at the end of summer, from the shore? We knew all the lyrics to "Shenandoah," Jeremy and I. We knew mostly all of "Go Down, You Blood Red Roses." We could hum our way through "The Girls Around Cape Horn" and moan along with "Ranzo." My childhood nested in my son's, somehow. The girl I was is in the boy he's been. The past carried forward, planted, and sprouted, and not because it was merely good enough, but because it was whole, it was happy. Who are we after the first long sprint of motherhood is through? We are ourselves, carried forward.

It is something to be on the cusp of things, contemplating and projecting. Something to go back in time to consider who you were before you were a mother mostly or what you loved before a child stole your heart. Lately, when my son is at his job and my own work seems done or dull, I find myself remembering the not-quite-a-mother me. She is twenty-eight, this other me, and there is no gray in her brown hair. There are no punctuation marks in the skin around her eyes—no parentheses, no brackets, no exasperated semicolons. She likes fast things. Bikes on the downward leaning slope of the hill. Ice skates on an empty pond. Her own two feet, which take her everywhere—in and out of thrift stores, hunting; up and down the wide streets, snooping; onto the stoops of neighbors. She takes other people's children on as friends, miniature companions. She is responsible for little; she's not tired.

She writes fierce things in notebooks and calls herself a poet, and when she plays her music, she plays it loud and dances, unafraid to be seen, or to be found out.

There is an exuberance about this me that I find enviable, appealing. There is a fearlessness that seems naïve, incautious, and terrific. This me does not yet know what I now assuredly know about how fortifying, consuming, blinding, defining, and still somehow fleeting the childhood of one's own child can be. She does not yet know how glorifying and intimidating and political and personal motherhood is, nor does she know long nights and exhaustion, nor has she made the mistakes I've made, nor has she reveled as I have reveled, nor has she stolen so many gorgeous moments, snapshots, blessed details from a child's finally inexplicable life. She is not yet so riled with regret, so blasphemous with pride, so prone to lying awake at night, when she would rather be, she needs to be, sleeping. I want to have a baby, she turns to her husband and says. I want a baby, something she's longed for for years. And this night it is raining. It will rain that whole night long. It will rain. The color will be sweet and tender blue.

I have lived too many years to be that woman again. There is grammar in my skin, gray in my hair. There is less speed in my feet; the old bike is rusty; I walk where once I ran. I have learned not to call myself a poet anymore, and when I dance, I dance where nobody can see me, to music that I play at a drearily decent decibel. The exhaustion of motherhood is cumulative. Exuberance is tempered by the many choices a mother makes. Pathways narrow when a woman has a child, because incautiousness yields consequences, and irresponsibility is selfish, and the dreams one dreams on behalf of a child are the dreams one does not dream for one's self.

Still and nevertheless, I honor that not-yet-mother in quiet hours now. I remember her, and return to her, and restore what was never fully forsaken. Lately I find myself growing bolder when telling my own versions of my stories. Lately I grow ever more truly predisposed toward neighbor ladies who invite me into their homes. Lately I go hunting for things my son would never care to see. Lately, and more and more lately, I sit outside and dream.

We bring our own selves and stories forward when the first long sprint of motherhood is through. We reconcile who we were to who we'll be. We look at the face that has changed over time and seek the child who won ribbons, the young wife who loved to dance, the mother who gave her child both all she had and not enough. We bring ourselves, our stories forward, adding fractions to make a whole, singing our seafaring songs.

Dude, Where's My Family?

Margaret Remick

I met my husband at college when I was nineteen. Compared with my pale family of armchair dwellers and poetry readers, his golden boy athleticism and carefree, youthful outlook were utterly foreign and mesmerizing to me. Here was someone who didn't overthink or discuss everything. What clarity! Besides getting good grades, he was preoccupied with the hippest music and clothes, the hot parties on campus and in Manhattan. These seemed perfectly legitimate pursuits to me since they were mine as well. We were inseparable, whether up all hours cramming for exams or dashing around barefoot in winter from adventure to adventure, somehow untouchable by germs or bad luck. We were recklessly, stupidly in love.

Our fast life accelerated after college when we moved to Los Angeles and fell in with a crowd of blue chip heirs and young celebrities. A typical party took place over several days at a Malibu or Brentwood estate. No pool was left un–skinny dipped, or un-drained and skateboarded. We imbibed and smoked with abandon, 1920s style, as if no one had ever heard of lung cancer or addiction, and it was pure, irresponsible fun. At one particularly decadent party, we alighted on a mansion in the Hollywood Hills and were handed sledgehammers and crowbars. Although in mint condition, the house was to be redesigned, and we were encouraged to smash it to bits. Have a drink and take a swing at a sconce or a diamond-paned window. Rome before the fall. My husband and I, fiancés then, were team players, partners in harmless, pointless crimes.

Immaturity in my mate wasn't a drawback until we had babies. By then we had left Los Angeles. I was twenty-four years old, my husband twenty-six, when twins appeared on the ultrasound, and my life changed irrevocably. I took a swan dive into mothering, never understanding all the comments from people sympathizing about the hardship of having infant twins. I loved every minute of it. Never having had a solo baby, I had no point of comparison: these were my two beautiful boys, and I was so relieved the three of us had survived a tricky birth that the rest seemed easy. Although a trouper about diaper changes when the boys were tiny, my spouse generally continued in his merry ways, working as an animation producer while pursuing, with intense drive, a second career as a competitive windsurfer. He maintained a suntan, partied with his beach pals, and bought himself a motorcycle.

This was during the early nineties, when any self-respecting woman was expected to go barreling off to a job the instant her baby's mouth could fasten on a bottle. Generations of women before us had struggled to carve out their places in the work force, so it would be sacrilege to give up those gains now. I waited until the boys were eighteen months old to return to work, which at that time seemed preposterously, indulgently late. So began one of the most miserable, lonely stretches in my adult life. I dropped my darlings off at day care, and they cried. I worked, fetched the twins for hurried dinners and bedtimes, and then I cried—over missing them and over this wretched, unnatural arrangement. Meanwhile, Mr. Suntan worked, sailed, and partied. He was all smiles and happiness when present, and clearly loved his baby boys; he just wasn't around much. He saw nothing wrong with seeing his kids nominally during the week and partying through Fridays and Saturdays. A hung over, albeit cuddly and fun Sunday afternoon spent with his sons was plenty for him. To me, going out seemed absurd: weekends were the only real time I had to be with my boys.

The situation worsened when he invited one of his swinging single friends to move into our basement and said friend started bringing home loud sex partners. Their downstairs thrashing never actually woke the twins, but it was an odd background noise to rock a baby to sleep to. Forget about cherishing the sweetness and innocence of two bouncy boys: no, our household, our frat house, was too cool to acknowledge life evolving in that way, and I was too exhausted to do anything but plod on. I laugh now, but it was awful at the time. When you've had only broken sleep for two years, sensible clothes for three, and are permanently smeared with baby paste, it's disheartening to have some frowzy vixen stagger into your kitchen to get water or a piece of toast after her appetite-building sessions downstairs. "Hi, good morning, Donna/Rhonda/Jeanette! I haven't had more than a back-room quickie set to Looney Tunes music in ages, but, by all means, carry on. I'm glad you're here to highlight how very unsingle I am. Instead of peek-a-boo, let's play the walls aren't paper thin."

What became abundantly clear at this juncture was the disparity between my priorities and my husband's. His friends had always been important to him, but I had no idea how important. The nastiness between us went way beyond the usual parental scorekeeping. I ended up with the role of the teeth-gritter, the bitter domestic, the sometime hysteric, and this naturally justified even longer absences for my husband, whether he was skipping off to Burning Man with his buddies or flying to South America for a windsurfing race. The vicious cycle lasted four years. My resentment was made surreal by Mr. Suntan's continued ebullience and good humor whenever he was actually present. I would mock his effusive greetings to the kids, knowing that the louder the "Hiiiiii, boys," the less time he actually planned on being around.

The funny thing was, we all got used to this dynamic. The twins loved him like Santa, or some mythical, hard-to-spot creature. I loved him as I always had, despite being deeply angry. Eventually, my husband and I got used to our grinding differences, and what emerged was our alternative family, the core being my boys and me, with their father as a satellite; one son actually called him "Uncle." One of the perks of his 24-7 career and growing income was that I was able to reduce my working hours to part time. I made the most of the situation, figuring I was essentially a well-sponsored single parent. The twins and I became very, very close. As it is for many women with husbands in absentia, my children were, without a doubt, my central source of love and comfort, and I theirs. We went on all sorts of adventures, just the three of us, ransacking the city, museums, zoos, and parks. Looking back, I marvel at the ridiculous optimism a new mother has: I would go tent camping with two tod- dlers by myself, hauling coolers, lanterns, cookstoves, sand toys, books, diapers, and all the rest.

I also became ruthless about borrowing dads—meaning we tagged along with friends whose husbands weren't too busy to do things with their families on weekends. If all four of us did spend time together, it was at the beach, at windsurfing competitions. The boys and I, along with other windsurfing widows and orphans, hud- dled like Bedouins under blankets or inside vans to stay out of the flying sand. This was often great fun, and my husband's surf friends would play with the boys in the unmeasured, energetic way only childless people play. Occasionally we'd have pizza delivered to the beach, our family's version of the time-honored ritual of Sunday dinner—sort of Norman Rockwell meets *Baywatch*—happy wind- blown kids, exhilarated dad in a half-peeled wet suit, and me, glad all of us were together, if only for time scraps.

Cut to: The Dawning of a New Age, or Move Over, Shrunk Shanks!!

My boys are now teenagers and excelling so mightily at every- thing they do, it's almost spooky. They are handsome, ferocious on the soccer pitch, surpassing their teacher in chess. Their knees barely fit in the car, and one boy has a beautiful, low, gravelly voice, far deeper than his father's. My boys, now these young men, emanate potential and power just beginning to unfurl, and it's thrilling to witness.

Meanwhile, my husband and his swingin' cronies are pushing forty and beyond. The "buzzards" party on (although not as much), and do things like "pants" each other and get head injuries from wrestling. My husband showed up late to our family party, but at least he finally showed up. While not relinquishing his own boyish ways, he cherishes his kids and spends a lot more time with them. His many achievements now serve as an excellent example to our children.

The buzzards still enjoy spending time with our family, and they are always welcome. Very few have married, and several seem to envy us for having gotten through child-rearing, even if by the skin of our teeth. A couple of the guys have taken the conventional path but leap-frogged ahead a few steps and have married women who have children from previous marriages. Although juvenile in lifestyle, the buzzards are big-hearted. These core guys have become dear friends to all of us.

But their larger social crowd of ever-young singles is another kind of beast altogether. At a recent surf-snob party I attended, this tall, hulking Aussie jock pushed past me on his way to the kitchen for a "beah." His sunglasses were perched strategically on his thinning hair. His hair itself was artificially lightened—and not in an up-the-establishment way, but in an unconvincing, cover-the-gray way—and he was squeezed into a snappy, name-brand T-shirt that was a bit too snug, something perhaps from the juniors department. His pecs, no doubt once perfect shields of muscle mass, were gone soft. Yet the teen spirit was far from extinguished in this mid-lifer. He gave me a nasty, demeaning look, as if to say "What are *you* doing here? You must be thirty-five or, *gasp*, forty!" I am in fact thirty-eight, a solid ten years older than the women usually welcome at these bacchanals. And I do not resemble an inflatable pleasure doll. I glared back at him. He struck me as terribly funny—this middle-aged man trying so hard to look twenty, drinking his lite beers and clinging to raver status. Mutton dressed as lamb, man-wise! I kept picturing my boys, real youth—the real thing—next to this buffoon.

And then the other night my husband's new garage band was jamming when the boys returned from a museum costume party with their dates, one in belly dancer garb, the other in a green plastic go-go outfit, both fourteen years old. The girls filed past the band on the way to the boys' room, and the band nearly skipped a beat. The girls barely noticed them despite their racket of music and oh-so-hipness. I would be lying if I said I don't get a huge kick in the pants watching this phenomenon, watching the old men step down. I should be sympathetic to my husband's slowly being humbled by time, like all of us. But there's still this germ of bitterness from those lonely days with my little boys that makes me want to laugh meanly and revel in the fact that I may have missed some Saturday parties, but my stars are shining now.

My Surrogate

Charo Gonzalez

1.

I hold her clothes outside the changing room. We talk through the curtains about injections, side effects, and a new beginning for both of us. She calculates a possible due date. Was I late when I delivered my children? How much did they weigh? This is good, a pause; a respite from the past three weeks of groping my way through the fog of fertility drugs, preparing for the retrieval of my eggs and this procedure—the only way, I learned two years ago, that I would be able to have another baby of my own.

I am surprised at how comfortable and natural this physical closeness feels, just to stand on the other side of the curtain from this woman I have met only twice before. I pass her the gown and socks she needs to put on. She passes me her backpack. This is what you do for your sister, I think, for your best friend—you fold her clothes; you hold her hand through a surgical procedure. When I pass her the blue bonnet to cover her hair, she jokes about her newest, most immediate concern: to make it through the end of the procedure when, after having sipped four glasses of water in the last hour, she will finally get to pee. I tell her that I would happily trade her my trip to the bathroom for the Valium she got half an hour before.

2.

Four months ago, after reviewing several profiles from potential surrogate mothers, my husband and I met with her and her husband for brunch on a Sunday morning near their home. I was up at dawn with plenty of time to prepare, or so I planned. What do you wear to meet the woman who will decide whether or not to carry your baby? I tried on several outfits, but instead of confirming my choice, the mirror gave me back the sheer panic on my face. How would I be able to tell, from *her* physical appearance and a first meeting, whether she would honor an agreement to relinquish my baby?

The lawyer from the surrogacy agency would draft a contract between the surrogate (sometimes referred to as the "birth mother") and us (for the duration of the pregnancy, the "intended parents"). The scope of the agreement would be mainly financial, with stipulations for the compensation the surrogate would receive and all the other medical and personal expenses to be covered by us. The contract would also state our parental rights over the baby after the birth and over the medical decisions that might arise during the pregnancy.

Biologically—or more specifically, genetically—the surrogate would have no connection to our baby. The series of procedures required to achieve this pregnancy would be a blunt reminder of that, but how would that knowledge play out once she actually became pregnant? Although both parties would agree that we would become the child's parents at the moment of birth, it would not be until near the end of the pregnancy that our legal petition to be named on the birth certificate could be finalized. Surrogacy is a new and unsettled area of the law; there is a chance, however minute, that if the surrogate changed her mind, the agreement could not be enforced. Trust, and trust alone, is the very axis of surrogacy.

I had already talked to other surrogates and intended moms, trying to understand a surrogate's perspective and to anticipate what might worry mine. As hard as it was for me to imagine, one of the most consistent anxieties among surrogates is the possibility that the intended parents might split up and refuse custody of the baby after the birth, forcing the surrogate to either put the baby up for adoption or keep it herself, as was reported in a recent case.

When my potential surrogate arrived at the restaurant with her husband, I stood up to greet her. She smiled and waved, signaling me to stay at the table. She and her husband sat down across from us, holding hands under the table.

Throughout the lavish brunch we hardly touched, the four of us exchanging abbreviated and somewhat rushed stories about our lives. The meeting was an obvious, reciprocal interview. Though lively, the conversation sounded almost as if we were checking off bullet points of curriculum vitae.

Born in northern California, my surrogate and her husband had lived three blocks from each other during most of their childhoods, but did not meet until they were in their late teens. They had been together ever since. She works as a teacher's aide in her son's school and he as an electrician. They both have large extended families living close by. Acting as a surrogate was her way of contributing to her family's dreams—they were saving to buy a house—but it was also a way to help another couple experience the joy she and her husband knew through their own children.

She asked me for medical details about the partial hysterectomy I had undergone months after my son was born. "Did you have any form of cancer?" were the words she chose in lieu of, "Are you going to get sick and die after your third baby is born?" I responded to what I suspected was her real question, explaining the chronology of our decision to do a gestational surrogacy: the funky results of a routine Pap smear, the carcinoma in situ found in my endocervical canal, and the recommendation to remove my uterus as a preventive measure to secure my health. Once over that hump, free simply to learn more about us, she asked me about Buenos Aires, where I was born and raised, and Spain, where my parents are from and where we still spend many summers visiting my extended family. We talked about my husband's childhood in Moscow and about how we met in New York, where I had emigrated alone at twenty-one. (A maternally protective confession: I have changed my age to thirty when I tell this story to my two children, for the same reason my husband flatly assures them that the disco-inferno motorcycle helmet they found in the attic was, in fact, just a collector's item, not something *he* ever used.) She was curious to know about my previous life as a TV journalist and how my husband had emigrated at sixteen, a Jewish refugee from the Soviet Union, to study physics. After more than twenty years in the United States, he is still sometimes homesick for his roots, for the comfort of an extended family and the easy familiarity of an existence in one's own land. I knew that his desire for another baby, like mine—undiminished by the obstacles we faced—was in part because our children had anchored the fragmented pieces of our lives. They had become our center of gravity in the world.

The four of us were still casually yet diligently adding some colors to the applications we had both filled out for the agency. As my husband began telling the story of how we had moved to San Francisco after half-jokingly scanning a map of the world and circling the cities where we would like to raise a family, I pulled the pictures of my seven-year-old daughter and four-year-old son from my wallet.

That did it.

She let go of her husband's hand and produced several pictures of her own children, also a boy and a girl, close in age to mine, from her handbag. We lost ourselves in a slower conversation, shamelessly wallowing in stories of the children who had changed our lives. She told me how motherhood had affirmed and renewed her desire to go back to her teaching career, regardless of how thankless that profession can sometimes be. Without knowing how I got there, I was telling her about a cherished, intimate moment after I gave birth to my daughter, my firstborn.

Earlier that day, after twelve hours of induction medication in my IV, I had dilated from one to ten centimeters in less than two hours. The baby came out after three pushes. It was like one of those weird plane rides traveling west when you end up arriving at your destination an hour before the time of your departure. Transition time between *no baby* and *baby born*: minus zero. Immediately after, the doctor gave my daughter to me, and she latched onto my breast.

Hours later, with my husband curled up in a chair—dozing off the epidural that had not worked on me!—I lay in bed wide awake, dimly aware of the "It's a girl!" balloon wiggling above the ventilation outlet. As I held my daughter that night in the quiet of my room, I felt her warmth against my skin, the boundaries of my body contracting as my whole being expanded to welcome her, and the creeping sense that the very "foreignness" that had blanketed my existence for the last ten years was shifting. The dawn hours after my daughter's birth ushered in for me an easier connection to this country, as well as a renewed homage to my ancestry. Half a world away, I felt the closest I have ever been to my mother: As she did thirty years before, I had given birth in a foreign land to a daughter whose faintly familiar noises finally rocked me to sleep.

3.

My mother, unwittingly, had been the one who first exposed me to the concept of surrogacy. Of all aspects of the complicated decision to let another woman carry my child, the question that kept popping into my head was: who are these women? I longed for a general profile, something reliable and time-tested, along the lines of those detailed descriptions of personality types used by career counselors.

On our last trip to visit my family in Spain, my parents and I sat in my grandmother's kitchen in the stillness of siesta time, sipping our coffee. We talked about immigration, cultural assimilations, and the containing power of families through that life-long process. That's when I broke the news about pursuing a gestational surrogate to my seventy-year-old parents, who now live in a country where surrogacy is taboo and, until recently, illegal.

I rambled through "the profile" I had constructed from books and conversations with doctors, psychologists, family advocates, and people who had gone through the experience. The picture that emerged was of a woman who was already a mother, had easy pregnancies, and was thinking of the financial gain of surrogacy as an investment in her own family's future; above all, these women wanted to help other women become mothers. Some of the surrogates cherish the fantasy of giving the gift of life to a childless family. Others prefer to work with families who already have children—they embark on the journey as one family's labor of love for another family. Many surrogates have carried children for other couples more than once.

"The 'tit surrogate' coming to help you," my mother said.

Of course, I thought. She had told that family story several times to my brother and me, usually as an illustration of my brother's famously insatiable appetite, but she had never used the term "tit surrogate" before.

After thirty-six hours of labor, two hours of pushing, and a forceps delivery, my brother, at eleven pounds, was born. At that time in Argentina, after a baby's delivery the new mothers were put in rows of beds separated by curtains in the hospital maternity ward. Families were allowed two hours of visitation time. Once in her "room," my mother tried to nurse my brother, who made it loud and clear that colostrum barely passed as an appetizer. The nurses repeatedly told my mother, who was now crying together with her baby, to breast-feed him and try to hush him, because the rest of the mothers needed their rest. After some time, a woman standing behind the curtain whispered to my mother to let her in. She had two children at home and had labored a stillborn baby two days before. She offered to nurse my brother.

"He slept through the night and then some more, in time for my own milk to come in. I was overwhelmed with gratitude for this woman, for my baby, and for what she did for me," my mother said. "Women have shared bodies for a long time, *Nena,*" she added, gazing inwardly, now contemplating this old memory in a whole new light.

In the hospital the next morning, my father woke my mother with a bunch of roses. She asked him to deliver them, instead, to the other mother. But she was already gone. Even though my parents explained to the staff that they just wanted to send flowers to this woman, the hospital never disclosed her name.

Could a woman really give up to another woman a baby she has carried for nine months? Yes, answered all the surrogates I spoke with. The tigress instinct I already know from being a mother myself wondered, *how*? I asked a "repeat" surrogate. She told me that she felt as protective of the baby as she had felt when pregnant with her own children. She did everything she could to ensure the baby's health. However, she recalled the moment right after the delivery as her happiest memory from the experience. She felt infinitely successful, proud, and moved beyond words as the intended parents held their baby in the delivery room, and the genetic mother cut the umbilical cord.

4.

I was driving across the Bay Bridge from San Francisco's East Bay, where I had gone to the lawyer's office to pick up the signed contracts with the surrogate, when it hit me full force. What am I doing to her family? How are her kids going to understand this? Fear, the sheer terror of having metamorphosed into a desperate monster, ate at my whole being. I bungled in my bag for the cell phone and dialed her number. Then I froze at the break of another, equally disturbing thought: Why do I assume I know better? How do I get off with the moral superiority to question her choices or her family's? I could barely see straight. I found a parking spot as she picked up the phone. What would be the quickest, most polite way to tackle this?

"I wonder how you are going to present this to your children?" I asked, fumbling for words. What I really wanted to say was: How are you going to tell your children that you're carrying someone else's baby? And when that baby is born, that it will be going home with me?

Pause.

"Are you really asking how you should present this to *your* children?" she questioned me gently.

I guess I was. Is motherhood now negotiable? Will my children feel threatened by a sibling who, to their minds, instantaneously appears? Will they feel more or less special because they came out of my body, requiring no superhuman efforts to bring them into the world? How will they think of the mysterious woman who gives birth to their sibling—is *she* the mother? What will they think of *me*? For two years I had argued these nagging issues with my husband, my family, my friends, mainly with myself. As reconciled as I mostly was to the idea of surrogacy, still there lingered these worries.

Since our first meeting over brunch, my surrogate and I had stayed in constant contact, having almost daily conversations over e-mail or on the phone. I got to know her. I went from skepticism to admiration and gratitude for her willingness and excitement to carry my baby because I knew she, too, had deeply considered what surrogacy really meant to us both. Somehow, we had found ourselves committed to it together, despite how "unnatural," counterintuitive, and weird it was.

We talked for a while about different suggestions that we had both heard of, yet neither of us would consider. For instance, we could use a recently published children's book on sexual education that illustrates the mechanics of surrogacy and other assisted reproduction technologies without going into too much detail. However, on the following pages, there are elaborate explanations and graphics of masturbation and other equally uncomfortable parent-child topics we both hoped to delay a bit longer, thank you very much.

Because we live in diverse communities, our children already live among different kinds of families. We both marveled at how naturally they had reacted when we explained to them what surrogacy was about. They were more blasé about the idea of one mother growing a baby for another than most of the adults we had talked to. We tried out our own ideas on each other, in preparation for conversations with our kids about the joint journey our two families would now be embarking on. Once again, we treaded on the common ground between us.

"Will you let your daughter come to visit with mine once I get pregnant? I am afraid she won't have any other friend to talk with about this," she said.

"Of course," I assured her. "Listen, my baby will miss your body after the birth . . . the noises of your children, the rhythms of your home . . ."

"I know," she said, pausing. "I have an idea," she continued, sounding as clear and close as if she were sitting in my car with me. "Make a tape with your children's voices, yours and your husband's, and I will play it for the baby when I am driving by myself."

The lawyer's contracts were still on the seat beside me, but the bond I could feel was taking place elsewhere, in a place without words. The regimen of fertility drugs would soon make us a team, our bodies cycling as one. Emotionally, we were already in sync.

5.

The nurse comes into the changing room and smiles at me with routine understanding. My surrogate emerges from behind the curtain and the three of us walk into the room where the doctor will transfer three of my embryos to the top of her uterus. To be present at the transfer procedure is my way to "conceive" this pregnancy, so different from those intimate moments I had previously shared solely with my husband.

Once she lies down on the stretcher, I cover her with extra blankets. The nurse places her feet in the stirrups, making sure she is comfortable enough so she will not move during the transfer, then dims the lights and turns on the sonogram machine before she leaves the room to get the doctor and embryologist. I can feel the chilliness in the room, the unique temperature of antiseptic environments, of shiny, gelid instruments. As I look at her lying on the table with her eyes closed and her legs open, I want to cover her with even more blankets, to protect the body she is surrendering so I can have a baby.

In preparation for this day, for the past three weeks, miles away from each other but in perfect unison, we have each locked ourselves in the bathroom after putting the children to bed, mixed a line of tiny vials of powdery drugs into one of distilled water and injected it into our bodies. In the mornings we have popped pills and gone to doctor's appointments for blood tests and sonograms, all the while trying to stay focused (or at least pretend with authority) in the pick-up lines at school, while supervising homework, at sports practices. For an entire menstrual cycle, her body and mine shared a "protocol calendar": we acted as one unit—(surrogate's uterus) + (mother's eggs) + (father's sperm) = baby—of an unconventional equation.

So much is going through my head, so many things I would like to say to her, but we are united in silence. Words might dilute the staunch female will we hold together inside our fragile equation, the primal instinct, two tigresses watching over a cub. For a fleeting moment, we share the same body.

"Find a place to sit, honey, so you can watch the screen," the nurse says as she returns to the room. "Is your husband coming in as well?"

"No, he'll stay outside with her husband," I answer. She nods, betraying nothing but professionalism, and proceeds to unwrap the speculum and other medieval-looking instruments women know too well. I move my chair closer to my surrogate's bed and offer her my hand. She holds it tightly.

What do men do while their wives are in an operating room together, trying to conceive a baby?

Her husband had elected to sit in the waiting room, where a game of football was playing on the TV. "I'll be here when you come out," he said before kissing her good-bye. My husband hadn't known what to do. He had wanted to be at the transfer, but what if her husband wasn't there? What if he was? Either way, it would have been awkward. So he sat with her husband in the waiting room, mystified by football like many foreigners, trying, as he explained to me later, both to "blend in with the furniture and make small talk about the game."

Inside the transfer room, the embryologist cradling the catheter now walks up to the doctor. Following standard and legal procedure, speaking into a tape recorder, he says my name, my husband's, the surrogate's, and the names of the three embryos to be transferred: #2, #8, and #14. The doctor then introduces the catheter into the uterine cavity, where the embryos are released. "Watch out for three dots on the screen. You cannot see the embryos but you will see the three bubbles of air in between," the embryologist says, soon handing me a printout of their picture taken under the microscope. I show it to my surrogate. "Look. Smart, huh? They look like three little brains," I say. She smiles.

Two hours later, I hold the door open for her and my husband, who carries her bags. Her husband waits inside their car with the engine running, looking ahead. As she steps out onto the parking lot, she squints to the noon sun, then turns to face me. We lock unguarded eyes, hers glassy and steady, a blue surrender to the unleashed new life inside of her, and mine, vulnerable—the eyes of a mother relying on another mother's womb.

"Please call me for whatever you need. Promise?" I whisper in her ear as we hug.

"Yes," she nods, then gets into the car.

My throat closes on me as she drives off with my three embryos.

6.

Ten days after the transfer, my surrogate would go in for her first blood test, where she would be tested for the base level of the pregnancy hormone HCG. A rise in the hormone level would mean that implantation had occurred ("chemical pregnancy"). Once these results were confirmed by ultrasound two to four weeks later, it would become a "clinical pregnancy."

For now, it was time to wait.

During those ten days, I dreaded the hours while my husband was at work and my children at school. To concentrate on my daily routine was virtually impossible. These days were definitely not going to be "normal." So I tried to teach myself to knit. I did yoga, baked, took several baths, and cleaned closets. I reread the IVF cycle review chapter from the booklet published by the fertility center—several times, as if it were some kind of oracle. I avoided newspapers and their bad news, and pretty much avoided everybody but my surrogate.

"I think we'll hear good news soon. I am so tired, just like I've been in my previous pregnancies," she said in a hollow voice.

In the back of my mind, I knew that fatigue, like other symptoms of pregnancy, is also a common side effect of the progesterone injections she was still getting daily. But I chose not to give in to that possibility.

7.

On the afternoon when we would get the result, I sat at a restaurant downtown across from my husband, checking my phone every two minutes to see whether I was still getting cellular reception. The phone rang, and I saw on the screen that the call was coming from the fertility clinic.

It was the nurse. She explained, again, the meaning of the results of the first blood test. "Unfortunately, Charo . . ."

I heard no more; nothing, for the rest of the day.

8.

That night our doctor spoke in detail with my husband. According to the results of the test, the HCG levels were flat, suggesting an immunological problem with our surrogate. The doctor was confident the results could have not been caused by a problem with the embryos. Could our surrogate be treated? Yes, but she would have to undergo a complicated treatment involving medications derived from blood products, which could compromise her overall health. After a long and hard consideration of our case, our doctor recommended that we change surrogates.

9.

The nurse at my clinic offered to explain the diagnosis to my surrogate, but I wanted to do it myself. She had already called the lab for results and had left a message on my cell phone, asking me to call back. I wondered whether it would be better to get together in person to talk. I was drenched in a sadness that left me wearing my loss inside out. There was still some time before I had to pick up my children from school that day, then I would not be back home until the evening. I decided to call her from my car and offer to meet her later.

"I am so sorry. I feel so bad, so guilty. My body could not hold your three 'best' embryos," was the first thing she said. I do not recall what words of consolation I must have mumbled. What I remember most distinctly was the sound of the wind tunneling along the street past the sides of my car. She preferred not to meet in person. It was time, we both knew, to say good-bye.

The complementary piece we had been to each other for the last six months crystallized for a moment. "I will miss your calls, sharing this with you." Her voice trembled. Instead of bonding with the baby as I had feared, she had bonded with me, with the unique warmth and intimacy of our unconventional equation of trust: two mothers sharing their bodies to bring forth a new life.

At the mercy of unyielding nature, the unit we had become began to dissolve. I told her how sorry I was for the new diagnosis she was walking out with.

"I am not going to worry about this immunological thing. I've gotten pregnant easily before," she said, protecting me from the only thing she could: the guilt of having put her body through so much, to end with no reward. There was no shielding either of us from the stark emptiness left by our hope for a baby for me.

I asked her what she was going to do next. As she spoke

about her future plans—of how she would give all of this a rest before deciding what to do next, of how she now needed to spend time reconnecting with her children and family—I also thought about my family, my future. Now, it was time to let go.

"Thank you," I said. "I am forever grateful to you and I will always remember you."

"I know," she answered, claiming her body back.

It was my turn; I had to settle back into mine. During the weeks that followed, I was too raw to recognize what I would soon know with every cell of that same body. The disappointment ran so deep, it illuminated the opposite—I couldn't give up.

Six months later, I would fly to Los Angeles to sign new contracts with another surrogacy agency. Three months after that, at a different restaurant, I would meet another surrogate and her husband. Once we talked about our children, I would look into her eyes and know.

Then, with trust as the only guarantee, one mother relying on another, I will hold her clothes outside the changing room.

The Belly Unbuttoned

Susan Straight

It's not the stomach we see everywhere now, not the innocuous soft abdomen or even the dimple of navel, the vestige of our infancy and need. No. What we see—on college girls at the university where I teach, on girls at the high school and junior high my daughters attend, on elementary school girls who stand on the stage with my youngest daughter to perform in "Mice from Outer Space", on Catherine Zeta-Jones in her cell phone ads—is not the stomach, where our food lands, where undignified gastric breakdown and distribution occurs.

What we see now is the belly. We see sex.

The expanse of skin not above the navel, but below it, the smooth skirt of flesh between hipbones, the concave bowl where babies will curl. We even see the taut cords of muscle that lead to the groin. We see the shining rim of a cup, the allure of what's below.

And it's accessorized, of course, in this age of over-accessorization. The navel with jeweled rings, the front hipbones with "tan tattoos" (a decal is placed on the skin before the subject enters the tanning salon, leaving a white image of, say, a Playboy bunny, as on a twelve-year-old girl who plays in the junior high band with my daughter), and the back belly—oh, there we have butt cleavage accentuated with the de rigueur real tattoo (your name, someone else's name, Celtic symbols, roses and birds and dolphins all rising from the cleft between your buttocks). Don't forget the top of the thong, which might show to the point that the pockets of skin below the stretchy material are also tattooed. (How do you plan for that? Squat in front of a mirror and see what is exposed on a regular basis when you sit down?)

We know all this. But I've tried, at junior high band performances or high school orientations, or just walking around the mall, to figure out why these bellies are not the bellies of my young womanhood, and how the belly itself became the new icon of sexual allure, the part of the body that girls and even their mothers are showing off.

In the 1840s, a "well-turned ankle" was the glimpse of a woman's body that excited men, the lovely bone showing like a tiny face, I imagine, when the foot moved out from under the voluminous skirt. In the 1940s, the foci of sexual presence were shapely calves that showed off the stocking seam, à la Betty Grable. The 1950s were about sweater girls, which required a full bust, but as I recall from movies and family stories, tissue paper and padded bras, not permanent surgery, did the trick. And in the 1960s, with hot pants and hip-huggers, a flat butt and thin frame were sexy to most Americans. Think Twiggy. The androgynous look was difficult to achieve for most American women, who stuck with capris and camp shirts while their daughters worked hard with the shag haircuts and hot pants. Though it may have seemed that it was the hot pants that were on display, it was the exposed thighs that signified sex, teasing with their never-before-displayed access.

I grew up in the 1970s, and my own daughters love to tease me after watching *That '70s Show*. Okay—we had Farrah Fawcett wings, a tough hairstyle to pull off given gravity and the unnatural position of the curls, and Afros, which required blowing out and a lot of combing. I may have shown my stomach in the seventies. I got out my junior high and high school yearbooks to check. I saw hot pants and hip-huggers (what my daughters call flares and low-rise) and I saw baby-doll smocked shirts and spaghetti-strap tanks. But what showed, even, I discovered, on me, was only a part of our abdomens. The navel sometimes, but more often the skin above it, at the ribcage, which was definitely not ripped abs. We didn't do ripped abs. Think Goldie Hawn in *Laugh-In*, saying "Sock it to me." Maybe a circle of her abdomen waist showed in a mini dress. Think Chaka Khan on the album cover of *Rufus*, her strong hips and thighs in tight bell-bottoms, her navel showing in a slice of brown skin, and maybe her two bottom ribs.

Our jeans, though short-zippered, seemed somehow more forgiving. Let's put it this way: we didn't have butt cleavage.

I got married in the 1980s, the disco years, when sexy was all about the total look, the makeup and hair and leg warmers and scarves, *Flashdance* body parts exposed between the manufactured tears of the Jennifer Beals sweatshirt.

In the 1990s, the bosom became the undeniable sexual focus of our culture, and then big American breasts were marketed globally, through our magazines and movies and television and commercial dominance. In fact, the 1990s transformed natural sexual allure into the marketing of products as never before. You could buy breasts. In earlier decades, women couldn't purchase slimmer ankles, lovely collarbones and shoulders (the height of feminine appeal in the 1820s), or Twiggy's thinness. But now cleavage was required, and it was within reach for everyone. Push-up bras and water-filled enhancers were ubiquitous, and then even that wasn't enough: plastic surgery was suddenly necessary. Breasts grew everywhere, and were displayed in all their planetary inconsistency with the rest of the body; the hard, sculpted spheres rose like Tupperware bowls attached to perfectly ordinary chests. It wasn't sufficient that American culture improved American women: suddenly women in other countries, such as Brazil, where they'd been happy with average breasts, great buttocks, and overall sex appeal, thought they needed *Baywatch* breasts.

I had three babies by then. I remember watching my average breasts turn into stripper breasts, to do their assigned tasks of feeding my daughters for a year each, and then return to their previous size. I remember wondering how, if the nipple was moved during augmentation, breasts could still feed. And I remember looking at women's bodies differently by then, as mine had morphed so many times from 100 pounds to 150, from 34-24-34 to manatee-shaped to what I am now: average. I studied women's breasts in advertisements and in celebrity magazines. Nature is balanced: large breasts usually go along with large hips and medium waists. Hourglass figures. Now boy hips, man abs, Bardot breasts, and that concave under-navel belly are required to be an ideal woman. This is, for most women, a physical impossibility.

Maybe in 2000, big breasts became so ordinary, so easily attained, that allure went south to the belly. The navel rings, the tattoos, the Christina Aguilera/Britney Spears low, low, low-rise pants.

It's awfully hard to buy a concave belly.

Recently I walked around Disneyland with my three daughters and a friend with her kids. We could have been anywhere in the United States; a male friend had mentioned preteens showing navel rings and tattoos in Los Angeles and Detroit at sport arenas, and another friend mentioned six-year-olds showing their underwear elastic with pushed-low skirts at an elementary school in San Francisco.

We saw bellies at Disneyland. The archetypes—the Paris Hilton/Christina/Britney/Olsen Twins wannabe girls—were all present, blonde and preternaturally thin. Girls of every other size and shape were also on display. And what I couldn't help but notice was how different all of these bodies were from those of my youth. We had waists and then hips. These girls had long, long waists, with interesting pads of muscle/fat above the back pelvis, pads that made me think of my favorite chicken part: the back. Those soft tender pads of meat beside the vertebrae, the ones my mother-in-law taught me to savor because that unwanted piece was usually what we women were left with after the platter was passed around.

Yes. The place where fat is stored after we have children, and now that we are an increasingly overweight society, often before we have children.

The girls and women who were not Paris Hilton still wore

ultra-low-rise jeans and skirts the size of manila envelopes. I saw shining rims of skin, marked with the delicate silvery filigree of stretch marks, with the angry red of sunburn, with tattoos and elastic marks from where the shorts rode up. I saw striving and desire and the shrugs of defiance: I don't care if my tender girl-fat trembles when I walk. I'm still sexy.

I saw women my age whose stomachs hung over their belts the way men's beer bellies do, when their shirts ride up unexpectedly. I saw women my age who had obviously done Pilates and yoga and Yogilates and thousands of sit-ups, who wore low-rise sweat pants with JUICY stenciled on their butts, just below the pads of skin showing with downy fur along the arrowhead-shaped end of their vertebrae.

The chicken back ends with that—do you remember? The vertebrae end in that soft triangle of the butt. I stared at all the daughters and mothers walking with friends; pushing strollers; bent over, working hard; strolling, sexy and nonchalant; waiting in line. All races and sizes and ages. Some pulling their shirts down again and again, letting them ride up again and again, as if shy but not really, as if feeling the brush of illicit air between their hipbones.

What were we wearing, my daughters and I? They wore basketball jerseys and shorts, their everyday attire, and they glared scornfully at the other girls. But their friends wear low-rise, and now and then, so does my fifteen-year-old, though she is shaped like Beyoncé and therefore has a hard time with buttless jeans.

Me? I wore capris and a T-shirt, and if I reached up to grab a bar in a ride, some of my stomach showed. When that happened, my middle daughter, extremely judgmental at twelve, would pinch the hem of my shirt like a curtain and yank it down.

I suddenly thought of how all these teenage girls must feel watching their mothers try to adopt the public belly—the one body part you'd think would be off-limits to women whose stomachs had stretched from giving birth.

Standing in line for Pirates of the Caribbean, watching a woman my age with a deep, bought tan and her lower back exposed, a faint trail of hair like a second spine, images of my mother's magazines came to me. The seventies wasn't the most tasteful decade, and those moms must have shown off bad fashion, too, in their ponchos and no bras and paper dresses and Earth shoes. But regular moms in my neighborhood, of all races and sizes, wore mom clothes or work uniforms. I never saw a mother's cleavage or belly or the soft lower back. I'm sure women of my mother's generation wanted men to notice them. But magazine covers showed Jackie Kennedy and Coretta Scott King and Lena Horne and Audrey Hepburn, Janice Dickinson and Lauren Hutton. My mother and her contemporaries admired these women's eyes or brows or hairstyle, their coats or jewelry or regal bearing or volunteer work. My mother and her friends didn't expect to be confronted with the buttocks or abs of Jackie Kennedy, or to be expected to show off their own.

Quirky, generous beauty seemed a realistic expectation for mothers only a few years ago. Our impossible, celebrity-charged standards now: Cindy Crawford, Sarah Jessica Parker, Catherine Zeta-Jones, Madonna. Belly-baring as soon as possible after giving birth; no alteration in the body—and for most of the rest of us, guilt or disbelief at the amount of flawless skin exposed for our instruction. Those abs, those below-navel planes of flesh with no stretch marks or after-baby pooch, require hours of gym time and personal trainers, which requires nannies, which would require entirely different lives for most mothers, not just different postpartum bellies.

Even for young women who haven't had children, the standards of beauty seem impossible. Jeans require no hips and flat buttocks, the better for butt cleavage. We are even over-accessorized below the knees, where requirements for feet are French pedicure, toenail decals, toe rings, ankle bracelets, tiny ankle tattoos, and, yes, toe cleavage. On the Jungle Cruise, while the wisecracking safari guide shot a cap gun into the mouth of a descending plastic hippo, I saw high-heeled flip flops, but at least I didn't see any Manolo Blahniks.

There at Disneyland, though, I realized that I was wrong about one thing: Women can buy a belly. I'd forgotten the graphic scene on television where I saw the marker lines on a woman's stomach for her tummy tuck.

That night, so tired I couldn't move from the couch after the girls had gone to bed, I made the mistake of watching for the first time, and last, *Extreme Makeover.*

A woman my age, with a husband who apparently loved her enough to take care of their four small children while she was gone for two months(!), remade her entire face and body. Face: nose job, eyelid tightening, lip contouring, liposuction on cheeks, teeth whitened, scars laser-removed, and new hair sewn to her existing hair. Body: tummy tuck, liposuction on thighs and buttocks, breast augmentation and lift, and two months' worth of diet and rigorous workouts with a personal trainer.

I learned a new term: Brazilian butt lift.

Let's not talk about the clothes or makeup.

Let's just stick with this: after the four kids, she felt that her breasts had sagged, her stomach was disfigured with stretch marks and excess skin, and her face was haggard, her eyes swollen and bleary.

Well, yeah. Those are standard results of pregnancy and childbirth, not to mention the sleepless nights of strep throat, coughs and colds, and childhood illnesses. She hadn't even gotten to the long nights of waiting up for those who are dating and driving.

I have.

We're in our thirties, our forties. We have given birth to and are raising children. Who expects us to look like this? Our men? I don't think so. Yes, there are trophy wives and second wives and third wives. There are men who leave their first wives for someone younger. But among my friends, in my middle-of-the-road existence, that has hardly ever happened. Men leave, but often for someone their age and often for no one at all. For solitude and no kids. And other men don't leave. They might look at the billboards or the models in Victoria's Secret catalogs, they might even fool around, but usually not with that kind of woman.

Women tend to say, "I do it for me. Not him."

Mothers have fallen for the marketing—the marketing and advertising of our lives, advertising to other women, along with men, that we are perfect, we will always be perfect, even after having children. We will never have flaws on our bellies or faces or appearances or lives.

A friend recently passed on a clever advertisement in a catalog called "As We Change" (for "older" women, certainly, though no change at all would be the goal). "Don't blame yourself if your tummy is suddenly out of proportion. Beginning in your early 20s, nature conspires to redistribute adipose (fat) tissue." (I had no idea that women of twenty-two, say, are now considered to be gracefully aging, or that nature was actually sneaky, rather than merely matter-of-fact.) "Sovage Tummy Flattening Gel works by forcing stored fat out of abdominal fat cells and into the bloodstream to be burned as energy." (Yeah, and I'll just have one little square of chocolate.) A four-to-six–week supply was $119. But if you're "changing," and you're only in your forties, that's a lot of money over the estimated weeks you'll live, still redistributing, making up for the life you've had, still with a life to come.

Why do so many women want to erase all evidence that they've had children, or eaten well, or gotten older? I often think of the question Ann Landers once posed to mothers: If you could go back and choose again, would you have kids? Readers were surprised by how many women said no. Somehow, this new obsession with tummy tucks that tighten an upper abdomen, leaving scars elsewhere, seems that kind of defiance, even denial. Women want to look forever young, or to look like their daughters' friends, rather than the mothers they are, inevitably older and therefore not desirable, not even visible.

What I couldn't stop thinking about, when I saw women who had transformed themselves into females who apparently had never had children, who showed off their new bodies made unrealistic and their new not-their-own hair: what did their children think? The smaller children of the *Extreme Makeover* woman looked frightened, as if a total stranger had appeared before them. And the face of one teenage daughter on another show was dubious, to say the least.

My girls are appalled by women my age who try to look like their own Extreme Makeover. They shake their heads at the mothers who wear false eyelashes to the store, who have obviously enhanced busts spilling out of shelf-bra tanks, who wear Candies shoes (another seventies revival!) and hot pants to pick up their kids from school, revealing crescents of flesh not usually seen.

I watched the mothers at a school assembly recently, and I watched the kids' reactions to us, and I believe that children want us to look like mothers. That doesn't mean shabby and resentful and uncaring, but it doesn't mean a leopard-print thong and a sun tattoo around the navel and a shirt that says PORN STAR.

We are animals, with many body parts. But mothers have produced offspring, and when mothers are actively trying to attract men, even their own husbands, with constant displays of overt sex, I think baby and even adolescent animals feel threatened, or at least uneasy.

There is unease at the sight of our sexualized, public bellies. Most of the girls I know don't want their mothers wearing JUICY or SWEET across their butts, or dolphins or hearts rising from the nether regions. Daughters do not want to think about our nether regions.

Which is what the belly is all about. In a recent issue of *Redbook*, in an entire section devoted to depilation, women are admonished not to forget to remove "your goodie trail." Goodie trail? I squinted at the explanation: "The line of hairs that leads to, well, your goods." That would be the hair on the belly that people didn't used to see. The hair that's sexy on men who wear their jeans down low, showing their boxers.

So it's all about the goods. The swath of flesh between the hipbones, the groin itself, that is the actual repository of our species. Under that decorated skin is the receptacle of uterus and ovaries, the place where the baby will lie curled and waiting.

Then the baby will grow into a child who certainly doesn't want to see her mother's belly, or cleavage, high or low.

My friend, who walked beside me at Disneyland, also has three kids, the same ages as mine. I studied myself in her sunglasses. We have marks. Lots of them. We wear capris from Target and colorful tees and flat shoes. We have soft stomachs because, well, babies were in there. We have fans of fine lines around our eyes because it's sunny and we squint when we watch kids practice or wait for them outside the classroom or the orthodontist. We have not-snowy teeth because we drink coffee and tea to keep us awake in the morning while we make lunches and get ready for work or housework or dirty work—what women do.

As I watched all the girls walking the asphalt trails of Disneyland with thousands of other animals—none of whom, I will guess, wanting to see their mother's belly on display—what I saw were their burnished lower backs, their trembling too-pale bellies, their fake tattoos peeling off disconsolately from the lower spines, or their elaborate real tattoos pointing the way into their jeans, toward goodies they may not fully understand, and dangers for which they may not be ready. And I thought, *I feel the same way about you.* I see your hipbones like little goal posts poking through your skin, and I see in my memory the sketches of the reproductive organs from school lessons mapping you, and I see in my imagination the flaws and scars, the resignation and knowledge that will eventually leave their marks, and I see the delicacy of that belly skin, the elasticity that will allow you to become me, someday.

Mother of the World

Kate Moses

Mother of the World

I arrived at three o'clock in the morning, but even then Cairo's notoriously polluted air was thick with lingering heat. Though the city's lights glittered against the desert's distant darkness, it was far too early to go to my hotel. As we drove on empty highways, the taxi driver, who spoke some English, said he would take me to a café where I could have tea and wait. "In Cairo, you will be treated as a man," he reassured me. I had heard this before: Western women are typically relegated to the status of "honorary men." I wasn't convinced; being treated as sexually invisible seemed closer to the truth.

Left on a corner with my luggage, dressed in modest, baggy clothing, I was at the edge of the labyrinthine Khan al-Khalili, a fourteenth-century neighborhood famous for its historic, bustling market sprawling over a square mile of medieval streets and alleyways. Beyond the corner sidewalk café, the thousand-year-old Al-Azhar University and the Al-Husayn mosque—holiest of all in Cairo—rose behind walls on either side. Even that early, many people were wandering about, mostly men but also some women and children. The women I saw sat in family groups at the café, veils carefully pinned close to their heads as they sipped spicy, fragrant

Egyptian coffee or hot, scarlet tea—*karkaday*, made from steeped hibiscus flowers—while the men smoked flavored tobacco from *sheeshas*, ornate, brass-fitted water pipes. Or they strolled slowly with their families through the crowds, mildly looking around, sleeping babies draped limply over their shoulders.

Pulling my suitcase along as discreetly as I could, I turned down an alley lined with market stalls, lights blazing. There were tourist-trap bazaars crammed with faux Egyptiana and gaudy belly-dancing outfits alongside craftsman's shops selling hand-embroidered tribal tents and rugs woven of camel hair. There were huge rush baskets brimming with spices, donkey carts loaded with burlap sacks of roasted nuts, tired salesmen with piles of cheap plastic toys laid out on blankets in the street. I looked at everything and everyone surreptitiously, obliquely, not wanting to make eye contact, not wanting to be noticed. I felt a tug behind me and heard laughter. I turned around: A group of beggar children, barefoot and wearing shreds of clothing, were skipping away, giggling, having just touched my uncovered hair. Behind them was a man with no legs, only bare, black-encrusted feet, using his hands to walk. Along the sacred mosque's high crenulated wall, a merchant had stacked cages of restless, hissing wild animals, their tails brushing the wire bars, and on top of the cages, dead animals—taxidermied, grimacing creatures I couldn't identify, their glass eyes soulless.

I hurried back to the corner where the taxi had dropped me. I sat at one of the café tables surrounded by men smoking *sheesha*, the sickeningly sweet smoke from their apple-scented tobacco making me dizzy and ill. For the first time I admitted to myself that this trip might be fruitless, a bad idea. I'd never before in my life gone anywhere alone, ever. I had always managed to bypass any chance I'd ever had to move independently through the world; the truth is that my identity had always been largely dependent on others—my parents, my family, my friends, ultimately my husband and my children, motherhood being my self-hood's galvanizing force. I felt confident and solid as long as I was the caretaker or the mother, the provider of comfort or the solver of problems. During the spring of 2004, though, my self had become someone I found unreliable.

A few days before Christmas, at the age of forty-one, I lost my third baby.

Five weeks later, a dear friend was diagnosed with a rare form of metastasized cancer. She is the fourth of my beloved, trusted friends—all women, all mothers—to face a cancer diagnosis in three years.

Now in summer, trying to remember the Arabic words the taxi driver had taught me, awkwardly ordering another scalding cup of mint tea when my last one had cooled, I was not entirely sure I was up to this. For months I'd lived as if skinless, utterly vulnerable. Overwhelmed by human frailties, especially my own, I didn't know what to do, but I had to do *something*. I had come to Egypt to see a painting, a portrait of a woman whose face haunted and consoled me.

With each sip of tea, my fingers trembling around the glass, I tried to coax myself back from the ledge of panic. I tried to focus on something I'd read in a novel by Egypt's Nobel laureate, Naguib Mahfouz, who had grown up in this neighborhood. Mahfouz wrote several of his books in the "Closed Treasure Room" at el-Fishawi's café, a Khan al-Khalili institution for hundreds of years. The line I remembered was one I loved for its ambiguity, its multiple layers of meaning and possibility: Cairo, wrote Mahfouz, was "like meeting one's beloved in old age." It was almost a riddle. Did "meeting" mean for the first time, or after a lifetime's separation? Is it the beloved or the lover who is old? Or both? In my head, I mentally fingered the variable answers.

Cairo itself embodies contradiction, a city widely acknowledged as bewildering, seductive, filthy, operatic, vast, decadent, glorious. The prehistoric mythology of the ancient Egyptians says that life began at the spot that is now Cairo, born out of universal nothingness by the creator god, a radiant orb whose tears became mankind—though Cairo is known in Arabic as *Misr um al-dunya*, "Mother of the World." The creator god's wife was the resourceful goddess Mut, protectress of the innocent, righter of wrongs, and patroness of women, especially mothers. The hieroglyphic form of the word *mut* is the huge, powerful vulture of the African desert. In Egyptian, *mut* means both "mother" and "death."

From my sidewalk table at the café I watched the sky, deep indigo when I arrived. As the sun's rising light bled up through the shadows, minarets and domes materialized before me in high, gilded relief. At five o'clock, the recorded voices of the *muezzins* broke the morning's relative silence as loudspeakers came on at mosques all over the city, calling the faithful to prayers.

The Fayum Portraits

Her name was Demos, a word meaning "the people"; she was twenty-four years old. She lived and died in Egypt in the first century A.D. Her portrait was painted to decorate her mummified body after her death, for two reasons: to give her *ka*, her life force, a symbolic portal into eternity; and to give her loved ones a tangible focus for their grief. The mummy of the baby girl found with her was almost certainly her daughter. Both had died shortly after their portraits were painted. A scarlet ribbon edged in gold had been laid across Demos's mummified breast by the people who loved her; written in Greek, the common language of her time, was her name, her age, and a single phrase: *always to be remembered.*

Despite my letters and e-mails and calls, the Egyptian Museum had never confirmed that the portraits of Demos and her baby, two of the masterpieces in the museum's collection of so-called Fayum portraits, would be on display when I arrived. The portraits had been restored, then shown in a special exhibit at another Cairo venue a year before; since then, they had disappeared.

The thousand or so Fayum portraits scattered through museums around the world are the only significant body of painting to survive from classical antiquity. Most of them were found in the late eighteenth century in Egypt's Fayum oasis region, unearthed in Roman-era cemeteries where they had been buried in shallow

sand graves, the thin wooden panels and wax encaustic medium
of the fragile portraits preserved thanks to Egypt's dry climate
and burial customs. Amazingly, the colors and luminosity of the
portraits are said to be just as fresh today as they were in the first
four centuries A.D., when they were created as memorials to capture the unique individuality of their subjects.

Most of the portraits were painted quickly from life and displayed in the home until the subject's death; the portrait was then
removed from its frame, cut down, and affixed to the mummified
body, a pictorial representation of the deceased meant to ensure
their body's journey from life to immortality, in keeping with the
highly ritualized Egyptian religious beliefs. A majority of the portraits are of people in what we would consider the early stages of
life; some have the hunted look of illness, their skin sallow or their
eyes sunken in dark circles, or their faces disfigured by unknowable
maladies. Since life expectancy during Egypt's Greco-Roman period
was dismal for children and less than thirty years for women—
childbearing being a commonly lethal risk—most of the portraits
were painted in anticipation of an expected death.

The Greek painter and art historian Euphrosyne Doxiadis,
who spent ten years documenting the portraits, has called them
"great monuments to mourning." I came across Doxiadis's book
when I was also in mourning—for my baby, my friends' uncertain
futures, the competent, effective self I used to trust. I needed distraction and solace. The immediacy of the portraits, the candor
and elegiac dignity of their moving, numinous faces, were mesmerizing. They were paintings of the long-dead, but they continued, as André Malraux wrote, to "glow with the flame of eternal
life." They were as vivid, as life-affirming, as anything I'd ever
seen—as the faces of my children.

There were faces more breathtaking, more beautiful than
Demos's. There were handsome, shirtless young men going off to
join the Roman army, their loved ones knowing they would likely
never return. There were women whose dazzling portraits were
embellished with gold leaf. But humble Demos immediately possessed me. She looks back at the artist from the slightest angle,

over her left shoulder, her face girlishly rounded, its youthful soft-
ness betraying her age despite the intricate styling of her dark
hair. Her lips are slightly parted, as if she were about to speak,
but hesitates. Demos's somber-faced baby, who shares her dark,
questioning eyes and poignantly tender double chin, is impossible
to mistake as anyone but Demos's child.

Even as I studied the book of Fayum portraits last spring, as I
explained to my patient family and friends how and why they
were painted—feeling a little more animated, a little less ground
away by grief—I didn't know how to articulate what *I* saw. How
was it that Demos, confronting the end of her life, was luring me
away from my own despair? It was my husband who suggested I
go to Egypt to see her. I had a long-standing business commitment
in London in June; I could extend my trip by a few days. It would
be good for me, he said, speaking to me in the low, calming tones
one would use on a frightened animal or a child. I didn't know
whether it was crazy for me to go, or not to. Within a week I'd
bought my plane tickets.

Like Niobe, All Tears

In the classical Greek myth, Niobe was a Theban queen who
offended the gods by her maternal hubris. Blessed with seven
graceful daughters and seven strong sons, she dared to boast: how
could any mother be as lucky as she? Even the worshipped goddess Leto had only two children. Furious at the slight, Leto called
to her twins to exact revenge. The deadly archer, Apollo, and the
divine huntress, Diana, took aim at Niobe's children and shot
them all dead. Niobe's grief was so great that she turned to stone.
Only her tears continued, unstoppable. "Like Niobe, all tears,"
wrote Shakespeare in *Hamlet*.

Through the fall of 2003 I relished in selfish privacy what I
knew would be my last pregnancy. I was greedy for this long-
awaited baby—my payback, I felt, for triumphing, however slowly,

over marital ambivalence. My second marriage had been like a good wine opened too soon: The first seven years were tannic, but not undrinkable. It needed to breathe. After allowing my marriage to decant, putting a third child on hold as it matured, a decade after our wedding my relationship with my husband had finally become delicious. Our other two children—our seven-year-old daughter and my fifteen-year-old son from my first marriage—were sheer delight. A third! We couldn't believe our luck, late though it had arrived. We joked that we would tell people we'd planned our family with this age gap in mind: Where other parents might think two or three years is the perfect span between kids, we'd settled on eight.

My husband and I decided to wait until "everything was okay," after the amniocentesis, to break the news about this baby. It never occurred to me that anything might *actually* go wrong—I was only forty-one; some of my friends had had their first babies at thirty-nine, forty, even forty-three. Still, we opted for the magical landmark of that assessment as a knee-jerk caution against vague catastrophes we never even thought to discuss. Meanwhile, alone with my body through school days and after bedtime, I lived inwardly, just feeling my pregnancy and its cavalcade of coursing hormones. I gloated. I stared down at my expanding body and marveled at its power. I fell asleep at my desk and walked the dog in a self-satisfied daze, free from the necessity to hide how tired, fat, nauseated, and biologically distracted I was, a ruse I reinstituted while driving kids to school dressed in unremarkable overalls or ransacking my closet to find some sort of reasonable getup to disguise the obvious fact of my unannounced pregnancy at the family Thanksgiving gathering.

In fact, I loved keeping my baby to myself. I was so much older, my life so much more evolved, than when I'd first become a mother at twenty-six, or again at thirty-four. This was my chance, at last, to be fully present in my life and in my female body. This would be the pregnancy unmarred by a shaky marriage or by my apprentice status as a mother and a woman. This time I even had a house, a washer and dryer, a tiny space to work at home; I wouldn't have to catch glimpses of my newborn's babyhood as I rushed off somewhere else. I was good at this now. Not merely wine but champagne, this eleventh-hour pregnancy. I savored the tender ache, the percolating sensation of my baby growing cell by cell—like bubbles rising in a champagne glass.

The routine sonogram I had in December in preparation for genetic testing showed that something was wrong with my baby. It took three more sleepless weeks to get a diagnosis. For weeks after my baby died, my emotions were so paralyzed I could hardly feel them. Kept a secret for its entire duration, my pregnancy and all its attendant fantasies felt like a ghost event, something I had heard rumor of. I mimicked an adequate, if vague, version of myself. I brushed hair. I fed animals. I drove to basketball practice. I nagged people about homework.

But when I heard the news of my friend D.'s cancer, I started crying and I couldn't stop. Literally, perpetually. Walking the dog at the beach on the moodiest of gray February days, tissues crumpled in my fist. In the pickup line at schools, leaking tears through March, through April. Like Niobe, all tears. Broken down, helpless, wiping my face on the back of my sleeve.

Whatever restraint I had that winter and spring I put toward keeping my composure in front of my children. My daughter was deep in a maternal phase of her own. For months Celeste had been talking wistfully about wanting to be a big sister, not just a little sister, and she'd written to Santa for a particular cuddly cloth baby doll with a cap of mohair curls. On Christmas morning she found "Lora" wrapped in a blanket under the tree. Celeste and I sat on the rug in our nightgowns undressing Lora to her dimpled bottom and trying out all the tiny outfits in her flannel layette. As I cradled the doll in my lap while Celeste dressed her, I slanted my mind away, refusing the creeping awareness that I was doing something more than acting a part in my daughter's game.

Celeste had also asked for a set of twin toddler dolls for her birthday. Along with Lora, "Brian" and "Claire" became my responsibility during school days. It was my job to get them up from their naps, move them around the house, and help them pass the time until Celeste got home to take over. I didn't go so far as to actually play with them while she was gone, but I felt a renewed stab of inadequacy if I saw them slumped on their faces on Celeste's bed. "I'm so glad you love Lora and Brian and Claire as much as I do, Mommy," Celeste once said as we drove home from school on an afternoon scented with new grass and blossoming trees, her dolls strapped into a single seat belt as she'd instructed, my shattered face, by then, hidden behind sunglasses. "You're really good at this mommy stuff," my daughter continued, the echo of my earlier arrogance ringing hollow.

I could no more tell my son what had happened to me than I could tell his sister. Even while I was still pregnant I hadn't looked forward to breaking that particular category of news to a teenager who'd just started dating. Zachary had been seeing another high school freshman, a sweet girl with braces on her teeth. Over the holiday break we'd forced a fascinated Celeste ahead of the rest of the family on a beach walk so Zachary and his girlfriend could enjoy a modicum of privacy. They strolled barefoot far behind us, their fingers knitting and separating as their awareness of the rest of us ebbed and flowed. One night I drove to pick them up after a movie. When I reached the fast food place where we'd agreed to meet, I spotted them through the restaurant's plate glass window, heads tenderly inclined toward each other as they whispered and kissed. I could see them, but they couldn't see me. I made a noisy racket as I entered, slamming the door of the newspaper kiosk, standing with my back to them as I pretended to read the paper, giving them time to register my presence. A few days before Valentine's Day, Zachary told me his girlfriend had broken up with him. He shook his head, repeating over and over her inexplicable reason, and for weeks I listened and offered what advice I could as he sorted through his pain and frustration. My son didn't need to know my problems. He had a heartbreak of his own.

Searching for Demos

The Egyptian Museum was just a short, straight walk down a single street from my hotel in Cairo's haphazard, confusing downtown. What I didn't account for, that first morning, was the endless stream of randomly honking vehicles passing Midan Tahrir, the city's central intersection, a traffic circle around which six or eight or eleven lanes of cars weave tooting past. I could see the pink edifice of the turn-of-the-century museum rising in neoclassical grandiosity on the other side, beyond a police barricade I would also have to cross. For half an hour I stood at the curb waiting for a window of opportunity, the ferocious sun's hundred-degree heat baking my skull, watching blasé Egyptians walk out in front of careening trucks, then finally I made it myself, running and hesitating by turns, across the street.

Despite its high security, the Egyptian Museum is legendary for the stupefying immensity of its disorganized collection, the almost total lack of curatorial information for visitors, and the poor conservation inside the building. In contrast to the super-heated glare outside—light that had the quality of stripping one back to defenselessness—the light inside felt grainy, filtered through centuries of grit. There were no maps or museum guides or membership propaganda evident in the museum's lobby, but I knew my destination: a gallery on the second floor.

I walked briskly through a gallery of colossal sarcophagi and up the stairs past the royal mummy rooms, into a long hall displaying the seemingly innumerable, priceless treasures of Tutankhamun, all gold. Near the very end of the hall, in a gallery built around a balcony open to the room below, I thought I saw her. At first glance it could have been Demos: in a mauve tunic, three-tiered pearl earrings, three necklaces of gold and emerald. But this woman's face had an expression of poised elegance, as if she were aware of the opulently bejeweled mummy case to which her portrait was still attached. I scanned the room and saw a glass case on the next wall in which three shelves of detached portraits were propped up against a linen backdrop. Looking carefully at each portrait, I saw that there were empty spots in the case where at least two paintings might have been—a noticeable layer of disturbed dust on the glass shelf indicated that objects had been removed—and that Demos and her baby were not there.

There was a sonogram, and another the next week, and another the next, my baby fading more each time. After they told me that my "fetal tissue was not viable," while I was resisting whatever terrible thing they wanted to do to my baby and me next, I began to contract and bleed at home. It hadn't seemed so dramatic, the bleeding; I held it, bulky and hot and contained, in my cupped hand, before it sank heavily through the water and I flushed it down. At the next sonogram, there was simply nothing there. My baby had slipped out of me, and I hadn't known. What mother would not have been ashamed?

I had lost my baby like a set of car keys. Lighter than car keys, actually—two inches long and the weight of fifty paper clips, or so I read on the fetal development e-list I'd signed up for and that, after my miscarriage, I could not manage to get myself deleted from. Even at that I was a failure.

At my age, the rate of fetal death from natural causes rises precipitously, I was told by the young obstetrician who couldn't remember my name from one appointment to the next. At my age, seven years between pregnancies was not a hopeful sign. At my age, first-tier treatment drugs to boost fertility, like Clomid, were unlikely to be helpful, because my eggs were already old. She counseled me to think "good and hard" about how much money, time, and energy I was willing to put toward getting pregnant again, at my age; after all, she said, consulting my chart, I already had two healthy children.

At my age, I had grown complacent about the femaleness of my body. The shock of monthly blood and developing breasts were long past; so too the mysteries of birth control, the awkwardness of discovering sexual satisfaction, the righteous indignation of the first experiences of blatant mysogyny, all replaced, over the course of adulthood, by a sense of relief in the unshakeable reliability of my female body: its rhythms, its sensations, its varied physical, emotional, and intellectual capacities. Being a woman, having a mother's body, had become the seat of my power in the world. I thought I still had the luxury of assuming that my sexuality had purpose—the erotic a means of procreation and influence, my femaleness something inexhaustible and primitive, like the flooding of the ancient Nile.

Yet all of my friends had developed cancers in the cells that made them womanly: in their breasts, in their wombs, in the cushioning flesh that had comforted children in their laps, that had fed or grown their babies. After the counterattack of chemicals and scalpels, the flesh that remained was different, no longer what we think of when we think of a mother's welcoming, enveloping body. The flesh that survives is scarred, knotted, hardened, tight; the emotions, in some cases, equally embrittled.

When had our bodies so viciously turned on us? I wasn't a young, fertile Venus of Willendorf with long honey-colored hair, not anymore. When I looked in the mirror I was fat and not pregnant, a tired, dumpy, forty-something mother going gray, who could walk unnoticed down any city street. How I defined myself had changed, slipping away from me unknown, unseen, like my baby, like the cells shifting ominously in the bodies of my friends.

I remember seeing D. before she was diagnosed with cancer, all self-possession and refinement on a university stage, preparing to give a lecture—wearing different colored shoes! One black, one red—an audacious expert, in even the most staid circumstances, at maintaining her feminine originality, her personal flair. I remember a series of black-and-white nude photos taken years before my friend C. saw a strange and minatory bruise on one of her breasts: her body turned toward the window light behind her, her legs twisted together in shadow, her skin as perfect and shapely as the contours of a Noguchi sculpture.

And I remember myself at a time that seems not so long ago, looking down at my own breasts three days after the birth of my daughter: in a matter of hours my milk-engorged breasts had ballooned exponentially, literally before my eyes, each growing to the size and taut firmness of a child's rubber ball. The absurdity of it, the outrageous disproportion to the rest of me and to my tiny baby, was hilarious. My breasts, then, like the scarred and irradiated and poisoned flesh of my friends with cancer now, were hard, melon-thumping hard. But they were full of milk. They were meant to sustain life. I have rarely, before or since, felt more truly feminine, or more vital. Just as with her older brother, long after my daughter stopped breast-feeding I continued to lactate. My milk continued for years, seemingly unstoppable.

I needed to find a curator or a director, someone who could lead me to Demos. I pestered disinterested guards at the endless security checkpoints, brandishing color photocopies of the portraits of Demos and her baby, trying to follow the confusing, contradictory instructions I was given, the indiscriminate honking of traffic at Midan Tahrir in the background a soundtrack, relentless. I wandered the museum into the afternoon, finally stumbling into the administrative wing. Veiled women in aprons passed by with trays of tea, and men in shirtsleeves were crowded into a broom closet eating their lunch. Under a low arched doorway another bored guard watched a small television, his feet up on an ugly desk. Behind him, a bearded Western man in Indiana Jones garb spoke earnestly to a clean-shaven Egyptian wearing ordinary street clothes.

"I need to speak to the curator of the Fayum portraits," I said, holding up the photocopied Demos for the relaxing guard. I repeated my request twice before I managed to gain his attention. The guard jerked his head sideways, not taking his eyes from the TV screen.

"Mrs. Tawfic," he said.

"This way?" I asked.

The guard jerked his head again.

At the end of the hall, through an open door, there was a room full of women. All veiled, they sat together around numerous desks crowded against the walls, sharing tuna sandwiches and drinking milky tea. One of them spoke quietly on the solitary telephone. Flies ambled in esoteric, repeating patterns in the center of the shabby, nondescript room: the curators' office.

"Mrs. Tawfic?" I said, all the women turning to look at me as I entered. One well-dressed woman sitting in a chair with her back to one of the file cabinets, her purse in her lap, looked quizzically at me. I'd broken into a profound sweat. I dabbed at my face with a tissue from a packet I kept in my pocket; already I'd noticed many Egyptian women doing the same.

I held out the photocopy of Demos's portrait, like an offering in exchange for a blessing. My request, however indistinct its reasons, tumbled forth: that I'd come from America, that I'd written and called, that I wanted to see this portrait, but it wasn't in the gallery.

"You want to see the portraits?" Mrs. Tawfic replied, standing up. "Yes, yes. Nobody comes to see the portraits. They all want to see the old things." She edged herself gracefully through the narrow space between her desk and the next one, taking the likeness of Demos from my hands. "She is in storage," she continued. Though she looked to be about my age, she was taller than me, meticulously made up, and she carried herself with serene authority. "But if you want to see her, I will bring her out for you."

"You will?" I answered, disbelieving. "Yes! Please. I've come all the way from America," I said pointlessly again.

"Can you come back?" Mrs. Tawfic asked. "I can't . . ." she hesitated, searching for the English words. "I will need papers. I will need a letter."

"That's fine," I said. "I can come back any time. I'm here until Thursday. I have all of my papers here. What do you need?"

Mrs. Tawfic looked at everything I had: the photocopies of the portraits along with my stack of unanswered correspondence, my passport, my California driver's license, the card from my hotel, and the half-bogus press pass my son had concocted for me the night before I left home. I sat at an empty desk and handwrote a new letter to the museum's director, waving away a persistent fly as I wrote.

"This is good," said Mrs. Tawfic, smiling warmly at me as she finished reading the letter slowly. "Can you come back, umm . . . Wednesday? Two days, at ten o'clock?"

Walk Like an Egyptian

Before the building of the Aswan Dam in the 1900s, June had been the time of the Nile's annual flood. All life in Egypt was reliant on the Nile's flooding and receding. The right amount of flooding meant fertile fields and healthy harvests; too little or too much meant desperation and starvation. My experience of Cairo, of waiting to go back to see Mrs. Tawfic, wavered equally between extremes, ecstatic and despairing by turns.

I left the museum, stunned and excited by finding Mrs. Tawfic and the prospect of seeing Demos, only to be stranded again at the edge of the Midan Tahrir. Even worse, it was just before Cairo's rush hour, and drivers were taking advantage of any free space in the nonexistent lanes, gunning their engines to get as far toward their destinations as possible before the vehicular deadlock that would soon come.

I could see no way to get back across the street. Even the local pedestrians were avoiding any attempt to cross on foot. Suddenly someone grabbed my elbow, an old Egyptian man with a face shriveled to leather, wearing a stained *galabiyya* and rubber flip-flops. "Walk like an Egyptian!" he urged me. I almost burst out laughing, thinking of the insipid eighties pop song with that title—was it the Bangles or some other girl group?—but there wasn't time. My escort pulled me straight into oncoming traffic, walking, not hurrying, gripping my elbow firmly, holding his other hand out toward speeding cars and buses as he wove me between them; they passed us within inches. I held my breath; I kept walking. "Welcome!" the man shouted as he left me on the opposite curb.

Not all the Egyptians I met in the next thirty-six hours were so magnanimous. My elbow was grabbed many times, often to force me toward someone's "art gallery," which would turn out to be a shop selling hideous paintings on ersatz papyrus, or by hucksters who opened their wallets to show me dubious photos of friends and relatives in America before trying to drag me to their "family shop." After being reluctantly pulled down a few alleys I learned to stop their hard sells immediately by saying, "My husband will kill you!" with a smile, a strategy that worked every time. I knew they only wanted my business; diminished as I felt—as well as grimy and perpetually sweaty—attracting sexual attention, desired or otherwise, from men seemed an almost laughable absurdity. Most Egyptians were merely friendly, acknowledging my presence in their country with whatever English they had at their disposal: sometimes "Texas?" or "Hollywood?" but also "Okay!" "Yes, yes!" and once, "Yankee doo doo!"

Still, Cairo was exhausting, dirty, and overwhelming, difficult almost everywhere. Maps were useless against the intricacy of the city's many narrow, name-changing streets, and cash was hard to get: The ATM keyboards were in Arabic (of course!) and even the bank exchanges at major hotels were open for mystifying, unpredictable periods. I spent hours searching for money, a necessity in Egypt's largely cash economy, and for phones that would work with the international phone cards I purchased. When I did manage to get through to the United States, I resorted to leaving long, rambling messages for my family, knowing they had no way to reach me: The grubby phone in my hotel room didn't work.

Finding Demos

Mrs. Tawfic was waiting for me at the door when I reached her office on Wednesday morning. "I am still meeting with my director. Can you come back in one hour?"

"Of course," I said, fighting off my auto-response of skepticism, the low gnawing of disappointment anticipated. "I'll come back in an hour."

I have an hour, then, I encouraged myself, standing unexpectedly in the penetrating morning light in the museum courtyard. I crossed the alley to the Nile Hilton, thinking I would get some money and try to call my family again. But I spent most of the hour walking back and forth between the unattended bank exchange office and the hotel operator's booth, until I finally gave up. I had some cash; it would have to last me indefinitely. As I turned into a breezeway leading out of the hotel's main lobby, I passed a bookshop. In the window was a copy of *The Mysterious Fayum Portraits* by Euphrosyne Doxiadis, the same book in which I first saw Demos.

"Can you take a credit card?" I asked the bookshop clerk. The answer was yes. Success! I bought the book—for moral support, even if I didn't end up needing it to shore up my application to see the portraits—and crossed the Hilton's garden back to the museum.

When I arrived at the curator's office for the second time, Mrs. Tawfic had a stack of papers for me to sign. I exhaled. Again I surrendered my passport, my press pass, everything, while Mrs. Tawfic went to the director's office for his final approval. When she returned, impeccably dressed, her dark hair barely showing at the hairline under a navy scarf, her eyes lined in blue, I thought for a moment of how crude I must look to her, in my dusty pants and shoes and my enormous, baggy cotton shirt—my daily Egyptian getup. "Now we can go," she said, holding the stack of signed, sealed forms. "What is that?" she asked, pointing at the book of Fayum portraits.

"This is how I discovered Demos," I said, handing her the book. Immediately, hungrily, she started to page through the volume.

"I have never seen this," she said, almost breathless. "I need this! How can I get a copy? I need this to write the catalog for my new exhibit."

The portraits of Demos and the baby, as well as many of the other portraits in the museum's collection, were in storage, Mrs. Tawfic told me, because she wanted to mount them in a newly curated exhibit, something that would lend them more honor than the neglectful way that some of them were currently displayed. But without more information she could not develop a catalog, and without a catalog, the director would not schedule the dates for the exhibit. She was gleeful, almost giddy, as she pored over the faithful reproductions and careful scholarship in Doxiadis's book.

"Take this book," I said. "It's my gift to you."

Mrs. Tawfic gasped and looked at me, hugging the book to her chest like a child, holding it up to show the other curators, who had gathered around to see. Mrs. Tawfic turned to me, her kind face beaming. "We can help each other, yes?" she said.

Our entourage had assembled at the door. Led by Mrs. Tawfic, we entered the museum through the director's entrance, trailed by four or five men brought along to move the portraits out of storage, a guard, Mrs. Tawfic's assistant, and a museum official. We walked down the halls of the ground floor, past befuddled tour groups, and into a gallery where there was a padlocked door leading to a storage room.

The door opened onto an unlit space crowded with precious antiquities in what appeared to be desultory order, like the average garage or basement. Just inside was a tall wooden chest of drawers. Mrs. Tawfic began giving directions in Arabic, her voice maternal and firm, as the workers pulled the knobs on the first drawer.

I could feel my emotions begin to spill over, welling since I left the hotel that morning, since December, since last fall—about everything: the elated, stunned amazement; the gloating anticipation and self-satisfaction; the shame and confusion; the fear of mortality's darkness rumbling toward me and my friends; the crushing sense of powerlessness and inadequacy against the responsibilities of my life. The realization that I couldn't count on myself or on the identity I'd taken for granted, and how ineffectual, fraudulent, simply used up I'd come to feel. And then, in that bleak and colorless time, how something rich had begun trickling back, something essential, because of an ancient face.

Inside the first drawer were Plexiglas cases padded with thick white flannel. Fitted into the cases were taupe-colored wooden boxes lined with linen display boards, and on the linen the portraits rested. The workers brought out Demos first, two of them mindfully carrying her case, which they set upright on the floor in the open gallery. Demos, in her lavender tunic, looked out at us, her deep brown eyes caught in an eternal moment of melancholy wonderment. My eyes started to burn.

Mrs. Tawfic was still giving instructions, now in Arabic and English. "The baby, too," she called to the workers.

I turned to look at Mrs. Tawfic—her lovely, open face. "She's so beautiful," I said, my ability to communicate emaciated, what this meant to me ineffable. And then I burst into tears. "Thank you, thank you . . ." I muttered, wiping my eyes with a wadded tissue.

Mrs. Tawfic hugged me, smoothing my hair back from my dripping face, keeping her arm around my shoulders as she took my tissue to dab it at my cheeks. "You love her, too," she said. "You love her, too."

Two workers brought out the baby's portrait and placed her on a scuffed cube of painted wood, while the others unscrewed the Plexiglas covers from the display cases and set them aside.

There was Demos's serious baby girl. As delicately rendered as Demos, her face was more thickly impasto than her mother's, as if the artist had had to work all the more quickly to capture a still moment in the life of a busy little child. The rough lines created by the quickly drying pigmented wax left the impression of arrested energy in the baby's face, as if at any moment she might have crawled away or hidden herself in her mother's lap. I had to keep digging into my pocket for more tissues to keep from dropping tears and beads of perspiration onto the lustrous wax.

As Mrs. Tawfic studied the book I'd given her, sitting in the middle of the gallery with her assistant and the museum official on a chrome-sided bench that the workers had lugged in, I knelt on the floor in front of Demos. Since I first saw her face that spring I had wondered what happened to her—she was so young, her baby so small! Now in the same room with her, what mattered most to me was imagining how she felt as she met the intensity of the artist's gaze with her own. Demos's expression was not so simple as obligation filtered through religious belief and culture. Hers is the face of a woman who knows she is confronting the end of her life, and the end of her child's. In her eyes is a profound knowledge of loss, of sorrow and pity. All of it, soon, will be lost to her: the tenderness of her loved ones, the suckling of her baby, the Nile's reliable cycle of ebb and flow, the calling of birds, and the scent of honey and mint. She knows that life itself has brought her to this moment; painful as it is to face, she does not look away. To deny this moment is to deny all the moments before.

I had not been able to understand how my friends could face the heightened possibility of death; it was unthinkable to me that my friends and I were walking the downward slope of our lives. How could they—these vibrant women I love—stand to live with it, the inescapable reminder of mortality that cancer drags in its wake? Neither could I bear to know that my body was aging—complicit in my baby's death, less and less the body that had made me feel so potently alive. Everything in me, all I had come to feel about being a mother, a fertile woman, fought against this knowledge. I wasn't ready—I wasn't ready to give it all up, all the beauty and astonishment that living in my womanly skin had given me.

But there was Demos, gazing back at me. Notably absent from the complicated emotions washing over her face was anything resembling resignation. She had prepared for this moment in the ways available to her: She had dressed and perfumed her dark hair, coiling it at the top of her head, securing the braid with a gold pin, winding curls about her face. She wore her jewels—her dowry, her inheritance?—and adorned her daughter with a magical necklace, a chain hung with *lunulae*, feminine fertility symbols, to protect her as well as she could. And so she faced the truth of her life: her lips slightly parted with something she needed to express, the look in her eyes incandescent. *See me,* her eyes seem to say. *This is me.* It was her deliberate expression of mortality—of being a woman, a human, a mother, fleetingly alive—that made her eternal. And gave me, I now understood, a redeemed trust in my own worth, mortal and human as I was. What I saw in Demos's eyes was not acceptance of death, but acknowledgment: of death, of loss, of suffering, as well as of desire and remembered joy, all of it part of living.

"When I look at their faces," Mrs. Tawfic told me hours later, as we sat in her office together, "I see life. Not death. I see their eyes. Some are so sad. Some are so many different things." So many different things, just as in the enigmatic quote from Mahfouz: like meeting one's beloved in old age. If you could embrace all that you loved, all that you had lost and could lose, all that you were, however late it might seem—wasn't that also an answer to the riddle?

Mrs. Tawfic and I were having tea at her desk. "Now I will show you *all* of my favorites," she said. She unzipped her purse and pulled out a stack of photographs, which she carries around with her like baby pictures: all of the Fayum portraits in the museum. We looked at them together, pointing out their similarities and differences, reveling in the eloquence of these strangers we could know only across the gap of two thousand years. I told her about my tall, contemplative boy and my ardent little girl, and she told me about her three sons: the one in university and the one in secondary school, like my son. And the third, who doesn't go to school; he had an accident, a brain injury.

"You have a friend here," Zienab Tawfic said, squeezing my hand.

"Yes, I know," I said, returning her grip.

"When you come back, we will show each other more," she added.

"*Insha'Allah,*" I answered, *god willing.* We sat quietly together, intimates, our glasses of tea steaming.

The Closed Treasure Room

On my last day in Cairo, I went back to the Khan al-Khalili. There was so much more of Cairo to discover, impossible in a day. After a couple of hours investigating the edges of the *khan*, analyzing my pointless map, unwilling to lose my sense of direction, I hadn't found anything I'd intended to see: the crafts center, el-Fishawi's, palaces I'd read about. But I was in Egypt—I gave up my plan. I would spend the day wandering deeper into the labyrinth, wherever it took me.

The streets of the Khan al-Khalili smelled of incense and mint and shit, of sweat and thousands of years of human grime, of waste and unexpected sweetness. I let the perfume sellers dab their heady oils on my wrists with their long glass wands. A spice merchant, after lighting crystals of frankincense in a clay burner, filling his shop with musky, aromatic smoke, gave me pinches of spice in my palm to smell; not to waste it, I rubbed each handful onto my arms. A strolling flower salesman held a thread of fresh jasmine blossoms out to me on his fingers; I bought it and put it on, raising it to my nose periodically, taking in the intoxicating scent.

"May I take your picture?" I asked over and over again. I took photographs of a lime seller and her smiling toddler squatting before their pyramid of green fruit, the young calico cat that followed me through the garbage-strewn passageways all morning, a girl before her display of floral paper boxes filled with confections of ground nuts and honey, a man selling fresh, puffy Egyptian pita breads stacked in a crate of crisscrossed sticks that looked like the frame of a kite.

Everywhere, I purchased presents for my family and friends: backgammon boards inlaid with camel bone, a red tasseled fez of thick felted wool, alabaster animals, bags of spices, tiny ornate perfume bottles of blown glass wrapped in cotton-filled boxes to keep them from breaking, powdery coffee ground with cardamom and allspice. I picked out semiprecious stones—peridot, raw emeralds, rose quartz, aquamarine, all mined in Egypt—and waited while the jeweler strung them. My many bags already heavy, I wore the necklaces out of the shop.

Late in the afternoon, laden with my purchases, I passed under the Badestan Gate, deep in the heart of the Khan al-Khalili.

A canary in its cage was trying out its notes from a window on the second floor. On the steps were carefully folded stacks of deeply dyed Egyptian cotton scarves. I fingered the pleasing heft of a scarf, thinking how easily they would pack in my suitcase, a perfect present to give each of my friends.

"You like?" said a young man. "I have more in my shop. Come." He started climbing the steep stone steps beside the gate, beckoning me to follow him up the vaulted passage.

At the top of the stairs he led me through a closed door, into a shop stacked floor to ceiling with brilliantly colored textiles—cottons and silk, see-through chiffon, gold-embroidered finery, as well as tribal bags, clothing, tasseled belts, even well-made T-shirts with tasteful, traditional patterns in silkscreen, totally unlike the Cleopatra faces and Tut-wear I'd seen all over Cairo. Another man folded textiles with his back to us, undisturbed by our entrance.

The young merchant and I started pulling out scarves of different sizes and patterns; we counted periodically as I remembered more and yet more women I wanted to bring them home to. Finally we had an opulent stack as well as an assortment of T-shirts, all tribal designs from the Red Sea, for my husband and children.

I opened my wallet. It was empty.

"Cash machine downstairs. I will show you," the young man said.

"It won't work," I said. "I've tried, but the machines are all in Arabic."

The second man in the shop, who had been folding scarves all this time, turned around. "Let him take you to the machine," he said. "I know your problem. This machine will work."

I looked at him; impossibly, he seemed familiar.

"I don't think so," I said doubtfully. "My code is my cat's name. I only know it in English."

"Trust me," the second man said. He was, I suddenly registered, incredibly handsome, with curly hair graying at his temples, a shadow of beard on either side of his sculpted jaw, and breathtaking, light green eyes. There was something else about him, but I didn't know what. Nodding toward the younger man, he said, "He'll walk you down to the machine and bring you back. It will work, I promise. You can leave your bags here."

"Okay," I said, not quite persuaded, but hypnotically willing to do whatever the second man said. I left my many bags in a heap on the floor of the shop and followed the young guy through a maze of streets, turning again and again. Finally he waved his hand in front of himself to urge me forward, and stopped: There was an ATM machine with a keyboard in English. I collected my cash, and we returned to the shop.

"It worked?" the green-eyed man asked.

"It worked," I said. "Thank you."

"Your cat's name," he said, shaking his head in mock dismay, amused.

"I know," I said, feeling exquisitely ridiculous, smiling as well at myself.

"What *is* your cat's name?" he asked.

"Minerva."

"That could be your problem. You should have named it Athena."

I got it, then, who he was, or who he reminded me of—the Roman, one of the earliest Fayum portraits, painted when Ovid and Augustus Caesar were alive. Though the portrait was of a man in his virile prime, his mummy, when examined, turned out to be that of an old man with a white beard. The Roman had lived for many years after his portrait was done.

"And what is your name?" the green-eyed man asked me.

"Kate," I said. "What is yours?"

"Well," he began, clearly pleased with himself, "my name is Hussein. But I got so tired of jokes about Saddam Hussein, I gave myself another name."

"What is that?" I asked.

"Franco," he replied.

I laughed. "One dictator to another," I said.

"Yes," he said, grinning. "Nobody gets it."

We started talking, then, about politics. He asked me where

I was from in the United States, and how I felt Arnold Schwarzenegger was doing as governor of California. Like everyone I met in Cairo, he hoped the American people would elect John Kerry. I told him of my husband's writings about conflicts in the Middle East, and I told him about my children. The shop was his, he told me, and he had learned to speak English from his customers over the years.

The young merchant stood patiently by. I got out my wallet to pay.

"What more would you like?" Franco asked me. "You have gifts for your husband and your children and the children of your friends. What about for you?"

I realized he had listened to everything I'd said in his shop. I felt utterly relaxed, truly enjoying myself. "I don't need anything more," I said. "I've got everything I want."

"You can't leave Egypt without something to remember her by," Franco said. "What about a Bedouin blouse. You should get something beautiful for yourself." He turned around and picked up a thick cotton blouse delicately embroidered at the neckline and sleeves. When he turned around again, holding the blouse out to me, all I could see were his eyes. Not emerald. Not peridot. Not Nile, that green. Celadon?

"What?" he said finally. I realized I had been staring at him, staring at me.

"Oh, nothing," I said, scurrying for cover. "Just—thank you." I felt my face turn hot. But I couldn't stop myself; I looked up, again, at him.

The room suddenly contracted, electric.

"Something is happening here," Franco said quietly, almost whispering to me. "Have tea with me. I know you are married. Let's have tea, keep talking."

"I can't," I said, feeling dangerous. I glanced at my watch, a reflex. My god, it was already six o'clock. I had to pack, I had to go to the airport. "I really can't," I said. "I have to leave."

"Then come back tomorrow," Franco said. "Meet me for tea tomorrow."

"I can't," I said. "I'm leaving tonight. I'm going home."

"Tonight?" he said. "But—we should have tea." I was dimly aware that there were other people in the shop, somewhere far, far away. Franco looked at me, his eyes penetrating. His countenance softened, earnest. "There is feeling here," he said, his voice low.

I couldn't speak. He was right, and I knew it. I fumbled with my purse, standing on a precipice. He was unbearably handsome, charming, witty, funny. "I know," I said. "And I really, really have to go."

"You really, really have to go," Franco said, his voice yielding. "I know." He laid down the blouse, unfolded.

"May I take a photo of your shop, at least?" I asked, knowing the answer.

"Of course," he said, and I got out my camera. "Here," he said, calling to a little boy who had been wandering in and out of the shop. "You can take a picture of us." I gave the little boy my camera and showed him how to press the button firmly. I stepped back. Franco stood next to me, pressing two fingers lightly into the small of my back as the little boy squinted into the viewfinder. Two fingers.

Nothing happened. No click, no flash.

"Press harder," I said to the little boy. Franco's fingers on my back. I could feel them through my sweaty shirt.

Again nothing happened. No flash.

"Oh well," I said, taking the camera back. I hid behind the lens, my heart racing. I took a photo of the little boy, another of the shop. Franco didn't move from his spot near the door, next to me. He was assessing my bags.

"You can't carry all of this," he said. He nodded toward the boy. "He's a good boy. He's in school. I'll give him a pound to carry your bags. He'll be happy." He looked, smiling, at the boy. "Tell Madame Kate how old you are."

"Eleven and one," said the boy.

"No!" Franco said, roughing the boy's thick black hair. "You're twelve!"

The little boy's face erupted into a gorgeous dimpled grin, and he ducked away from us, gathering my bags.

I turned toward the front door, open now. Franco reached into his pocket and got out his own wallet. "If your husband ever wants to talk politics with an Egyptian, give him this," he said, slowly handing me his business card, handing me, with diplomatic grace, back to my life.

"Thank you," I said, "I'll tell him."

He stepped away, toward the neatly stacked piles in the shop. "Take this as a gift," he said, holding the Bedouin blouse lightly by the shoulders. He shrugged. "My last one," he said, "I couldn't sell it anyway. Not now."

The boy had all of my bags in his hands. I took a couple back from him and held the blouse. Franco was admonishing the boy to take me straight to the taxi stand, not to dawdle or make me late for my plane, and I pulled the door shut behind us. We walked down the steep steps, out to the Badestan Gate, where the canary was still singing its random song. The boy led and I followed, blood beating in my ears.

"You're in school," I said, making conversation, feigning normalcy. "What studies do you like?"

"I like history," he said, beaming his dimpled smile. We were passing shops and merchants, all of them calling out "Madame, madame!" or "I make you a deal!" The boy used his narrow shoulders to block their entreaties, protecting me, maneuvering my bags through the alleys and slow-moving crowds as I trailed behind.

"We're a good team," I said to the boy, whose name I still did not know. "You make me homesick for my children." The boy smiled again, then settled his face, serious now, all business.

All at once I recognized the street where we walked, near the same corner where my taxi had dropped me on my first morning in Cairo. Around us, beyond the hanging festoons of leather sandals and stuffed camel toys, people were sitting at café tables out in an alley, the *sheesha* smoke rising around them. As I passed an unoccupied wooden bench with striped pillows on the seat and an ornately framed, horizontal mirror hung on the wall behind it, I looked up and saw the sign over the carved alleyway arch: el-Fishawi's.

"I'll stop here," I said quickly to the boy. "This is good. We can set the bags here," I added, dropping my own load on the empty bench. Hesitating, he set my bags down. He didn't want to disappoint Franco. I watched his brow knit.

"It's okay," I said. "Really." I knew that Franco had already slipped him a pound as we left the shop. But I reached into my purse and pulled a ten-pound note from my wallet. When I handed it to him he took it in both hands, his entire face lighting once more with that unforgettable smile before he skittered away, folding back into the crowds.

Still racing, my heart. I needed to sit. I could hardly breathe. A waiter approached me, instantaneously bringing me hot mint tea in a chipped enamel pot. What had happened to me? All around me laughter, voices, water bubbling in the bowls of the *sheeshas*, music, shouts. I tried to focus on my tea. The large crystals of sugar made a deafening sound as the little spoon scraped through the bowl. Another spoonful, *ziyada*, sweet, and I stirred the sugar in, the leaves of mint swirling in the glass. Every table around me was full, the café spilling out from the yellow-walled room I could see through the *mashrafiyya* lattice windows. Couples were sitting close together, their foreheads nearly touching, talking and smoking. Waiters leaned against the walls watching the tables, arms folded, relaxed but attentive. Groups of tourists sat in sweaty abandon at tables pushed together, loads of overfilled bags like mine slumped on the ground at their feet, taking photographs of one another; like the Egyptians around them they greeted friends newly arrived, or called and waved as others left. I reached into my purse for my camera and turned it on, scrolling back through the digital images. There was the shop, the boy, the photos I'd taken all afternoon and morning . . . that was all. My body pulsed, alive, urgent, under the sweat-damp cotton I wore. I tried to drink from my burning cup. I could see his green eyes, still, seeing me.

It really was, I knew, time for me to go. I had to go back to the hotel to pack, I had to go—I wanted to go—home. I ached for my family. I waved for the waiter and paid my bill. *Shukran*, I said, "thank you." I picked up the Bedouin blouse and folded it neatly, pressing it smooth with my hands before I put it inside one of the bags. The attar of roses and sweet pea perfumes I tested had warmed on my skin; my arms were saffron yellow, dusted with cinnamon and cloves. I was fragrant with perfume, with spice, wearing jewels and flowers, like a bride. *Like meeting one's beloved in old age*, I thought again, rising to leave. I turned around to gather all of my gifts in their wrappings and stood, face to face now, with the mirror. I saw her there, her hair long and loose, the sun shining down on it, and all the people behind, drinking their tea, saying their hellos and good-byes, living and dying.

CONTRIBUTORS' NOTES

Jennifer Allen is the author of *Fifth Quarter: The Scrimmage of a Football Coach's Daughter*, a memoir of life as the youngest child and only daughter of legendary NFL coach George Allen, and the short story collection *Better Get Your Angel On*. Allen's work has appeared in the *New York Times Magazine, New Republic, Rolling Stone, Men's Journal*, ESPN.com, NFL.com, and *George*. In 2002, she was a writer on the HBO series *ARLI$$*. She lives in Los Angeles with her husband and their three sons.

Cecelie S. Berry is a freelance writer and a former lawyer. She is the editor of *Rise Up Singing: Black Women Writers on Motherhood*, and her essays have appeared in the *New York Times*, the *Washington Post, Newsweek, Child, O—the Oprah Magazine*, and *Salon*. Her commentaries have been broadcast on National Public Radio's *Morning Edition*. She lives in New Jersey with her husband and sons.

Rosellen Brown is the author of ten books, most recently the novels *Half a Heart* and *Before and After*. She has been married to teacher/educator Marv Hoffman since (gulp!) 1963, and has two grown daughters and one calico cat. Having lived in too many places, she has come to ground (for now) in Chicago.

Ana Castillo, one of the original contributors to the online Mothers Who Think, is a novelist and poet who divides her time between teaching in Chicago, where she shares a duplex with her twenty-one-year-old son (and their dog), and her desert home in New Mexico, where she writes, paints, and runs around "nekid" to her heart's desire.

Mari Leonardo is the pseudonym for a woman who immigrated to San Francisco from Guatemala in 2001. She has three children, sixteen, fourteen, and thirteen years old.

Janet Fitch's first novel, *White Oleander*, has been translated into twenty-eight languages. She is the mother of a now fourteen-year-old, who in the end chose to attend a liberal, Catholic girls' high school a short six-minute drive from their home in Los Angeles. Fitch is currently finishing a second novel. Her daughter does not intend to be a writer.

Charo Gonzalez was born in Buenos Aires, Argentina. She is a journalist and writer whose interviews and articles have appeared in Latin American publications, and a former producer, editor, and reporter for an international Spanish-language television news network in New York. She lives in San Francisco with her husband and two children, Camilla and Nico. Gonzalez is currently working on her first novel.

Ariel Gore (www.arielgore.com) is the editor and publisher of *Hip Mama: The Parenting Zine (*www.hipmamazine.com) and the author of three parenting books—*The Hip Mama Survival Guide, The Mother Trip*, and *Whatever, Mom*—as well as a novel/memoir, *Atlas of the Human Heart*. She is a contributor to the *Mothers Who Think* anthology. She lives with her family in Portland, Oregon.

Andrea Lawson Gray is a native New Yorker who moved to San Francisco in 1989. She has three children, Andre Gabriel Gray, eighteen; Armand Alexis Gray, twelve; and Cienna Georgia Gray, seven.

Ann Hulbert, a senior editor at the *New Republic* for many years, is the author of *The Interior Castle: The Art and Life of Jean Stafford* and *Raising America: Experts, Parents, and a Century of Advice About Children.* Her writing has appeared in various publications, including *Slate,* the *New York Times Magazine* and the *New York Times Book Review,* the *New York Review of Books,* and the *New Yorker.* She lives in Washington, D.C., with her husband and two children.

Nora Okja Keller, a contributor to the *Mothers Who Think* anthology, is the author of the novels *Fox Girl* and *Comfort Woman*, which won an American Book Award in 1998. She is the recipient of a Pushcart Prize for the short story "Mother Tongue," a portion of *Comfort Woman*. She lives in Hawaii with her husband and two daughters.

Beth Kephart is the award-winning author of five nonfiction books; her most recent is *Ghosts in the Garden*. Her first book, *A Slant of Sun*, was a 1998 National Book Award finalist and a Salon.com Best Book of the Year. Her second, *Into the Tangle of Frienship*, earned an NEA grant. Frequently anthologized, Kephart's essays have appeared in the *New York Times*, the *Washington Post Book World*, the *Chicago Tribune, Real Simple*, and elsewhere. She is a partner in a marketing communications firm. A contributor to the *Mothers Who Think* anthology, she lives in Devon, Pennsylvania, with her husband and teenage son.

Christina Koenig, formerly a print, radio, and television journalist, is now director of communications and media relations for Y-ME National Breast Cancer Organization, which provides information and support for breast cancer patients and their families. She lives in Chicago with her eight-year-old daughter, Rebecca . . . and husband Bill, whom she met at a bar over a margarita.

Jean Hanff Korelitz is the author of three novels, *The White Rose, The Sabbathday River*, and *A Jury of Her Peers*, as well as a novel for children, *Interference Powder*, and a collection of poems, *The Properties of Breath*. She is one of the original contributors to the online Mothers Who Think. Korelitz lives in Princeton, New Jersey, with her husband, Paul Muldoon, and their two children.

Constance Matthiessen, one of the original contributors to the online Mothers Who Think, is a journalist and writer who lives with her three children in San Francisco.

Denise Minor is a doctoral candidate in Spanish Linguistics at the University of California, Davis, where she also teaches Spanish composition. As a news reporter and freelance writer, she wrote for the *San Francisco Examiner, Pacific News Service*, and *Image* magazine, among others. She lives in Davis, California, with her husband, Alex Milgram, and her sons, Max and Nathan. Her essay, "There's No Being Sad Here," is dedicated to her mother, Pat Minor.

Mary Morris is the author of twelve books, including the novels *Revenge, Acts of God, The Night Sky,* and *House Arrest*; the story collection *The Lifeguard*; and the travel memoirs *Nothing to Declare: Memoirs of a Woman Traveling Alone* and *Angels and Aliens: A Journey West*. She and her husband, Larry O'Connor, are coeditors of *Maiden Voyages*, an anthology of women's travel literature. Morris's short stories and travel essays have appeared in the *Paris Review,* the *New York Times, Travel & Leisure,* and *Vogue*. The recipient of a Guggenheim fellowship and the Rome Prize in Literature from the American Academy of Arts and Letters, she teaches writing at Sarah Lawrence College and lives in Brooklyn with her husband and daughter.

Kate Moses is the author of *Wintering: A Novel of Sylvia Plath,* recipient of the Janet Heidinger Kafka prize and translated into thirteen languages. She is the coeditor, with Camille Peri, of the national bestselling, American Book Award–winning *Mothers Who Think: Tales of Real-Life Parenthood,* and was a cofounder of *Salon*'s Mothers Who Think. She lives in San Francisco with her husband, Gary Kamiya, and their two children, and is currently writing her second novel, inspired by the Fayum portraits described in "Mother of the World."

Asra Q. Nomani, born in Bombay, India, is a journalist and the author of *Tantrika: Traveling the Road of Divine Love,* selected by Beliefnet.com as one of the best spiritual books of 2003. She is also the author of *Standing Alone in Mecca: An American Woman's Struggle for the Soul of Islam.* A former reporter for the *Wall Street Journal,* she has written essays about Islam for the *Washington Post,* the *New York*

Times, Time, and *Salon*; her work has also appeared in *Cosmopolitan* and *Sports Illustrated for Women.* She lives in Morgantown, West Virginia, with her son Shibli, who has taken eight keys off her keyboard at last count, and near her supportive parents, Sajida and Zafar.

Debra Ollivier, a contributor to the *Mothers Who Think* anthology, is the author of *Entre Nous: A Woman's Guide to Finding Her Inner French Girl.* Her work has appeared in numerous publications, including *Salon, Harper's, Playboy, Le Monde,* and *Les Inrockuptibles.* Ollivier and her family divide their time between France and the United States.

Mariane Pearl is the author of the memoir *A Mighty Heart.* She is an award-winning writer and documentary film director who produced and hosted a daily radio show for Radio France International and has written for *Télérama,* the *New York Times,* and *Salon.* She lives in New York with her son.

Camille Peri is the coeditor, with Kate Moses, of the national bestselling, American Book Award–winning *Mothers Who Think: Tales of Real-Life Parenthood.* She is a former senior editor at *Salon* and founding editor of Mothers Who Think. She lives in San Francisco with her husband, David Talbot, and their sons, Joseph Lyle and Nathaniel Augusto Talbot.

Marina Pineda-Kamariotis is an immigration attorney who worked at La Raza Centro Legal in San Francisco before going into private practice in 2001. She lives with her husband, Jim, and daughters Justine, seventeen, and Jasmine, fourteen, in South San Francisco.

Margaret Remick is the pseudonym for a San Francisco writer prone to hyperbole and subjective thinking. She has written for *Salon,* the *San Francisco Chronicle,* and *Publishers Weekly.* An active advocate of public schools, she is currently working on a twisted vocabulary workbook for kids and a low-brow mystery. She lives with her three children and patient, inspiring husband.

Rahna Reiko Rizzuto is the author of the novel *Why She Left Us*, which won an American Book Award in 2000. She is also a recipient of the U.S./Japan Creative Artist Fellowship, funded by the National Endowment for the Arts, and is a contributor to the *Mothers Who Think* anthology. She has two children, lives in Brooklyn, New York, and is currently working on her second book.

Mary Roach is the author of the *New York Times* bestseller *Stiff: The Curious Lives of Human Cadavers.* She is a former *Salon* columnist and contributing editor at *Discover* magazine; her writing has also appeared in *Outside, Wired, The Believer, GQ,* and the *New York Times Magazine.* She lives in Oakland, California, with her husband, Ed, and has two stepdaughters, Lily, who is nineteen, and Phoebe, fifteen. She is at work on her second book.

Dr. Karin L. Stanford is a writer and professor of Pan African Studies and African American Politics at California State University, Northridge. Her most recent book is *Black Political Organizations in the Post–Civil Rights Era,* coedited with Ollie Johnson. The author of numerous articles on black women and black politics, Dr. Stanford is the former director of the Washington, D.C., bureau of the RainbowPUSH Coalition and a former Congressional Black Caucus fellow. She and her daughter reside in Los Angeles.

Susan Straight, a contributor to the *Mothers Who Think* anthology, has published five novels, including the most recent, *Highwire Moon,* a finalist for the National Book Award, winner of the Commonwealth of California Gold Medal for Fiction, and named one of the year's best novels by the *San Francisco Chronicle* and the *Washington Post.* Her new novel, *A Million Nightingales on the Branches of My Heart,* will be published in 2005. Straight's essays, articles, and short fiction have been published in numerous magazines and journals, including the *New York Times Magazine,* the *Los Angeles Times Magazine, Harper's, Salon, Zoetrope All-Story,* and *McSweeney's.* Her short story, "Mines," was chosen for the collection *Best American Short Stories 2003* and won a Pushcart Prize in Fiction. Her commentaries are frequently heard on National Public Radio's *All*

Things Considered. Straight was born in Riverside, California, where she still lives with her three daughters.

Margaret Talbot is a staff writer at the *New Yorker* magazine. She is one of the original contributors to the online Mothers Who Think. Talbot lives in Washington, D.C., with her husband, Arthur Allen, and their children, Ike, eight, and Lucy, five.

Kristen Taylor is a writer and cognitive psychologist. Her work has appeared in the *Los Angeles Times Magazine*, the *Christian Science Monitor*, and in her column for the *Ventura County Star*. She lives in Los Angeles with her husband, Christian Gaines, and their two children, Lola and Luke.

Lisa Teasley is the author of the story collection *Glow in the Dark*, winner of the 2002 Gold Pen Award and the Pacificus Foundation Award, as well as the novels *Dive* and the forthcoming *Heat Signature*. Her other awards include the May Merrill Miller Award; the National Society of Arts & Letters Short Story Award, Los Angeles; and the Amaranth Review Award. A painter as well as a writer, Teasley has exhibited widely throughout the country. She is the mother of Imogen Teasley-Vlautin, who is nine years old. They live in Los Angeles.

Fufkin Vollmayer is a lapsed journalist who worked for public radio and CNN. She now lives and writes in San Francisco, and tends to her children, her garden, and her sanity. She is the parent of two testosterone-filled toddler boys, Joaquin and Javier. Sleep permitting, she occasionally gets work done.

Ayelet Waldman is the author of the novel *Daughter's Keeper* and of the Mommy Track mystery series. Her novel *Love and Other Impossible Pursuits* will be published in 2006. She lives in Berkeley, California, with her husband and four children.

Katherine Whitney is a writer and museum consultant. She lives in San Francisco with her husband and two children.

ESSAY CREDITS